A THEOLOGICAL INTRODUCTION TO THE Old Testament

Second Edition

Bruce C. Birch

Walter Brueggemann

Terence E. Fretheim

David L. Petersen

ABINGDON PRESS
NASHVILLE

A THEOLOGICAL INTRODUCTION TO THE OLD TESTAMENT

Library of Congress Cataloging-in-Publication Data

A theological introduction to the Old Testament / Bruce C. Birch . . . [et al.].—2nd ed.
    p. cm.
    Includes bibliographical references and indexes.
    ISBN 0-687-06676-X (alk. paper)
    1. Bible. O.T.—Theology.   2. Bible. O.T.—Introductions.
    I. Birch, Bruce C.
    BS1192.5.T43   2005
    230'.0411—dc22

                                                                                2004022219

05 06 07 08 09 10 11 12 13 14—10 9 8 7 6 5 4 3 2 1

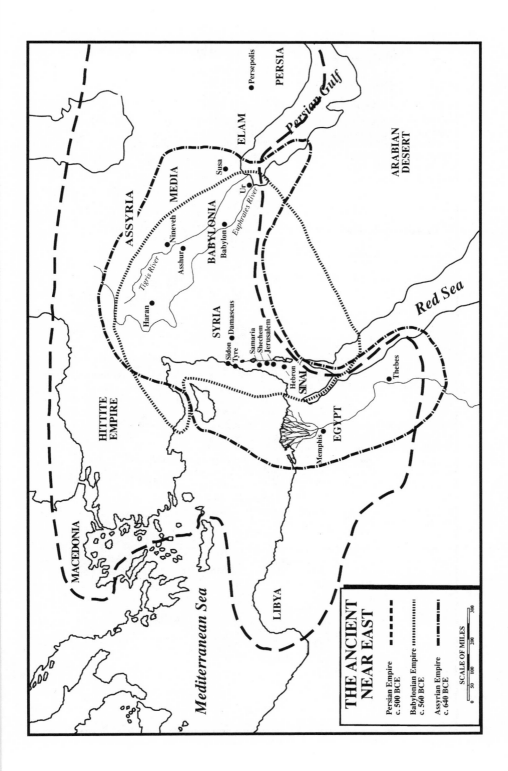

THE ANCIENT
NEAR EAST

Persian Empire
c. 500 BCE

Babylonian Empire
c. 560 BCE

Assyrian Empire
c. 640 BCE

SCALE OF MILES
0   50 100   200   300

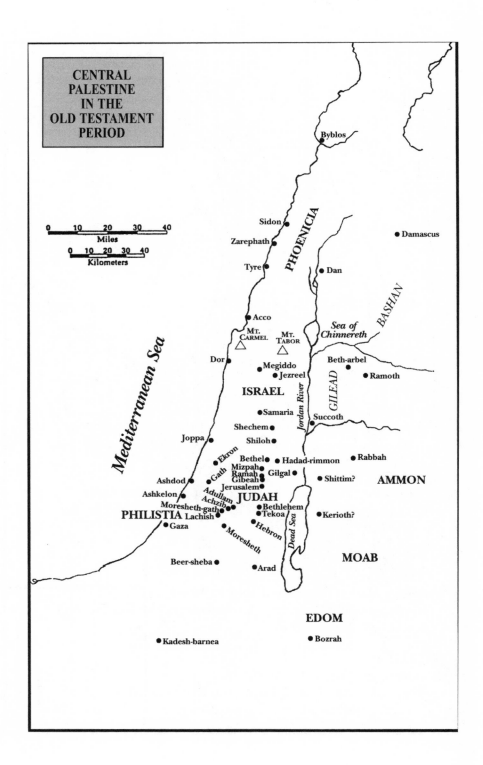

CENTRAL
PALESTINE
IN THE
OLD TESTAMENT
PERIOD

Miles
0 10 20 30 40

Kilometers
0 10 20 30 40

Byblos

Sidon
PHOENICIA
Zarephath
Tyre
Dan
Damascus

Acco
BASHAN
MT. CARMEL
MT. TABOR
Sea of Chinnereth
Dor
Megiddo
Jezreel
Beth-arbel
GILEAD
Ramoth
ISRAEL
Samaria
Shechem
Succoth
Shiloh
Jordan River
Joppa
Ekron
Bethel
Hadad-rimmon
Rabbah
Mizpah
Gath
Ramah
Gilgal
Ashdod
Gibeah
Shittim?
AMMON
Jerusalem
Ashkelon
Adullam
Achzib
JUDAH
Moresheth-gath
Bethlehem
Lachish
Tekoa
Kerioth?
PHILISTIA
Gaza
Hebron
Dead Sea
Moresheth
MOAB
Beer-sheba
Arad

Mediterranean Sea

EDOM
Kadesh-barnea
Bozrah

CONTENTS

PREFACE TO THE SECOND EDITION

This second edition of our text grows out of the gratifying response to the publication of the first edition. We are pleased that so many colleagues have commented to us on their use of the first edition in seminary courses, as well as in some college and university settings. We have had the opportunity to use this text in our own teaching as well. Reviews have offered challenging and helpful suggestions. Out of this response we believe we have some ideas for making this volume even more useful, and accessible to introductory students, and some revisions and expansions that more adequately cover the range of theological issues we hoped to discuss. The changes do not dramatically alter the approach or character of the volume, but we hope the changes will make it more adequate to the purposes for which it was written.

In an effort to enhance the use of this volume as a textbook, we have added additional maps and charts throughout the volume. We also have expanded the endnotes in some chapters in order to give a fuller guide to students who wish to explore further key issues and discussions in Old Testament studies. This will make more visible our own engagement with those issues, although limited space in a single volume will not allow a full airing of many complex ongoing scholarly discussions. Bibliographic suggestions for further reading at the end of each chapter have been expanded and updated to reflect the continued appearance of excellent resources.

We still believe that in teaching an introductory course this volume must be supplemented by additional resources. We have not tried to make this volume cover all of the purposes served by appropriate histories of ancient Israel, treatments of material culture, discussions of linguistic evidence, or examinations of ancient Near Eastern texts. All of these matters have been influential in our work and are touched upon but not given full treatment. We know that most introductory Old Testament courses use a variety of resources already, and they do so with different operative pedagogical approaches by our teaching colleagues. We simply hope to offer a volume that provides a theological perspective on the biblical texts that has often been missing in textbooks that have given more comprehensive treatment to other matters. We still do not believe we can take up this wider range of issues without diluting the particular voice we believe we might add to the mix.

Some reviewers of the first edition of this book suggested that we devoted too much space to the Pentateuch. While we thoughtfully considered this observation, on reexamination we think the theological themes that emerge from the Pentateuch are too significant to be given shorter shrift. Setting aside the introductory chapter, the texts of the Pentateuch occupy only four of the remaining eleven chapters. The themes of creation, brokenness, promise, deliverance, covenant, and wilderness simply seem too major and defining of Israel's experience of God and the church's reading of Israel's witness to that experience for us to deal with in less than four chapters. Five of the remaining chapters use the historical framework of Joshua through 2 Kings and take up the individual prophetic voices of Israel at appropriate points in that framework. We have tried to give a fuller treatment to many individual prophets rather than simply the more general discussion of the prophetic movement in Israel. Two chapters deal with material drawn from the final segment of the Hebrew canon, the Writings.

Although we undertook this volume because we shared a common and congenial approach in our own teaching, we are fully aware of the importance of listening to and letting ourselves be informed by perspectives divergent and supplemental to our own. We have tried to make our conversations and indebtedness to these diverse voices of biblical interpretation more visible in this new edition. We have included new material in the discussions, endnotes, and bibliographies that reflect our awareness of the importance of gender and cultural perspectives on the texts of ancient Israel. We take note of major critical discussions now taking place among scholars, and give students fuller information on where they might find additional information on those discussions. We try to make our own critical choices clear without suggesting they are the only possible choices.

Finally, we are aware that no one text can be suitable to all who might use it. Some have not found a "theological" introduction to be a useful or pertinent genre. Some have even argued that such "theological" approaches have passed their usefulness and should be abandoned. We respectfully disagree with this judgment. Our own experiences with our students and the responses we have heard from many colleagues convince us that such an approach was needed, timely, and appropriate to those who wish to teach the texts of the Old Testament as important ongoing resources for the life of the church in our contemporary world. We believe the richness and diversity of the witnesses to Israel's experience of God may give important perspective to the challenging issues of our troubled world. We know that even this second edition can do only partial justice to the challenge of claiming Scripture anew for our day. We hope our effort may encourage others to take up the task as well.

September 2004
Bruce C. Birch
Walter Brueggemann
Terence E. Fretheim
David L. Petersen

PREFACE TO THE FIRST EDITION

This book grew out of the conversations among friends and colleagues concerning the teaching of introductory Old Testament courses in the context of a theological school. We all shared a deep affection for the excitement and challenge of introducing Israel's testimony to seminary students as a resource for their own ministry and the life of the church. However, we all shared some degree of frustration that the textbooks available for use in introductory courses treated the Old Testament as evidence for the religious experience and witness of ancient communities but seldom as theological resource for contemporary confessing communities. The biblical text is used as descriptive of ancient faith, not as scripture speaking a word to modern faith. This is understandable, since most of these texts are also intended for university courses where a scriptural perspective would not always be appropriate. Nevertheless, we often found it necessary to supplement chosen textbooks with additional articles or chapters that introduced a theological perspective into our introductory courses, or we simply tried to supply such a perspective in our own lectures.

In discussion over our common desire for a different kind of text, we resolved to author jointly a book that introduced the Old Testament both as the witness of ancient Israel and as a witness to the church and synagogue through the generations of those who had passed these texts on as scripture. The result is this book, which seeks to discuss the Old Testament in theological terms at a level appropriate to introductory seminary students. We also hope that it might be of some value in college and university courses interested in a more theological approach.

The book we offer is organized with attention both to the history of Israel and to the shape of the canon of the Old Testament. We begin with creation and move through the narrative course of events in the Pentateuch because that is the way Israel has passed on its own faith story. We progress through the story of Israel reflected in the historical books from Joshua through 2 Kings and relate the various books of the prophets and the writings to appropriate moments in that story. We are aware that the compositional history of this material might order things very differently, and we refer to standard critical judgments concerning such matters. Nevertheless, we think that the narrative story of Israel and its faith experience as now reflected in the shape of the Hebrew canon is the most appropriate framework for a study directed to the use of the Old Testament in the life of the church.

Our intention is that this book of theological essays on segments of Israel's life and literature be used alongside other resources in an introductory course. This volume does not offer comprehensive coverage of all matters appropriate to the introduction of the Old Testament. Thus, the reader will not find extensive maps or historical timelines. Although we make use of historical and archaeological evidence, we do not attempt to give these matters thorough discussion. The debates about critical issues of composition, sociohistorical context, or literary genre will be utilized and referenced but not given detailed treatment. Our modest goal is to broaden understanding of the theological claims of the text and to stimulate thinking about how such texts handed on through generations in communities of faith can speak a pertinent theological word to the challenges of faith in our own time.

We have each contributed initial drafts of certain chapters. However, we have all read and commented on every chapter so that the final form of each one represents approaches and positions that we can all generally affirm. We have tried to write in a direct style that reflects the way in which we teach and avoids the more formal academic style. There is a minimum of endnotes, but each chapter closes with a list of works appropriate for further reading.

It goes without saying that we owe a great debt to the generations of students we have taught in our respective schools. They have challenged us to continue to grow as teachers. Thus, we gratefully acknowledge our students over the years at Wesley Theological Seminary, Columbia Theological Seminary, Luther Seminary, and Iliff School of Theology.

January 1999
Bruce C. Birch,
Walter Brueggemann,
Terence E. Fretheim,
David L. Petersen

ABBREVIATIONS

AB	Anchor Bible
ABD	*Anchor Bible Dictionary.* Edited by D. N. Freedman. 6 vols. New York, 1992
ABRL	Anchor Bible Reference Library
BRev	*Bible Review*
BTB	*Biblical Theology Bulletin*
CBQ	*Catholic Biblical Quarterly*
FOTL	Forms of the Old Testament Literature
GBS	Guides to Biblical Scholarship
IBC	Interpretation: A Bible Commentary for Preaching and Teaching
IBT	Interpreting Biblical Texts
Int	*Interpretation*
IRT	Issues in Religion and Theology
ITC	International Theological Commentary
JBL	*Journal of Biblical Literature*
JHNES	Johns Hopkins Near Eastern Studies
JPS	Jewish Publication Society
JSOT	*Journal for the Study of the Old Testament*
JSOTSup	JSOT Supplement Series
NIB	*The New Interpreter's Bible*
OBT	Overtures to Biblical Theology
OTG	Old Testament Guides
OTL	Old Testament Library
SBL	Society of Biblical Literature

SBLDS	SBL Dissertation Series
SBLMS	SBL Monograph Series
SWBA	Social World of Biblical Antiquity
TZ	*Theologische Zeitschrift*
WAW	Writings of the Ancient World
WBC	Word Biblical Commentary

CHAPTER ONE

THE OLD TESTAMENT AS THEOLOGICAL WITNESS

The Old Testament can be read from many different perspectives, and each contributes to the richness of meaning recognized in these texts by generations of readers. The Old Testament is a collection of ancient literature. These texts reflect the history of a people called Israel. Behind and beneath the texts lies a wide variety of social contexts that gave rise to and shaped the text. Current biblical studies have benefited from decades of generative scholarship that has illumined the literary, historical, and sociological dimensions of our understanding of the Old Testament. This book has been deeply informed by such scholarship and will reflect it at many points. But this book will focus on the Old Testament as a theological witness to the experience of ancient Israel.

What does it mean to read and interpret the text of the Old Testament theologically? At its most fundamental level such reading and interpretation means taking seriously the claim of the text that it is speaking about encounter and relationship with God. Claims are made by and for these ancient texts that make them more than the literature, history, and sociology of an ancient people called Israel. These texts were written, collected, and passed on through generations as the witness of a community of faith shaped in relation to the character and actions of the God of Israel.

To read and interpret the Old Testament theologically is, however, a complex and multifaceted task. For us, such work means standing within several sets of creative, interpretive tensions that we will discuss in the remainder of this chapter. Our intention here is both

1

to illumine what is meant by theological perspectives on the Old Testament and to clarify the perspectives at work in this volume.

Ancient Testimony, Enduring Scripture

The Old Testament is the collected faith testimony of ancient Israel. Yet, at the same time, this collection is regarded in Judaism and Christianity as scripture through which God's word becomes a reality and a resource to the modern synagogue and church.

1. Whose book is this anyway? On the one hand, we can answer that this is obviously Israel's book. The first community to which the text of the Old Testament is addressed is the community out of which the text arose. That community was ancient Israel. Voices from different periods and social contexts of Israel's life address the wider community of which they were a part. Since the experience of ancient Israel stretches over many centuries, the Old Testament is a library that includes faith testimony, moral admonition, liturgical remembrance, and religious story. The ancient communities decided that these texts were the authoritative witness to their experience of God and their life as the community of God's people. The texts of the Old Testament were initially words addressed to an audience in Israel, but they have been judged by the community as worthy of preservation and reading through subsequent generations.

2. Since ongoing communities of faith, Jewish and Christian, have claimed these texts as scripture, there is a sense in which the Old Testament is not just ancient Israel's book but belongs to the church and synagogue as well. To claim these texts as scripture is to acknowledge authority in these texts for the ongoing life of the religious community and its individual members.

To read the Old Testament theologically is to recognize that when we read as people of faith within a confessional community, we are interested in more than conveying information about an ancient community. The events of Israel's history and the witnesses to Israel's experience of God contained in the Old Testament are of interest because we read as a part of communities that still seek to stand in the presence of that same God. To read the Old Testament theologically is to seek in its texts wisdom on the ways of God that allows us to submit ourselves and our actions to that same God in the effort to be faithful communities in the world. The Old Testament as scripture gives us imaginative categories for discerning God's presence and will in the deeply troubling challenges of our own time.[1]

Every reading of an Old Testament text involves at least two distinct audiences: the audience to whom the text was originally addressed and the audience supplied by the reader and the context that informs the reader. To read the Old Testament as scripture is to suggest that the ancient story intersects our contemporary stories in ways that inform and transform lives and communities. To read these texts as scripture is to expect such informing and transforming power. To read these texts as scripture is to bring the multiple voices and contexts of ancient Israel into dialogue with the complexities of our own reading communities and the world in which we read.

This book is written from the perspective of the Christian church and its reading of ancient Israel's testimony. We write as those engaged in teaching these biblical texts to those who will draw upon them as a scriptural resource for Christian ministry. We are deeply informed and grateful to the ongoing reading of these texts in the Jewish community, and we are aware of the shaping influence of Jewish tradition on the church, particularly its influence on Jesus and the earliest church. Nevertheless, we cannot escape the particularity of our exposition of the biblical text as Christian interpreters. We continue to use the term *Old Testament,* though we are aware of its problematic character in interfaith contexts. Alternative terms seem equally problematic in other ways and have achieved no wide use or recognition in the church.[2] We reject the destructive implications of any form of supercessionism and affirm the ongoing debt and necessary interrelationship of the Christian church to Judaism, both ancient and modern. We have tried to be open to contemporary Jewish interpretive voices and readings in our encounter with these texts. We are convinced that commonalities between Christians and Jews in reading these texts are more important than differences. But Christians and Jews alike must allow for readings that reflect the particularities of distinct religious traditions and their communities. This is part of what it means to read these texts as scripture for church and synagogue. The concerns we bring to our dialogue with the Old Testament are the concerns that are provided by the Christian church and the challenges to its identity and mission in our world at the beginning of the twenty-first century. For us this means there is a continuity between the texts of ancient Israel, the person and work of Jesus, the formation of the early church, and the ongoing history of the Christian churches with their diversity of tradition. We reflect this trajectory in our discussions, but this is not the only trajectory of these texts; and our discussions are also influenced by an ongoing conversation with Judaism, its claim on these texts as scripture, and a trajectory in Judaism that moves from Tanak to Talmud.

Critical Understandings

The Old Testament as the literature of ancient Israel must be understood critically. Likewise, the claims of authority for the Old Testament as scripture in the church must be critically assessed. In both of these arenas a variety of critical approaches contributes to the discussions in this volume, and this book is greatly informed by generations of productive critical scholarship. These critical approaches are not without tensions and competing claims, and it is important to discuss some of our perspectives on these issues.

Historical Criticism and Beyond

Historical criticism rose to the height of its influence in the nineteenth to the mid-twentieth century as an effort to apply Enlightenment epistemological assumptions to the biblical text and to escape the dominance of church authority in biblical interpretation. Its various methods (e.g., source criticism, form criticism, traditio-historical criticism, redaction criticism) collectively assumed the possibility of objective and scientific interpretive results that would not be affected by prior dogmatic assumptions about the biblical text. The use of these methods allowed the development of a more detailed understanding of the complex processes through which our biblical texts developed into their present form. The rise to dominance of historical criticism in biblical interpretation fit with the spirit of modernity, which prevailed through the mid-twentieth century, even though significant battles continued with those who held to more restrictive views of ecclesial authority in interpreting the Bible. Much of the interpretive literature available and used in the church still today is deeply influenced by historical-critical approaches.

More recently some of the assumptions and results of historical criticism have become widely viewed as problematic.[3] Some have claimed that historical criticism is bankrupt, and some have argued that these critical methods have been superseded. We would agree that there are significant issues to be raised about historical-critical approaches to biblical interpretation, but these are often issues posed by the more extreme claims made for historical-criticism. Or these are sometimes issues that arise with the inability of some to acknowledge the legitimacy of interpretive methods that go beyond or build upon the historical critical method.

(a) Few would any longer defend the possibility of genuinely "objective" interpretive readings of biblical texts. We agree with those who would argue that there are no disinterested readings of biblical texts. Every reader or reading community brings a set of contextual assumptions, perspectives, and values into the interaction with the biblical text. Thus, interpretation must critically reflect on the context of the reader as well as the text. In this volume, we offer our theological interpretation of the Old Testament as a reading informed by our particular contexts, but also as aware of and in conversation with interpretive voices from other contexts dissimilar to our own. While we do not believe there are totally disinterested "objective" readings of texts, we do not consider this an invitation to uncritical relativism in reading the biblical text. We have attempted to approach this theological introduction to the Old Testament with a disciplined and critical awareness of the text, the context out of which its witnesses arose and the context out of which we read it. To do this we necessarily continue to gratefully use historical-critical tools and methods.

(b) Historical criticism has also at times become problematic for developmental assumptions that have regarded as valuable only what resembled, moved toward, or could be reduced to the prevailing patterns and assumptions of twentieth-century Euro-American intellectual life. Thus, for example, some scholars viewed the period of second-temple Judaism as a degeneration into legalism from the high watermark of the prophets—a view that fostered disregard for the creative response of Judaism to the challenges of the time

5

after the return from Babylonian exile. As a further example, the developmental assumptions of some advocates of historical criticism, fearful of supernaturalism, relegated theological claims about the activity of God in Israel's story to a secondary level of importance less significant than the investigation of literary and social processes at work in the formation of the text. Many of the theological claims of the text were, accordingly, explained away or regarded as early, more primitive religious expressions. Such a perspective is, of course, contrary to the claim of the text itself that the activity of God—including all of God's mysterious, hidden, and alien aspects— is at the heart of any meaning ascribed to these texts. The movement beyond historical criticism in recent interpretation attempts to read the text with attention to all of its claims, including those that seem odd, alien, or difficult but are nevertheless part of the text that is to be read as scripture by the church.

(c) Positivistic philosophical assumptions, operative in the exercise of much historical-critical work in the twentieth century, often resulted in a search for *the* meaning of a biblical text. This led to a tendency to value the discovery of underlying sources, and supposed original intent, more highly than the completed text of many biblical books. In the approach of this volume we believe that critical understanding of the development of a text through complex processes may inform our understanding of the text, but never to the exclusion of interest in the witness of the final form of the text as we now have it.

Some of these criticisms of the way in which the historical-critical method dominated previous generations of biblical scholarship are justified. New methods of interpretive encounter with the text are demanding and receiving attention, and our approach is influenced by some of these as discussed further in this chapter. But historical-critical methods cannot be set aside and are still an important part of disciplined critical study of the Old Testament, even one that stresses the theological address of the text.

If this volume reflects interpretation that moves beyond historical criticism, it nevertheless cannot interpret as if we stood prior to the contributions of historical criticism. We continue to use many historical-critical tools of analysis and continue to be informed by the contributions of historical criticism to our knowledge of the text and the world out of which it came. In particular, historical criticism has given us a respect for the complexity of the process that produced the biblical writings of ancient Israel. It has made us aware of the patterns and propensities of various genres of ancient literature. It has heightened our awareness of the shaping influence of various social, economic, and political factors that define the contexts out of which biblical texts are formed. In short, even as we move beyond historical criticism, we remain engaged in and indebted to its contributions and perspectives.

History, Language, Story, Song

There is increasing recognition that interpretation now takes place in a postmodern context, one in which the previously settled assumptions of the modern world have become unsettled and must, therefore, be reassessed.[4] One of those assumptions, closely allied with the claims of historical criticism, was that history was the primary category for assessing the truth claims of the biblical text and the reality assumed to "stand behind" the text. In our view, the search for a historical reality behind the text sometimes did violence to the imaginative and rhetorical integrity of the text itself. In particular the confessional speech of Israel about God was often judged to be lacking a ground in historical reality, and much of this speech about God was placed either to the side or on the margins of efforts to describe biblical "truths."

As a category for assessing the claim to authority for the texts of ancient Israel, history has become a battleground. Only a generation ago, scholars were confidently writing histories of Israel using the biblical text itself as a primary resource and supplementing that with ancient Near Eastern and archaeological data. There was some recognition that texts, particularly those telling the story of early Israel, were shaped by confessional tradition. Nevertheless, Israel's testimonies were confidently believed to have a base in historical reality, and this claim was considered important to the theological authority of the text.[5]

For over thirty years this claim has been under serious attack. At present there are many scholars who regard most of the texts of the Old Testament as having no basis in historical reality. Most of these scholars regard the bulk of the Old Testament narrative tradition as a fiction generated by the community of post-exilic Judaism.[6] For most making this argument, this lack of historical basis undermines the authority of the theological claims of the text as well.

This is not the place to assess the poles of this debate in detail. The Old Testament was not written and passed on primarily as historical record but exists as theological testimony. Thus, the use of the text to reconstruct the history of ancient Israel does present serious critical problems. But the abandonment of all historical connection behind the texts of ancient Israel is itself a position with assumptions that are not disinterested. Already serious challenges to the extreme minimalist reading of Israel's history have emerged to challenge the notion that historians must choose between critical and confessional perspectives. These voices argue that a history of Israel that is more than a fiction can be written and the biblical texts can contribute to such a critical history.[7]

In our view, the God of Israel and the claim that God may make on the communities that continue to regard the Old Testament as scripture can be known only by taking seriously the full reality of the imaginative language through which that God is presented in the biblical text. Thus, interpretation is as much a rhetorical as a historical enterprise.[8] The recent explosion of literary approaches in biblical studies has significantly aided such interpretation. To encounter Israel's God requires not the discovery of some hidden history behind the text but serious entry into the world of biblical testimony about this God with its claims and counterclaims. Narrative (i.e., story) and poetry (i.e., song) are the central forms of this testimony about God. Even the nonstory elements of the Old Testament characteristically assume the framework and knowledge of Israel's story about encounter and relationship with God. We are invited, indeed required, to enter the story and to hear the song and to respond according to the shape of the story and the transactions appropriate to the song. We are to value the imaginative power of the narrative or poem more than its correspondence to some external, empirical reality. We are to discover in the world of Old Testament texts tensions and struggles that challenge settled claims about God and God's community, Israel. It is the power of imaginative language to give rise to metaphor that allows us as modern readers to find our entry into the settled claims and the competing witnesses of the Old Testament. In that encounter with Israel's imaginative language we find perspectives on the claims and witnesses of our own experiences as persons and communities. Such entry into the literary worlds of Israel and its subsequent impact on our own lives has a power that no accumulation of historical data could ever have. The reality of God cannot be disclosed, past or present, apart from the boldness of those who speak that reality into the realm of their own experience. Our treatment in this volume tries to honor the boldness and creativity of that speech.

Social World and Theological Dynamics

Even as we have come to appreciate the theological value of creative story and song, we have also become aware of the diverse circumstances in which the people of Israel lived. Study of these circumstances has had a profound impact upon our understanding of the theological developments reflected in the Old Testament. The past several decades of Old Testament scholarship have seen a remarkable number of studies devoted to the social worlds of ancient Israel. Issues such as gender, social status, political structure, and ideology have become part of the discussion in an entirely new way. Such analytical categories have provided new ways to reflect theologically about the Old Testament.

At the same time, biblical scholarship has grown in its awareness of the social context of biblical reading and interpretation. The community within which one reads and understands the meaning of a biblical text has a profound impact. We are affected by the perspectives of gender, ethnicity, religious tradition, and cultural setting. A theological reading of Old Testament texts must be self-conscious and critical in its awareness of the effect of social context within the world that produced the text and among the communities that read the text in our own time. Part of the power of these texts as scripture affirmed by faith communities over generations lies in their ability to speak meaningfully to multiple contexts and to be interpreted helpfully from differing perspectives. To interpret these texts theologically is to enter a dialogue with the many voices that speak from the text and with the generations that have read the text faithfully from their own times and places in the world.

Attention to social context, ancient and modern, has resulted in scholarship aimed at calling our attention to perspectives that might be overlooked or undervalued.

Gender studies, as well exemplified by *The Women's Bible Commentary*,[9] offer readings that emphasize how differently the stories and roles of men and women have been treated in the biblical text and in the history of interpretation. In the patriarchal world of ancient Israel, women were seldom the central focus in the stories. Images of women in the stories and in non-narrative materials often reflected social roles that were limited and sometimes harmful. Interpreters, until recently almost entirely men, often overlooked the importance of women in biblical stories or failed to consider that the genders may have perceived divine reality and the relationship of God to the world differently. Gender-sensitive scholarship has called our attention to previously ignored or undervalued elements of the Old Testament story. For example:

- Hagar, a slave to Sarah, mother of Abraham's first son, and outcast into the wilderness, becomes the recipient of a divine theophany and promise.
- Tamar, Rahab, and Ruth, although women in marginal roles and positions in their societies, become the mothers from whose line comes David, Israel's greatest king. These same women, along with Bathsheba, become the mothers named in the genealogy of Jesus in Matt 1.
- Prophets such as Hosea and Ezekiel regularly use images of Israel as an unfaithful wife deserving abuse and humiliation for her unfaithfulness. Although reflecting the treatment of wives in ancient Israel, such images are not a part of the prophetic message we want to uncritically affirm.[10]
- Women such as Miriam, Rahab, Deborah, Hannah, Abigail, Huldah, and Esther do play important roles of leadership and bold initiative that affect the future of Israel and advance God's purposes. Renewed attention to their stories often suggests alternative patterns of influence and leadership that depart from customary styles and practices.

Socioeconomic status and class provide another important variable for theological reflection. The Old Testament regularly depicts the people of Israel on the move. At one key point, early on in the story, God liberates the people from slavery in Egypt and, after a sojourn in the wilderness, a later generation is able to move into the promised land. There has been much theological reflection about the importance of this paradigm through which many in subsequent generations have encountered a God who liberates people from oppressive situations.[11] In contrast, later in the story, many of the people of Judah are forcibly removed from their land into exile in the early sixth century BCE. Here God is depicted as acting in accord with principles of justice, righteousness, and sole loyalty to Yahweh that were constitutive for the covenant community. The theological experiences of the people of God at these two radically different moments in the story are, not surprisingly, quite different. Exodus focuses on the experience of the dispossessed and the oppressed, but exile arises from the failures of those who possessed power and failed to heed prophetic warnings. Such differences challenge readers today to make certain that their theological understandings can accommodate the full range of social condition and experience that God's people have known and which is attested in the canon.

Reading with attention to *ethnicity and culture* can bring out elements of texts and stories that would otherwise be missed.[12] For example, Israel's attitude toward the nations reflects universal or exclusivist viewpoints depending on Israel's own experience and the voices speaking in the text (cf. Amos 9:7 to Nah 3:19). Contemporary reading of the Old Testament from within differing ethnic or cultural communities calls attention to elements of Israel's story and witness that would otherwise be missed (e.g., the simple but important insight that the stories of Joseph and Ruth are immigrant stories). Readings attentive to ethnicity and culture can also provide a corrective to past readings that have distorted the text in the service of racism or cultural bias (e.g., the historic and tragic use of the story of Cain and the mark of God to justify racism and slavery).

Theological reflection on *geographical/historical differences* (e.g., a people in the wilderness versus a people in the land) or on the different *polities and political realities* in effect (e.g., monarchy versus colonized province; people in cities versus people in rural areas; people in Judah versus people in Israel) stimulates a complex portrait of God in the life of Israel. And yet, such diverse experiences offer a template by means of which the people of God today, also in diverse settings, can relate to the God they worship.

Canon and Church

The Old Testament would not have been handed down to the present apart from a process within Jewish and Christian communities that settled on an authoritative collection of texts, known as a canon. The extent and shape of the canon have varied somewhat from one tradition to another. Even today multiple translations of the text result from differing judgments about the varying manuscript traditions on which translations must rely.

Beyond the canon itself, church doctrine and ecclesial authority have influenced the theological interpretation of the biblical text and the authority it exercises within the community of faith. Critical analysis and assessment must also be directed to differing claims about the nature of biblical authority and the modes of interpretation appropriate to the theological interpretation of the Old Testament.

One of the first challenges to the early church was a reductionist attempt to restrict the church's authoritative canon by leaving out the Old Testament and many parts of the New Testament (particularly those that reflected the Jewish context of the early church). In the early second century, Marcion and his followers argued for a biblical canon consisting of only the Gospel of Luke and a few of Paul's Letters. He rejected the Old Testament entirely and argued that it depicted a God completely unlike the Christian God. His views were opposed and eventually claimed heretical by the early church. Many see his views as a stimulus for the early church in this period to determine which books would be in an authoritative canon. For this volume, an important element of this effort to determine the extent and shape of the canon was the decisive affirmation as scripture of those books we now call the Old Testament, and the affirmation that the God of those scriptures was the same God from Genesis through Revelation.

Although forms of virtual Marcionism, which ignore or downgrade the importance of the Old Testament canon, persist until the present, the church has at many crucial points in its various traditions affirmed the inclusion of the Old Testament as a part of the canon of authoritative scripture. This firm commitment to the Old Testament as scripture has played no small role in maintaining a vital interest in the preservation, transmission, and ongoing interpretation of the Old Testament in and for the life of the church. It is in the context of this church commitment that theological interpretation finds importance beyond the exercise of academic interest in ancient traditions. Contemporary communities of faith have a stake in theological interpretation of these ancient texts, and this church context influences decisively the expectations of the interpretive task. Interpretation in the context of the church expects an ongoing transformation of lives and communities that arises from genuine encounter with the text of the Old Testament and the God to whom the text bears witness.

Canon refers to the authoritative collection of writings affirmed and passed on by the church. All Christian traditions agree on the canonical status of the Hebrew writings organized at first in the Jewish tradition into Law, Prophets, and Writings. Traditional English translations since the seventeenth century, following the lead of translations during the Protestant Reformation in Europe, have embraced an altered ordering of these books. Roman Catholics and some Eastern Orthodox traditions have also given canonical status to the intertestamental books commonly called the Apocrypha (see Tables I–IV, pp. 25-28). The Hebrew canon Christians call the Old Testament arose out of the experience of ancient Israel and reflects not only the end point of an authoritative collection but also a record of the witness of a community reflecting at many points on its own multifaceted journey with God.

The medieval church, and in large measure the later Reformation churches, preserved the canon of the Old Testament but largely subsumed its theological voice to categories taken from systematic or dogmatic theology. The result was, in considerable measure, a monochromatic view of the canonical witness. The polyphonic voices of the Old Testament with their unsettled diversity of witness were often pressed into artificial unity through systematic categories brought from outside the text itself. Attempts to describe the Old Testament's theological witness often used the categories common to systematic theology. Elements deemed inconsistent with church doctrine were ignored or treated as marginal to the theological understanding of the Old Testament. Historical criticism, which helped uncover the diversity of ancient Israelite religious tradition, helped free the text of the Old Testament from this reductionist use by the church. However, it has not always been easy to integrate such analysis with the use of the Old Testament by the church. The result has sometimes been a distancing of biblical scholarship from the theological concerns of the church.

Recent work in Old Testament theology has emphasized the importance of the process that produced the canon and the canonical form of the text as the tradition passed on by Jewish and Christian communities of faith.[13] The authors of this volume affirm that emphasis as welcome for its seriousness about the entirety of the Old Testament tradition and the importance of interpreting the text as it stands in its final form. But we are also clear that recognition of the important role of the church in affirming and passing on the Hebrew canon does not justify interpretations of canonical literature that limit our ability to hear the canonical polyphony of voices in order to conform to patterns of acceptable church doctrine. Nor does the importance of the canon in its final form eliminate the need for critical study of the processes that brought the text to its final form.

In our theological analysis of the Old Testament, we understand our task as the presentation of interpretive readings that are honest to the religious experience given witness by ancient Israel and accessible to encounter by contemporary Christians. It is not appropriate to attempt to make these readings conform to any particular pattern of church doctrine. The goal is not conformity but open and honest encounter with the church's doctrinal traditions. Some readings of the Old Testament text will undergird and give foundation to church doctrine. But some of the honest reading of Israel's witness will present troublesome issues to Christian faith and difficult portraits of God's character and work. Where narrow doctrinal readings may try to present settled affirmation, honest readings of the Old Testament (or the New) may "trouble the waters" or disturb comfortable certitude. This is one of the ongoing functions of the Bible with its diverse voices and perspectives. What we seek is a theological reading of the Old Testament engaged critically and honestly with church doctrine in ways that contribute to the biblical foundation of the church's beliefs and the ongoing transformation of the church in its relationship to God and the world.

Since for Christians the canon of scripture includes the books of the New Testament, there have been prominent modes of interpretation that seek to find some form of overt witness to Jesus Christ in the Old Testament. We do not believe this is ever the intent of the Hebrew text. Israel's witness to its experience with God possesses its own integrity, which does not allow us to identify specific texts as part of the church's Christology in their initial context. We do, however, think it is important to recognize the ongoing traditions as they live and receive reinterpretation in later Jewish and Christian contexts. Old Testament texts have trajectories of transmission and reinterpretation that for Jews stretches from Hebrew canon into the Talmud and for Christians from Old Testament into the New Testament. Such recognition of Old Testament texts and themes, used and reinterpreted by the early church, serves to integrate the Old and New Testament witness as testimony to the reality of the same God.

The Public Context of Theological Reading

Although it is primarily the community of faith that reads the Old Testament theologically, it does not read in a vacuum. The church does not exist as an end in itself. It is called to discern and join in the exercise of God's justice, righteousness, and love in the world. Thus, any adequate theological reading of the Old Testament must critically engage the public context within which the church reads, interprets, and proclaims these texts. To read theologically is to go beyond our legitimate and important reading for the purposes of individual piety or for the needs of institutional ecclesiastical interests. The theological significance of the Old Testament rests in the conviction that these texts constitute a witness in behalf of the God of Israel that can make a difference in the public issues and crises of our time. There are public as well as ecclesial possibilities for the message of these texts.

We unavoidably write from the perspective of twenty-first-century, North American, Protestant Christian interpreters, representing four different religious traditions. But it is apparent to us that the churches and the culture of which we are a part are undergoing profound challenge, struggle, and change. We observe the end of dominant privileged positions of race, class, culture, and gender. Traditional centers of economic and political power have eroded, and new power structures are taking their place. We live in what some have called a postcolonial world, but corporate and consumer economic forces and structures threaten new forms of domination. We live in an increasingly global and multiethnic world, but we experience the wrenching violence of nationalist extremism and ethnic intolerance. We live with a new awareness of race, class, gender, and sexual orientation, but with growing expressions of intolerance and hatred directed at differences in the human community. We live in a world grown smaller and more interrelated by virtue of travel and technology, but with increased divisions of wealth and poverty and growing crises of environmental exploitation. We live in a time of spiritual hunger but with challenges to our spiritual integrity that arise out of self-interest and consumer values. We live in a society with vast new opportunities to enrich the lives of families and children, but with increased pressures that sometimes break fragile family structures or put our children at risk. At the time of this writing we live in a world plagued by terrorism, but in a nation pursuing security through a war that much of the world condemns.

If we are to read the Bible theologically, then our reading cannot be indifferent to these public crises. The church reads the Old Testament faithfully only if its reading is not for its own sake but for the sake of the broken world to which it is sent—the world God loves and seeks to judge and redeem. This volume seeks to present the Old Testament theologically out of a conviction that its surprising stories, its diverse voices, its unflinching involvement with the moral issues of power, its willingness to face human ambiguity, its constant testimony to a demanding and complex God, can make a difference in the way the church engages the public crises of our time. Our hope is that a theological engagement with the witnesses of ancient Israel in the Old Testament will provide perspectives on our contemporary world out of the conviction that the God of Israel is the same God active today. The Old Testament is not simply about ancient religious communities. It concerns God's justice and redemption at work in the world of economic and political power and in the midst of the living and dying of human communities. Thus, the Old Testament is not to be read today for the sake of in-house religious purposes in the church. It is to be read to make the reality of God's power amid the issues of human power clear for our time, as it was for Israel's time. Such a reading is complex and multifaceted to be sure, but to read for any lesser purpose is to cut ourselves off from the enduring power of God's word (cf. Isa 40:6-8).

Diversity and Continuity

Any adequate theological reading of the Old Testament must take into account the diverse theological voices that speak through its texts. This diversity has been viewed by many as a theological problem that undermines the possibilities of any use of the Old Testament as authoritative scripture for the church. Some have tried to deal with this problem of diversity by imposing an organizing theological pattern on the Old Testament. These efforts have failed to attract enduring support because they either force material into an artificially unified schema or relegate some Old Testament voices to a devalued margin.

Diversity as Gift and Danger

No one who has read the Old Testament can fail to notice the great diversity of voices that speak through its texts. Narrative and poetry, peasant piety and royal archive, priestly ritual and prophetic utterance, apocalyptic vision and wisdom saying—all of these voices, and many more, witness to the polyphonic nature of the Old Testament as a whole. It is one of the great gifts of the Old Testament as a theological resource to the community of faith that almost any person in any role or circumstance can find a voice within the Old Testament witness that seems to offer the reader common ground.

This collection of polyphonic voices does indeed enrich our perspectives on the biblical experience of God. The Old Testament does not present a narrow harmony of voices. There is, however, a danger in this affirmation. Our affirmation of this diversity should not be understood as a settling for pluralistic voices as an end in themselves or as a selection from which we simply make congenial choices. The God of the Hebrew Bible is one God, although experienced in many ways and depicted through multiple images. The presence of such diversity in the same Hebrew canon is an invitation to consider these voices in relation to one another and as witness to diverse, even inconsistent, experiences of the same God. Such an invitation draws us into dialogue with these voices. We cannot settle for atomistic description of each witness in isolation but are drawn to consider how so many diverse stories are collected into a canon that insists these stories be in dialogue together. We are asked to consider what Walter Brueggemann has called testimony and counter-testimony as a necessary tension within which religious readers seek to discern God's word.[14]

Coherence and Continuity

We do believe, however, that there is a coherence and continuity in the Old Testament that transcends the diversity of its voices. This cannot be thought of as an imposed unity that would obscure, diminish, or deny the dialogue among the polyphonic witnesses of the Old Testament. The dialogue within the Old Testament is not, however, without unifying elements. We would suggest that the polyphonic voices of the Old Testament have a common focus on the character, activity, and will of Israel's one God and a common framework in the story of Israel as the people of that one God.

Esther and the Song of Songs are the only books in the Hebrew canon that do not mention God, and they were controversial for this reason at the time the final section of the canon (the Writings) was being fixed. Throughout the rest of the Old Testament, every type of material gives overt testimony to Israel's experience of God. Sometimes, as in covenant and commandments or prophetic utterance, the emphasis is on *God's will* as revealed to Israel. At other times testimony is to the *actions of God* as Creator of all things, as deliverer/judge/redeemer of Israel, and as sovereign over all nations. And throughout the Old Testament there are witnesses to the experienced *character of the God* to whom Israel is related—a God in whom Israel has known holiness, justice, righteousness, compassion, wrath, love, mercy, and wisdom. Although diverse, the texts of the Old Testament nevertheless participate in testimony about, to, and against a common God.

If God is the common focus, the *story of Israel as a people* related to this God is the common framework for the diverse texts of the Old Testament. The Old Testament is not abstract, philosophical discourse or dispassionate, historical narrative. The Old Testament is the faith story of Israel or testimony from within the context of that faith story. Some of the Old Testament is composed of the narrative texts that simply tell Israel's story, although sometimes from multiple perspectives and always as faith witness rather than neutral history writing. Nonstorytelling materials, such as law codes or collections of prophetic preaching, are to be understood in the context of particular times and places in Israel's story. The psalms are Israel's worship materials. Even the Wisdom literature is not presented as commonly held international literature but as a part of Israel's testimony to Yahweh, who as Creator is the source of all wisdom. If there are divergent and sometimes clashing voices in the Old Testament, they nevertheless remain a part of Israel's story as the people of God and judged by Israel worthy to pass on as its testimony to its God.

Even in the diversity of voices in the Old Testament, one may discern a creative tension that is itself an element of continuity and coherence. Voices that witness to God as the power that sustains creation and orders the lives of the community are constantly challenged by voices that critique the existing order of the status quo in behalf of those left in the margins and testify to God as the power that brings revolutionary possibility for change and transformation. It is a part of the theological character of the Old Testament that the reader is constantly forced back into this creative tension. God who blesses and orders our lives is also God who disrupts in order to make new. We can count on this dynamic. Our theological reading of the Old Testament as scripture of the church will both comfort and disturb us. It will support our cherished faith visions and challenge us to give them up for new and different ones. It will affirm our place in relationship to God in community and judge our unwillingness to make place for others. It will provide resources for comfort in time of trouble and trouble us when we settle into comfort.

A final word must be said about *continuity*. Readers tend to read the Old Testament in isolation as if it did not stand in continuity with their own faith traditions and communities. The Old Testament ends abruptly. There is no carefully crafted conclusion or summation. We are in the midst of a story and it simply breaks off. As Christians we have most often resumed reading with the New Testament. The result is a sense of discontinuity. Christians often treat the Old Testament as distant background and the New Testament as a fresh start. We know little of the intertestamental literature that tells the story of the continuing journey of God's people—the Jews—in various parts of the ancient world. We know little of the story of Judaism and the rich literature that provides the context for the life and ministry of Jesus and the emergence of the early church.

We must move beyond this sense of discontinuity in favor of a new recognition of continuity between the Old Testament's witness and our own faith identity. We must do this with an awareness that the continuity of Israel's witness with our own Christian tradition is but one of several continuous traditions that grow from Israel's texts. Both Judaism and Islam are lively and creative, historical and contemporary religious traditions that share with Christianity a foundation in the testimony of ancient Israel.

As Christians we are still connected to the story and witness of ancient Israel. It is theologically important to recognize several dimensions of that connectedness.

There is a *continuity of God*. The God of Israel is the same God made known in Jesus Christ and the early church and given testimony in the New Testament. This is the same God with whom the church has lived in relationship down to the present. Our God is Israel's God. Thus, all of the aspects of God's character and activity given witness in the Old Testament are in continuity with the experience of God reflected in the New Testament and the centuries of Christian tradition. God's power, love, justice, redemption, judgment, compassion, and faithfulness are all known first in the Old Testament. It is sometimes suggested that we meet a different God in the New Testament. The caricature often suggests that the Old Testament gives us God's law, but we encounter God's grace only in the New Testament. We want to assert unequivocally that God's grace is already manifest in the pages of the Old Testament and does not wait to be introduced for Christians in the New Testament. The God of Israel is the same God seen as incarnate in Jesus Christ, and it is our recognition of God's grace in creation, promise, deliverance, covenant making, judgment, and redemption in Israel's story that allows us to understand more fully the divine grace we see in Jesus Christ. Recognition of this continuity of divine grace would help put an end to caricatures that associate the Old Testament only with law and judgment and the New Testament with grace and love.

There is a *continuity of God's world*. The potential of God's creation is the same gift to every generation, ancient and modern, Jew and Christian, believer and unbeliever. The ancient cosmologies of Genesis are not the same as the Greek understandings of the cosmos in the background of the New Testament and are certainly different from modern scientific understandings of the cosmos. But testimony by the faith community to the gifts of God's creation and the challenge to live as stewards in that creation are continuous in spite of changed cosmologies. To claim continuity with the testimony of ancient Israel that the world is God's created world is to choose a way of relating to the world that transcends changes in cosmology. We also, however, share with ancient Israel the conviction that the world God created in wholeness has become broken. The reality of broken creation faces the faith community, ancient and modern, with the same challenges. There are, of course, great differences in the social contexts of ancient Israel, the early church, and our own time. Yet, there is a continuity of human sinfulness and social brokenness that makes the issues of ancient Israel our own. Behind the reality of changed social context is a continuity of human nature and human interrelatedness that allows our story to be intersected by the biblical story. We experience the common struggle we share with ancient Israel to face issues of meaning and faithfulness in the midst of broken lives and broken social communities, to face issues of justice and redemption in the midst of settled and sinful patterns of power.

There is a *continuity of God's people.* God's people do not cease to exist at the close of the Old Testament only to resume existence for Christians at Pentecost. There is a continuing story of God's people through the story of second-temple Judaism extending beyond the canon through the literature we now call the Apocrypha and witnessed in other early Jewish writings. Jesus and the early church were an inseparable part of this early Jewish tradition. To comprehend early Christians adequately we must understand more fully the continuity of Christian tradition with its Jewish roots. The community of God's people was not created at Pentecost but emerged as a living branch of a lively Jewish tradition that bridges in continuity from the Old Testament to both later Judaism and the early church.

There is a *continuity of God's work.* We hope that through this theological interpretation of the Old Testament, readers will emerge with a sense that God's work, attested so richly in the writings of ancient Israel, will be recognized as in continuity with the work of God in our own world. Thus, such study of the witness of ancient Israel is not an end in itself, but instead enables the Old Testament as scripture of the church to serve as a resource that empowers us as God's people for our own faithful response to the needs of a broken world.

Notes

1. Numerous recent publications suggest a revival of interest in reading and teaching the Old Testament (and the New) theologically—reading the biblical texts as scripture. Representative of these resources are Ellen F. Davis and Richard B. Hays, eds., *The Art of Reading Scripture* (Grand Rapids: Eerdmans, 2003); and John P. Burgess, *Why Scripture Matters* (Louisville: Westminster John Knox, 1998).

2. A lively recent discussion of terminology for the collection of ancient Israel's texts has not resulted in any general consensus, and it is clear that none of the alternatives are ideologically neutral or without interpretive pitfalls. See the helpful discussions of this issue in Jon Levenson, *The Hebrew Bible, the Old Testament, and Historical Criticism* (Louisville: Westminster John Knox, 1993); John J. Collins and Roger Brooks, eds., *Hebrew Bible or Old Testament? Studying the Bible in Judaism and Christianity* (South Bend: University of Notre Dame Press, 1990); and Christopher R. Seitz, *Word Without End: The Old Testament as Abiding Theological Witness* (Grand Rapids: Eerdmans, 1998), 61-74.

3. There is a lively literature available debating the merits and liabilities of the historical-critical method in this postmodern era. See Levenson, *The Hebrew Bible, the Old Testament, and Historical Criticism;* John Barton, *The Future of Old Testament Study* (Oxford: Oxford University Press, 1993); and "Historical Critical Approaches," *The Cambridge Companion to Biblical Interpretation* (Cambridge: Cambridge University Press, 1998), 9-19; Leander E. Keck, "Will the Historical Critical Method Survive?" in R. A. Spencer, ed., *Orientation by Disorientation: Studies in Literary Criticism and Biblical Literary Criticism* (Pittsburgh: Theological Monographs 35, 1980), 115-27; Francis Watson, *Text, Church, and World: Biblical Interpretation in Theological Perspective* (Edinburgh: T. & T. Clark, 1994).

4. See Walter Brueggemann, *Texts Under Negotiation: The Bible and Postmodern Imagination* (Minneapolis: Fortress, 1993).

5. The most widely used treatment of Israel's history in this vein is John Bright, *A History of Israel* (4th ed.; Louisville: Westminster John Knox, 2000).

6. The following quote represents this school of thought: "There is no more 'ancient Israel.' History no longer has room for it. This we do know. And now, as one of the first conclusions of this new knowledge, 'biblical Israel' was in its origins a Jewish concept." T. L. Thompson, "A Neo-Albrightean School in History and Biblical Scholarship?" *JBL* 114 (1995): 697. See also P. R. Davies, *In Search of "Ancient Israel"* (JSOTSup 148; Sheffield, JSOT, 1992); and K. W. Whitelam, *The Invention of Ancient Israel: The Silencing of Palestinian History* (New York: Routledge, 1996).

7. Particularly impressive as a comprehensive response to minimalist historical approaches is Iain Provan, V. Philips Long, and Tremper Longman III, *A Biblical History of Israel* (Louisville: Westminster John Knox, 2003). Students will find in its opening chapters a comprehensive review of the debate over Israel's history, and a convincing challenge to the minimalist assumptions for writing Israel's history. Another effort to affirm alternatives to the minimalist perspective can be found in Michael D. Coogan, ed., *The Oxford History of the Biblical World* (Oxford: Oxford University Press, 1998). See also William G. Dever, *What Did the Biblical Writers Know and When Did They Know It? What Archaeology Can Tell Us About the Reality of Ancient Israel* (Grand Rapids: Eerdmans, 2001); and V. P. Long, G. J. Wenham, and D. W. Baker, eds., *Windows into Old Testament History: Evidence, Argument, and the Crisis of "Biblical Israel"* (Grand Rapids: Eerdmans, 2002).

8. Walter Brueggemann refers to this as "imaginative remembering" in his *An Introduction to the Old Testament: The Canon and Christian Imagination* (Louisville: Westminster John Knox, 2003).

9. Carol A. Newsom and Sharon H. Ringe, eds., *The Women's Bible Commentary*, rev. ed. (Louisville: Westminster John Knox, 1998). Many of the articles in this volume include bibliography for reading further in the growing volume of feminist and womanist biblical studies. See also Phyllis Bird, *Missing Persons and Mistaken Identities in Ancient Israel* (OBT; Minneapolis: Fortress, 1997); and Tikva Simone Frymer-Kensky, *Reading the Women of the Bible* (New York: Schocken Books, 2002).

10. See Renita J. Weems, *Battered Love: Marriage, Sex, and Violence in the Hebrew Prophets* (OBT; Minneapolis: Fortress, 1995).

11. See Michael Walzer, *Exodus and Revolution* (New York: Basic Books, 1985); and J. Severino Croatto, *Exodus: A Hermeneutics of Freedom*, trans. by S. Attanasis (Maryknoll, N.Y.: Orbis Books, 1981).

12. See Cain Felder, ed., *Stony the Road We Trod* (Minneapolis: Fortress, 1991); and R. S. Sugirtharajah, ed., *Voices from the Margin: Interpreting the Bible in the Third World*, new ed. (Maryknoll, N.Y.: Orbis, 1995).

13. See Brevard S. Childs, *Introduction to the Old Testament as Scripture* (Philadelphia: Fortress, 1979); James A. Sanders, *Canon and Community: A Guide to Canonical Criticism* (GBS; Philadelphia: Fortress, 1984); and Rolf Rendtorff, *Canon and Theology* (OBT; Minneapolis: Fortress, 1993).

14. Walter Brueggemann, *Theology of the Old Testament: Testimony, Dispute, Advocacy* (Minneapolis: Fortress, 1997).

Bibliography

Alter, Robert, and Frank Kermode, eds. *The Literary Guide to the Bible.* Cambridge: Harvard University Press, 1987.

Barton, John, ed. *The Cambridge Companion to Biblical Interpretation.* Cambridge: Cambridge University Press, 1998.

Birch, Bruce C. *Let Justice Roll Down: The Old Testament, Ethics, and Christian Life.* Louisville: Westminster John Knox, 1991.

Brueggemann, Walter. *An Introduction to the Old Testament: The Canon and Christian Imagination.* Louisville: Westminster John Knox, 2003.

———. *Texts Under Negotiation: The Bible and the Postmodern Imagination.* Minneapolis: Fortress, 1993.

———. *Theology of the Old Testament: Testimony, Dispute, Advocacy.* Minneapolis: Fortress, 1997.

Childs, Brevard S. *Introduction to the Old Testament as Scripture.* Philadelphia: Fortress, 1979.

Collins, John J. *Introduction to the Hebrew Bible.* Minneapolis: Augsburg Fortress, 2004.

Coogan, Michael D., ed. *The Oxford History of the Biblical World.* Oxford: Oxford University Press, 1998.

Davis, Ellen F., and Richard B. Hays, eds. *The Art of Reading Scripture.* Grand Rapids: Eerdmans, 2003.

Gottwald, Norman K. *The Hebrew Bible: A Socio-Literary Introduction.* Philadelphia: Fortress, 1985.

Newsom, Carol A., and Sharon H. Ringe, eds. *The Women's Bible Commentary.* Rev. ed. Louisville: Westminster John Knox, 1998.

Perdue, Leo G., ed. *The Blackwell Companion to the Hebrew Bible*. Oxford: Blackwell, 2001.

————. *The Collapse of History: Reconstructing Old Testament Theology*. OBT. Minneapolis: Fortress, 1994.

Provan, Iain, V. Phillips Long, and Tremper Longman III. *A Biblical History of Ancient Israel*. Louisville: Westminster John Knox, 2003.

Reid, Stephen Breck. *Experience and Tradition: A Primer in Black Biblical Hermeneutics*. Nashville: Abingdon, 1990.

Rendtorff, Rolf. *Canon and Theology: Overtures from Old Testament Theology*. OBT. Minneapolis: Fortress, 1993.

Sanders, James A. *Canon and Community: A Guide to Canonical Criticism*. GBS. Philadelphia: Fortress, 1984.

Segovia, Fernando F., and Mary Ann Tolbert. *Reading from This Place*. 2 vols. Minneapolis: Fortress, 1995.

Sugirtharajah, R. S., ed. *Voices from the Margin: Interpreting the Bible in the Third World*. New ed. Maryknoll, N.Y.: Orbis, 1995.

THE CANONS OF SCRIPTURE

All Christian churches accept the thirty-nine-book Jewish canon for the Old Testament (Table I). The Roman Catholic and Orthodox traditions accept additional books into the Old Testament canon. Anglicans, Lutherans, and other Protestants call these books the Apocrypha.

Table I: The Jewish Canon

Jewish Scriptures are divided into three parts: Torah, Prophets, and Writings. First and Second Samuel, 1–2 Kings, 1–2 Chronicles, Ezra and Nehemiah, and the Twelve Minor Prophets are each considered a single book because each set of writings forms one complete scroll.

Torah	Prophets	Writings
Genesis	*Former Prophets*	Psalms
Exodus	Joshua	Proverbs
Leviticus	Judges	Job
Numbers	1–2 Samuel	Song of Songs
Deuteronomy	1–2 Kings	Ruth
	Lamentations	Ecclesiastes
		Esther
	Latter Prophets	Daniel
	Isaiah	Ezra
	Jeremiah	Nehemiah
	Ezekiel	1–2 Chronicles
	The Twelve	
	Hosea	
	Joel	
	Amos	
	Obadiah	
	Jonah	
	Micah	
	Nahum	
	Habakkuk	
	Zephaniah	
	Haggai	
	Zechariah	
	Malachi	

Table II: The Protestant Old Testament Canon

Most Protestant denominations accept the following thirty-nine books as the canon of the Old Testament in this traditional order.

Genesis	Isaiah
Exodus	Jeremiah
Leviticus	Lamentations
Numbers	Ezekiel
Deuteronomy	Daniel
Joshua	Hosea
Judges	Joel
Ruth	Amos
1 Samuel	Obadiah
2 Samuel	Jonah
1 Kings	Micah
2 Kings	Nahum
1 Chronicles	Habakkuk
2 Chronicles	Zephaniah
Ezra	Haggai
Nehemiah	Zechariah
Esther	Malachi
Job	
Psalms	
Proverbs	
Ecclesiastes	
Song of Songs	

Table III: The Roman Catholic Old Testament Canon

The Roman Catholic Canon includes all thirty-nine books found in the Old Testament in Table II, plus eleven additional books. These books are arranged variously in different Roman Catholic Bibles. The order below reflects that of the New Jerusalem Bible and the New American Bible. The names of the books in italics are those not found in the Protestant canon.

Genesis
Exodus
Leviticus
Numbers
Deuteronomy
Joshua
Judges
Ruth
1 Samuel
2 Samuel
1 Kings
2 Kings
1 Chronicles
2 Chronicles
Ezra
Nehemiah
Tobit
Judith
Esther *(with six additions)*
1 Maccabees
2 Maccabees
Job
Psalms
Proverbs
Ecclesiastes
Song of Songs
Wisdom of Solomon
Sirach

Isaiah
Jeremiah
Lamentations
Baruch (Baruch 6 = The Letter of Jeremiah)
Ezekiel
Daniel(*with three additions: the Prayer of Azariah and the Song of the Three Young Men, Susanna, and Bel and the Dragon*)
Hosea
Joel
Amos
Obadiah
Jonah
Micah
Nahum
Habakkuk
Zephaniah
Haggai
Zechariah
Malachi

[The Vulgate, or Latin, translation of the Roman Catholic Bible contains *3 Esdras, 4 Esdras,* and the *Prayer of Manasseh* in an appendix.]

Table IV: The Orthodox Old Testament Canon

The Orthodox tradition includes all thirty-nine books of the Old Testament found in Table III, plus fourteen additional books. In the Greek Orthodox Church, the traditional text for the Old Testament is the Greek Septuagint (LXX). The Slavonic translation of the Septuagint is the traditionally used Old Testament text for the Russian Orthodox Church. The names of the books in italics are those not found in the Protestant canon.

Genesis

Exodus

Leviticus

Numbers

Deuteronomy

Joshua

Judges

Ruth

1 Kingdoms (= 1 Samuel)

2 Kingdoms (= 2 Samuel)

3 Kingdoms (= 1 Kings)

4 Kingdoms (= 2 Kings)

1 Chronicles

2 Chronicles

1 Esdras (= Esdras in the SRSV Apocrypha = 2 Esdras in Slavonic Bibles)

2 Esdras (= Ezra; in some Orthodox Bibles 2 Esdras also includes Nehemiah)

Nehemiah

Tobit

Judith

Esther *(with six additions)*

1 Maccabees

2 Maccabees

3 Maccabees

Psalms *(with Psalm 151)*

Job

Proverbs

Ecclesiastes

Song of Songs

Wisdom of Solomon

Wisdom of Sirach (= Ecclesiasticus)

Hosea

Amos

Micah

Joel

Obadiah

Jonah

Nahum

Habakkuk

Zephaniah

Haggai

Zechariah

Malachi

Isaiah

Jeremiah

Baruch

Lamentations

Epistle of Jeremiah

Ezekiel

Daniel *(with three additions: the Prayer of Azariah and the Song of the Three Youths, Susanna, and Bel and the Dragon)*

[Greek Orthodox Bibles contain 4 Maccabees and the Prayer of Manasseh in an appendix. Slavonic Bibles add 3 Esdras to this appendix.]

CHAPTER TWO

THE CREATED ORDER
AND THE RE-CREATION
OF BROKEN ORDER

Gen 1–11

The Old Testament begins at the beginning—not of Israel, but of the cosmos. Its opening chapters move from the morning of the universe to the ordering of families and nations to the birthing of the fathers and mothers of Israel. God was there "in the beginning," but this is a new day for God, too. Given the divine commitment to relationships with the creation, God will never be the same again.

Genesis 1–11 enjoys an especially high status in those communities for whom the Bible is authoritative, especially the Christian church. Books and videos on Genesis attract a steady stream of buyers. This popularity has not been achieved because of an interest in these chapters elsewhere in the Old Testament, where only rare reference is made to these texts (e.g., Isa 54:9-10). Yet, this is true of Genesis texts generally (e.g., Gen 22), so it is difficult to assess what role these chapters may have played in Israel's reflections.

New Testament texts, especially Paul's references to Gen 3 and the "fall" (e.g., Rom 5:12-21), are perhaps most responsible for the attention given these chapters in Christian circles. These Pauline texts have been extended by elaborate churchly reflections about creation, sin and evil, the nature of the human, and the relationship between God and world. Immense theological edifices have been built squarely on interpretations of these chapters, and differences among interpreters continue to animate many a conversation and to generate debate within the Christian community. From another angle, the stories as stories continue to attract; the seven days of creation, the garden of Eden, Adam and Eve, Cain and Abel, Noah and the animals in the ark, and the tower of Babel have all become deeply rooted in Christian consciousness and culture and even beyond. These chapters no doubt will continue to provide readers with foundational resources for their storytelling and their theological reflection.

Modern experience has also generated much interest in these chapters: the discovery of ancient Near Eastern creation and flood accounts; new approaches to literature and historiography; and issues raised by scientific research, environmentalism, and feminism. These developments have sharply complicated the interpretation of these chapters: What kind of literature is this? How old is the earth? How and when did human life appear? Does Gen 1 commend the exploitation of the earth? Are these texts inimical to the status of women in church and society?

In addressing such issues responsibly, we must go beyond Genesis and draw on insights from other parts of Scripture and from our own experience—in and through which God continues to work. We are encouraged in this endeavor in that not every concern in these chapters is collapsed into a theological framework. For example, Gen 1–2 provides considerable evidence of what might be called "prescientific" reflection. Israelite theologians were interested in "how" the creation came to be, and not just questions of "who" and "why." Such "prescientific" knowledge is evident in God's use of the earth and the waters to mediate further creations (1:11, 20, 24), the classification of plants into certain kinds (1:11-12) and a comparable interest in animals (1:20-25), as well as the ordering of creative acts. The authors utilized whatever data was available about the natural world from their context to shape these chapters, integrating "secular" knowledge and theological perspectives. This sophisticated move recognized that all spheres of knowledge must be drawn into the conversation in any effort to understand the way the world has come into being. Readers in every age are implicitly invited to do the same.

Difficulties arise when it becomes evident that not everything in Gen 1–11 corresponds to modern knowledge about the world (though no field of inquiry has achieved full understanding). We have learned truths about the origins, development, and nature of the world of which the biblical authors never dreamed (e.g., the source of light; the age of the world). We must take whatever additional knowledge has become available over the years (e.g., some form of evolution) and integrate it with theological and confessional statements. We are not called to separate theological material from "scientific" material in Gen 1–11 and rewrite the chapters from the perspective of present knowledge (though that must be done for other theological and ethical purposes). Rather, the Genesis text remains an important paradigm regarding the way in which to integrate theological and scientific knowledge in a common search for truth about the world.

Critical Study of Gen 1–11

A captivating array of interests and issues enlivens current scholarly study of these chapters. This liveliness is due at least in part to the fact that the critical study of Genesis (and the Pentateuch generally) is in disarray. Long-standing hypotheses about the origins and development of these chapters have been found wanting; new theories of various sorts have been proposed, but no comprehensive alternative has yet captured the field. We sketch some of the more basic developments pertinent to Gen 1–11.

Source Criticism

This literary-historical approach engages in study of the origins of the text, including such matters as authorship, the oral and written sources used, and the editorial stages through which it may have passed. This approach has long been the dominant scholarly approach to Gen 1–11. The study of Genesis from this perspective has commonly been included in a study of the Pentateuch as a whole.

Genesis is usually seen as a composite work, drawn up from various sources and edited over the course of many centuries. The classical consensus, emergent in Germany in the late nineteenth century (associated especially with the name of Julius Wellhausen), spoke primarily of three interwoven sources for Genesis—Yahwist (J), Elohist (E), and Priestly writer (P), dating from the ninth to fifth centuries BCE. Two of these sources (J and P) were seen to be present

31

in chapters 1–11, at times placed side by side (chaps. 1–2) and at times interwoven (the flood story, chaps. 6–8). The recognition of two creation stories (1:1–2:4*a*; 2:4*b*-25) has long enjoyed a special place in demonstrations of the virtues of a source-critical approach.

Much scholarly energy has been expended in seeking to refine this "documentary hypothesis," with frequent probes regarding the identity, unity, scope, and dating of these (and other) sources. While much remains uncertain, and scholarly focus has moved on to other paradigms, general agreement continues that Gen 1–11 is a composite work, consisting of a patchwork quilt of traditions from various periods. More particularly, the Priestly tradition continues to be associated with the first creation story, most genealogies, and portions of the flood story. These texts may have been written either as a supplement to the rest of the material (commonly identified with J) or as a separate account, later integrated with the older material to provide a unified story. This chapter will focus on the present form of the text.

The primary concerns of these traditions are theological and kerygmatic, transmitted by persons of faith in order to speak a word of God and about God to other persons of faith. As such, however, Genesis is not socially or historically disinterested; it was written—at each stage of transmission—with the problems and possibilities of particular audiences in view. Yet, determination of those audiences has been notoriously elusive, though the Babylonian exile has often been suggested as the setting for one decisive moment in the history of this material (for both J and P).

One source that lies behind these traditions needs special attention. Israel was not the only people in the ancient Near East with creation and flood stories. Sumerian, Mesopotamian, and Egyptian accounts have been unearthed in the last two centuries. One example, the Babylonian *Epic of Atrahasis* (about 1600 BCE), presents a creation-disruption-flood sequence, a structure similar to Gen 1–11. As a result of comparing these texts with the biblical account, it is apparent that Israel participated in a culture with a lively interest in these questions. While some have claimed that Israel used one or more of these accounts directly, it is now more common to speak of a widespread fund of images and ideas upon which Israel drew for its own account. Important differences are evident in Israel's use of them: the absence of a family tree for God (theogony) and a conflict among the gods, the lack of interest in primeval chaos, the prevailing monotheism, and the high value given human beings. Yet, these resources from Israel's environment must not be viewed simply in polemical terms, as if Israel were concerned only to speak against them. The theology of these "outsiders" made genuine contributions to Israel's reflections on creation.

Form Criticism

This approach focuses on the identification of the type(s) of literature and the settings in life where they may have been produced and functioned. Scholars generally agree that Gen 1–11 consists of two primary types of literature, narratives and genealogies, into which a few poetic pieces have been integrated (2:23; 3:14-19; 4:23-24; 9:25-27).

1. *Genealogies.* Ten genealogies (six in chaps. 1–11) constitute major portions of seven chapters in Genesis, providing its most basic structure: 2:4 (heaven and earth); 5:1 (Adam); 6:9 (Noah); 10:1 (Noah's sons); 11:10 (Shem); 11:27 (Terah); 25:12 (Ishmael); 25:19 (Isaac); 36:1, 9 (Esau); 37:2 (Jacob). These Priestly genealogies are supplemented by others (e.g., Cain, 4:17-22). Their historical value is debated, but families and tribes no doubt relied upon them to track family "pedigrees" for social or political purposes. More generally, the genealogies show that every person—chosen and nonchosen—is kin to every other; even more, in view of 2:4, human and nonhuman are linked together in one large extended family. Theologically, the genealogies stress God's ongoing creational activity—bringing new lives into being and ordering them into families. While these genealogies witness to order and stability, narrative pieces within their flow (e.g., 5:24, 29; 10:8-12; cf. 4:17-26) introduce elements of disequilibrium and unpredictability into the story of families.

2. *Narratives.* The narratives are more difficult to assess. No precise designation for them has been agreed upon; *saga, legend, myth, folktale, etiology, story,* and *theological narrative* have all been candidates. The designation *story* (or *story of the past*) is perhaps most helpful in determining how these materials functioned.

The stories are told in such a way that they could become the stories of each generation; people come to recognize themselves at the juncture of past story and present reality. By and large, the world reflected in them is ordinary and familiar, filled with the surprises and joys, the sufferings and the troubles, the complexities and ambiguities known to every community (6:1-4 is an exception). At the same time, they are God's story. These stories disclose a world with which God has entered into relationship and is deeply engaged in its ongoing life. This admixture of the human story and God's story provides much of the drama that these stories present.

While these texts often mirror human life in every age, the past and the present are not simply collapsed into each other. These texts do purport to tell a story of the past—note their cumulative character and chronological framework—yet, they are not historical in any modern sense ("history-like" is a term sometimes used). This concern for the beginnings of things is evident in the atypical aspects of some texts (e.g., the long-lived patriarchs belong to an irretrievable past, as does the reality of one language, 11:1) and in the interest in genealogy and chronology (e.g., 8:13-14). On the other hand, that which is typical in human life may be reflected in the use of the word *'ādām*, which refers to generic humankind (1:26-27), the first man (2:7), or Adam (4:25). The interweaving of the typical and the atypical in these texts provides for a richness and depth in the story and carries important *theological* implications. For example, Gen 3 speaks both of a past, *subsequent* to the creation, when sin and its evil effects emerged into the life of the world, *and* of a typical encounter with the reality of temptation. The tendency in recent scholarship has been to emphasize the latter. But, if the reader does not attend to the presentation of these materials as *past,* and views them only as ever-present and typical, then any distinction between God's creation and the entrance of sin into the world is collapsed, and one is faced with a dualistic perspective. Sin would then be viewed, not as a disruption of God's good creation, but as integral to God's intention for the world. Sin would be a divine rather than a human problem.

The interweaving of genealogy and narrative provides the basic structure of Gen 1–11. The narratives move in parallel panels: (a) One panel moves from beginnings (1:1–2:25) to sinful individuals (3:1-24), through family (4:1-26), through ten generations (5:1-31), out into the larger world (6:1–8:19), ending in catastrophe. (b) A parallel panel begins anew after the flood (8:20–9:17), moving again through sinful individuals and family (9:18-27), out into the world

(10:1–11:9), only this time into a world that Israel clearly knows (e.g., Babel). The genealogy of Shem (11:10-26) also provides an individual point of reference that reaches through ten generations to the family of Abraham and out into the larger world (12:3*b*).

A Universal Frame of Reference

As with any effective literary work, the opening pages of the Old Testament are key to a proper discernment of the whole. How would the reader experience this "opener"? This material is not laid out simply to give the reader some information about the world or the beginnings of things. The story does not begin with the chosen people or even with the human race. The strategy is to catch the reader up into a universal frame of reference. Readers are invited to view a screen that is cosmic in its scope and to engage in an act of the imagination that carries them beyond—far beyond—their little corner of the world, wherever that may be.

In serving this strategy, Gen 1–11 presents a rhythmic interweaving of story and genealogy that focuses the mind on certain recurring images, especially those of God and the world. They set the tone and direction for *reading all that follows* in the Old Testament. New images and ideas will emerge over time (e.g., divine forgiveness in Exod 34:6-7), but the reader is to work with such new developments against the backdrop provided by these opening chapters.

Regarding God

Genesis assumes that God does not have to be introduced (1:1); even the name Yahweh is assumed to be known (2:4; 4:26). God is the subject of more activity than any other character in Gen 1–11: God creates, blesses, gives laws, judges, grieves, saves, elects, promises, makes covenants, provides counsel, protects, confers responsibility to human beings, and holds them accountable. And we are not yet to Sarah and Abraham! These activities reveal God's core character and the basic divine way of relating to the world. This language is testimony to the kind of God who is active in the world more generally, not just in Israel. Abraham and Israel are called into a world within which God is already deeply and pervasively engaged. Such has been the case with every calling since that time.

Through the lens of these images, the God of the opening chapters of Genesis is portrayed as a relational God. Most basically, God is present and active in the world, enters into a relationship of integrity with the world, and does so in such a way that both world and God are affected by that interaction. God has chosen not to remain aloof from the creation but to get caught up with the creatures in moving toward the divine purposes for the world. For example: God involves the human in responsibilities for the creation (1:28; 2:15); God walks in the garden and engages the human in dialogue (3:8-13); God gives counsel with respect to human behavior (4:6-7); God ameliorates judgment (4:15); God suffers a broken heart (6:6); God limits the divine options in relating to sin and evil (8:21-22); and God paints a reminder in the sky for whenever the clouds of judgment thicken (9:8-17). The rest of the Old Testament witnesses to this kind of God.

More particularly, Israel conceptualized God's creative activity and told creation stories in several ways:

1. God's creation by means of the word. This is majestically presented in chapter 1. Yet, it is important to note that God's speech does not stand isolated from divine deeds (1:6-7; see Isa 48:3; Ezek 37:4-6). A wedge must not be driven between God's speaking and God's acting; these must be kept together for any proper discussion of creation. It is not enough to say that the divine word goes forth and creates what has been articulated. God's spirit and action accompany the word and complexify the creative process; moreover, the text speaks of receptors of that word (1:11-12). The fundamental purpose of the emphasis on divine word is to indicate that creation was not accidental or arbitrary, but a deliberate act of the will of God. The word personalizes the will of God at work in creating (see John 1).

2. God's use of that which has already been created as a means to bring still further creations into being. This is present in both chapters. In 1:11-12 the earth brings forth vegetation (cf. 1:20, 24); God forms the man out of the dust of the ground and the woman out of the side of the man (2:7, 22); and the man joins God in naming the creatures, thereby ordering the world (2:19-20; see below for further theological reflection).

3. Creation through conflict, a common ancient Near Eastern creation motif. Some have thought this to be present in this text,

particularly in connecting the "chaos" features of 1:2 with other passages (e.g., Ps 74:12-15). Yet, the poetic and metaphoric character of such references suggest that the conflict with chaos motif plays no important role here or elsewhere in the Old Testament (see below on "chaos").

Regarding the World

God brings the cosmos into being and the result is, as they say, awesome. The reader is immediately introduced to a world that is filled with "all things bright and beautiful." We are asked to keep this bountiful and flourishing creation in our minds as we read on, and the Old Testament will return to such grandeur from time to time (e.g., Deut 8:7-10; Job 38–41; Pss 19; 104; 148). The reader of Gen 1 must not get lost in literary, historical, and scientific questions. First and foremost, we are called to pause and wonder at the jewel of a world that God has created. This world is "very good" indeed.

The doxological character of the opening of Genesis is fitting for such a world. At the same time, the text does not lose itself in rapturous praise of God. Woven into the doxological strains are strong words of command for the human creatures in particular: Be fruitful, multiply, fill the earth, have dominion, subdue the earth (1:28). The future shape of this beautiful world is placed quite directly in human hands. God engages humankind in a risky enterprise on behalf of the creation (as we can see from what happens), and God will relate to these appointed stewards with integrity in the ongoing divine commitment to the world.

The powerful images of God in this chapter must not be allowed to obscure this high place given to the human in God's creation. Human beings are presented as good and responsible creatures. Created in the image of God (see below), as well as from the dust of the ground, they are given work to do in God's world; indeed, they are called to be cocreators with God. Though they sin, they remain God's good creation, in the divine image (5:1-2; 9:6), with the same summons to responsibility (3:22-24; 9:1-7). Faithfulness remains a human calling (5:24; 6:8-9) and how human beings respond will make a difference—for both God and world.

Sad to say, human beings do not do so well with the charge; sin issues in a breakdown of relationships at multiple levels, including devastating effects upon God's good world. Sin creates disharmonies between human beings and God, among human beings (men and women; brothers; parents and children), between human beings and the animals and the land ("thorns and thistles"), and within the self (shame). Sin affects adversely the spheres of family and work (3:14-19; 9:20-27), of culture and community (4:17-24), of national life (10–11), of the larger created order (the flood), and even intrudes upon the heavenly realm (6:1-4). In fact, sin is so deep-seated that "every inclination of the thoughts of their hearts was only evil continually" (6:5); even the flood does not change that (8:21). Yet, human beings can act against such inclinations (4:7; cf. Deut 30:11-14) and in favor of that which is life-giving rather than death-dealing. The stories that follow will narrate this human predicament from every angle, especially among God's chosen people.

The Priority of Creation

To begin the Old Testament with such powerful and pervasive images of Creator and creation bespeaks several theological emphases:

1. Such a beginning reflects the actual order of God's activity in the world. God was at work in the world and in the lives of all creatures on behalf of God's creational purposes long before Israel existed or articulated what creation was all about. Israel does not bring God into any of the places into which it is dispersed across the face of the earth. God is there to meet them, and God's work in those "unchosen" places will have been rich and pervasive.

2. Such a beginning gives priority of place to God's actual engagement with the world, rather than to human knowledge of such divine activity. Human beings—as individuals or communities—receive life from the Creator quite apart from any knowledge of its source. Israel's later understandings of creation only "catch up" with what God has long been about in the world.

3. Such a beginning parallels the human experience of God's activity. All human beings have experienced God's creative work (e.g., conception and birthing) prior to (and concurrent with) God's redemptive work. God's promissory and redemptive activity does not occur in a vacuum, but in a context shaped by the life-

giving, life-enhancing work of the Creator. God's work in creation is necessary for there to be a people whom God can redeem and a context within which they can live well.

4. Such a beginning demonstrates that God's work in the world has to do with more than human beings. Most of Gen 1 portrays the creation of that which is other than human; indeed, human beings have to share the sixth day of creation with the animals. Moreover, God involves the nonhuman in creative activity (1:11, 20, 22, 24). In addition, the human and nonhuman orders are deeply integrated, so that human sin has devastating effects on the nonhuman (3:17; 6:5-7; 9:2). And so the nonhuman creatures are caught up in God's saving work (6:19–7:3), God's remembering (8:1), and God's promising (9:10). Readers of the rest of the Old Testament should be attuned to the important place of the nonhuman in God's economy.

5. Such a beginning makes clear the intentions of God's redemptive work. Genesis 1–11 demonstrates that God's purposes in redemption move beyond Israel; they are universal in scope. Israel appears on the scene only within the context of all the nations/families of the earth (Gen 10–11); the promises given to the chosen people are grounded in God's promises to the world (8:21-22; 9:8-17); Israel's election is specifically tied back into this world family in Gen 12:1-3, "in you all the families of the earth shall be blessed." All these families, laboring under sin and its effects, are the ultimate concern of God. God's initially exclusive move with Abraham and his family is in the interests of a maximally inclusive end—a new creation. God's redemption of Israel serves this divine intention with respect to the creation in its entirety. This universal mission informs more of the Old Testament than has been commonly recognized.

Two Creation Stories Become One (1:1–2:25)

Many students of Gen 1–2 think that these chapters consist of two creation accounts, assigning 1:1–2:4a to the Priestly writer and 2:4b-25 to the Yahwist. Differences in type of literature, structure, vocabulary, style, and center of concern have been noted. Yet, while the two accounts have different origins and transmission histories, they have been brought together in a theologically sophisticated fashion to function *together* as the canonical picture of creation. As such, they reveal key points of complementarity: God as sole Creator of a good and purposeful world; the key place of the human among the creatures in a cocreative role; the social character of the human as male-female.

In the following paragraphs these chapters are read as a unified whole in seeking to draw out some of these emphases, and to give evidence of both creative tension and complementarity in this complex story of creation.

Traditional and churchly understandings of creation have tended to favor the presentation of chapter 1; this preference has been reinforced by critical decisions that have often portrayed chapter 2 as more naive and less sophisticated theologically. The result is an image in the theological tradition of a Creator who is radically transcendent, operating in total independence from the creation, speaking the world into being. But if the two chapters are kept in an interactive relationship with one another, a more relational view of God emerges.

We will see in what follows that both God and creatures have an important role in the creative enterprise, and their spheres of activity are interrelated. God is not presented as powerful and the creatures powerless. In spite of the risks involved, God chooses the way of less than absolute control, for the sake of a relationship of integrity in which power is shared with that which is other than God. In the very act of creating, God gives to others a certain freedom and independence, and catches them up in creativity (from the earth in 1:11 to the man and woman in 1:28 and to the man in 2:19). Creation is process as well as event (see especially 2:18-23); creation is creaturely as well as divine. God has established a relationship with human beings such that their decisions about the creation truly count—both for God and the creation.

Signaled by the shift in 2:4 from "heaven and earth" to "earth and heaven," chapter 2 focuses on the earthly context and the human characters; it may be intended to describe in detail several days of chapter 1, especially the sixth day. In this linkage, diversity and complexity in the imaging of creation are valued more than strict coherence. God is characterized as one who creates *(bārā')* and makes *('āsāh)*, who speaks and separates, who forms and builds from existing material, and who engages that which is already created in the creational process (1:11; 2:19). Analogies from human creating are common, and the verb *bārā'*—God is the only subject and it carries no object of material or means—may be used to affirm that no earthly analogy adequately portrays God's creative activity.

Although ordering (usually of material specified in 1:2) is the primary effect of this divine activity, the diverse images, the less than perfect symmetry (e.g., eight creative acts in six days), and the call to the human to "subdue the earth," convey a sense that this creative order is not forever fixed. The creation is presented as basically in place, but still in the process of becoming. In view of this reality, appeals to the "orders of creation" or natural law (on, say, ethical issues) must be handled with considerable care.

The opening verses of chapter 1 are difficult to translate, and hence interpretations will vary more than is usually the case. The most convincing (and common) position is to translate verse 1 as an independent sentence (so RSV; NIV; contrast NRSV) and to interpret it as a summary of the chapter (and so it would be parallel with the other genealogies in 5:1; 6:9; 10:1; and 11:10); verse 2 describes a state of affairs prior to God's ordering, a state that is not *yet* consonant with the divine purposes in creation; verse 3 reports the first creative act.

The "chaos" of verse 2 ("a formless void") refers, not to some divine opponent (as it does in Babylonian parallels), but to raw material that God uses to create what follows. At that point, the "chaos" ceases to exist; it does not persist as a negative backdrop or potential threat to God's creation. Allusions to "chaos" in later literature (always poetry), do provide deeply negative *images* for the world (e.g., Jer 4:23-26); but these images are subsumed under the wrath of God in response to creaturely wickedness, not to some independent threat to the creation. In the flood story, which soon follows and witnesses to God's judgmental response, the fountains and windows of heaven function intensively, but as created realities; this is no return to the chaos of 1:2. When the floodwaters abate, the created order of chapter 1 emerges into the light of day.

The "formless void" is neither nothing nor an undifferentiated mass; the earth, the waters, the darkness, and the wind are discrete realities—the "stuff" that God uses to bring about a new order. The earth (which in v. 9 "appears") is so described because it is desolate and unproductive (not unlike the portrayal of 2:4-6). The author does not deny that God created all things, but the origin of what is specified in verse 2 is of no apparent interest, except that God was present and active there. Any comprehensive doctrine of "creation out of nothing" must be grounded in other texts (e.g., 2 Macc 7:28; Rom 4:17; Heb 11:3) or theological perspectives.

Verse 2 does claim that, whether one translates *rûaḥ* as spirit or wind, God is present and active with this undifferentiated mass. The "hovering" suggests an ever-changing velocity and direction, and because God is involved this movement is purposeful. This use of the language of movement rather than static categories, as at a key juncture in the flood story (8:1) and at the Red Sea (Exod 14:21), suggests creative activity in this verse, a bringing of something new out of a chaotic situation.

The word *beginning* thus is not the absolute beginning of all things, but the beginning of the ordered creation, including both spatial and temporal orders. The seven-day order (climaxing in the sabbath, 2:1-3) establishes a temporal pattern to be observed by all human beings, so that human life will be in tune with the creative order. This concern for a work-rest weekly rhythm (which grounds the sabbath commandment in Exod 20:8-11) makes it likely that the days of creation are to be understood as twenty-four-hour periods. Efforts to understand this temporal reference in terms of, say, evolution, by interpreting "day" as an extensive period of time, betrays too much of an interest in harmonization. This text reflects early "prescientific" reflection, and moderns must consider perspectives from various scientific disciplines to discern a fuller truth about the origins of the world.

The basic content of the eight-act, six-day structure is ordered in terms of parallels between spaces and their inhabitants: days 1 and 4 (light/luminaries), days 2 and 5 (waters/firmament; fish/birds), days 3 and 6 (dry land/vegetation; land animals/people/food). Among the repetitive phrases associated with these creative acts, "God saw that it was good" is especially noteworthy. Here God reacts to the work, making evaluations. One such evaluation occurs explicitly in 2:18 ("it is *not* good") and implies that such an evaluative assessment was part of an ongoing process for God, within which creational change is possible. The use of the verb *subdue* (1:28) implies that "good" does not mean perfect or static or in no need of development, but appropriate for God's intended purposes and for creaturely life and well-being. The divine naming (1:5-10) stops with the earth's appearance, and human beings pick up that task in 2:19.

For both God and human beings, naming denotes a discernment of the creatures' place within the creation, not authority (so Adam's naming of Eve does not entail subordination, demonstrated by Hagar's naming God in 16:13). Such an ordering activity through naming is coordinate with God's naming and hence is an integral part of the creative task, involving human beings in an ongoing cocreative responsibility.

Although the creation of humans does not require an entire day, a change in rhetoric signals the importance of their creation. The "let us" language (1:26; see 11:7) images God as a consultant of other divine beings (for the heavenly council, see Jer 23:18-22). The creation of humankind results from a dialogical act, an inner-divine communication. This language reveals the richness and complexity of the divine realm. God is not in heaven alone, but is engaged in a relationship of mutuality and chooses to share the creative process with others. Human beings are thus created in the image of one who creates in a way that shares power with others, which would be congruent with the command in 1:28.

While the meaning of *the image of God* is open to much debate, this phrase refers basically to those characteristics of human beings that make communication with God possible and enable them to take up the God-given responsibilities specified in these verses (this image remains intact after the entrance of sin, 5:1-2; 9:6). That human beings, like other creatures, are also created from the dust of the earth, either directly or indirectly (2:7, 21-22), constitutes the other pole regarding human identity.

As image of God, human beings function to mirror God to the world, to be as God would be to the nonhuman, to be an extension of God's own dominion. This text democratizes an ancient Near Eastern royal use of image language; all human beings are created in the image of God, not just kings. The result is that all interhuman hierarchical understandings are set aside; all human beings of whatever station in life stand together as image of God. That both male and female are so created (*'ādām* is here used generically, hence the translation "humankind") means that the female images the divine as much as the male. Likeness to God pertains not only to what male and female have in common but also to what remains distinctive to them. This provides a basis for the use of both male and female images for God in the Old Testament. While male images predominate, female images, especially those of mother-hood, are used, particularly in those texts and times where themes of divine closeness and comfort seem called for (e.g., Deut 32:18; Isa 42:14; 66:13).

The command to have dominion (1:28), in which God delegates responsibility for the nonhuman creation in a power-sharing rela-tionship with humans, must be understood in terms of caregiving, not exploitation (see the use of the verb *rādāh* in Ps 72:8-14; Ezek 34:1-4). The verb *subdue,* while capable of more negative senses, here has reference to the earth and its cultivation without parallel in the Hebrew Bible and, more generally, to the becoming of a world that is a dynamic, not a static reality. The indispensable character of this role for the human is also lifted up in 2:5, which remarkably claims that a precreation state remains, not only because there was yet no rain, but also because there was as yet no human being to serve (less than adequately translated "till") and to keep the ground (2:15; 3:23). This responsibility assigned to the human has not sim-ply to do with maintenance and preservation, but with intracre-ational development—bringing the world along toward its fullest possible potential. God intends from the beginning that things not stay just as they were initially created. God creates not a static state of affairs but a highly dynamic world in which the future lies open to various possibilities, and human beings are given a key role to play in developing them.

With this divinely ordained role, male and female, in turn, are placed in a garden in Eden (perhaps thought to be in the Jordan val-ley, 13:10; ancient Near Eastern parallels are minor). Rivers flow from Eden to give water to the world outside of Eden (2:10-14); so when the man and woman are excluded from the garden, they do not move from a world of blessing to one devoid of blessing. The garden has sometimes been described in overly romantic terms, but the text shows much restraint. Indeed, one might speak of various dimensions of suffering implicit in this text—for example, the pain associated with the limits of finitude, loneliness, temptation, and even anxiety (which become intensified and tragic in the wake of sin). The text emphasizes the basic needs of life: freedom, food, a home, a family, harmonious relationships, and a stable natural envi-ronment. The contrast with the situation in 3:7-19 is clear, if at times overdrawn, and to that we turn shortly.

God is imaged as a potter (2:7), whose hands work with the stuff of the ground *('ădāmâ)* in designing and creating the first human being *('ādām;* a male figure rather than an earth creature, as some have suggested [e.g., P. Trible], for this text is the only reference to the creation of the male). This image of a God with his hands in the dirt is remarkable; this is no naive theology, but a statement about the depths to which God has entered into the life of the creation. God's very life is then breathed into the man; something of God's own self becomes an integral part of human identity, enabling life to move from God out into the larger world (the animals may also have been so understood, see 7:22).

God is also imaged as a farmer, placing two trees in this garden; they are associated with life and death and human choices related thereto (see Deut 30:15-20). The tree of life is a means to continuing life, but from which God bars them after they have eaten of the tree of knowledge (3:22). The tree of the knowledge of good and evil, a knowledge that God has (3:22), presents a use of the law wherein certain creaturely limits are established by God as in the best interests of human well-being. These limits are associated with a divine knowing, by which humans are to acknowledge the decisiveness of the word of God for true human life; they anticipate the giving of the law at Sinai. To conceive of these matters in terms of an eating metaphor, so prominent in Gen 2–3, signifies taking something into the self that shapes one's total being ("you are what you eat"). The penalty for eating is death—capital punishment, not an ontological change (from being immortal to being mortal), for death as such is part of God's created order. If this were not the case, the tree of life would have been irrelevant.

The prohibition regarding the tree in 2:16-17 joins with the positive law of 1:28 to present a central place for law in the pre-sin created order of things. Law is given with creation, is seen to be integral to proper human life in the world, and enables law to be understood in basically positive terms as that which promotes life. Law is a gracious gift for the best possible life.

The phrase "it is not good" (2:18) is part of the ongoing divine evaluation of the creation, identifies a problem with the creation to this point—human aloneness—and moves to resolve it. That God first brings animals to the man demonstrates that the issue being addressed is companionship, not sexuality or procreation. That "helper" does not entail subordination is likely in view of its common use for God (e.g., Ps 121:1-2). That God gives such an important decision to the man—"whatever," without qualification (2:19)—shows the extent to which God delegates power to the human, engages the human in the creative process (cf. 1:11), and leaves room for human decisions that truly count in the shaping of the future. Such a commitment on God's part involves risk, since human beings may (and in time do) misuse the power they have been given.

God honors the first human decision and goes back to the drawing boards. God next brings to the man a personally designed and constructed woman—made from living flesh (perhaps "side" rather than "rib"). Being created from a part of the man does not entail subordination for the woman any more than man's being created from the ground does for the man. The man recognizes that the woman addresses the stated need, and his exultation counts for an evaluation that the situation has now moved from "not good" to good. His words (v. 23) stress mutuality and equality, with a new level of knowledge of his identity as a man in relationship to a woman. The concluding verses do not mention children, but focus on the man-woman relationship; they are now "one flesh," which refers to intimacy in the broadest sense of the term, not just the sexual. The man and the woman are now an indissoluble unit of humankind.

These various images regarding creation may be especially important for an audience in need of God's creative activity in the midst of the collapse of their ordered world. These chapters would thus parallel the use of creational themes on the part of key exilic prophets (Isa 40–55; Jer 31–33).

The Intrusion of Sin and Its Social and Cosmic Effects (3:1–6:4)

This section is generally assigned to the J writer (except the Priestly genealogy in chap. 5). Genesis 3 has played an extraordinary role in the history of interpretation, even if not within the Old Testament itself (Ezek 28:11-19 has some uncertain connections). This text probably did not gain this status until post–Old Testament times. But care must be used not to overdraw this point. The text's placement at the head of the canon gives it a certain theological stature.

At the same time, chapter 3 does not stand isolated, and its larger context should play a more important role than it commonly has. While the literary and thematic links with chapter 2 are often noted, less attention has been given to the chapters that follow. For example, similarities in the progression of chapter 3 and of 4:7-16 should keep these texts closely connected. This link should be extended through 6:1-4, where the cosmic effects of sin are mythically conveyed, with 6:5 summarizing the situation at that juncture: "every inclination of the thoughts of their hearts was only evil continually."

No such claim is made at the end of chapter 3, though that has been a common interpretation. Rather, chapter 3 describes the "originating sin," and the chapters that follow speak of a process by which sin became "original," that is, universal and inescapable (no genetic understandings are conveyed). When this processive understanding is combined with the primary imagery of separation, estrangement, alienation, progressively greater distances from Eden, and the decreasing ages of human beings, "fall" language is reductionistic and not entirely appropriate for chapter 3. To speak of a "fall" in the sense of falling "out" or "apart," however, would resonate well with the basic images used in these chapters.

While no ancient Near Eastern "fall" story has been uncovered, understandings of sin in the broader culture no doubt influenced Israel's reflections. A universal and pervasive understanding of sin can be discerned in several texts:

A Sumerian penitential prayer reads, "Who is there who has not sinned against his god; who has always obeyed the commandments? Every one who lives is sinful." Or a Sumerian wisdom saying: "Never has a sinless child been born to its mother." Or, this penitential lament, "My god, though my transgressions are many—free me of my guilt! Though my misdeeds be innumerable—let your heart be still! Though my sins be countless—show mercy and heal me!" Or, this remarkable invocation to the goddess Ishtar: "Forgive my sin, my iniquity, my wickedness and my offence . . . loose my fetters, secure my deliverance . . . Let my prayers and my supplications come to you and may all your grace be with me; then those who see me in the street will glorify your name." Or this song of thanksgiving to the Egyptian god Amun-Re: "If it is the nature of the servant to commit sin, it is the nature of the Lord to be gracious."[1] These profound understandings of sin are nothing peculiarly biblical, let alone

Christian. We are the inheritors of a rich theology of sin from the prebiblical world, though it is seldom acknowledged.

Some interpreters have suggested a quite different approach to this text, seeing it in terms of a "fall upward," which the becoming like God theme might suggest. Most have interpreted this "fall" negatively. Human beings transgress the limits of creatureliness and assume godlike powers for themselves; yet, this assumes a more basic problem, namely, mistrust (see below). Others have taken this theme in a positive direction (at least since Irenaeus in the second century). In this view, human beings move out from under the parental hand of God, a necessary move for the child on the way to true maturity. Yet, in such an interpretation, God becomes the problem in the text, setting arbitrary limits in the first place, opposing maturity, and overreacting when humans transgress them. The text gives few suggestions that the human lot improves, from either the divine or human perspective, as relationships at every level fall apart. If the sin of the humans is minimized, then the effects of the sin in verses 14-19 are minimized, including the patriarchy that now ensues.

No word for "sin" occurs in chapter 3; good storytellers don't have to name the game. The word *sin* first appears in 4:7, where it is given an enticing, possessive character. This absence has made it difficult to agree on the nature of the primal sin; what do the human beings do that is wrong? A closer look at some details of the story will assist readers with such a question.

Chapter 3 brings readers into the middle of a conversation between a snake and two human beings (3:6 makes clear that the man is present the whole time). Is the snake a malevolent or demonic creature, out to seduce humans away from God? This is not likely, though the claim has been made since intertestamental times (Wis 2:24; cf. Rev 12:9; 20:2). The text identifies the snake as an animal of the field which God had made, as in 2:19-20 and in God's sentence (3:14). The humans seem to so understand it; they express no fear or wonderment, perhaps because animals in the garden are given capacities of thought and speech (cf. Job 12:7-9).

The snake is an ambivalent symbol, associated with both life and death (see Num 21:4-9), and also with craftiness (cf. "sly fox"), perhaps because of its ability to sneak up on others. The verbal link (in Hebrew) between the "naked" humans and the snake's "craftiness" suggests that human beings may be *exposed* at times to shrewd elements in God's world—language appropriate for temptation. So, the snake is a metaphor, representing anything in God's good creation that could present options to human beings, the choice of which could seduce them away from God. The snake as a neutral observer facilitates the options the tree presents. True to life, the facilitator participates in the consequences of the choice and the metaphor of the snake is established as a negative one for future generations of humankind (3:14-15).

The reader overhears the conversation at the point it evolves into a question about God and the prohibition (3:1). The snake asks questions that carry the conversation along, and responds in ways that are truthful, or at least potentially so: they do become like God, knowing good and evil (3:22), and they do not die, at least physically; in fact, they could eat of the tree of life and continue to live (3:22).

The key phrase that leads to the eating is "God knows" (3:5). This claim highlights the fact that God has not told the humans the full truth. And the question is thereby raised as to whether God, having kept something from them, indeed something that seems beneficial, could be fully trusted with their best interests. The issue of knowledge at its deepest level is an issue of *trust*. Can the humans trust God while pursuing the truth about God? Can they trust that God has their best interests at heart even if they do not know everything? Can they trust that not all "benefits" are for their good? The primal sin may thus best be defined as mistrust of God and God's word, which then manifests itself in disobedience and other negative behaviors (e.g., blaming).

The snake has presented possibilities through words (only) and the humans draw their own conclusion. Rather than speak to God about the issue, they silently consider the tree and the wisdom it offers (without recalling the prohibition). The issue is not the gaining of wisdom in and of itself, however, but the way it is gained ("the fear of the LORD is the beginning of wisdom"). What this entails can be seen from the result. Only God can view the creation as a whole; the humans do not have such a perspective or the wherewithal to handle their new knowledge very well (a recurrent problem!). The woman takes of the fruit and—with no tempting words—gives it to her silently observing partner (3:6). Even now, he raises no questions and considers no religious issues; he simply and silently takes his turn. The man and the woman are in this together (the interpretation of this text in 1 Tim 2:14 is deeply problematic and has fostered the idea that the woman is the culprit).

Their eyes are opened, that is, they see each other and the world differently—entirely through their own eyes; left to their own resources they are indeed naked, both literally and metaphorically. Their human resources—loincloths—prove inadequate, as they hide from God (3:10). Their clothing reveals more than it conceals (as does God's clothing the already clothed in v. 21). In 3:8-13, the man is the primary subject, balancing the female subject of verses 1-7. The Creator of the universe—no aloof God this—does not leave the humans alone or walk elsewhere. God seeks a response from the fearful and ashamed human beings, but they move to the "blame game" rather than confession. The sin has led to dissonance in inter-human relationships, between humans and God, between human and nonhuman, and within the self (shame).

Most would say that 3:14-19 is descriptive (of what happens in the wake of sin) rather than prescriptive (divinely established orders for the future). Yet, the language of divine judgment is appropriate if understood as God's *announcement* of what the sinful deeds (including those in vv. 8-13) have wrought. They reap the consequences of their own deeds in terms of their primary roles in that culture; God midwifes the connection between deed and effect. Every aspect of human life is touched: marriage and sexuality; work and food; birth and death. It is especially remarkable that the "rule" of the man over the woman is seen as a consequence of sin; hence it stands over against God's creational intention. More generally, they wanted control over their own lives; they now have control in grievously distorted and unevenly distributed forms. They wanted to transcend creaturely limits; they have found newly intensified forms of limitation. They now have the knowledge they desired, but not the perspective to handle it well.

But this state of affairs has not been put in place for all time to come; no new orders of creation are established. Indeed, as with any consequences of sin, or divine judgments (witness the rebuilding of Jerusalem), effort should be made to relieve the toil, pain, patriarchy, and negative effects on nature ("thorns and thistles"). Such endeavors (from anesthesia in childbirth to laborsaving devices in farming to efforts to overcome patriarchy) harmonize with God's intentions in creation, though continuing sinfulness impedes the effort.

Even in the wake of these effects, God remains in relationship with the creatures, and hopeful signs for the future emerge though expulsion from the garden becomes necessary. The naming of Eve anticipates that life will go on; God acts to cover their shame with more substantial clothing (3:21); even exclusion from the possibility of never-ending life could be interpreted as gracious given what they had become. The humans leave the garden with integrity, and are not described in degrading terms; they are still charged with caring for the earth. While being "like God" (in a way different from the likeness to God in 1:26-28) severely complicates life, it also bears some potential for good and advancement. The expulsion mirrors later Israelite banishments from the land because of disloyalty to God (see Lev 26).

The effect of these garden events on family life now follow, initially in the story of Cain and Abel (4:1-16). Life now takes place outside the garden, though God seems as available to Cain as to Adam and Eve in the garden. But life outside the garden is life away from one's true home. The story of the world's first children in chapter 4 presupposes a more densely populated world (Cain's wife, building of a city, and concern for his life). Yet, the text may belong with those (e.g., 2:24) that collapse the distance between the "then" of the story and the "now" of the reader. The story portrays how the effects of sin cross generations, afflict even families (a basic order of creation), and lead to intensified levels of violence (4:23-24; 6:11-13). The story also sets in place key themes for the rest of Genesis: family conflict, primogeniture (God's not choosing the elder son), sibling rivalry, and divine promises given to the non-chosen (e.g., Ishmael, Esau).

The story of Cain and Abel begins positively with responses to God's commands to be fruitful and multiply (Eve), to have dominion over the animals (Abel), and to subdue the earth (Cain). The initial focus on worship—represented as integral to creation—sees the brothers bringing appropriate offerings. God, however, rejects Cain's offering, for reasons unknown; Cain's dejected response to God's choice is not the problem so much as his interaction with God about it. God makes clear that Cain is able to master his anger (4:7), but he kills Abel anyway. God, having been called by the blood of

51

one unable to seek justice, calls Cain to account for the murder. When Cain deflects the question, God more intensively applies to Cain the earlier curse on the ground (3:17), the banishment, and the distancing from God's presence. When Cain objects to what amounts to a death sentence, God mercifully ameliorates the sentence by promising (!) to be Abel's brother's keeper and sealing the promise with a mark (its nature is uncertain). Ironically, the restless wanderer proceeds to build a city. Such an image again mirrors the experience of a dispersed people, who settle in a place that is less than truly home.

The genealogies portray two different family lines (Cain, 4:17-24; Seth, 4:25–5:32) that flow from this conflicted family. Both positive and negative effects are portrayed. A powerful rhythm within life that works for good persists: intimacy, which brings new life into being; creative advances in the arts of civilization; the invoking of the name of Yahweh (by those who were not Israelites!); people who walk with God, such as Enoch (5:24). Yet, violence becomes more intense (Lamech), and the diminishing age spans may depict the effects of sin (see also the ages in 11:10-27). Long lives are also characteristic of other ancient Near Eastern lists of kings and patriarchs. Comparatively, the ages in Gen 5 are much more modest, but sufficient to carry this point. Progress in civilization is always accompanied by progress in sin and its effects, so that "progress" becomes an ambiguous reality.

The effects of sin and its aftermath now are extended to the cosmic sphere, first in 6:1-4 and then in the flood itself. The first text has never been satisfactorily explained by interpreters. Its depiction of the crossing of boundaries between the heavenly and earthly realms may portray the cosmic effects of sin, with new possibilities for violence. This would, then, be a natural lead into the flood story, in which the entire cosmos is caught up in the effects of violence and is threatened with extinction.

The Flood: The Great Divide (6:5–8:22)

This text is usually recognized as an interweaving of J and P stories. That Israel would have preserved more than one version of the flood is not surprising since flood stories circulated widely in that world, of which the one in *The Gilgamesh Epic* is the most well known.

The basis for these stories is probably a severe flood in the Tigris-Euphrates valley (one occurred ca. 3000 BCE), which in time was interpreted by Israel's theologians as a flood that covered the then known world as a judgment of God on human sin.

The focus of the present text is signaled by the repeated conviction about human sinfulness (6:5; 8:21) and the associated disclosures regarding divine sorrow, regret, disappointment, mercy, and promise. God appears, not as an angry judge, but as a grieving and pained parent, distressed at developments; yet, the judgment announced is thorough and uncompromising. This inner-divine tension is resolved on the side of mercy when God freely chooses Noah (6:8). Noah's faithful walk with God, exemplified by his obedience (6:22; 7:5, 9, 16; 8:18), becomes a vehicle for God's new possibilities for the creation.

The flow of the story leads up to and falls away from God's remembrance of Noah and the animals in 8:1. The story itself gives repeated attention to the boarding of the ark, to lists of people and animals/birds that are saved, to what God does to bring salvation rather than judgment, and to the chronology of the event. Remarkably little notice is given to the disaster itself, to the plight of its victims, and to the feelings of the participants; no dialogue is reported and Noah does not speak. The flood is described in natural terms—"what goes around comes around"—with no divine act of intervention; only with the subsiding of the waters is God's explicit activity stated.

The ecological themes in the text are significant. Humans have had a deeply adverse impact on the creation; thorns and thistles (3:18) grow to cosmic proportions and the world's future is endangered. God's assigning temporal limits to the flood (7:4) assures that the orders of creation will not break down completely, and God's remembrance of the animals and birds (6:19; 8:1) belongs to the same initiative as God's remembering Noah.

Scholars have proposed overlapping purposes for the flood:

1. God intended to *purge* the world of its corruption. Water would thus be understood as a cleansing agent. The language of blotting out (6:7) suggests a wiping clean of the slate of the world and beginning anew. Yet, 8:21 makes clear that human beings are just as sinful before the flood as after. If the purpose was to cleanse, it was in some basic sense a failure.

2. God intended to *undo* the creation and begin again. Water would thus be understood as an instrument of destruction. The references to a return of the watery chaos (7:11) and the use of *rûaḥ* in 8:1-2 issuing in the return of the dry land (8:13-14) and the blessings of 8:17 and 9:1, 7 suggest this. Yet, the "old" creation was not destroyed; major continuities with the original creation remain (vegetation; light; firmament; luminaries; ark occupants). There is a beginning again, but the preflood creation remains intact, including a sinful humanity.

3. The flood story represents a *typical judgment.* The floodwaters symbolize a threat to ordered life, always lurking at the edges of existence. Water is thus used as in, say, the lament psalms (see Ps 69:1-2), as an image of difficulty and suffering and catastrophe. Yet, while flood *imagery* may be used to depict such moments, God's promises at the end of the flood indicate that the flood was an event that would not be repeated. Hence, the flood should *never* be used as a type or illustration of divine judgment. Rather, it functions as an illustration of the certainty of God's promises (as in Isa 54:9-10).

4. The flood story represents a *polemic against other religious understandings.* Hence, efforts have been made to show the "obvious" superiority of the biblical flood against the polytheistic stories current elsewhere. But this hegemonic agenda is often overplayed. Israel learned much from the peoples round about, and the purpose of the flood story was certainly more than a negative point.

5. The flood story focuses on *God and God's commitment to the world.* This God expresses sorrow and regret; judges, but doesn't want to; goes beyond justice and decides to save some, including animals; commits to the future of a less than perfect world; is open to change in view of experience with the world and doing things in new ways; promises never to do this again. What God does here "recharacterizes" the divine relation to the world. God ameliorates the workings of divine judgment and promises an orderly cosmos for the continuation of life. God will never do this again! God is the one who has changed between the beginning and the end of the flood, not human beings.

God's regretful response assumes that humans have successfully resisted God's will for the creation. To continue to interact with this creation involves God's decision to continue to live with such resisting creatures (not your typical CEO!). In addition, God's regret assumes that God did not know for sure that this would happen (as elsewhere—see Gen 22:12; Deut 8:2). The text provides no support for a position that claims that God knew, let alone planned, that the creation would take this course.

What God does recharacterizes the divine relationship to the world, but God is not simply resigned to evil. God must find a new way of dealing with the problem of evil. Two complementary directions are taken:

(a) For God to promise not to do something again—and God will keep promises—entails a self-limitation regarding the exercise of divine freedom and power. God thereby limits the divine options in dealing with evil in the life of the world. The route of world annihilation has been set aside as a divine possibility. Divine judgment there will be, but it will be limited in scope.

(b) Genesis 6:5-7 suggests that God takes the route of suffering. Deciding to endure a wicked world, while continuing to open up the divine heart to that world, means that God will continue to grieve. God thus determines to take suffering into God's own self and bear it there for the sake of the future of the world. It is precisely this *kind* of God with whom sinful readers have to do, and it is primarily the divine commitment to promises made that they need most to hear.

We find an admixture of realism and promise here. On the one hand, human beings remain sinful creatures through and through. The flood cuts them off from any Edenic paradise; access to that world cannot be bridged by gradual improvement or sudden insight. On the other hand, human beings remain in the image of God (9:6); they are so highly valued that commands are put in place to conserve their lives, and they retain fundamental responsibility for the larger created order (9:1-7). But sinful human beings do not possess sufficient resources for the task; only God can assure the creation's future. To this end, God ameliorates the workings of divine judgment and promises an orderly cosmos for the continuation of human and nonhuman life. Humans may, by virtue of their own behaviors, put themselves out of business, but not because God has so determined it or because the created order has failed.

A New World Order (9:1–11:26)

The post-flood account of the Priestly writer (9:1-17) picks up the theme struck by the narrator in 8:21-22: God now speaks directly to the flood's survivors regarding his changed relation to a still-sinful world. This world is no new Eden, but every creature—human and nonhuman—is assured that God is still the Creator and that the basic divine relationship to the world still holds, with its blessings and (adjusted) commands.

The basic creational order still remains, but the dominion charge is complicated by sin and its effects: the "fear and dread" of the animals because of human violence, the human diet's being supplemented with meat as a concession in a famine-ridden world (a theme in chaps. 12–50), and the proscription regarding blood (see Lev 17:11) stand as a sharp reminder that killing animals must not be taken lightly, for God is the source of their life. Moreover, the high value of human life is affirmed; an understanding of the human as image of God still pertains in the post-flood world. The lifeblood of human beings is not to be shed. Indeed, murderers are directly accountable to God for their actions. At the same time, human life is not absolutely inviolable; humans can forfeit their right to life if they take someone else's life.

God makes a covenant with those who have endured the flood (9:8-17). Covenant in this text is simply a promise, wherein God publicly states the divine commitment of 8:21-22. The repetition of words and phrases in this text emphasizes its promissory character—never again!—and its inclusiveness of its recipients through all generations. This unilateral and unconditional covenant is an obligation that God alone assumes; it will be as good as God is, and so human beings can rest back in its promises. The sign of the rainbow serves *God's* remembering, that is, action with respect to a prior commitment (see Exod 2:24), but it becomes a secondary sign for people in which they can take comfort and hope. This divine restraint in dealing with evil is an eternal limitation of God's exercise of power; it sets the direction for a different approach to dealing with sin and evil and to the redemption of the world, beginning with Abraham and Sarah.

The remaining segments in chapters 1–11 (9:18–11:27) serve several purposes in preparing for God's choice of Abraham.

1. These sections bring the reader into a world whose peoples and places reflect known historical realities (e.g., Babel), though not all of the names can be identified. A kind of secularity is introduced, for God does not speak or act in 9:18–10:32.

2. These sections extend human relationships beyond the family into the world of nations, where problems and possibilities of various sorts—both good and evil—take on a communal aspect.

3. It becomes clear that the flood has not cleansed the world of sin and the curse; the new Adam (Noah) and his sons get caught up in their spiraling effects. The theme of dysfunctional families continues and sets the stage for the rest of Genesis.

4. Goodness persists alongside human failure. The blessings of God's creation continue to abound in the proliferation of families, the development of cities and nations, and the appearance of the family of Shem. Abraham emerges from within this family and this kind of world, and it is for their sake that he and his family are called, so that "all the families of the earth shall be blessed" (12:3).

The first text in this section (9:18-29) contains difficulties that cannot be pursued here. One key is that Noah's sons are presented both as individuals and as ethnic units (e.g., the Canaanites), as in chapter 10. God's post-flood blessing begins to take effect amid the world of the curse, ameliorating its effects, for instance, the vineyard and its wine, which symbolize God's blessings of life and fertility (see Ps 80:8-16). At the same time, human sin (drunkenness and parental disrespect of some sort, perhaps the public disgrace of the father) and intrafamilial conflict abound, leading to communal difficulties—including slavery—among the descendants (9:25-27). The move from individual behaviors to systemic forms of evil is an ongoing pattern.

The second text (10:1-32), the table of nations, delineates all the known peoples of the world eponymously, that is, in terms of their descent from Noah's three sons. Such multiplying and ordering of the peoples into an international community is witness to God's continuing creational work. Problems of identifying the nations in the genealogy remain, but basically the horizon of the list extends from Crete and Libya in the West to Iran in the East, from Arabia and Ethiopia in the South to Asia Minor and Armenia in the North (the world then known). The recurrent use of the word *families* (10:5, 20, 31-32) links this chapter to 12:3.

The third text (11:1-9), centered on the city/tower of Babel, seems out of place after the table of nations, where people are already scattered (10:18) and Babel is named (10:10). But the two sections are not in chronological order; 11:1-9 reaches back and complements chapter 10 from a negative perspective. Links with later Israel in Babylonian exile may be seen in the scattering of the people from the city—note the typicality of the "whole earth" reference (11:1).

The basic human failure in this text is not easy to discern, but seems focused in the motivation, "otherwise we shall be scattered abroad upon the face of the whole earth" (11:4). Largely because of this, building a tower and making a name become problematic, namely, as an attempt to secure their future isolated from the rest of the world. This constitutes a challenge to the divine command to fill the earth (1:28; 9:1) and fulfill the charge to have dominion; human concern for self-preservation places the rest of the creation at risk. God counters these efforts by acting in such a way—confusing languages—that they have no choice but to scatter and establish separate linguistic communities. God thereby promotes diversity at the expense of any kind of unity that seeks to preserve itself in isolation from the rest of the creation and thereby places that creation at risk.

From one of these scattered families Abraham is raised up for God's mission with respect to all such families.

The thematic direction of Gen 1–11 may now be summarized. The recurrent litany that God has created everything good stands as a beacon regarding the nature of God's creative work and God's intentions for the creation. The *subsequent* entrance of sin, while not finally effacing the God-human relationship or the key role human beings play in the divine economy, has occasioned deep and pervasive ill effects upon all relationships, human and nonhuman. These effects issue in a universal disaster for the earth, and dramatically evidence the need for a reclamation of creation. On the far side of the flood, God rejects annihilation as the means to accomplish this reformation and graciously chooses a more vulnerable, long-term engagement, working from within the very life of the world itself. The world continues to live and breathe, and to establish families and nations, because God makes a gracious, unconditional commitment to stay with the world, come what may in the wake of human sinfulness. And that commitment shortly becomes evident in a new divine strategy to work through one family to save and bless all families.

AGRICULTURAL AND CIVIL CALENDAR

The Gezer Calendar	Season	Labor	Babylonian Numbering	Months		Israelite Numbering	Religious Festivals	
Two months of [olive] harvest;	Former (autumn) rains	*Olive, grape, fig harvests	1st	Tishri (*Ethanim)	Sept/Oct	7th	**High Holy Days** Trumpets	1 Tishri
							Day of Atonement	10 Tishri
							Booths-Ingathering	15-22 Tishri
		*Plowing	2nd	Marchesvan (*Bul)	Oct/Nov	8th		
Two months of sowing;		*Sowing of wheat, barley, and spelt	3rd	*Chislev	Nov/Dec	9th	Hanukkah	25 Chislev (eight days)
	Winter rains 70% of yearly precipitation	(Second plowing) Late planting	4th	*Tebeth	Dec/Jan	10th		
Two months of late sowing;		(Sheep shearing) Flax harvest	5th	*Shebat	Jan/Feb	11th		
			6th	*Adar	Feb/Mar	12th	Purim	14 Adar
A month of hoeing weeds;	Latter (spring) rains	*Barley harvest	7th	*Nisan (*Abib)	Mar/Apr	1st	Passover	14 Nisan
							Unleavened Bread	15-21 Nisan
A month of harvesting barley;		*Wheat harvest	8th	Iyyar (*Ziv)	Apr/May	2nd	First Fruits	
A month of harvesting and [measuring];		Early figs ripen Grapes ripen	9th	*Sivan	May/June	3rd	Weeks (Pentecost)	7 weeks after Passover
Two months of cutting [grapes];	Summer Dry Season	*Date, fig, grape, and pomegranate harvests	10th	Tammuz	June/July	4th		
			11th	Ab	July/Aug	5th		
A month of [collecting] summer fruit.			12th	*Elul	Aug/Sept	6th	[Vintage Festival at Shiloh]	

*Times of intense labor demand.

*Used in the Bible

Note

1. These references are to W. Beyerlin, ed., *Near Eastern Religious Texts Relating to the Old Testament* (Philadelphia: Westminster, 1978). See index under "sin."

Bibliography

Brodie, Thomas L. *Genesis as Dialogue: A Literary, Historical, and Theological Commentary.* Oxford: Oxford University Press, 2001.

Brueggemann, Walter. *Genesis.* Atlanta: John Knox, 1982.

Fretheim, Terence E. "The Book of Genesis: Introduction, Commentary, and Reflections." *NIB,* vol. 1. Nashville: Abingdon, 1994.

Gowan, Donald E. *From Eden to Babel: A Commentary on the Book of Genesis 1–11.* Grand Rapids: Eerdmans, 1988.

Rad, Gerhard von. *Genesis: A Commentary.* OTL. Philadelphia: Westminster, 1972.

Towner, W. Sibley. *Genesis.* Louisville: Westminster John Knox, 2001.

Trible, Phyllis. *God and the Rhetoric of Sexuality.* OBT 20. Philadelphia: Fortress, 1978.

Wenham, Gordon J. *Genesis 1–15.* WBC 1. Waco: Word, 1987.

Westermann, Claus. *Genesis 1–11: A Commentary.* Minneapolis: Augsburg, 1984.

For general books on the Pentateuch as a whole, see the bibliography at the conclusion of chapter 5.

CHAPTER THREE

PROMISES MADE, THREATENED, AND FULFILLED

Gen 12–50

Introduction

There is, perhaps, no more problematic phrase in Hebrew bible studies than *the patriarchal period*. Many standard introductions to the Old Testament and histories of ancient Israel written in the mid-twentieth century routinely equated Gen 12–50 with a historical period, the so-called Middle Bronze Age, ca. 1800–1600 BCE. Time lines were sketched in which the phrase *the patriarchs* was inked onto this several-century moment in the ancient Near East. Now, such an exercise seems problematic for at least two reasons—historical and literary ones. First, there is little incontrovertible evidence that these chapters were composed, either in oral or written form, during this period. Further, figures like Sarah and Abraham or Rebekah and Isaac are impossible to root firmly in this particular historical context. In fact, it is difficult to discern anything in the Hebrew Bible that might stem from this time, since Israel, even what one might call pre-Israel, emerged in Syria-Palestine only at the beginning of the Iron Age, ca. 1100–1000 BCE.

Some readers may raise questions about how one understands such literature apart from a particular historical context. For example, it would be helpful if we knew what century lay behind the particularities of Gen 14 or the more general features of Gen 22. Still, as with many of the psalms, it is possible to comprehend literature even when there is much one would still like to know about its origins.

One theological issue raised by this absence of a clear historical context is that involving the authority of the biblical text. In the case of psalms, the primeval history, and these family stories, the authority of the text does not derive from its role as reporter of either events or history. Instead, the text presents poetry and prose that later religious communities have found not only useful but essential for thinking about their own lives. The stories in Gen 12–50 became canon even though they had no firm anchor in specific historical waters.

Second, the term *patriarchal* does not do justice to the nature of this literature. The stories involve fathers and mothers, sons and daughters, aunts and uncles—simply put, families. The genealogy may be patrilineal (see below), but the stories do far more than focus on fathers. Hence, we prefer to term this literature "family stories."

Nonetheless, there is something palpably "patriarchal," in the contemporary sense of this word, throughout Genesis. Sons, rather than daughters, receive most property. To this extent, these texts do mirror a kind of society—one that favors males in the public arena—if not a particular society that we can place at one historical moment.

After reviewing a number of methods available for the study of this literature, we will investigate Gen 12–50 in three basic sections. Each section is introduced by a genealogical formula, "These are the descendants/generations of," which may be found in Gen 11:27; 25:19; 37:2. These markers provide evidence for the way in which the biblical authors and editors understood this material to be organized. Although we usually think about Abraham, Isaac, and Jacob as particularly prominent, the three names that appear in these formulae are Terah, Isaac, and Jacob. Attention to these particular names will provide an important key to understanding the significance of these chapters.

Critical Study of Gen 12–50

The book of Genesis has served as an anvil upon which many of the methods of biblical study have been wrought. We can think of no critical perspective that has not been exercised on this material. So we offer an overview of these perspectives in order that students of the Bible may know the options available to them. Also, those interested in a theological assessment of this literature have often used one or another of these perspectives to make their cases. This has been particularly true for the first method, source criticism.

Source Criticism

As we demonstrated in the previous chapter, Gen 1–11 is a composite work, reflecting the hands of various authors, who had quite different literary styles and theological perspectives. Genesis 1:1–2:4*a* has been attributed to someone known as the Priestly writer, whereas Gen 2–3 has been traced to the so-called Yahwist. Most of Gen 1–11 can be divided between these two "sources,"[1] i.e., a Priestly source [P] and a Yahwistic source [J]. Those who advocate such an approach to understanding the composition of Genesis have maintained that these same sources, but now with a third, the so-called Elohistic source [E], may be discerned in Gen 12–50, especially Gen 12–36. The case is particularly compelling in the case of "duplicate" episodes, the same basic story told from the perspective of the two different authors. The so-called "wife-sister" stories offer the best example. Genesis 12:10-20; Gen 20; and Gen 26:1-16 appear to present the same basic motif, a husband who passes his wife off as his sister when they reside in a foreign land. In the first two instances, the story is told about Abraham and Sarah; in the final case, about Isaac and Rebekah. The first two versions are, perforce, the more interesting, since they provide the same story about the same people. The most convincing explanation for this phenomenon is that the same basic story was related by two different authors or storytelling traditions, and that, over time, each version achieved a measure of distinctiveness, including that of theological perspective. The version in Gen 12 seems to focus on the conflict between human plans and the divine purpose, whereas Gen 20 seems particularly concerned with the "fear of God." The former concern appears in a number of J or Yahwistic texts, whereas the latter is characteristic of E or the Elohistic tradition. One can make a similar case about the two versions of God's covenant with Abraham, though this time the sources are different: Gen 15 is Yahwistic, Gen 17 is Priestly.

To read the family stories in this manner allows one to focus on the theological distinctiveness of each "source." In fact, Hans Walter

Wolff and Walter Brueggemann have provided insightful articles which do precisely that.[2] One may identify theological hallmarks for each source, such as the fear of God in E, the blessing of all humanity through Abraham in J, land as blessing in P.

However, the scholarly consensus about source criticism in its classic form is no longer as strong as it once was.[3] Two other competing paradigms to explain the origins of Genesis have emerged. One suggests that there was a primary source or story that was added to and edited over time. However, none of the additions are of a scale or scope comparable with the primary or "original" story. The other maintains that there are no "sources" that extend the length of Genesis. Instead, the constitutive building blocks had independent existences and only relatively late in the book's composition were they combined to create the version as we now have it.[4] The primary blocks of tradition in Genesis have been identified as the primeval history (Gen 1–11), the family stories (Gen 12–36), and the Joseph short story (Gen 37–50).

This debate about the origins of Genesis has clear implications for the theological assessment of this literature. If one adopts the former approach, then one would try to identify the theological features of the primary story and then those of the later additions. If one adopts the latter approach, then one would compare and contrast the theological elements of the three constituent blocks that make up Genesis. The approach we adopt here is most like this latter one. In sum, the model one uses for the book's formation will almost certainly influence the way one approaches the book theologically.

Form Criticism

As with Gen 1–11, genealogy and narrative constitute the two major literary types present throughout the remainder of Genesis. Those scholars concerned with the formal features of literature have investigated both types. Genealogies have not received as much attention as have the stories. Still, recent work has helped us understand that there are two basic types of genealogy: linear and branching.[5] Many genealogies in Genesis are linear, that is, they trace a family over time—through many generations (Gen 11:10-26). In contrast, branching or segmented genealogies report relations and statuses within a family at one time. This kind of genealogy is embedded in Gen 29:31–30:24 and is reflected in poetic form in Gen 49. This genealogy concerns the sons of Jacob and their relationships.

These two types of genealogies are designed to do different things. The linear genealogy helps enfranchise or simply identify a particular individual as belonging to a group, (e.g., Israel or Moab), even to a group with special prerogatives (e.g., to a royal or to a priestly lineage). The segmented genealogy indicates the relative power and status among people at the same time. So, genealogies can do different things. And, as we shall see, they bear not only children but theological significance.

The relation of genealogy to story in Genesis is vexed. Some scholars have suggested that the stories were earlier and that they were secondarily linked by using genealogies to integrate characters in the stories. Alternatively, one could claim that the genealogies came first, and that certain genealogical nodes, such as twins, spawned stories about them (e.g., Jacob and Esau). Whichever model one prefers, there can be little question that most readers of Genesis are more interested in the stories than they are in the genealogies.

Hermann Gunkel has had a remarkable influence on the ways in which the Genesis stories have been read.[6] His name is associated with the form-critical interpretation of these stories, since he gave them a name—in German *Sage* (not equivalent to the English term *saga;* even less to the term *legend*). In so doing, Gunkel defined what this type of story is in Genesis. It is not a long entity; for Gunkel, there is no Abraham story. Instead, the *Sage* is a short episode with few characters, often focusing on a particular place or problem, such as birth, death, or conflict. For the most part, the *Sage* deals with family life. Gunkel thought the narratives in Genesis were the product of oral storytelling. He also judged that many had an etiological intent, that is, they were interested in explaining the origins of some name or practice (see, e.g., Gen 32:30-32).

The terms *narrative* and *story* have been applied to larger texts. So one hears about the Jacob and Laban story or the Abraham story, even the story of Genesis. All such claims deserve to be heard and tested. One good way to assess whether a story is present is to ask if there is a plot at work, and not simply a sequence of events; not all reports are stories.

It would be difficult to overestimate the importance of Gunkel's contributions to the study of Genesis (and biblical studies in general). Many who approached Genesis were concerned about either historical matters—whether the events narrated had actually happened—or doctrinal issues—whether that which was reported squared with religious understandings, such as *creatio ex nihilo* (creation out of nothing). Gunkel reoriented the conversation by focusing on aesthetic matters. He was interested in describing the special features of ancient Israelite literature, a feature of biblical studies that came to full bloom in the late twentieth century.

Tradition History

Tradition history is a logical outgrowth of a form-critical approach to Genesis. And it is associated in the study of Genesis with the work of Martin Noth.[7] Noth was interested in knowing how the individual stories were collected and then developed into the literary configurations in which we currently have them. He postulated that over time they were told and collected at particular places, for instance, those tales about Abraham were preserved at Beersheba, those about Jacob at Bethel. And he presumed that what were originally unrelated characters—Abraham, Isaac, and Jacob—were only later connected by means of a fictive genealogy. Noth's primary focus, however, was on the collections of literature associated with these key individuals. In this chapter we, too, will adopt a similar approach. However, we will focus on the family in which that individual was embedded and not simply on an individual patriarch. The reader interested in theological issues should ask how the concerns in the Abraham narrative are similar to and different from those in the Jacob narrative.

Redaction Criticism

Redaction criticism works out of the judgment that the book of Genesis grew out of originally distinct parts, whether sources or stories. The redaction critic is concerned to learn what principles or interests guided that process of forming those sources and/or stories into the book we now have. For example, if the individual stories circulated independently, why does Gen 12 come before Gen 20?

It has generally been assumed that the so-called priestly material has been added to an earlier version of the essential literature. Moreover, a number of formulae that include the Hebrew word *toledot,* "generations" or "descendants," have been introduced into the emerging literary tradition (e.g., Gen 5:1; 10:1; 11:10; 11:27; 25:19; 37:2, etc.). These formulae can also be attributed to the Priestly tradition. Also, they typically introduce that which follows and relate it to that which has gone before. The basic assumption at work in the use of these formulae is that all people, even the universe, are related in an inextricable manner. To understand Israel, one must understand the way in which Israelites are related both to those who came before them and to those who live with them.

History of Religions

As we noted earlier, it is difficult indeed to speak about a historical context for the family stories, a social world behind the text. Nonetheless, a social and religious world is presented in that literature. Those interested in the theological dimensions of the text have a special interest in the religious world of these families.

The religious universe in Gen 12–50 is remarkably complex.[8] To be sure, the names for the Deity that had appeared in Gen 1–11 occur here as well (Yahweh—the LORD—and Elohim—God). However, that vocabulary is enriched in the family stories. On the one hand, there are references to "the god of the father," apparently an expression deriving from devotion to a clan or family god. The text depicts this feature most clearly in the scene during which Laban and Jacob make a covenant (Gen 31:43-54). As a part of the ceremony, each person takes an oath by his family god. Laban swears by "the God of Nahor," and Jacob swears by "the God of Abraham." (Interestingly, in neither case do they swear by the god of their own father.) They swear by the same kind of god, but not the same god. Religious pluralism is a hallmark of this world.

One has a comparable sense of religious diversity when one looks in detail at the deities venerated by Abraham, Isaac, and Jacob. In each case there is a noun associated with the god of the patriarch: Abraham—*magen* or "Shield" (Gen 15:1), Isaac—*paḥad* or "Fear" (Gen 31:42), and Jacob—*'abir* or "Bull" (Gen 49:24). These titles suggest that the god of each individual possessed a distinctive identity, as one might expect with a clan deity. Deity and family were inextricably linked.

The case seems to be different with another theological vocabulary, that which includes the word *'el,* the general term for god and, as well, the name of the Canaanite high God, El. In each case, the Hebrew text includes the noun *El,* along with some other term or phrase. The texts include Gen 14:18-22, El Elyon, "God Most High"; Gen 16:13, El Roi, "God of seeing"; Gen 17:1, El Shaddai, "God Almighty"; Gen 21:33, El 'Olam, "the Everlasting God"; Gen 33:20, El Elohe Israel, "El the God of Israel"; Gen 35:7, El Bethel, "El of Bethel." If the phrase *god of the fathers* reflects a clan-god type of religion, which is known in many different places and settings, then the El language fits what we know about religious traditions native to Syria-Palestine, especially the Canaanite traditions as exemplified in the Ugaritic texts.[9] It is, therefore, not surprising that these El-named references often occur with references to specific places (so Gen 32:30 and Peniel) in Syria-Palestine.

In the face of such a diverse religious world, it is interesting to note that biblical writers themselves forged claims about the overall coherence of this system. When the biblical author writes, "I am Yahweh, the God of Abraham your father and the God of Isaac," that individual is clearly claiming that Yahweh is the God of the various fathers (Gen 28:13). Moreover, in Exodus, biblical writers were interested in making a comparable claim, namely, that despite different names, Israel's God has remained the same across the generations and in different geographical settings (Exod 6:2-3).

As readers work their way through the family stories in Genesis, they should attend to the various explicit theological vocabularies that the text presents. At the risk of oversimplification, we suggest that clan-god language is often related to specific family issues, whereas El-god language focuses more on place.

Literary Criticism

There is no more natural approach to the family stories than to read them as stories, as literature.[10] Still, such an interpretive style has been developed only fairly recently. Attending to the issues of theme, motif, characterization, plot, and dialogue, among others, can assist the reader in discerning elemental features of this literature. One can compare and contrast the characters of Abraham and Jacob and even study God as a character in these texts.

One of the greatest challenges to the literary study of Genesis is deciding what are the boundaries of the text to be studied. Does one focus on an individual *Sage,* à la Gunkel? Should one focus on cycles of stories, such as the Abraham and Sarah stories, à la Noth? Should one focus on the major compositional building blocks, the Joseph story or the family stories as a whole, à la Rendtorff? Or should one view Genesis as one long story? Of course one could do any or all of these things—and people have proceeded in all these ways.

Social-World Analysis

We have had occasion to note earlier that there is no obvious historical or social context for the family stories. Nonetheless, there is a clear social world conveyed in the text. The text describes means of transport, diet, housing patterns, weather, agriculture, and kinship structure, among other things.

Such information can be studied using the perspectives developed by sociologists, anthropologists, and economists. For example, the kinship structure that stems from Terah is one well known to students of human culture; it is one termed patrilineal endogamy, a pattern in which both husband and wife must be derived from an earlier family headed by a male. Similarly, the marriages between various individuals might seem strange to contemporary eyes. However, the relationship between Abraham, a wife, and a concubine is known elsewhere. The same is the case with the marriage between a man and two women who are sisters. Cross-cultural study reveals that such marriage practices occur in societies in which it is imperative to achieve a male heir to whom property might pass. Such social-world study of texts in Genesis does not have a long history, but the results of such study will profoundly influence future studies of Genesis.[11]

As should be clear, each method or perspective attends to a different set of questions or concerns. And each one can assist the reader in exploring the manifold religious and theological issues present in these family stories.

"These Are the Descendants of Terah" (Gen 11:27–25:18)

The boundary between the primeval history and the family stories is indistinct. Drawing a line between Gen 11 and 12 does not do justice to the particularities in Gen 9:27 (e.g., the relationship of Canaanites to Israelites), nor does such a line allow for the broad scope of texts like Gen 12:1-3, which carry forward issues broached in those earlier chapters.

Narrative Overview

The plot of these chapters focuses on Abraham and Sarah securing and then preserving progeny. The plot is not driven by any self-stated urge of that couple to propagate. Instead, God's signal speech (Gen 12:1-3) makes one ask: will a people, much less a great nation, stem from Abraham? There is, as well, a subplot involving Abraham's nephew, Lot, which results in the creation of space for Abraham's primary heir to settle.

The author uses geographic movement to assist in the telling of this family's story. On occasion, such movement is directed by the Deity (Gen 12:1), and on occasion, such movement results from exigency (12:10-20). Moreover, one has a sense that certain motifs that will become prominent in Israel's life are foreshadowed in this literature involving movement, for example, the move to Egypt in time of famine (so Gen 12:10).

Israel Among the Nations

Unlike the other two primary bodies of family stories, this one commences with a genealogy, one that situates Terah in the primeval post-flood generations. Again, the boundaries between the family stories and primeval history are permeable. The ancient authors were interested in testifying to the "roots" of Israel. Though relative newcomers in the ancient Near East, especially when compared with their Mesopotamian or Egyptian neighbors, Israelites could point to a genealogical connection with the flood survivor. As a distant descendant of Shem, Abraham was a "son" of Noah.

As a corollary to this placement among the nations, the Terah/Abraham story also highlights the place of Israel among its national neighbors. One might call this the international dimension of the family story. The Terah family does not live in isolation, but is bound—in its earlier history and in its contemporary reality—to others. Moreover, from a genealogical and theological perspective, those others are part of the "extended" family.

One could read the Terah/Abraham story as a statement about the origins of various Syro-Palestinian communities. Moab and Ammon come to exist in 19:30-38; Midian in 25:2; Aram in 22:21. The Ishmaelites stem from the story of Hagar and Ishmael (Gen 21). To be sure, Israel will stand in a relationship of enmity with many of these groups, but it is always possible to view this as a familial relationship, which may help explain the occasional intense animosity.

Genesis 14, the truly odd chapter in the Terah/Abraham story, attests to this international side to the family stories. Abraham, viewed here as a warrior, defeats a military coalition, rescues Lot, and is blessed for his deeds by Melchizedek, king of Salem (Jerusalem?). This episode is surely of a piece with the theological tradition attested in Gen 12:3, "in you all the families of the earth shall be blessed." Not only is Abraham related to all the families of the earth; he and his family have a calling, to be a source of blessing for all those to whom he is explicitly—through recent genealogy— or implicitly—through ancient genealogy—related.

A Promise Offered and Ratified

God is the first character to speak in the Terah/Abraham story. And it is a momentous speech:

> Go from your country and your kindred and your father's house to the land that I will show you. I will make of you a great nation, and I will bless you, and make your name great, so that you will be a blessing. I will bless those who bless you, and the one who curses you I will curse; and in you all the families of the earth shall be blessed. (Gen 12:1-3)

Here one finds God offering promissory notes of two different sorts. On the one hand, God promises to make a great nation out of Abraham. Such will require Abraham (and presumably Sarah) to bear an heir. On the other hand, God promises to show—and presumably give—Abraham land in which to live. Land and progeny constitute the two primary elements of the promise.

71

The language of promise may seem neutral, even banal. Anyone can make promises, so why not God? In order to understand the real significance of these promises, one must set them in their Genesis context. Promises had occurred earlier. For example, God had promised Noah that he would remember the covenant that he was making with all life (Gen 9:15-16). God had "promised" to punish humanity (Gen 3:16), and God had promised not to undertake certain kinds of punishment (Gen 8:21). (See our discussion of these texts in chap. 2.) But Gen 12:1-3 represents the first occasion during which the Deity promises to do something truly affirmative and for specific people. God provides direction within the context of the dispersal created by the aftermath of the tower of Babel episode. God offers the prospect of land to a group that had hitherto been without such a form of property.

The promises in Gen 12:1-3 must also be understood from the perspective of that which comes later in the Terah/Abraham story, namely, the creation of a covenant between Abraham and God (Gen 15 and 17). The vocabulary of covenant provides a powerful set of symbols throughout the Hebrew Bible. We have already discussed the covenant that God makes with all life (Gen 9:1-17). In the Terah/Abraham story, covenant becomes far more palpable.

Covenants are not just something the Deity says to an individual. They are virtual contracts—rooted in the discourse of real-life economic, political, and social transactions. For example, Abraham and Abimelech, king of Gerar, make a covenant in order to solve a problem, namely, to determine who has rights of ownership and use of a particular well (Gen 21:25-34). This covenant involves the taking of an oath, and the payment of fees by livestock. A legal relationship is established by such action.

The writers of Genesis offer two versions of a covenant between Abraham and God.[12] However, one might ask why either version of this covenant is necessary, since God has already promised land and progeny to Abraham. It may be that promise is not enough—that the legally binding explication of such a promise through the contraction of a covenant is necessary.

Though both Gen 15 and 17 have been characterized as "the Abrahamic covenant," they are not identical. Both these covenants articulate and refine the promises made in Gen 12:1-3. Genesis 15, which has typically been attributed to the Yahwist, addresses both components of the covenant. As for the promise that he will become a great nation, Abraham complains that such an entity would need to stem from a member of his house who is not even his son, Eliezer of Damascus. God responds by affirming that "no one but your very own issue shall be your heir" (Gen 15:4). This covenant results from Abraham's questioning of the Deity. The original promise (Gen 12) did not suffice as God's final word to Abraham concerning the growth of his family into a great nation.

The text goes on to treat the issue of land.[13] It not only identified the boundaries of that territory over which Israel will assume control, but it also explains that there will be a delay in the allocation of the land. The current inhabitants, the Amorites, must live in the land for a longer time in order for them to have committed enough iniquitous acts to justify their dislocation.

In all this, there are no requirements placed on Abraham. In fact, one has the sense that this covenant is a response not only to his questioning of God, but also to Abraham's willingness to "believe the LORD." However, Gen 15:6 is ambiguous. Without question the text indicates that Abraham believed or trusted the Lord. But the subject of the next verb is unclear; it could be either Abraham or God. One could say that Abraham reckoned it to God as righteousness or one could claim that God reckoned it to Abraham as righteousness. In either case, both parties were prepared to trust each other, which is a hallmark of covenants, whether between Abraham and Abimelech or Abraham and God.

Genesis 17 bears the traits of the Priestly source. One should ask, if a covenant between God and Abraham has already been established in Gen 15, why is Gen 17 necessary or even appropriate? An answer emerges when one examines the specific features of this covenant.

At the very outset of this text, God challenges Abraham to "walk before me and be blameless." "Walk before" signifies a style of life, not simply approaching an altar. One senses that this is a condition of the covenant, which is then offered to Abraham and his offspring, whereupon reference is made to a grant of land. Imperative language continues: every male in an Israelite household should be circumcised. This, too, is a requirement for Abraham, but it is more since this rite allows each new generation of those in the Israelite household to become part of this covenant community.

Finally, the covenant in Gen 17 makes specific one feature of the promise for progeny that had hitherto been ambiguous and that had resulted in the family complications reported in Gen 16, namely, who was to be the mother of Abraham's direct heir. Genesis 17:15 states that an individual will be born to Sarah—she rather than Hagar will be the mother of kings.

In sum, the language of promise feeds into the language of covenant. Genesis 15 and 17 refine and make specific the more general promises of Gen 12:1-3. Together, these texts depict an obligating God, a God who promises certain things and who expects a style of life—walking before one's God—in return.

The Fate of the Promise

As we have just seen, it is possible to speak about a twofold promise, which involves land and progeny. How does such a promise, ratified by covenant, work itself out?

The promise of land does not explicitly involve land ownership, but rather a place to live. Only in the covenant does possession of the land become an issue. In this regard, it is interesting to trace Abraham's movement in and legal status vis-à-vis land. After hearing the promise, Abraham moves by stages into the Negeb, and then down to Egypt, and subsequently back to Palestine, to Mamre, where he builds an altar. Abraham remains at Mamre until he leaves for Gerar (Gen 20). We are not told explicitly when he returns to Palestine, but he is in the southern part of Palestine again according to Gen 21. Here we hear that he gained control of a well, but also that he "resided as an alien many days in the land of the Philistines" (Gen 21:34). Then, Gen 23 reports that Abraham is able to purchase a field and cave near Mamre appropriate for the burial of his wife and, finally, himself (Gen 25:10).

Such an overview suggests Abraham was able to gain a tenuous toehold in the land. However, his efforts to secure water and burial ground did not result in the fulfillment of God's promise. The promise of land was not fulfilled in Abraham's lifetime, nor for that matter was it "fulfilled" at the end of Genesis or even at the end of the Pentateuch. Israel remained, in consequential ways, a people of promise.

The situation is different with the promise of progeny. One might even say that this promise, rather than that of land, drives much of the Terah/Abraham story. It is helpful to review those episodes that have an impact upon the working out of this promise.

Soon after the promise of progeny was made, Abraham and Sarah are in Egypt, with Sarah in Pharaoh's household. Such a situation threatens the ability of that family to produce an heir. By the end of the story, the couple is reunited. Then, soon after the first version of the covenant, Sarah adopts the ploy of polycoity. A member of the household, Hagar, will serve as a surrogate spouse and conceive a child with Abraham. Cross-cultural studies indicate that such a child, in this case Ishmael, would have been a legitimate heir. This plan worked, only to be followed by another version of the covenant, according to which Sarah herself would have a son. Then, the second wife–sister episode jeopardizes Sarah's role as wife to Abraham and potential mother for his son. But, after they are reunited, she bears a son, Isaac. Potential conflict with Ishmael made it necessary for him and his mother to be removed from the scene. But with Isaac alone in place, the very survival of this heir comes under question, when God commands Abraham to kill him. After Isaac survives and after Sarah dies, the necessity of finding an acceptable wife for Isaac comes into play. In order to preserve the family structure, he must marry someone from the lineage of Terah. Hence, he travels to that group and finds Rebekah. That marriage choice sets the stage for the next story, which involves the descendants of Isaac.

Special note must be made of the ambiguous Hagar and Ishmael and all that they represent.[14] Ishmael could have borne the promise, as a son of the household. Abraham holds deep affection for the lad, whom he had named: "The matter was very distressing to Abraham on account of his son" (Gen 21:11). Further, God made promises to Hagar (16:10). She, in turn, offered a new name for "the LORD who spoke to her" (16:13). This Egyptian slave girl will become the mother of a multitude.

Still, Ishmael and Hagar are tangential to the Israelite kinship structure. Though abandoned by the household, the author notes that "God was with the boy" (Gen 21:20). The tradition attests that God is concerned for more than just Isaac. The Deity's care for Hagar and Ishmael is consistent with the motif struck in Gen 12:1-3, namely, that there should be blessing beyond the household of Israel. The Old Testament recognizes this motif as in some way manifest in Israel's relations with the Ishmaelites; they are never at war with each other, a peaceful relation symbolized when Ishmael and Isaac bury their father (Gen 25:9).

The Terah/Abraham story unfolds as one and then another impediment to the birth and then survival of the heir is resolved. The promise of progeny is continually threatened and yet ultimately comes to fruition. The Israelite writers understood this to be a theological story. Though Abraham treated his wife as his sister and though Sarah advocated the ploy of polycoity, God, in covenant, affirmed that Sarah would be the mother of the son who would symbolize the promise.

Theological Reflection in the Story of Terah/Abraham

Claus Westermann has argued that a certain level of theological reflection is present in this literature.[15] His roster includes Gen 15:6; 16:6; 18:16-33; 22. Though we do not necessarily agree with him that these verses are late developments in the Terah/Abraham story, we do think that Westermann has identified an element that is distinctive in this literature and is resumed in the story of Joseph, namely, overt theological statements.

The story of Terah/Abraham puts Abraham and the Deity in a dialogic position. They talk, and their conversations address major theological issues. Genesis 15:6, though ambiguous, appears to present God's judgment that, because Abraham trusted Yahweh, he would be viewed as righteous by the Deity. This judgment is more unusual than it might appear. Righteousness (and justice) often appear as ethical norms in ancient Israel. Certain individual actions or social modes of behavior can be construed as righteous or just. In Gen 15:6, however, Abraham is deemed righteous because he responds to God by "believing." Such a view expands the notion of righteousness to include disposition or attitude, not just behavior in the social or family sphere.

Genesis 18:16-33 provides a remarkable theological dialogue between patriarch and Deity. After God reveals to Abraham that he is going to examine Sodom and Gomorrah, Abraham poses a question to God: "Will you indeed sweep away the righteous with the wicked?" Though one might view this query as Abraham's use of a theological smoke screen to protect Lot and his family, the discourse that follows indicates that the biblical author is pursuing nothing less than the issue of theodicy, as do other biblical voices (Job, Jeremiah, Habakkuk). The dialogue, which is driven by repeated questions from Abraham, results in God's concession that if ten righteous people are found in the city, then it would not be destroyed. God's justice can be made specific. Moreover, that specificity, once affirmed, will enable the Deity to act when fewer than ten righteous people were found in the city.

Finally, if Gen 15 focuses on righteousness, and 18 on justice, Gen 22 moves on to a nexus of issues—God's testing of humans and the fearing of God. At the outset, the reader is informed that God tested Abraham, something that the reader knows, but Abraham presumably does not. At the end of the story, the reader learns, along with Abraham, that God now knows Abraham fears him. The notion of fearing God is complicated. Fear and veneration are closely linked. And the Hebrew Bible includes language about fear with that of acquiring knowledge—the fear of the Lord is the beginning of wisdom (Prov 1:7).

There have been so many learned and sensitive interpretations of Gen 22 that one hesitates to add more. In the context of this introduction, it is perhaps enough to identify several features of this text. It is a well-written text. Readers may ponder the way individual characters are drawn, the way dialogue works, the way in which resolution is achieved, if indeed it is achieved. It is a text that raises ethical issues. Readers may ponder whether Abraham's willingness to kill Isaac would result in a good act.[16] Is obedience to God always good if it were to result in the death of an innocent child? Such a question is particularly difficult since the act of killing would occur within the familial context. It is a theological text, since it raises questions about the sort of Deity who would command a parent to do such a thing. And, more generally, it identifies Elohim (God) as a Deity who tests individual human beings (typically in the OT, God tests Israel, not persons). After this episode, Abraham, who has spoken to God so often, speaks to him no more.

In sum, the notion of promise drives the Terah/Abraham story. Promise develops into covenant; promise, particularly the promise of progeny, works itself out in various discrete episodes, which together make up the Terah/Abraham story. God works through promise into covenant and, on occasion, in spite of human endeavor.

In addition to the power of those promises ratified in covenant, the Deity requires that Israelites work in common, whether put in general terms—walking before God—or specific terms—the act of circumcision.

The authors of this story understand that promises work themselves out over long periods of time. Individuals belong to family that will continue over time. The quintessential theological motifs of that faith—promise into covenant—make sense not to the individual in isolation, but to the individual in family. Family—particularly, in the Terah/Abraham story, the relation between the parent generation and the next generation—symbolizes the coming to fruition of the promise of progeny, though without the final form of the promise—nations and kings—having been fulfilled.

"These Are the Descendants of Isaac" (Gen 25:19–37:1)

The story of the descendants of Isaac is made up of short episodes, as was the previous cycle. However, they are grouped into two primary blocks, Jacob and Esau (Gen 25–28; 32–33) and Jacob and Laban (Gen 29–31). Further, one has a stronger sense of a story about the primary character, Jacob, than one did about Abraham. Such literary concentration may be due to the authors' interest in the person who achieves the status of Israel.

Narrative Overview

These chapters cover two of the "patriarchs and matriarchs," Isaac and Rebekkah; Jacob, Rachel, and Leah. (Though Isaac has appeared earlier, he undertakes no significant independent action.) Jacob predominates, whereas Isaac offers a shadowy presence. Rebekkah seems more clearly drawn than her husband. The relation between father and son, Isaac and Jacob, becomes far less important than between brother and brother, Jacob and Esau. Genesis 4:1-16, the Cain and Abel story, has alerted the reader to the potential incendiary consequences of a fraternal relationship gone awry.

This story about Jacob commences with a birth narrative, introducing him as a younger twin to Esau. That relationship drives the story, until Jacob must flee the land to escape Esau's anger. Therewith begins the Jacob-Laban story, which is also the story about Jacob's search for an appropriate spouse along with the reporting about the birth of his twelve sons. Once Jacob's family has been established and he must leave Laban's household, the story about Jacob and Esau resumes. The Jacob-Laban episode is, therefore, surrounded by the story of twins.

The second section of the Jacob and Esau story leads up to their meeting/confrontation (33:1-16) and subsequent separation. The story involves both violence—the rape of Dinah and ensuing murder of males in Shechem—and resolution—Jacob's settling in Bethel and the death of Rachel.

Place looms large in this story. Whereas Abraham was moving about in the South (Beersheba, Hebron, and Mamre are mentioned explicitly), place-names are more prominent in the stories within which Jacob plays a prominent role. Jacob is located in or near Bethel, Peniel, and Shechem, that is, farther north than the Abraham stories. Together these two sets of stories spell out the breadth of God's promise of land. And, of course, Jacob lives for a time in the land of Laban.

Bethel seems especially important; Jacob discovers it and returns to it. Bethel is not just another city; the name means "God's house." Jacob becomes a forerunner of other Israelites who will want to live near God—in Jerusalem—where the temple, literally, "house of God," was built.

The Continued Story of Promise and Covenant

Unlike the story of Abraham, that about Jacob begins with neither divine direction nor promise. Isaac "prays," the Deity responds; Rebekah "inquires," God answers (Gen 25:21-22). Human initiatives are prominent here. In fact, what God did earlier, the patriarch Isaac attempts to do now. There is a commingling of human and divine blessing (and cursing). Whereas in 12:1-3, Yahweh said to Abraham, "I will bless those who bless you, and the one who curses you I will curse," Isaac says to Jacob, "Cursed be everyone who curses you, and blessed be everyone who blesses you" (27:29). The Deity is, quite simply, less present as a character in the Jacob than in the Terah/Abraham story. This tendency will become even more pronounced in the story of Joseph.

This narrative presumes, even builds upon, the earlier promises and covenant. Those promises require multiple generations for their fulfillment. Jacob's family is of critical importance for that part of the story, since it reports the birth of twelve sons and one daughter (Dinah). The family is growing into a multitude.

The very fact that no covenant is made between Jacob and Yahweh sustains the notion that the covenant between Yahweh and Abraham continues on in the story of his grandson. Still, the essential elements of the divine promise—progeny and land—are rehearsed (Gen 28:13-14; 35:11-12).

The Theme of Conflict and Its Theological Significance

The first episode of the story of Isaac focuses on the pregnancy of Rebekah and the birth of her two sons. When the writer states, "the children struggled together within her" (25:22), the reader has been alerted to a motif that will continue through these chapters, namely, the struggle between various parties and alliances. Moreover, such conflicts seem to be a way in which the Deity is working out the divine purpose in this family. Among other things, this story attests to conflict as a regular element of human existence, particularly in the familial setting. (Unlike the conflicts in the Joseph story, the ones here seem more unavoidable.) These conflicts occur within two primary contexts: the household and the extended family.

Struggle within the household of Isaac and Rebekah commences in the womb and continues outside it. Two verses of crisp description and narration underline the full nature of the conflict:

> When the boys grew up, Esau was a skillful hunter, a man of the field, while Jacob was a quiet man, living in tents. Isaac loved Esau, because he was fond of game; but Rebekah loved Jacob. (25:27-28)

Esau and Jacob are simply different sorts of people. Their parents respond to these differences by creating alliances within the household: father and older twin, mother and younger twin. The full implications of these alliances are not worked out by the author until chapter 27. In the meantime, the two twins interact with dire consequences, at least for Esau. The author continues his characterizations; Esau is portrayed as impetuous and rash, such that he despised his birthright (25:29-34).

The place of God in this set of alliances is not spelled out. God did speak to Rebekah about the children she would bear (Gen 25:23). And then, only after Jacob had achieved both birthright and blessing did the Deity appear to him and repeat the promises made originally to Abraham.

The conflict between Jacob and Esau, which originates inside the household, develops into a quite different phenomenon. After Esau sells his birthright to Jacob, but before Rebekah dupes Isaac in the scene of blessing (chap. 27), the writer reports that Esau married two Hittite wives. This act has a significant impact upon the way in which this story will play out. Whereas Abraham and Isaac had sought (and Jacob will seek) wives from the lineage of Terah, Esau married outside that lineage and hence disinherited himself in yet another way than just the sale of his birthright. Esau is lost to the family as a potential heir and becomes a "foreign" entity, which is symbolized by the name of Edom.

In this story, the author explores the various ways in which individuals become part of the family of promise and leave that family of promise. Conditions for remaining part of this family/covenant involve more than the explicit requirements of the covenant, such as circumcision. Marital choices are part of those requirements (see Gen 27:46–28:2), as they will be again in the time of Ezra and Nehemiah (Ezra 9–10).

The blessing of the father plays a key role in the working out of the promise. Genesis 27 conveys a scene in which Isaac gives the blessing of the firstborn to Jacob. Rachel's plan to secure that blessing for her favorite son worked. That blessing (27:27-29) and corresponding speech to Esau (27:39-40) provide poetic versions of the relative status of the two nations that Israel understood to derive from these two brothers, Israel and Edom. To this extent, Jacob and Esau, like Ishmael and Lot before them, function as symbolic or eponymous ancestors. Israel told these stories to offer explanations for the ways in which the peoples of Syria-Palestine (Edom, Moab, Ammon, Ishmaelites, Israel) came to be in their various relationships. From Israel's perspective, Edom was to live in less-prosperous territory and in a position of servitude to them.

Esau's murderous intent was thwarted when Rebekah heard about it, whereupon Jacob was ordered by both father and mother to flee the country. His return marked the necessary encounter with his brother, Esau. Some have described this final act of the Jacob and Esau narrative as one of reconciliation. We do not think that the text allows that claim. Fear precedes the encounter; careful dialogue and wary separation conclude it.

Genesis 32:3–33:16 depicts Jacob's attempt to appease Esau by the presentation of gifts. Esau, accompanied by four hundred men, comes to meet Jacob, who has gone ahead of his family, which had been divided into sections, some of whom might survive an attack (32:8). The two encounter each other and embrace. Moreover, Esau accepts the gift of livestock offered by Jacob (Gen 32:14-15). Then, Esau proposes that he accompany Jacob, a suggestion that Jacob carefully refuses. Esau suggests that some of his men remain with Jacob, but Jacob is able to escape this as well. Hence the two men and their respective groups separate.

Accommodation rather than reconciliation seems to have taken place. There is no covenant; there are no oaths. Instead, based on payment in livestock and adroit negotiation, the two groups are able to disengage and avoid violent confrontation.

The relationship between Isaac and Rebekah does not receive much overt comment. Rebekah's plan for Jacob becomes God's plan for Israel. Moreover, it becomes a plan that Isaac accepts (28:2-4). Ultimately, the human plans and the divine plan coalesce in the person of Jacob.

The second major conflict occurs in "the land of the people of the East." Jacob encounters the family of Laban, another family within the lineage of Terah, which could be the only source of a genetically proper spouse for Jacob. The narrator reports that Jacob loved Rachel, who was such an acceptable spouse. But this time he is deceived. Laban engineers Leah into Jacob's bed, with the result that Jacob must marry both Leah and Rachel (Gen 29). So, at the outset of this sojourn with the extended family, there is conflict between Jacob and Laban. This conflict continues as Laban and Jacob engage in various trickery regarding the development of their respective flocks (Gen 30).

A new "household" has been created, and here too there is conflict—between Rachel and Leah, over their ability to produce children. As with Abraham and Hagar, substitute wives—Bilhah and Zilpah—play roles in this intrafamilial set of tensions. Moreover, there is conflict between this new household and the originating household of Laban. Laban's daughters, now become Jacob's wives, claim that their father treats them like foreigners (31:15). This attitude results in Rachel's willingness to take the "household gods" (31:19). Deceit is really a hallmark of these episodes and even occurs in the very last one—"Jacob deceived Laban the Aramean, in that he did not tell him that he intended to flee" (31:20). Jacob flees but Laban tracks him down. Violence is, however, avoided because the two camps are able to achieve accommodation, here by covenant. The promise to and covenant with Abraham still seems to be in force. Isaac and Rebekah, Jacob, and Rachel and Leah now live on the basis of that agreement. Whatever covenants need to be made are now between humans, in this case Jacob and Laban, and not between God and humans.

The covenant scene (Gen 31:43-55) is instructive since it depicts parties who make an agreement, one in which both sets of gods function as witnesses to the contract (see above). Jacob and Laban take an oath not to cross a boundary that separates the two parties. Another oath—sometimes known as the "Mizpah benediction"—calls for God to observe both parties and requires that Jacob not mistreat Laban's daughters. For whatever reason, the Jacob-Esau accommodation did not require such oaths and accompanying covenant.

In sum, the story of Isaac's descendants reports numerous occasions of conflict. These conflicts do not go away. The complicated relationships that Israel will have with people to the east are addressed in the covenant between Jacob and Laban. The spiteful and strident relationship between Jacob and Esau//Israel and Edom is addressed by careful watching and division, a partition of terrain, as had been the case with Abraham and Lot//Israel and Moab and Ammon. People work to accommodate, to arrest conflict, but the roots of the conflict remain. The promises and covenant do not work themselves out automatically or without problems. Rather, God's purposes to this family can come to fruition only through the conflicts inherent in families where there are multiple spouses and multiple potential heirs.

Jacob and God

We have already observed that Jacob stands in a different relation to the Deity than had his grandfather. Vigorous encounter, even conflict, replaces conversation.

There are two key episodes, which flank both sides of Jacob's journey to the East. It is as if Jacob must meet his god both at the time he leaves the land and when he returns. Journey—one might even say pilgrimage—is a precondition for divine encounter in the Jacob story. On the first occasion, Jacob simply lies down to sleep at "a certain place." Unbeknownst to him, it is one of those liminal places where humans can encounter the world of the gods. Hence his act of sleep and dreaming is an unpremeditated act of incubation (incubation is the act of sleeping at a holy place, usually a temple, with the hope of receiving information from the Deity; cf. Samuel in 1 Sam 3 and Solomon in 1 Kgs 3).

What Jacob discovers in his dream is essentially twofold. First, he hears for himself, and for the first time, the promises that had been made to Abraham. Second, God assures him of divine accompaniment on this journey and the assurance of return (something fairly ironic, since to return is to face the prospect of a murderous Esau). Nonetheless, Jacob recognizes what sort of place he has encountered, namely, the house of God (a literal rendition of the Hebrew word *Beth* [house] *el* [God]). Moreover, he makes a conditional vow. If the Deity brings him back as the Deity has promised, "then the LORD shall be my God" (28:21). This is classic Jacob. Whereas Abraham might ask about the implications of the promise, Jacob puts it to the test. Jacob wants to hold God accountable.

Jacob does return, and again, without intending to, encounters the Deity (32:22-32). At a river ford, also a liminal spot in many religious traditions, he must wrestle with a creature of the night. Jacob acquits himself well, so that the mysterious person must use a trick move to disable Jacob. Though injured, Jacob becomes Israel and receives a blessing from one who must be the Deity. Jacob becomes Israel because of his ability to stand successfully in conflict with God.

One way to compare and contrast the significance of the Terah/Abraham and Isaac stories is to ask which character is the true eponymous ancestor of Israel. Is it Abraham or is it Jacob? Though there is no wrong answer to such a question, a strong case can be made for Jacob, renamed Israel (this renaming is recounted twice, in 32:22-32 and 35:9-15). Struggle and conflict are captured in the meaning of the name Israel, which means "one who strives with God" (Gen 32:28).

Just as in the episodes of human struggle, where we saw various forms of accommodation, so too there is no reconciliation per se in the encounter between the Deity and Jacob. God and Jacob accommodate each other—Jacob must accommodate the one who disabled him, God must accommodate the titanic Jacob, whom he could not defeat. Jacob's prize is his new name and the literal birth of Israel. God's prize is the preservation of the Deity's divinity, which is here symbolized by the necessity of appearing only at night.

Conflict and struggle are evaluated positively in this story. They are understood to be essential for the emergence of Israel. Strife is valorized both within the human dimension and within the human-divine relationship. Accommodation, too, is offered as a way to deal with severe strife.

"These Are the Descendants of Jacob" (Gen 37:2–50:26)

This final section of Genesis is regularly associated with the name of Joseph. So, we may again be surprised that a major character's name does not appear in the title. Still, as we shall see, the emphasis in that title on the multiple descendants of Jacob helps us understand one essential issue of these chapters: once Abraham's descendants start to become numerous in one generation—twelve sons as opposed to only two—how will they fare, particularly when they must live in a foreign land?

The answer to this question works itself out in literature utterly different from the foregoing two sections of the ancestral texts. Instead of a series of separate stories that have been edited together into the two "cycles" that we have just examined, Gen 37–50—particularly chapters 37–47—is one long, carefully structured short story. (The story of Tamar and Judah is loosely related to the Joseph story. Moreover, Gen 48–50 provides a complex ending to the story.) Although there are distinct episodes, each of which has its own narrative structure—for instance, that involving Joseph and Potiphar's wife (chap. 39) or Joseph as dream interpreter for Pharaoh (chap. 41)—these episodes are carefully built into the larger story.

Because the Joseph story is so different from the foregoing chapters in Genesis, critical study of it has proceeded along other lines. To be sure, some scholars have tried to identify the classic sources, especially J and E. But such attempts have not generated wide agreement about the presence of earlier and different versions of the story. Instead, the very fact of the difference between Gen 37–50 and the rest of Genesis has driven scholars to offer explanations for that difference. One such answer, namely, that Joseph reflects the concerns of literature such as Proverbs and Job, that is, Wisdom literature, has been particularly important.[17] And this is an argument that can help us explore some of the theological implications of the Joseph story.

The argument runs something like this. The story of Joseph is informed by a world in which success in the royal court is important. Such is the case in the book of Proverbs (e.g., Prov 29:12, 14). Joseph, as a character, fails when he does not follow what wisdom dictates, as by boasting about his future status to his brothers. Moreover, he succeeds when he follow typical wisdom norms, as by rejecting the sexual advances of a woman, by serving as loyal subordinate, by planning ahead. Joseph is not so much a wise character as an instructive character. Moreover, a belief in God's providential care pervades both Proverbs and the Joseph story (see below). In sum, the story of Joseph breathes different theological air than do the earlier portions of Genesis, air often found in the book of Proverbs.

More recently, a number of literary assessments of the Joseph story have appeared. Scholars have attended to plot, theme, characterization, and other narrative elements. As well, the Joseph story has been compared to short stories found in the Hebrew Bible and elsewhere. In this context, it is possible to suggest that the Joseph story is a *Diasporanovelle,* literally, a short story oriented to life in exile. Two other biblical texts, Daniel and Esther, are set in a foreign land. They, too, narrate the ways in which an Israelite or Jew can exist in and around a foreign court. This international dimension present in these three short stories may well reflect Israel's own life in a foreign land, particularly after the defeat of 587, a time after which some Yahwists did live outside the land. Moreover, such an international dimension may also be related to the last portion of God's promise to Abraham, which was also a promise to people beyond Israel, "in you all the families of the earth shall be blessed" (Gen 12:3). According to the Joseph story, Egypt was blessed due to Joseph's prudential saving of grain during the years of plenty.

Narrative Overview

The story of Jacob's family unfolds in a series of scenes. Even before the first scene, the prologue (Gen 37:2-4) sets the stage. All the critical family relationships are depicted in the first verses. And the dream scene that follows offers a picture of Joseph's elevated status, which seems impossible to imagine at the end of chapter 36. Slowly, however, Joseph rises from the fate of the "pit," and achieves high rank in the Egyptian government (by the end of chap. 41). Once Joseph is so positioned, the story returns to the issue of family. Now, again at a deliberate pace, the family moves back together through multiple journeys to Egypt. The book of Genesis concludes with reports about the deaths of Jacob and Joseph. However, the end of the Joseph story is blurry, perhaps ending earlier than the final chapter of Genesis.

Alienation and Reconciliation

We think the Joseph story, as befits a complex short story, involves multiple theological dimensions. Here we identify a primary and a secondary one. The first, which we term alienation and reconciliation, is related to certain dimensions of the Jacob story (conflict and accommodation). However, the fractures in the Joseph story are stronger, more intense, and more fully developed by the author. The author uses a new set of vocabulary to describe the intensity of human feelings, such as "his anguish" (Gen 42:21) or "bears a grudge" (Gen 50:15). Attention to human emotions appears here in Genesis for the first time.

This story, as the title indicates, is still essentially a story about family—the family of Jacob. However, this is family quite different from the families of Abraham and Isaac. In both the previous households, there had been two potential heirs, Ishmael and Isaac in the first, Jacob and Esau in the second. In both these cases, the narrative removed one of the two claimants physically from the line of succession. Though there had been conflict (and it would continue in the international arena: Israel and the Ishmaelites, Israel and Edom), the conflict would no longer occur within Israel. Here lies the critical point of difference between the first two families and the family of Jacob.

Jacob's family is forced to wrestle with the relative status of multiple heirs who remain together in the household and, subsequently,

87

in the land. (Genesis 49 offers poetic testimony to the issue of relative status—e.g., 49:8, "Judah, your brothers shall praise you.") The story line requires the twelve sons to remain together or at least in close relation. As a result the potential for serious conflict is exacerbated.

One may read the story of Jacob's family as one of family alienation and reconciliation. It is a story about a family God has chosen and to whom promises have been made and repeated, but it is not a family whose members—in this story—interact directly with the Deity as a character. Instead, they confront God through each other (Gen 45:7).

The unraveling of Jacob's family occurs due to multiple human dynamics. No one party is responsible. Jacob favors one son over others. Joseph is an unwise braggart and tattletale. Jacob's other sons are jealous of the favored son; "they hated him, and could not speak peaceably to him" (Gen 37:4). Moreover, the brothers ultimately disagree among themselves about what should be done with Joseph. Most think he should be killed, though Reuben suggests that he should be deserted and then rescued, and Judah proposed that he be sold into slavery. Responsibility for this "dysfunctional family" is multiple. Still, this radically alienated family does not engage in murder or engage in inappropriate marital choices, though Joseph does marry Asenath, an Egyptian woman (Gen 46:20).

In addition, one should note that the household depicted in the story of Jacob stands without benefit of the matriarch. Rachel had died to the family in the previous story. About the relative chronology of Leah's, Bilhah's, and Zilpah's deaths we are not informed. However, none play a role in this story.

The family moves toward reunification due to the exigency of famine. Living in the same place does not necessarily mean reunification. That only happens as the result of multiple initiatives. The brothers, as symbolized by Reuben (42:37), are willing to offer up their own progeny in order to work out a solution to their plight. Moreover, as symbolized by Judah, they make a special plea to Joseph. The father is willing both to let his remaining favored son, Benjamin, go to Egypt, and then to go to that foreign land himself. Finally, Joseph moves beyond the role of tough interrogator and judge, when he "could no longer control himself" (45:1). The same parties that contributed to the dissolution of the family also help it become reintegrated.

The biblical author recognizes that the deep alienation, particularly between Joseph and his brothers, would not magically disappear. In the final chapter of Genesis, the brothers, when reflecting upon the implications of their father's death, said, "What if Joseph still bears a grudge against us and pays us back in full for all the wrong that we did to him?" (50:15). Even at this point in the story, there is some tension between these two parties, which may have been resolved when Joseph "reassured them, speaking kindly to them" (50:21).

The story of Jacob (and Joseph) demonstrates how difficult it will be for the promise and covenant to work itself out in the lineage of Terah, especially in this new kind of family with so many sons in one place. The explicit language of promise and covenant virtually disappears (cf. Gen 48:15-16). Implicitly, the story deals more with progeny than with land, which is, at least temporarily, lost to Israel by the end of this biblical book.

Providence

Early on in the story, the narrator offers a general comment at the end of the scene involving Joseph and Potiphar's wife: "the LORD was with him [Joseph]; and whatever he did, the LORD made it prosper" (39:23). The Deity is at work in and through Joseph's life. This claim helps us understand the theologically understated approach throughout most of the story. The Deity can work through humans, even though such may not always be said explicitly.

Still, the Deity was not interested simply in Joseph's prosperity. In two of Joseph's speeches to his brothers, we learn about a larger purpose. In the first, just after he has informed his brothers about his identity, he says: "Do not be distressed, or angry with yourselves, because you sold me here; for God sent me before you to preserve life" (Gen 45:5). God was with the brothers in their actions as the Deity was with Joseph later. Moreover, the goal was to preserve "life." Given the context of the story, such preserving of life involved far more than Israelite existence. "All the world came to Joseph in Egypt to buy grain" (Gen 41:57). Here, again, one hears echoes of Gen 12:3. But Joseph goes on (45:7-8): "God sent me before you to preserve for you a remnant on earth, and to keep alive for you many survivors. So it was not you who sent me here, but God." The language of a remnant reverberates with that of defeat and exile in 587, whereas the language of survivor may allude to a Noah-like motif, someone who survives catastrophe. God is concerned for all life, but especially the survival of this family. God has made a special commitment to the lineage of Terah, with whom there is a relationship based on promise and covenant.

Near the end of Genesis, Joseph speaks again to his brothers, when they express concern about their fate, "Even though you intended to do harm to me, God intended it for good, in order to preserve a numerous people" (Gen 50:20). Joseph's God is a God who acts behind the scenes and through the work of many people. This outlook, which one might term providential, is shared by the wisdom writers. They, too, imagine a universe in which God's ways may be difficult to discern, but which is directed toward some divine goal (cf. Prov 16:4).

In sum, the Jacob story offers new theological emphases to the earlier stories about the Israelite family. There is a deep sense of providence, which is hardly a facile judgment about things always working themselves out easily or happily. In addition, there is a move from alienation toward reconciliation. At first this move appears to work simply as human endeavor. But when the story is read from the perspective of providence, the reconciliation can be understood as part of God's larger purpose for Israel.

Conclusion

Genesis 12–50—the story of the descendants of Terah/Abraham, the story of the descendants of Isaac, and the story of the family of Jacob—is driven by family concerns. This family was the bearer of God's promise and partner in a covenant with the Deity. Things will change in Israel, especially when Israel as nation or as religious community becomes the bearer of that promise and covenant tradition. However, the theological motifs worked out in these stories— promise into covenant, conflict and accommodation, providence, alienation and reconciliation—remain potent in varied social and political settings. These promises appear with remarkable prominence in literature that postdates the fall of the monarchy. We sense that the language of promise spoke with special depth to those who had experienced God's apparent recanting of those promises as symbolized by military defeat and exile. The promise to Abraham and Sarah offered grounds for hope, a theological motif the biblical roots of which have been explored in remarkable ways by Jürgen Moltmann.[18] Finally, the family, whether in tribal league, nation state, exilic settlement, or religious community, remained a critical context for the development of Yahwism, which in turn moved into Judaism, Christianity, and Islam.

Notes

1. For a convenient display of such divisions, see, for example, the appendix in *Noth's History of Pentateuchal Traditions* (Englewood Cliffs, N.J.: Prentice-Hall, 1972) or A. Campbell and M. A. O'Brien, *Sources of the Pentateuch: Texts, Introductions, Annotations* (Minneapolis: Fortress, 1993).

2. See W. Brueggemann and H. W. Wolff, *The Vitality of Old Testament Traditions* (Atlanta: John Knox, 1982).

3. For a good overview of the current discussion, see J. Blenkinsopp, *The Pentateuch: An Introduction to the First Five Books of the Bible* (ABRL; New York: Doubleday, 1992); and D. Carr, *Reading the Fractures of Genesis: Historical and Literary Approaches* (Louisville: Westminster John Knox, 1996).

4. R. Rendtorff, *The Problem of the Process of Transmission in the Pentateuch* (JSOTSup 89; Sheffield: JSOT, 1990).

5. See R. Wilson, *Genealogy and History in the Biblical World* (New Haven: Yale University Press, 1977).

6. Gunkel's two studies of Genesis have been translated: *Genesis* (Macon, Ga.: Mercer University Press, 1997) and *The Legends of Genesis* (Chicago: Open Court, 1907).

7. M. Noth, *History of Pentateuchal Traditions*.

8. For a classic study, see F. Cross, *Canaanite Myth and Hebrew Epic: Essays in the History of the Religion of Israel* (Cambridge: Harvard University Press, 1973).

9. The Ugaritic literature dates to c. 1400 BCE and reflects the Canaanite culture of the Late Bronze Age as preserved in texts found at a site on the Mediterranean coast. For a convenient translation of the major epic and mythic texts, see S. Parker, *Ugaritic Narrative Poetry* (WAW; Atlanta: Scholars Press, 1997).

10. We recommend R. Alter, *The Art of Biblical Narrative* (New York: Basic Books, 1981) as an introduction to this way of reading biblical texts.

11. See the study of N. Steinberg, *Kinship and Marriage in Genesis: A Household Economics Approach* (Minneapolis: Fortress, 1993).

12. Westermann does not think Gen 15 reflects a covenant—see *Genesis 12–36* (Minneapolis: Augsburg, 1985).

13. In fact, a number of things are promised to Abraham and his descendants, for example, that they will become "a great nation" (12:2), that "kings of peoples shall come from her" (17:16). The royal and national connotations are obvious and may reflect composition during the period of the monarchy.

14. We do well to remember that many Arab Muslims trace their descent from Abraham through Ishmael. As a result, Jews, Christians, and Muslims all read the Terah/Abraham story as their own story, but each religious tradition accomplishes this reading in a different way.

15. Westermann, *Genesis 12–36*, 576.

16. S. Kierkegaard's treatment in *Fear and Trembling* remains unsurpassed.

17. G. von Rad (Genesis [OTL; Philadelphia: Westminster, 1972]) was apparently the first person to argue on behalf of this connection.

18. J. Moltmann, *Theology of Hope: On the Ground and Implications of a Christian Eschatology* (New York: Harper & Row, 1967).

Bibliography

Blenkinsopp, Joseph. *The Pentateuch: An Introduction to the First Five Books of the Bible.* ABRL. New York: Doubleday, 1992.

Brueggemann, Walter. *Genesis.* IBC. Atlanta: John Knox, 1982.

Brueggemann, Walter, and Hans Walter Wolff. *The Vitality of Old Testament Traditions.* 2nd ed. Atlanta: John Knox, 1982.

Carr, David M. *Reading the Fractures of Genesis: Historical and Literary Approaches.* Louisville: Westminster John Knox, 1996.

Coats, George W. *Genesis: With an Introduction to Narrative Literature.* FOTL 1. Grand Rapids: Eerdmans, 1983.

Fretheim, Terence. "The Book of Genesis: Introduction, Commentary, and Reflections." *NIB*, vol. 1. Nashville: Abingdon, 1994.

Rad, Gerhard von. *Genesis: A Commentary.* OTL. Philadelphia: Westminster, 1972.

Steinberg, Naomi. *Kinship and Marriage in Genesis: A Household Economics Perspective.* Minneapolis: Fortress, 1993.

Westermann, Claus. *Genesis 1–11: A Commentary; Genesis 12–36: A Commentary; Genesis 37–50: A Commentary.* Minneapolis: Augsburg, 1984–1986.

CHAPTER FOUR

BONDAGE, EXODUS, WILDERNESS

Exod 1–18, Selected Psalms

I t would be hard to overstate the central importance of the Exodus experience for Israel's understanding of itself and of its faith. In many ways the narrative of Exod 1–15 may be considered the birth story of Israel as a people. The book of Exodus opens with Israel suffering oppressively as slaves in Egypt, but in the climactic moment of the story (Exod 14–15), they are delivered by God's hand through the sea to new life. The struggles of wilderness begin (Exod 16–18), but they are on the way to Mt. Sinai where they will become God's covenant people (see chap. 5).

God's victory is seen in Exodus both as a cosmic victory over forces of chaos that threaten God's creation and as a defeat of human oppressive power in history. The liberation of Israel is a central event giving identity to the community of God's people throughout ongoing generations in both Jewish and Christian traditions. Frequent references to the Exodus experience are found throughout the literature of the Old Testament (see further discussion below), and the annual observance of Passover serves as a reclaiming of the Exodus story by each generation of the Jewish community down to the present.

The Exodus experience has also held central significance for the Christian community. Early Christians were baptized with a remembrance of passing through the waters to new life. The Gospels are permeated with Exodus themes and references, and the New Testament in general makes frequent use of the Exodus tradition. Like Israel, Jesus is "called out of Egypt" (Matt 2:15). He teaches

93

Israel on the mountain like a second Moses (Matt 5–7), and is himself identified as the "Passover lamb" (1 Cor 5:7; 11:25). Christian liturgy for the Eucharist declares "Christ, our Passover, is sacrificed for us; therefore, let us keep the feast." The victory of God at the sea is identified with the victory of God over the powers of death in resurrection, and Exod 15 is one of the scripture readings in the lectionary for Easter Sunday. In Christian history the Exodus story and its hope for oppressed people have come to special prominence whenever the community found itself in desperate circumstances of poverty and oppression, for instance, in the spirituals of black slaves in the American South or the modern liberation theologies of Latin America.

To read the story of the Exodus experience is for both Christians and Jews to touch the origins of community identity as God's delivered people. "Once you were not a people, but now you are God's people" (1 Pet 2:10; see Hos 2:23).

Reading the Book of Exodus

Because of the significance of both deliverance from Egypt and covenant at Sinai for Israel's life and the literature of the Old Testament, we will treat these themes in separate chapters. Yet, the two experiences are interrelated thematically and structurally in the book of Exodus. Hence, some perspectives on reading the book of Exodus in its entirety are appropriate at this point.

Context in the Canon

The book of Exodus does not stand as an independent piece but is intended to be read as a part of the Pentateuch. From a historical perspective, it is not at all clear that the Hebrew slaves of the Exodus story had any direct historical connection to the ancestors of the Genesis stories.[1] Nevertheless, the literary and theological presentation of events in Exodus assume a continuity between Genesis and Exodus that is defined by promise and fulfillment. God's promises in Genesis are moved toward fulfillment in Exodus. These promises are located in two different arenas in Genesis. On the one hand, God gives to humanity a promissory mandate in creation to "be fruitful and multiply, and fill the earth" (Gen 1:28). Now, in Exodus,

94

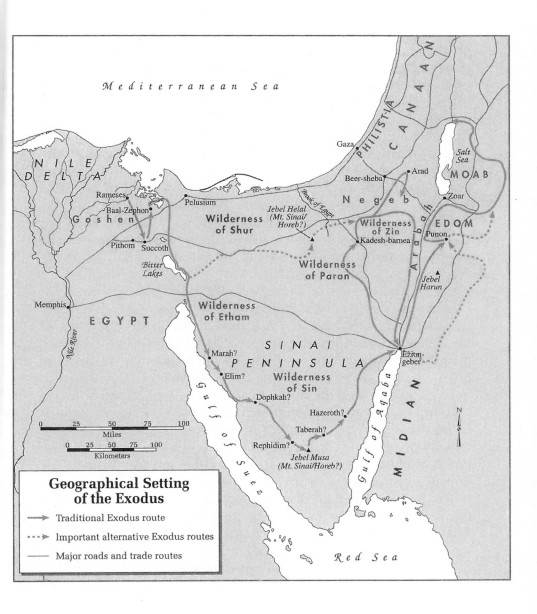

**Geographical Setting
of the Exodus**

→ Traditional Exodus route

‥‥► Important alternative Exodus routes

— Major roads and trade routes

we read that "the Israelites were fruitful and prolific; they multiplied and grew exceedingly strong, so that the land was filled with them" (Exod 1:7). Indeed, this Israelite fulfillment of creation promise becomes the source of threat to the pharaoh and motivates his genocidal policies (Exod 1:9-10), necessitating God's saving intervention. On the other hand, Exodus deliverance is related to God's fidelity to the promises made to Abraham, Isaac, and Jacob. Those promises involve land, descendants, and blessing to all the families of the earth (cf. Gen 12:1-3), promises that were affirmed in covenant with the ancestors (Gen 15). When God responds to the outcry of Israelite suffering, the divine response is characterized as remembrance of that covenant (Exod 2:23-24), and God repeatedly identifies the divine self to Moses as being in continuity with the God who made promises to the ancestors (Exod 3:6, 15-16; 6:2-3, 8).

On the other side of the book of Exodus, the legislation of Leviticus is presented as a continuation of Moses' mediation of the law to Israel at Mt. Sinai. Even though the legal traditions of Leviticus originated historically much later in Israel's life, they are presented as part of the authoritative understanding of Israel as delivered and covenanted people from the time of Moses onward. Indeed, the whole of the Torah (Genesis through Deuteronomy) is presented as Mosaic in its intention and authority, although many of its legal and narrative materials derive from Israel's later history. Exodus provides the center of this Mosaic authority, and it is the events of liberation and covenant making that provide the focus for the entire Torah (Pentateuch).

The Exodus tradition, particularly God's deliverance of Israel at the sea, is of crucial importance throughout much of the Old Testament canon, reflecting the centrality of that tradition in widely separated times and settings in the life of Israel. The breadth of this Exodus influence can only be sampled. It is:

—a part of the recital of God's saving deeds used by Joshua to summon inhabitants of the land into the service of Yahweh (Josh 24:5-7).

—a tradition that struck fear into the hearts of Philistines who had heard what Israel's God accomplished against the Egyptians (1 Sam 4:8).

—a source of hope in the worship materials of Israel, recited to encourage those in distress and trouble (Ps 77:14-20).

—a testimony to God's faithfulness by prophets confronting Israel with unfaithfulness (Mic 6:4).

—a source of hope for deliverance once again in the message of prophets during the Babylonian exile (Isa 43:16-17; 51:10-11).

The Composite Character of the Book

For most of the past two centuries scholarship on the book of Exodus has been preoccupied with source criticism and the complex literary history through which the text has been given its present shape.[2] There is a general consensus that the book of Exodus is a composite work brought together over the course of several centuries. Generally this has meant the recognition of at least three sources (J, E, and P) originating in different periods of Israel's life. Some unique materials, such as the Song of the Sea (Exod 15) and the Covenant Code (Exod 20:22–23:33) probably existed independently of these sources and were incorporated into the book at some stage of its development.

This "documentary hypothesis" has become increasingly controversial and less useful in recent scholarship. Few doubt the composite character of Exodus or question the complexity of its formation, but the details on the nature and dating of these sources or the process that brought them together are subject to vigorous debate and disagreement. Further, the development of literary and canonical approaches to the text have stressed the importance of the present, final shape of the text as *the* significant rendering of the story, which was finally affirmed and passed on by Jewish and Christian communities. This present form of the text is the appropriate locus of our efforts to read and interpret the book of Exodus.

This chapter and the next will focus largely on this final form of the text, although it is important to recognize that the complex literary process through which the text was formed is at times left visible. The seams and tensions of an account assembled through the telling and retelling of the Exodus story over generations are still apparent. Different views and perspectives have been allowed to stand together in the text. The result is a book that is the accumulated

97

testimony of a community over generations rather than the polished product of a single authorial point of view. This, in itself, is a testament to the vitality and importance of these Exodus experiences.

Historical Context and Theological Proclamation

The book of Exodus is not history writing; it is kerygma, that is, the book is theological proclamation seeking to tell the community's salvation story to subsequent generations so that they too will know and encounter the liberating God of the Exodus story. Modern interest in recovering the originating events of this story in historiographic detail is bound to end in frustration. There can be no doubt that the Exodus story assumes an originating series of events in the past, but the concern of the text is with the ongoing theological meaning of those events, not with the historical details of the originating context. The Exodus storytellers did not even bother to record the name of the pharaoh. While a majority of scholars hold that some of Israel's ancestors lived in Egypt along with other Semitic foreigners during the second millennium and that a general dating of the Exodus from Egypt must be placed in the early thirteenth century BCE, these and other historical details are uncertain and debated.[3] The story as it now stands in Exodus reflects not only the originating events but the meaning of the Exodus experience for subsequent generations of Israel over the course of centuries.

It does seem likely that the present and final form of the book of Exodus as a written text was fixed during the time of Israel's Babylonian exile (587–539 BCE). This final, exilic shaping may well be due to the work of priestly editors. Thus, we read of Israel's deliverance from bondage in Egypt and of covenant partnership with God from the urgency of reclaiming these traditions in a time when Israel was again in bondage in a foreign land and understood its desperate condition, unlike Egyptian slavery, as related to God's judgment on Israel's disobedience to covenant demands. Issues of bondage and deliverance, God's power versus the power of human empire, divine presence and divine absence, covenant obedience and disobedience, judgment and forgiveness, worship of Yahweh and accommodation to empire—all take on a new urgency in light of Babylonian exile and the crisis that the exile experience represents for Israel as the community of God's people. This final exilic shaping of the book of Exodus is certainly in view at times, but the appropriation of Exodus experience for such a time of crisis suggests the vitality of this tradition for all subsequent generations, including our own. This story refuses to be simply about ancestors in the thirteenth century BCE. It is about the experience of bondage, liberation, covenant community, and the presence of God's glory in our midst in every generation of God's people—that of Babylonian exiles or of today's church and synagogue.

Genre, Structure, and Narrative Flow

In this chapter we will be largely occupied with narrative traditions, although an important piece of ancient poetry appears in Exod 15. These storytelling traditions unfold a dramatic story with continuity of characters and plot, and a climactic resolution (Exod 14–15). However, the book of Exodus in its entirety has been noted for its juxtaposition of narrative and legal traditions. The covenant and its association with the law will receive full treatment later, but at this point we should note that even the law codes of the book of Exodus are placed in the narrative setting of covenant making with the God who delivered Israel from bondage in Egypt (cf. Exod 19:3-6). In addition to narrative and law, the book of Exodus shows the influence of liturgy. Parts of the narrative tradition show the influence of use in the worship life of subsequent generations. This context has reshaped the telling of the Exodus story to reflect the remembrance and recital of the Exodus story in the community of faith. This liturgical background is especially evident in the Passover narratives (Exod 12:1–13:16), the Song of the Sea (Exod 15), the wilderness story of manna (Exod 16), the covenant-making rituals (Exod 24:1-18; 34:10-35), and the plans for and building of the tabernacle (Exod 25–31; 35–40). The larger structure of Exod 1–15, in particular, may reflect a common Israelite liturgical pattern. The movement from bondage to liberation to praise suggests the relationship of lament, salvation, and doxology that the Psalms show to be a common pattern in Israel's worship.

The narrative flow of the book of Exodus reflects a series of connected foci around which the story is organized.

1. *Bondage.* Although God's promises at creation and to Abraham are fulfilled among Jacob's descendants in Egypt (1:1-7), the future of God's promises and of Israel's ancestors is endangered by the oppressive power of Pharaoh, who fears the Hebrews and seeks to enslave and control them by policies that border on genocide (1:8-14). In this context of bondage God seems absent, but hope for the future is preserved through the courageous action of five women who thwart Pharaoh's actions (1:15–2:10, further discussion below) and enable the birth, preservation, and first stirrings of social conscience in Moses, who will become God's agent to deliver Israel (2:11-22). At the end of this section we are told that God hears Israel's outcry (2:23-25).

2. *Confrontation with Pharaoh.* God becomes active in the story. First, God calls and commissions Moses, in spite of his objections, to act as God's agent in confronting Pharaoh and demanding Israel's freedom (3:1–4:31). Moses' initial efforts bring intensification of Pharaoh's oppressive policies (5:1–6:1). The focus, however, is not solely on Moses' role or effectiveness. The narratives reflect a self-disclosure of God, including a revelation of the divine name, Yahweh (esp. in 3:1–4:31 and 6:2-30). Although Moses plays an important role as revolutionary agent, it becomes increasingly clear that the crucial confrontation is between the liberating power of Yahweh and the oppressive power of Pharaoh. Through a series of plagues, Yahweh's sovereignty is made clear, and the genocidal policies of Pharaoh's tyranny are shown to have cosmic as well as historical consequences (7:1–11:10). God's opposition to Pharaoh is not only for the sake of Israel but reflects God's battle with chaos to preserve the integrity of God's creation. The final plague, the death of Egypt's firstborn, is surrounded in the narrative by detailed descriptions of Passover observance that reflect the later liturgical remembrance of this event in Israel (12:1–13:16). In grief over the death of Egypt's sons, Pharaoh allows Israel to depart, and with jewelry and clothing given to them by the Egyptians they go out arrayed as free people and not as slaves (12:29-36).

3. *Liberation.* The pharaoh's change of heart (14:5) places Israel in danger, and God must intervene to decisively defeat Pharaoh's forces. Israel's liberation requires the defeat of oppressive power. The account of deliverance at the sea (14:1-31) combines language of God fighting as warrior in Israel's behalf (14:24-25), with God

working through Moses (14:16, 21, 26-27) and the elements of nature (14:21-22). The account is very dramatic in its profusion of images: the angel of God, pillars of cloud and fire, walls of water, pathways through the sea, Egyptian chariots bogged down and over-whelmed by waves, and dead bodies on the shore. Although the liberation of Israel is the obvious result, Yahweh has larger purposes in mind as well. "This is why I have let you live: to show you my power, and to make my name resound through all the earth" (9:16). "The Egyptians shall know that I am the LORD, when I have gained glory for myself over Pharaoh, his chariots, and his chariot drivers" (14:18). True sovereignty belongs to Yahweh and not to the oppres- ✓ sive power of human empire. This public recognition of God's sovereignty is further served by Israel's first response to deliverance in doxology, led by Miriam (15:20-21, perhaps the original song), and by Moses (15:1-18, a long poetic piece that reflects liturgical use and development). God's victory as warrior over Pharaoh is celebrated as both cosmic and historical triumph, ending in recognition of Yahweh's sovereignty by the nations, the establishment of Israel in the land, and the declaration of God's reign.

4. *Wilderness.* Liberation is not directly into the promised land but ✓ into the wilderness. The hardships of a landscape without food and water and of encounters with new enemies threaten the people's trust in Yahweh. They turn on Moses and complain bitterly about their fate, wishing for return to Egypt (15:24; 16:2-3; 17:2-3; this theme was anticipated by the people's complaints at the sea, 14:10-12). God responds to the people's needs in spite of their complaints and brings miraculous provisions of water (15:22-27; 17:1-7) and food (16:1-36) while protecting them from desert enemies (17:8-16, the Amalekites). An encounter with Moses' father-in-law, the Midianite priest Jethro, provides Moses and Israel with good counsel that begins the institutionalization of liberation in judicial and social structures and provides an occasion for non-Israelite recognition of God's deliverance of Israel from the hand of Egypt (18:1-27).

This chapter deals with the Exodus story only to this point, but the narrative flow of the book of Exodus continues on through *covenant making at Sinai and the giving of the law* (19:1–24:18) and the *planning and building of the tabernacle* (25:1–31:11; 35:4–40:38), which provides for God's glory to dwell in the midst of Israel. This material on the tabernacle is interrupted by a dramatic story of *Israel's apostasy with the golden calf* (32:1–34:35). Israel's idolatrous action results in divine anger and judgment. Only Moses' intervention allows for divine forgiveness and the renewal of the covenant. These episodes of the book of Exodus will be dealt with more fully in chapter 5.

The narrative flow of the book of Exodus seems carefully structured to move the reader through an account of events that radically alter the realities of Israel's life. In the book of Exodus we move from the seeming absence of God in bondage to the liberating power of God in victory over oppression to the full presence of God in Israel's midst; we move from building Pharaoh's cities to building covenant community to building the tabernacle for God's glory; we move from oppression to liberation to community to worship.

Theological Themes in the Exodus Tradition

Creation as Cosmic Context

God's redemptive activity in the Exodus experience is set in the framework of God's purposes as Creator of the cosmos. The work of Terence Fretheim has especially emphasized the importance of creation theology for understanding the book of Exodus.[4]

We have already noted above that Exod 1:7 places the prospering of Israel in Egypt as the fulfillment of the creation mandate to "be fruitful and multiply, and fill the earth" (Gen 1:28). The pharaoh's threat to the future of Israel that immediately follows (1:6-14) is thus a threat to the purposes of God the Creator. There are frequent references throughout the Exodus story to Israel's God as the Lord of "all the earth" (9:14; 9:29; 19:5). Even though the focus of God's redemptive activity is the liberation of Israel from Egyptian bondage, this activity is intended to serve God's larger creation purposes. "I will send all my plagues . . . so that you may know that there is no one like me in all the earth . . . to show you my power, and to make my name resound through all the earth" (9:14, 16).

The pharaoh represents not only the historic powers of oppression but the forces of chaos that oppose God's work in creation. The drama enacted in this story is cosmic as well as historic in character. Thus, the plague stories represent God's sovereignty over the nonhuman elements of creation directed against Pharaoh's subversion of God's creation purposes. God's deliverance of Israel is not an end in itself. It restores God's creation by bringing new life out of victory over Pharaoh's actions that oppose the full life God intended in creation. This cosmic dimension of the Exodus drama is especially evident in the Song of the Sea (Exod 15:1-18). God commands the elements of sea, wind, storm, and earth (vv. 8-12) to bring victory over Pharaoh's forces. In the end, all the nations of the earth are witness to God's sovereignty (vv. 14-16), and God's reign is established over all the cosmos (v. 18). God's victory is both liberation (see below) and new creation.

Oppression as Historical Context

Israel's birth story as God's people does not begin in a chronicle of national heroism and triumph or in testimony to cherished hope in divine providence. It is significant that the central redemption story of the Old Testament begins in the context of oppression and suffering marked by the absence of God from the narrative. The description of Pharaoh's use of slave labor for his own building projects (1:11), the fear of the oppressor toward the oppressed, and the genocidal policies that grow out of that fear (1:8-22), serve as a gripping reminder of the underside of human history. We are forced to the recognition that human history includes exploitation so cruel that it extinguishes even the possibility of hope: "they would not listen to Moses, because of their broken spirit and their cruel slavery" (6:9). Theological meaning in the Exodus story grows out of this social context in oppression. When human resources seem defeated by the oppressive and self-serving power of empire (Pharaoh), there is yet the power of God as a source of hope and possibility for new life.

Yet, the first signs of hope and life in the story come not from God but from unexpected human agents—through the courage and resourcefulness of five women, the antithesis, in the ancient world, to the pharaoh's power. Even in human terms, the power of an oppressive pharaoh does not define reality. The Hebrew midwives, Shiphrah and Puah, deceive the pharaoh and thwart his genocidal command to destroy Israel's male children (Exod 1:15-22). The infant Moses is saved by the defiant action of his mother and sister, and he is subversively taken in by the pharaoh's own daughter to be raised in the Egyptian court (2:1-10). The actions of these women precede and foreshadow the saving activity of God on behalf of the Hebrews in bondage and preserve the life of God's agent, Moses.[5]

The context of oppression and suffering is also emphasized by the Hebrews' own outcry, which mobilizes the liberating activity of God. "The Israelites groaned under their slavery, and cried out. Out of the slavery their cry for help rose up to God" (Exod 2:23*b*; cf. 3:7, 9; 6:5). The Hebrew verb *za'aq*, "to cry out," implies not only pain but complaint (sometimes even in a legal sense). Israel's outcry is recognition that even slaves are not resigned to things as they are and refuse to accept oppression and suffering as the final reality of their lives. The outcry is a public expression of hurt that directs criticism toward the dismantling of oppressive power and begins to suggest the hope of a new reality. It is important to note that the outcry is not directed to God; it is not public prayer. It is a human cry of pain, yet, God hears. God's direct action enters the story in response to Israel's cry of pain.

The Self-disclosure of God

Above all else, the Exodus story is a story through which the character of Israel's God is revealed. It is Pharaoh who poses the dramatic question at the heart of this story, "Who is Yahweh?" (Exod 5:2). Repeatedly, the narrative states that a primary motivation for God's self-disclosure and action in the Exodus events is to make Yahweh known—to Israel (Exod 6:3, 7; 10:2), to Pharaoh/Egypt (7:17; 8:10, 22; 9:14, 29; 11:7; 14:4, 18), and eventually to all the peoples of the earth (cf. 15:14-15; 18:8-12). In the Exodus story, features of God's character are revealed for the first time in the biblical story and established as centrally important for much of the rest of the Bible and on through centuries of the Judeo-Christian tradition. Perhaps above all else these chapters are about the identity of God.

Crucial aspects of God's identity (and intentions) are first revealed to Moses in his encounter with God on Mt. Horeb (an alternative name for Mt. Sinai) in 3:1–4:17, and subsequently confirmed and elaborated in the activity of God through the dramatic events of confronting Pharaoh and liberating Israel from slavery. We may use elements of this story to sketch a portrait of the divine character revealed in the Exodus story.

God's self-disclosure to Moses out of the burning bush begins with a statement of identification with the God of Abraham, Isaac, and Jacob. This expression affirms the *fidelity of God;* the God of Exodus keeps promises, and the events of deliverance are tied in this narrative to the promises given to the ancestors (cf. Gen 12:1-3). The larger story of the Pentateuch shifts from the promises of land, descendants, and blessing to all the families of the earth into a narrative that begins the fulfillment of those promises. Israel will move toward a land of its own (Exod 3:8; 6:4, 8), has already become a numerous people (1:7), and will become God's covenant partner in a mission to all the earth (19:4-6). Even though Israel's ancestors did not fully know this God and called upon God by names other than Yahweh (6:2-3), God remembers the promises made and will keep them (2:24; 6:5). God is faithful and trustworthy. does not forget

God continues the disclosure on Mt. Horeb: "I have seen the affliction of my people; I have heard their cry because of their taskmasters. I know their sufferings and I have come down to deliver them from the Egyptians" (Exod 3:7-8*a,* author's translation). The powerful sequence of verbs in this verse discloses a God at the heart of Israel's salvation story who, in significant ways, is unlike the gods and goddesses of other ancient Near Eastern cultures. In response to the oppressed condition of a group of slaves in Egypt, God takes initiative to open a new future for them. This initiative represents the sovereign exercise of the *freedom of God.* God's deliverance of Israel is an act of freely given grace; it is not compelled or made necessary by special merit on Israel's part or by ritual coercion of divine favor (cf. Deut 7:8). The Exodus story particularly contrasts the freedom of Israel's God to that of the gods of Egypt. In Egypt, Pharaoh himself is considered a god, and the gods are allied with the powerful and the wealthy. In Egypt, and also in later Mesopotamian empires, the gods are identified with the ruling classes. By contrast, the Exodus God of Israel is free from the fates of empires—free to take up the cause of slaves. The later stories of Joshua and Judges suggest an identification of the gods of Canaan with oppressive social power centers as well (see the discussion in chap. 6). To tell the story of Yahweh, who responded and acted in behalf of Hebrew slaves in Egypt, is to testify to a sovereign divine freedom that provides a radical alternative to the state-controlled and manipulated gods of the ancient empires. Walter Brueggemann points to the significance of this radically free God for an alternative pattern of community in Israel: "In place of the gods of Egypt, creatures of the imperial consciousness, Moses discloses Yahweh the sovereign one who acts in lordly freedom, is extrapolated from no social reality, and is captive to no social perception but acts from his own person toward his own purposes. The participants in the Exodus found themselves involved in the intentional formation of a *new social community* to match the vision of *God's freedom*."[6] It is divine freedom that Yahweh emphasizes in the midst of covenant-making later in Exodus by proclaiming, "I will be gracious to whom I will be gracious" (Exod 33:19). God's free choice of Israel becomes freedom *for* Israel rather than freedom *from* Israel. The apostle Paul later cites this same divine declaration of freedom and God's confrontation with Pharaoh to remind the early church that salvation comes as a gift of divine freedom in grace rather than as a result of meritorious works (Rom 9:14-18).

God's disclosure to Moses (Exod 3:7-8*a*) indicates that God has not only freely taken initiative but has done so in relationship to human suffering and need. God's "seeing" and "hearing" are not generalized expressions of omniscience, but focused divine regard for oppression and suffering. Divine response is attuned to and mobilized by human cries of pain. Perhaps the most remarkable self-disclosure in this verse is in the phrase "I know their sufferings." The Hebrew verb used here (*yada'* "to know") indicates something broader than cognitive knowledge. It indicates a participation in and experiencing of that which is known. Thus, God indicates a divine choice to enter into and experience Israel's suffering. It points to a quality of divine character that we might call the *vulnerability of God,* the willingness of God to be wounded in solidarity with human woundedness. This is a distinct contrast to the gods identified with the power centers in ancient Near Eastern religions. It is the beginning of a biblical witness to the suffering of God in relationship to human suffering that for Christians finds its fullest expression in the death of Jesus (God incarnate) on the cross in full experiencing of human pain and brokenness. In between the moments of Exodus vulnerability and cruciform suffering in the biblical story are many other witnesses to God as vulnerable. Expressions of God's anguish, mourning, compassion, and participating presence in human suffering can be found especially in the Psalms and the Prophets.[7] In the book of Exodus we read the contest of power and sovereignty between Yahweh and Pharaoh knowing that divine power is tempered by divine suffering with the oppressed, but Pharaoh's power is self-serving and genocidal. The question is not simply "Who is sovereign?" but "What purposes does that sovereignty serve?"

Such a radical divine identification with human suffering and the plight of the dispossessed at the heart of Israel's birth story makes understandable the constant return throughout the canon to themes of God's special regard for the powerless, the poor, the oppressed, and the marginalized. At many points in the remaining chapters of this book we will see the reappearance of testimony to this aspect of the divine character.

It is important to note that God's word to Moses from the burning bush (Exod 3:7-8a) does not treat God's identification with human suffering as an end in itself. God freely chooses to be *active* in human history in behalf of those who suffer: "I have come down to deliver." God acts to make a new future possible for those who saw only a future without hope. To Moses, God declares a divine intention, and much of the narrative that follows is testimony to God's action in fulfillment of that intention. We will consider the climactic drama of God's salvation/deliverance/liberation further below.

God's character is further illuminated in the encounters with Moses by the revealing of the *divine name, Yahweh* (Exod 3:13-18; 6:2-9).[8] Moses objects that he cannot come to Israel and have credibility as one sent by God if he does not know the name of that God (Exod 3:13). Although the name Yahweh is used for God in some of the narratives of Genesis, the understanding of the Exodus tradition is made explicit in 6:2-3, "I am the LORD [Yahweh]. I appeared to Abraham, Isaac, and Jacob as God Almighty [El Shaddai], but by my name 'The LORD' [Yahweh] I did not make myself known to them." In response to Moses' insistence God reveals the divine name, Yahweh, to him (Exod 3:14-15).

The act of revealing the divine name is itself remarkable. In the ancient world, the giving of one's name is an act of intimacy that establishes relationship. It is related to vulnerability as well, for to know God's name is to have access, communication, and relationship by those who name the name. To know the name of God opens the possibility of honoring God more deeply in relationship, but for God runs the risk of abuse and dishonoring of the divine name as well. One of the commandments of the Decalogue is devoted to the protection of the divine name from such abuse (Exod 20:7; Deut 5:11). In later Israel the developed reverence for God's name (see the formula in Exod 33:19; 34:6) bespeaks a sense of Israel's belonging to God, and identification of themselves as people who carry God's name (see Num 6:27). Later Jewish reverence for God's name led to the practice of never vocalizing the name Yahweh but using the Hebrew word 'adonai, which means "lord." This continues as a practice of Jewish piety today.

The content of God's revealing of the divine name to Moses involves a play on words that has been extensively discussed, both linguistically and theologically. The divine name Yahweh is somehow linked to the Hebrew verb "to be" (hayah). The traditional translation of God's word to Moses in verse 14 is "I am who I am." This suggests a relationship of God to the state of being itself or a God whose reality is stable at the core of the divine being. Such a view is not in keeping with the more active view of God revealed in the Exodus story. Most scholars prefer a translation of the phrase that suggests a more dynamic relationship to existence—either "I will be what (who) I will be," or "I will cause to be what I will cause to be." The force of these translations is to relate the character of God to the unfolding of existence. [In the immediate context of the Exodus story, it is Israel's salvation and birth as a people that is coming to be.] God's character is at the heart of what is emerging in human history. At the same time, the statement of God's name in terms of what is, what will be, or what is caused to be reminds us that, in Exodus, God the deliverer is also God the Creator. God is the God in whom both cosmos and history originate, and it is this God who reveals the divine name to Moses and to Israel and establishes intimate relationship. → Human agency - God depends upon human action

It must be noted that the English convention of translating the divine name Yahweh as "LORD" is an impediment to fully appreciating the significance of God's name in biblical texts. The practice originates from the post–Old Testament Jewish custom of reading 'adonai ("Lord") in the place of Yahweh out of respect for the divine name. In the later Hebrew text, alternative vowels were written with the consonants for Yahweh as a reminder not to pronounce the holy name. The result was the peculiar hybrid title *Jehovah*. Out of respect for this ancient Jewish practice, most modern English translations continue to translate Yahweh as "LORD" (always printed in caps), but this suggests we are reading a title rather than a proper name and suggests masculine gender, which is not a part of the name Yahweh. In this volume we will most often use the proper name Yahweh unless quoting a particular translation.

Exodus 6:2-9 presents a further reflection on God's name, marked by the repeated refrain "I am the LORD" (Yahweh).[9] Most scholars think this passage comes from the Priestly tradition and especially reflects the importance given to the name of Yahweh during the time of the Babylonian exile. In the contrast between the theme of God's name in Exod 3 and here in Exod 6, we can see the evidence of multiple sources that led to the documentary hypothesis. Each passage reflects a theology of the name of God that speaks to a different generation in Israel. We have already discussed the emphasis on God's name as connected with the emergence of Israel, a theme appropriate to the period of Israelite monarchy when Israel was establishing its identity and place in the world (J and E sources). Exodus 6 relates the name of Yahweh more directly to themes of God's keeping of promises and making of covenant, themes important to an exile generation that has experienced broken covenant but hopes for renewal born of God's fidelity to promises.

In the context of the Exodus story as it now stands, this powerful passage (Exod 6:2-9) strengthens the connection of God's name to the covenant commitments of God—the fulfillment of promises made to the ancestors. The outcome of that fidelity to promises will unfold in the dramatic Exodus events that lie ahead in the story. Those events are anticipated in a series of powerful verbal phrases in verses 5-8: "I have heard the groaning. . . . I have remembered my covenant. . . . I will free you . . . and deliver you. . . . I will redeem you. . . . I will take you as my people. . . . I will bring you into the land. . . . I will give it to you." Four times throughout this recital God says, "I am Yahweh" (vv. 2, 6, 7, 8). The name Yahweh is being filled with this Exodus salvation and liberation content. The phrase "I will take you as my people and I will be your God" is a formula that is associated with the covenant at Sinai and anticipates that unique covenant relationship beyond liberation. It is easy to see how Israel in exile drew hope from devotion to Yahweh, whose name carried this hopeful content. It is also easy to understand how this has been true for generations of Jews and Christians, especially in times of distress and hopelessness.

God's Salvation as Liberation

God's salvation in Exodus does not focus on saving Israel from sin but is experienced as liberation of Israel from the oppression of a tyrant. Thus, the Exodus story is a major biblical corrective to a spiritualized notion of God's salvation.

The story does not proceed directly to the climactic moment of liberation (the dramatic passing through the sea), but first engages the reader in an extended drama of *God's confrontation with oppressive power, historical evil, and cosmic chaos.* This drama is a struggle to demonstrate whose power is sovereign in creation and history, that of Yahweh or of Pharaoh. Many scholars have felt that the episodes of confrontation between Yahweh (with Moses as active agent) and Pharaoh (5:1–11:10) have been liturgically shaped, probably through generations of Passover remembrance. Thus, the episodes are formally styled, with repetitive formulas and themes (e.g., "let my people go," "that you may know that I am Yahweh," the hardening of the pharaoh's heart).

It is not accidental that the pharaoh of these stories is not named. The concern of the narrative is less on the original historical moment of confrontation with a particular pharaoh than with Pharaoh as representative of those forces that constantly oppose the sovereignty and purposes of Yahweh. On the one hand, the fearful, oppressive, near genocidal policies of the pharaoh are documented as an evidence of historical evil, using political power in self-serving and demeaning ways that crush hope and break the spirit (cf. 1:8-22; 5:1-22; and esp. 6:9). On the other hand, the pharaoh is seen as a personification of the forces of chaos that oppose the intended order of God's creation and the intended well-being of God's creatures.

Yahweh opposes the oppressive power of the pharaoh in both its historical and its cosmic dimensions. With Moses as agent (see further discussion below), Yahweh begins a dramatic reversal of power that will culminate with the oppressed of Israel having the upper hand and the seemingly invincible pharaoh rendered powerless.

The realities of power in the world are not what pharaohs and their admirers imagine. What we commonly call the plagues (the text refers to them as "signs and wonders," 7:3) are evidences of disruptions in the cosmic order in response to Pharaoh's sin. These elements of the created order are evidences of the chaos that ensues when God's created order is threatened. Yet, even in their disturbance, these elements of creation stand under Yahweh's sovereignty and are directed to Yahweh's purposes. Fretheim calls the plagues "ecological signs of historical disasters."[10] The outcome of this drama is that all should "know Yahweh," sovereign as Creator and liberator.

The section on the plagues brought against Pharaoh (7:8–11:10) reflects a complex tradition history that has undoubtedly been shaped by liturgical practices. Comparison with Pss 78 and 105 makes clear that a seven-plague tradition was known in Israel. Those concerned with source analysis have all found evidence of at least three interwoven strata in these chapters, although the extent of each is debated. In some plagues God alone plays the decisive role, in some Moses and/or Aaron, and in some God and Moses. In short, these chapters show a complex literary and tradition history that cannot be recovered with certainty.[11] The result is a narrative in its final form that interweaves divine and human agency in opposition to oppressive power. Creation itself is disrupted and the chaos that results is used by God, Moses, and Aaron to oppose the tyrant who disturbed God's purposes for the world by acts of oppression. The plagues show the chaos unleashed by the pharaoh directed against his own hold on power.

There are consequences for those who serve the purposes of evil and chaos in opposition to Yahweh's sovereignty. Liberation of oppressed Israel and restoration of disrupted creation is not achieved without human cost to Pharaoh and to his people, Egypt. The consequences of oppression are not limited to the oppressors alone but extend to those the oppression was intended to benefit. It is a harsh lesson taught by these texts to those who think avoidance of direct oppression of others is enough to allow them to avoid culpability. The cost of oppression is seen especially in two difficult themes: *the hardening of the pharaoh's heart* and *the death of Egypt's firstborn.*

Some readers experience difficulties with God's action in the plague stories because God hardens the pharaoh's heart.[12] Does this not make Pharaoh the victim of a fate made inevitable by God's action? A careful reading of the references to Pharaoh's hardness of heart presents a more complex picture. There are three verbs used to indicate the hardening of Pharaoh's heart: "to be heavy," "to be strong," and "to be hard." They indicate varying degrees of obstinacy, single-mindedness, stubbornness, and lack of regard. Ten times God is the subject of these verbs, but ten times Pharaoh (or Pharaoh's heart) is the subject. Significantly, God becomes the subject only in the sixth plague (9:12; God's hardening is anticipated as a future action in 4:21 and 7:3). Prior to the sixth plague it is Pharaoh who hardens his own heart. Pharaoh's obstinence is due to his own predilections and willful resistance to God's desire for Israel's freedom. God becomes the hardener of Pharaoh's heart as an intensification of the pharaoh's own character. Pharaoh's resistance to God's word made known through Moses accumulates through the pharaoh's own obduracy until God enters the process to give the pharaoh up to the irreversible consequences of his own persistent sin. The last reference to Pharaoh's hardening of his own heart occurs in the seventh plague (9:35). God does not originate pharaonic persistence in sinful refusal of God's will, but there comes a point when God seals the fate of the oppressor and makes his fall from power inevitable.

The story of the final plague, the death of Egypt's firstborn (12:29-39), is surrounded by liturgical materials providing for and reflecting the celebration of Passover in Israel (12:1-28, 40-51; 13:1-16). This tragic, final act of the struggle between Yahweh and Pharaoh is understood in Exodus as the ironic, perhaps inevitable, rebounding of Pharaoh's own deadly intent toward Israel to take its toll on Pharaoh's own people. Pharaoh had commanded the death of all firstborn Israelite sons as an ongoing genocidal policy. God refers to all Israel as God's own firstborn and declares the death of Egypt's firstborn as the appropriate penalty for Pharaoh's crime (4:23). Pharaoh has set in motion the violence that finally takes the sons of oppressed and oppressor alike. One need look no further than the great wars of the twentieth century to realize the terrible truth of such an equation. Oppression exacts its cost on victims and beneficiaries alike. God's involvement is not a statement of divine lack of compassion but of divine unwillingness to soften the consequences of oppression's inevitable demise. To tolerate or benefit from the power of oppression is exposed as a risky course, and even the innocent, such as children, are placed in danger by the reckless disregard for God's purposes on the part of an oppressor. Those who rely on the brutalizing power of Pharaoh, even innocently, are at risk.

In chapters 14 and 15 we come to the stunning climax of this liberation story. God's will for freedom and justice for Israel becomes reality in a dramatic escape from bondage through the midst of a divinely parted sea and through the destruction of the pursuing Egyptian force. God's *salvation is experienced as liberation.*[13] Israel passes through the sea to new life, and the powers that would consign Israel to death are defeated. The story is told in a complex prose narrative (14:1-31), and the event is celebrated in song by Moses and Miriam (15:1-21). Both narrative story and poetic celebration represent the dramatic events at the sea as the culmination of a public struggle to determine the source of true power in the world. It is Yahweh who emerges as victorious. The sovereign God who suffers with the oppressed is more powerful than the brutal, seemingly invincible oppressor.

In this climactic moment, the emphasis is firmly on Yahweh as the source of liberating power, and the key image for Yahweh in these texts is that of divine warrior.[14]

"The LORD is a warrior" (15:3a). It is Yahweh who fights and wins the victory; Israel is summoned to faith and trust in this divine power to new life: "Do not be afraid, stand firm, and see the deliverance that the LORD will accomplish for you today; for the Egyptians whom you see today you shall never see again. The LORD will fight for you, and you have only to keep still" (14:13-14). The weapons available to a divine warrior include the elements of the cosmos: wind, water, darkness, clouds. No human warrior could stand the waters of the sea up in walls to come crashing in on the Egyptian enemy (14:22-29; 15:8-10). The warrior and battle language of these texts has sometimes seemed harsh and offensive to modern ears. Why must the moment of salvation come in terms of such violence? It is true that such military metaphors for God may be (and have been) used to authorize violence in God's name, often for less than noble purposes. Nevertheless, the truth of this text is that God is implacably opposed to the violent powers of oppression

113

and injustice in the world. To those victimized by oppressive power it is important to trust that there is a power capable of meeting and defeating the brutal powers that dehumanize, exploit, enslave, and marginalize. This text is not easily available to those who wield their own violent power in the name of God. It is directed to those marginal, suffering people who, having no power to oppose the violence against them, nevertheless trust in the "right hand" of the Lord to "shatter the enemy" (15:6).

The salvation wrought by Yahweh is liberation in the sociopolitical order. Israel is delivered from the hand of a flesh-and-blood, historical tyrant. We should resist softening the importance of this dimension of God's saving work by spiritualizing the text, making it a metaphor for God's overcoming of spiritual enemies or even death. God is at work to bring wholeness to those who are broken and dehumanized in the sociopolitical order, to bring hope to those broken of body and not just of spirit. It is in recognition of this concrete liberating activity of God that the Exodus story has functioned for generations to bring hope to those victimized by oppressive power.[15] In our own time the liberation theologies of African American, Latin American, Asian, and African voices have drawn deeply on Exodus themes for foundational understandings of God as liberator. These theologies, born in the experience of powerlessness and marginalization, understand what it means to view the activity of God from the perspective of Israelite slaves liberated from bondage—from the underside of history. The good news of this Exodus story is that God can be trusted to oppose and defeat all power arrangements directed against the full experiencing of human well-being.

It is important, however, that this text also identifies the liberating God as Creator. God's victory, depicted through imagery of water and sea, alludes to God's constant creative power opposing and pushing back the powers of chaos. Salvation in the Exodus story is liberation, but it is also re-creation—the reordering of God's creation and the life God intended for all within it. The good news is not only sociopolitical but ontological in character. We can trust the power of God to make possible the reordering of our lives in the face of all powers that bring brokenness and chaos. Pharaoh is defeated, but so also are Pharaoh's gods (12:12; 15:11; 18:11). Deliverance is a cosmic as well as a sociopolitical victory.

Exodus as Formative and Paradigmatic — Liberation

The full significance of the Exodus story cannot be understood in terms of the experience of Israel in the originating events alone. The narrative of Exod 1–15 already reflects a process of appropriation and reappropriation of the Exodus story by succeeding generations of the community of faith. The canonical text does not end this process; it continues beyond the fixing of the canon through the generations of Jewish and Christian communities down to our own. Every generation tells the Exodus story as its own. The story is both formative—calling community into being—and paradigmatic—reflecting and shaping each generation's experience of God's deliverance.

1. *Event, Response, and Meaning.* The Exodus experience does not stand as an isolated moment in Israel's past. God's liberating action immediately demanded response, and out of that response community was formed. Through the generations the community's Exodus witness generates new and accumulating response. Thus, the meaning of Exodus grows beyond its originating moment and demands response from every generation in the ongoing community of faith—from Israel to the present. The narrative itself indicates elements of the response to Exodus deliverance that forms community—both for Israel and the ongoing generations of God's people.

The initial response of liberated Israel is *doxological.* The joy of Israel in their new freedom spontaneously bursts forth in praise. Miriam and Moses lead Israel in singing:

> I will sing to the LORD, for he has triumphed gloriously;
>   horse and rider he has thrown into the sea.
> The LORD is my strength and my might,
>   and he has become my salvation;
> this is my God, and I will praise him,
>   my father's God, and I will exalt him.
>   (Exod 15:1*b*-2; cf. also 15:21)

The initial community of liberated Israel is a community of praise. Praise remained central and constitutive of Israel. This can be especially seen in the Psalms where praise is Israel's natural response in celebration of God's acts of grace in their behalf. Such praise at the heart of Israel's worship often included the praise of subsequent generations for the Exodus deliverance from bondage.

> Praise the LORD!
>> Praise the name of the LORD;
>> give praise, O servants of the LORD. . . .
> He it was who struck down the firstborn of Egypt,
>> both human beings and animals;
> he sent signs and wonders
>> into your midst, O Egypt,
>> against Pharaoh and all his servants.
>> (Ps 135:1, 8-9; cf. also 136:10-16)

Praise of God defines a central purpose for which God's people were formed, and Exodus themes are at the heart of Israel's praise. Israel is "the people whom I formed for myself so that they might declare my praise" (Isa 43:21). If we in the modern church would be God's liberated people in our time, then praise of God must be placed at the heart of the church's life.

Israel's response to Exodus liberation is also *kerygmatic.* Praise becomes proclamation. The Song of the Sea moves from doxology to tell the story of God's deliverance in stirring poetic detail. Community is formed in the act of recital. Israel is formed as community in part because they have a story to tell and a word of God's salvation to proclaim. Exodus is a central originating memory for Israel. Although the story of God's people grows, the central role of Exodus in that story remains clear throughout the generations. Thus, the kerygmatic recital of the Exodus events recurs throughout the Hebrew canon, attesting to the importance of such a story for the faith identity of subsequent generations in Israel. This may be seen in several creed-like recitals preserved in the biblical text. Deuteronomy 26:5-10 includes Exodus in a statement of faith to be used at the offering of firstfruits from the harvest. Joshua 24:5-7 makes Exodus a key element in recital of Israel's salvation story to those inhabitants of the land who are challenged to "choose this day whom you will serve" (Josh 24:15). The Exodus story is part of the identity of Israel known to the Philistines who face Israel in battle (1 Sam 4:8). It is a part of the proclamation of the prophets who call Israel back to obedience in service of the God who has saved them: "For I brought you up from the land of Egypt, and redeemed you from the house of slavery; and I sent before you Moses, Aaron, and Miriam" (Mic 6:4); "When Israel was a child, I loved him, and out of Egypt I called my son. The more I called them, the more they went from me; they kept sacrificing to the Baals, and offering incense to idols" (Hos 11:1-2). In time of exile, Exodus memory and recital becomes a source of prophetic hope for new life:

Thus says the LORD,
  who makes a way in the sea,
  a path in the mighty waters,
who brings out chariot and horse,
  army and warrior;
they lie down, they cannot rise,
  they are extinguished, quenched like a wick:
Do not remember the former things,
  or consider the things of old.
I am about to do a new thing;
  now it springs forth, do you not perceive it?
                    (Isa 43:16-19*a*)

Of course Israel's recital of Exodus liberation is most centrally focused in the Passover, which is celebrated every year in the spring. Each generation is formed anew in relation to the Exodus story as it is retold and celebrated. Each generation becomes the Exodus generation. The narratives of Exod 12:1-28, 43-49; 13:1-16 already reflect the liturgical practice through generations of Passover celebration. Moreover, such celebrations continue in the Jewish community until the present. In the gospel stories, Jesus' final supper with his disciples is a Passover meal, and Jesus' own death is understood through the metaphor of the sacrificial lamb of Israel's Passover and the tragic but necessary death of the firstborn to enable salvation. Liturgies today often declare, "Christ, our Passover, is sacrificed for us; therefore, let us keep the feast." Recital of the good news of God's deliverance lies at the heart of identity for the community of the people of God in the Jewish and the Christian communities. Passover (and its accompanying Exodus story) reminds each generation of the community of faith that their life originates in God's gift of life when they had no life. "Remember

117

that you were a slave in the land of Egypt, and the LORD your God redeemed you" (Deut 15:15).

Finally, Israel's communal response to Exodus is *covenantal.* It is not enough to sing praise and tell the story if there is no structure of community to carry on such doxology and recital. Thus, the story of the book of Exodus must continue on from the shores of the sea to the encampment at Mt. Sinai (Horeb) and the events that form the "mixed multitude" (Exod 12:38; "mixed crowd" in NRSV) of liberated Israel into a covenant people. The identity of God's covenant people presupposes the Exodus experience: "You have seen what I did to the Egyptians, and how I bore you on eagles' wings and brought you to myself. Now therefore, if you obey my voice and keep my covenant, you shall be my treasured possession out of all the peoples. Indeed, the whole earth is mine, but you shall be for me a priestly kingdom and a holy nation" (Exod 19:4-6). Although this portion of the book of Exodus is the subject of chapter 5, we suggest here that Exodus tells the story of Israel's freedom from the forced labor that built Pharaoh's treasure cities and that Sinai will call Israel to the covenantal labor that is necessary to build the faithful community of God's people. The move from Exodus to Sinai, from salvation to covenant, from freedom to obedience, is a necessary journey for every generation seeking to be God's people.

2. *The Pattern of Exodus Faith.* Even apart from explicit references to Exodus memory, there is a pattern of faith, a paradigm for understanding the experience of God's grace, that grows out of the Exodus experience. There is an Exodus shape to the faith experience of God's people reflected throughout the Old Testament, into the New Testament, and on through the subsequent history of church and synagogue.

This pattern arises out of the climactic moment of deliverance at the sea and consists of three elements:

Situation of Distress ⇒ Unexpected Deliverance ⇒ Response in Community

All persons and communities experience situations of distress, moments, both personal and corporate, when, like Israel at the sea, every generation despairs of finding any way into the future. In these moments we, like Israel, experience grief and anger (the people turned on Moses, 14:11-12). We see no possibilities for life, believing that death has the upper hand. We are without hope.

It is the testimony of Exodus faith that into this despairing moment God has made possible unexpected deliverance. In the Exodus story what could be more unexpected than that a path should open through the sea itself, and that Israel would walk to freedom on dry ground? The Exodus pattern suggests that through God there is always a way into the future and a further word of life to be spoken in the face of death. It will often come in "unexpected" ways. Exodus faith does not mean that people of faith always receive the future they wish for, but in God there will be a way forward into new life. The wilderness stories of Exod 16–18 suggest that such new life in faith involves struggle (see further discussion below). The promise of the Exodus paradigm is that death never has the final word; God's grace will make new futures possible, often in surprising and unanticipated ways.

Community forms in response to this movement from distress to deliverance. The Exodus-initiated community celebrates and remembers the stories of God's saving/delivering/liberating grace, and responds to shape its life and practice differently in the world because of its experience of the saving/delivering/liberating God. We will discuss this shaping of community in chapter 5 in relation to the concept of covenant.

This pattern of distress, deliverance, and community is reflected in much of the literature of the Old and New Testaments. In Israel's literature the pattern may be seen most clearly in the Psalms. The psalms of lamentation speak movingly and candidly of distress in many forms, but, as is well known, most laments also move toward praise in anticipation of deliverance (see Ps 77, which includes an explicit reference to the Exodus). Psalms of thanksgiving look back on distress from the perspective of those who have experienced deliverance and new life (see Ps 33). Other types of psalms reflect the community—in its remembrance of the salvation story (Ps 136), in its festival celebrations of faith (Ps 24), in the ethical demands on God's community (Ps 15), and in the leadership expected of the king (Ps 72). For Christians, the pattern of faith reflected in the Exodus story may also be seen in the central salvation story of the New Testament. In the relationship between crucifixion, resurrection,

119

and Pentecost we may see a christological reenactment of the Exodus-shaped faith. On the cross, Jesus identifies with the deepest human distress and despair. In resurrection God speaks an unexpected word of new life to those who thought death had spoken a final word. And in Pentecost, a new community is birthed to witness to and live out the implications of this new experience of God's grace. In the early church, baptism is associated both with rising from death to life (resurrection) and with passing through the waters to new life (Exodus). The pattern of faith experience that is reflected in the Exodus story remains a central part of the identity of God's people through the generations down to our own. Brevard Childs concludes his treatment of the deliverance at the sea with this theological reflection on its paradigmatic character:

> The church lives in the memory of the redemption from the past bondage of Egypt, and she looks for the promised inheritance. She now lives still in the desert somewhere between the Red Sea and the Jordan. "Therefore let no one think that he stands lest he fall, but God is faithful and will also provide for us the way of escape."[16]

Moses and the Role of Human Agency

God's initiative and ultimate power accomplish Israel's liberation from Egyptian bondage. But God does not act alone in these events. The important role of human agency in partnership with the redeeming activity of God is acknowledged in Israel's own testimony at the very moment of their liberation: "So the people feared the LORD and believed in the LORD and in his servant Moses" (Exod 14:31*b*).

God's power does not operate independent of human agency in the Exodus events. As we have seen, the resourceful, saving activity of five women preceded even the explicit initiative of God in behalf of Israel's future well-being (Exod 1:15–2:10). Aaron also plays an important role alongside that of Moses: "See, I have made you like God to Pharaoh, and your brother Aaron shall be your prophet. You shall speak all that I command you, and your brother Aaron shall tell Pharaoh to let the Israelites go out of his land" (Exod 7:1-2). Aaron becomes the ancestor of a major line of priests in Israel (cf. Exod 28:1).

In addition, Miriam is given an important role of leadership in the wilderness period of Israel's journey from Egypt. The prophet

Micah lists her alongside Moses and Aaron, "I sent before you Moses, Aaron, and Miriam" (Mic 6:4b). She is first to lead Israel in praise after the crossing of the sea (Exod 15:20-21) and is central to important wilderness episodes, particularly the account of a rebellion by Miriam and Aaron against Moses' leadership (cf. Num 12:1-15; 20:1; 26:59; Deut 24:9).[17]

Nevertheless, Moses most centrally represents the partnership between God and human agency in the liberation enterprise. The influence of Moses extends beyond these deliverance events into the experience of Israel in the wilderness and in the covenant formation at Sinai. In the Exodus drama, God announces the divine intention to deliver Israel from bondage and, almost in the same breath, commands Moses to go to the pharaoh to effect this desired outcome: "I have come down to deliver them. . . . So come, I will send you to Pharaoh to bring my people, the Israelites, out of Egypt" (3:8a, 10).

Moses engages in the difficult face-to-face confrontations and negotiations with Pharaoh over Israel's fate (5–12), faces the abuse and rejection of his own people, who are too beaten down to choose the risk of their own freedom (5:20-23; 14:10-12), and mediates God's power in the decisive moment of victory and freedom (14:15-16). The signs and wonders in this story remind us of the power of Yahweh, sovereign over creation and history. But the courage and faithfulness of Moses remind us of the human and social struggles through which God is at work to effect the divine saving purposes. Moses is the revolutionary agent of God, who defeats oppressive human power and makes hope possible to the hopeless. Moses is the mediator of divine creative power, standing with God in opposition to the forces of chaos and demonstrating God's sovereignty over creation itself.

The motif of Moses, being raised in the household of the very oppressor he would oppose is an element recognized by political theorists as often present in events that lead to liberation. The oppressed are drained of energy and without the power of initiative in oppressive circumstances. A human agent, spared from the deadening effects of oppression and benefiting from the resources of the privileged, identifies with the fate of the oppressed and exploited. Such a person, equipped with resources drawn from the privileged, often becomes a catalytic agent in revolutionary situations. In Exod 2,

Moses is given a privileged upbringing and yet nourished in his own identity by contact with his mother and sister. As an adult he is forced to choose between these identities and demonstrates a predilection for justice (2:11-22), though one that is not yet channeled and focused for God's purposes. When he is sent by God to confront the pharaoh, Moses stands between two communities he has known, but neither broken in spirit by oppression nor hardened of heart by possession of power. He can represent God's new possibility for Israel.

Attention to Moses' role in this story is the antidote to a reading that would settle for passive human waiting for God's action alone to oppose oppression and injustice. Trust in God's liberating power requires human participation in the processes that call and send persons like Moses to engage the oppressive powers of every generation. The leadership required of those who attend to Moses' role in this story will involve confrontation and struggle in the sociopolitical order, facing the Pharaohs of every age.

Liberative leadership also may require mediation between God's purposes and the people of God. Moses often faced the skepticism and rebellion of his own people (5:20-23; 14:10-12; 16:2-3). He challenged them in the name of the liberating God he served, urged them forward when they would remain in bondage, and mediated God's forgiveness in the face of their stubborn refusals of divine purposes.

God does not liberate without also calling human agents to the task of liberation. God works with and through the gifts and the weaknesses of those agents—in Moses' time and in our own. Passive waiting for God's justice and deliverance does not fit the biblical model of the Exodus story. Neither can political readings of these texts argue for human agency alone or fail to see the centrality of God's initiative and sovereignty. It was Moses (and secondarily Aaron and Miriam), as well as Yahweh, who brought Israel out of Egypt (see Exod 6:13, 26-27; 32:7).

Liberation into the Wilderness

God delivered Israel not immediately into the promised land but into the wilderness. Following the Song of the Sea (15:1-21), the book of Exodus includes several chapters reflecting initial struggles in the wilderness prior to the encampment at Mt. Sinai (Exod 19). Although some later texts look back on the wilderness as a "honeymoon period" in Israel's life (e.g., Hos 2:14-15), this is not the perspective of the wilderness traditions in Exodus (or the somewhat different wilderness traditions of Leviticus, Numbers, or Deuteronomy). Although important shaping of Israel as a community took place in this period, it was a time of trial and struggle.

The wilderness traditions immediately following the deliverance at the sea include crises over adequate water (15:22-27 and 17:1-7) and sufficient food (16:1-36). There is also the story of an attack by an enemy, the Amalekites (17:8-16), and a narrative on Moses' reunion with his father-in-law, the Midianite priest Jethro, who helps him organize the governance of the people Moses now leads (18:1-27).

Although there will be further discussion of important wilderness experiences in the following chapter, we can briefly note several important themes that appear in these initial wilderness encounters.

1. God's salvation does not guarantee life without hardships. The world outside of bondage is also a world with dangers and struggles. Needs are not automatically supplied, and lack of food and water for Israel carries the threat to the people's welfare into the most basic of human needs.

2. In the context of such struggle, even bondage can begin to look attractive. Faced with the wilderness, some would choose the security of bondage over the struggle in freedom. "If only we had died by the hand of the LORD in the land of Egypt, when we sat by the fleshpots and ate our fill of bread" (16:3).

3. In the wilderness struggle, the people turn on Moses, Aaron, and God (15:24; 16:3, 9; 17:2-4). This conflict is the beginning of a complex set of traditions concerning the people's complaint and rebellion in the wilderness that continue on through the Pentateuch. The memory of Exodus deliverance is not enough to engender trust in the Lord's providence. Moses increasingly must intervene and mediate between his rebellious people and God (see 16:11-12; 17:4-7).

4. In these chapters God's response is gracious, merciful, and providential. Only later in the wilderness traditions does the people's rebellion evoke God's anger and judgment (e.g., Exod 32).

In the midst of these wilderness trials the biblical narrative emphasizes God's ability to provide for the people's needs. The resources to sustain life in wilderness struggle come from God and are trustworthy. God's victory over the chaotic power of Pharaoh, who opposed God's creation, is now reflected in God's use of creation to give life in the wilderness.

The manna story in chapter 16 is especially important. Israel returns often to reflect on this story of the people's need and God's providence (Num 11; Deut 8; Josh 5:12; Neh 9:20; Ps 78:24). Every day the people could trust that the manna would be available. Every day the people must gather and eat it. Important economic insights were drawn from the manna story. Manna always miraculously provided just enough for the people's needs: "those who gathered much had nothing over, and those who gathered little had no shortage; they gathered as much as each of them needed" (16:18). Resources were keyed to need and excess was not possible. Later covenant provisions for economic life reflect some of the lessons learned from reliance on the manna from God. Even in the New Testament, the apostle Paul appeals to this same story for the principle of providing for one another's needs and avoiding excess when he takes up his collection for Jerusalem (2 Cor 8:13-15).

It is Yahweh who gives the resources that provide life in the deadly dangers of wilderness, but Israel must trust in the reliability of God's provision and avoid the temptation to hoard or control the blessings God provides. The people of God must learn to receive God's gifts; to attempt to grasp these gifts is to lose them (16:20).

5. The odd story of Jethro's advice to Moses in organizing new leadership structures for Israel that relieve the burden on him (18:1-27) serves two purposes. First, it allows for acknowledgment by a non-Israelite of what Yahweh has done in defeating Egypt and bringing Israel to freedom. The nations are indeed beginning to "know" that Yahweh is God. Second, this ordering of Israel's life foreshadows the long and important work of shaping Israel as covenant community. The justice initiated with Exodus deliverance begins to be institutionalized in social structures within the community. The structuring of Israel as a new community in covenant with Yahweh begins in chapter 19 of Exodus and serves as the subject of our next chapter.

Notes

1. See the discussion of "History and Faith in the Book of Exodus" in Terence E. Fretheim, *Exodus* (IBC; Louisville: John Knox Press, 1991), 7-10.

2. For those interested in scholarly judgments on the source-critical history of the text, the commentary by B. S. Childs, *The Book of Exodus: A Critical, Theological Commentary* (OTL; Philadelphia: Westminster, 1974), is a magisterial commentary that gives detailed attention to previous critical work on the text of Exodus.

3. Some scholars also defend an earlier date for the Exodus events. See the excellent discussion of historical possibilities in the Exodus narrative in Iain Provan, V. Philips Long, and Tremper Longman III, *A Biblical History of Israel* (Louisville: Westminster John Knox, 2003), 125-32.

4. Cf. Fretheim, *Exodus.*

5. See Fretheim, *Exodus,* 36-41; and J. Cheryl Exum, "You Shall Let Every Daughter Live: A Study of Ex 1:8-2:10," *Semeia* 28 (1983): 63-82.

6. Walter Brueggemann, *The Prophetic Imagination* (Philadelphia: Fortress, 1978), 16-17.

7. See T. Fretheim, *The Suffering of God: An Old Testament Perspective* (OBT; Philadelphia: Fortress, 1984); and also B. C. Birch, *Let Justice Roll Down: The Old Testament, Ethics, and Christian Life* (Louisville: Westminster John Knox, 1991).

8. For a fuller theological discussion of God's self-disclosure in Exodus, with reference to key previous treatments, see Walter Brueggemann, "The Book of Exodus: Introduction, Commentary, and Reflections," *NIB*, vol. 1 (Nashville: Abingdon, 1994), 711-22, 733-37.

9. See W. Zimmerli, *I Am Yahweh* (Atlanta: John Knox, 1982), 1-28.

10. Fretheim, *Exodus,* 107-8; and T. Fretheim, "The Plagues as Ecological Signs of Historical Disaster," *JBL* 110 (1991): 385-96.

11. Childs, *The Book of Exodus* (pp. 121-70) gives detailed discussion and response to the critical historical, literary, and liturgical questions raised by the plague narratives. In the end, he insists that the address of these texts is theological, as do Brueggemann, "The Book of Exodus," 722-23; and Fretheim, *Exodus,* 105-12.

12. See excurses on the hardening of the pharaoh's heart in Childs, *The Book of Exodus,* 170-75; and Fretheim, *Exodus,* 96-103.

13. The work of George V. Pixley, *On Exodus: A Liberation Perspective* (Maryknoll, N.Y.: Orbis, 1987) emphasizes the importance of the liberation theme throughout the book of Exodus. See also J. Severino Croatto, *Exodus: A Hermeneutics of Freedom* (Maryknoll, N.Y.: Orbis, 1981) in this regard.

14. See P. D. Miller, Jr., *The Divine Warrior in Early Israel* (Cambridge, Mass.: Harvard University Press, 1973); and M. C. Lind, *Yahweh Is a Warrior* (Scottdale, Pa.: Herald Press, 1980).

15. See M. Walzer, *Exodus and Revolution* (New York: Basic Books, 1985).

16. Childs, *The Book of Exodus,* 239.

17. See Rita J. Burns, *Has the Lord Spoken Only Through Moses?* (SBLDS 84; Atlanta: Scholars Press, 1987); and Phyllis Trible, "Bringing Miriam Out of the Shadows," *BRev* 5 (1989): 14-24, 34.

Bibliography

Commentaries

Brueggemann, Walter. "The Book of Exodus: Introduction, Commentary, and Reflections." *NIB*, vol. 1. Nashville: Abingdon, 1994.

Childs, Brevard S. *The Book of Exodus: A Critical, Theological Commentary.* OTL. Philadelphia: Westminster, 1974.

Durham, John. *Exodus*. WBC 3. Waco: Word, 1987.

Fretheim, Terence. *Exodus*. IBC. Louisville: Westminster John Knox, 1991.

Gowan, Donald. *Theology in Exodus: Biblical Theology in the Form of a Commentary*. Louisville: Westminster John Knox, 1994.

Sarna, Nahum M. *The JPS Torah Commentary: Exodus*. Philadelphia: JPS, 1991.

Other Studies

Bloom, Harold, ed. *Exodus*. Modern Critical Interpretations. New York: Chelsea House, 1987.

Coats, George W. *Rebellion in the Wilderness: The Murmuring Motif in the Wilderness Traditions of the Old Testament*. Nashville: Abingdon, 1968.

Croatto, J. Severino. *Exodus: A Hermeneutics of Freedom*. Maryknoll, N.Y.: Orbis, 1981.

Daube, David. *The Exodus Pattern in the Bible*. London: Faber and Faber, 1963.

Pixley, George V. *On Exodus: A Liberation Perspective*. Maryknoll, N.Y.: Orbis, 1987.

Walzer, Michael. *Exodus and Revolution*. New York: Basic Books, 1985.

CHAPTER FIVE

THE STRUCTURES OF COVENANT LIFE

Exod 19–40, Leviticus, Numbers, Deuteronomy

This segment of the Pentateuch fundamentally has to do with the law. Yet, the law is not presented as a code, a list of laws to be obeyed. The law does not stand alone. Rather, the law is integrated with the ongoing story of Israel's journey from slavery in Egypt to new life in the promised land. The law functions as a dynamic reality within a living community; the law will not stand still any more than the community will.

To speak of "the structures of covenant life" can be a helpful way to speak of the law. The language of structure catches up the theme of creation; the ordering of community is in tune with God's ordering of the cosmos. Just as the law and structures, more generally, were an integral part of God's work in creation (Gen 1:28; 2:15-17), so God, in giving the law to Israel, provides structure for society. The law is good, a gracious divine gift, and is given for the sake of a well-ordered community.

Structure is important for life; indeed, it is indispensable for life within relationship, both with God and with all other creatures. God gives the law for the sake of the best possible life in community, a life of stability and well-being for all, especially the most disadvantaged. God gives the law "so that you may live, and that it may go well with you, and that you may live long in the land that you are to possess" (Deut 5:33). As such, the law is not understood in a static sense, as if the law were given once and for all. In view of Israel's ever-changing experiences on its journeys, laws will be given and revised and even taken away.

This chapter consists of two primary segments. The first reviews these texts in terms of their placement within discrete books. The second moves through the texts thematically.

Exod 19–Deut 34: A Theological Overview

Exod 19–40

Israel's arrival at Mt. Sinai (19:1) issues in a lengthy stay; nearly a year and fifty-eight chapters later Israel departs (Num 10:11). At the mountain God takes several key initiatives. God prepares the people for the divine appearance (19), teaches them by means of the Ten Commandments (20:1-17) and the book of the covenant (21–23), enters into covenant with them (24), and gives them instructions for building a tabernacle for God (25–31). After Israel's apostasy and God's forgiveness (32–34), the sanctuary is built (35–40). Key to this section of Exodus is the interweaving of law and story (see below).

The personal terms with which this unit is introduced are important: "I did; I bore you; I brought you to *myself*" (19:4-6). In its journey beyond liberation Israel is personally borne by God to the place of God's presence. At the same time, 19:4-6 insists that life with God is more than basking in God's presence. The personal language continues. Israel is to give heed to "*my* voice" and "*my* covenant," to be "*my own* possession" and be "*to me*" a kingdom of priests and a holy nation. Israel's response to God is conceived in terms of personal commitment to God, but this is not simply a vertical relationship. Israel's commitment will immediately entail service to the neighbor, indeed the entire creation.

After being prepared for God's appearance, Israel hears God give the Decalogue directly. Here, and in Deut 5:6-21, it introduces the two major bodies of law in the Pentateuch, that given at Mt. Sinai (Exodus–Leviticus) and that given on the plains of Moab (Deut 5–26). As such, the Decalogue provides in apodictic form (that is, a declaratory word directed to "you") the core values that undergird and inform the statutes that follow. These values promote and protect the life and well-being of the *community*. The individualized address from the Lord "your" God lifts up the importance of internal motivation within relationship rather than heteronomous imposition ("obey because God said so") or external coercion (no sanctions are stated). Originally, every commandment was probably brief and negative in formulation; the list has been expanded and adjusted through the years in view of changing community needs. Clear examples include a change in motivations (cf. Exod 20:9-11 with Deut 5:13-15) and the removal of "wife" from the list of property (cf. Exod 20:17 and Deut 5:21). These changes provide an inner-biblical warrant for ongoing change in post-biblical times (e.g., the coveting commandment should include husbands).

The collection of laws called the book of the covenant (Exod 21–23) is diverse in form and content. The form includes case law (21:26-27), apodictic declaration (22:28), divine exhortation (22:21-27), and promise (23:27-28). The statutes order a wide range of daily life: sexual ethics (22:19); care of the disadvantaged (22:21-27); worship calendars (23:14-17); loyalty to Yahweh (20:23). Developed over time, these statutes are not a list of laws in force, but basic principles for shaping the judicial task and the community's life. The admixture of sacred and "secular" matters testifies that life is a seamless web and that Israel's God will not be split off to care simply for the religious realm. All dimensions of life are included for the sake of the good order of God's creation.

Chapter 24 focuses on Israel's response to God in a covenant-making ritual. It includes a commitment to God's word (vv. 3, 8), various sacrifices (vv. 4-5), the reading of the word (v. 7), the sprinkling of blood—an atoning act (v. 8)—and a meal of fellowship in the presence of God (vv. 9-11). This God-initiated covenant stands under the umbrella of the Abrahamic covenant (see below). It provides a *closer specification* of what that relationship entails in view of what Israel has become as a *people*. The Sinai covenant is a matter, not of the people's status, but of their *vocation*. God hereby sets this people apart for a task: to be faithful to the word of God in their daily rounds for the sake of the creation.

In 24:12-18, Moses ascends to God's mountain abode and receives the instructions for the tabernacle, a portable sanctuary (25–31); it provides a place for God to dwell among the people (25:8; 29:45-46). It constitutes a change in the way God is present among them—ongoing rather than occasional; close, not distant; on-the-move, not fixed. The reason for the detail, much of which is repeated in chapters 35–40 during the construction, is not clear. While the dating of this material is uncertain, it may relate to the situation of exilic readers and their need for detailed future planning for a return to the land where the temple lies in ruins; such a plan could foster a sense of hope. At the least, the detail demonstrates the importance of God's descent to dwell among the people and the worship of the community now to be centered at this sanctuary. This divine move sets the stage for Leviticus.

Between the instructions for the tabernacle and its construction stand chapters 32–34. The Israelites take the future into their own hands and compromise their loyalty to Yahweh by constructing an image of Yahweh (or the divine messenger) in the form of a golden calf (32:1-6). The rest of this section works out the effects of this apostasy. It centers on a lively dialogue between God and Moses, whose intercession is key to preserving Israel from annihilation, if not from judgment altogether (32:9-14, 35), and to gaining assurance of God's ongoing presence in their midst (33:1-17). Israel's future rests in God, yet God honors human prayer as a genuine contribution to the shape of the future (32:14; 33:17). Most remarkably, God forgives this people and renews the covenant (34:1-10). Such divine responses are grounded in the nature of Israel's God: gracious, merciful, slow to anger, and abounding in steadfast love (34:6-7). Israel's future is possible only because God is this kind of God.

Chapters 25–40 have a creation–fall–re-creation structure. The story of the golden calf is the story of Israel's fall, followed by acts of divine graciousness and the renewal of covenant (Exod 34:9-10 parallels Gen 8:21-22). Emblematic of this new relationship, the tabernacle is built precisely according to the divine command, and God descends to dwell in Israel's midst (40:34-38).

The tabernacle and God's promise to dwell among the people constitute assurances (verbal and tangible) that God is among them, a gracious divine condescension to the need of the human for that which is concrete and focused. When this theme is combined with Lev 1–7, with its provision for forgiveness, these texts constitute a statement that God is both *with* them and *for* them.

This move from slavery to worship means a change in status for the people; it also entails change for God. For God to be so intensely present with Israel is a new divine experience. This move seems to be for God's sake as much as for the people's. God desires such a "home" among the people! No more mountain hideaways; no more palace precincts. This enhances the intimacy of the relationship with the people whom God loves. At the same time, it makes for greater vulnerability; God can be more easily hurt by advantages assumed and presumptions advanced. That God does this in the wake of the golden calf debacle indicates something of the risk God is willing to take for closeness. No longer are the people—or their mediator—asked to come up to God; God "comes down" to them. No more trips up the mountain for Moses! God begins a "descent" that John 1:14 claims comes to a climax in the Incarnation.

The Book of Leviticus

The book of Exodus ends with the sanctuary in place. In Leviticus it becomes operational on behalf of a sinful community. This focus is integrated with other statutes regarding Israel's life in worship and world.

The book of Leviticus is the center of the Pentateuch. This placement conveys the importance of worship for the life and well-being of the community. As God had been active in Israel's history, so God promises to be active in worship. Through these visible and tangible means, from sacrifices to dramatized festivals, God continues to overcome slavery and death and bestows life and salvation. Leviticus has more of a life-giving word and world to offer than its formal character suggests.

Leviticus is part of the Priestly (P) tradition. Distinctions within this tradition are often made (e.g., chaps. 17–26, known as the Holiness Code = H), but the whole consists of essentially compatible materials. Scholars commonly conclude that these texts reflect an exilic or post-exilic situation, though recent attempts at an earlier dating have been made.[1] Generally, these texts may reflect understandings and practices built up over the time of the first temple (957–587 BCE), but they were given a decisive shape during the exile (see 26:43-45), with subsequent redactions likely.

From early times Leviticus has been considered a priest's manual. And, certainly, chapters 1–16 focus on matters in which the priests are more directly involved, including sacrifices and offerings (1–7), ordination (8–10), discernments regarding clean and unclean (11–15), and the Day of Atonement (16). Yet, while some texts are words of God for the priests (6:8–7:21; 16:1-28), most are directed to

MAJOR INDIVIDUAL SACRIFICES PRESCRIBED BY LEVITICUS

Requirements (in order of presentation):

Reason for Offering	Atoning Sacrifices — Guilt Offering	Sin Offering	Burnt Offering	Grain Offering
For violations of the Lord's holy things (5:14-19)	A ram without defect Value of profaned item plus 20%			
For violations of human property rights (6:1-7)	A ram without defect Full restitution plus 20%			
For lepers (14:4f.) when cleansed	A male lamb and a log of oil (as a wave offering)	A male lamb	A ewe lamb a year old	3/10 ephah, mixed with oil
or if poor	A male lamb	A turtledove or a pigeon	A turtledove or a pigeon	1/10 ephah, a log of oil
Inadvertent Sins (4:3–5:10): for Priests		A young bull		
for Congregation		A young bull		
for Ruler		A male goat		
for Individuals		A female goat or lamb		
if poor		A turtledove or a pigeon	A turtledove or a pigeon	1/10 ephah, no oil or incense
For purification after childbirth (12:6)		A pigeon or a turtledove	A year-old lamb	
or if poor		A turtledove or a pigeon	A turtledove or a pigeon	
For discharges (15:1-33)		A turtledove or a pigeon	A dove or a pigeon	
Voluntary (1:3-17)			A male animal from the herd or flock or a turtledove or pigeon	Fine flour, oil incense, and salt If cooked, no yeast or honey Bread, no yeast, made with oil
Peace Offerings (3:1-17) Thank Offerings (7:12-15) Votive Offerings (7:16-18) Freewill Offerings			A male or female from the herd or flock	Wafers, no yeast spread with oil Cakes, mixed with oil

"the people of Israel" (e.g., 1:2; 26:46). Chapters 17–26, with their admixture of moral and ritual statutes, are more lay-oriented. But, even the materials addressed to priests are here made available for everyone to read. No secret priestly lore exists that is not shared with all; in a democratizing move, the laity are given ownership with respect to priestly matters.

The story of Israel's stay at Mt. Sinai, begun at Exod 19:1, continues through Leviticus. Chapters 1–7, which outline Israel's sacrificial system (see below), continue God's response to Israel's apostasy (Exod 32:1-6). These texts take the form of law, but in reality they constitute a word of good news; a gracious and merciful God (Exod 34:6-7) thereby provides a visible and tangible means by which the people's sins can be forgiven. This divine gift makes another dimension of God's saving action available to Israel; whereas the Exodus provided deliverance from the sin of others (Egypt), in the sacrifices provision is made for the forgiveness of one's own sin. Leviticus also provides means—dramatized festivals (e.g., Passover)—by which the Exodus type of salvation continues to be made available to Israel: God brought *us* out of Egyptian bondage (Lev 23:42-43).

The story line is resumed in Lev 8–10. These chapters report the ordination of members of the family of Aaron, precisely following the instructions given in Exod 29. The fundamental task of the priesthood in Exodus, to bring Israel "to continual remembrance before the LORD" (Exod 28:12, 29-30), stresses their intercessory role; this role is continued in Leviticus, but in view of the apostasy, their ministry focuses on the mediation of the word and deed of God to the people, especially forgiveness, "making atonement on your behalf" (Lev 4:20–6:7; 8:34; 17:11; 19:22; cf. 10:10-11).[2]

Chapters 11–15 (and elsewhere, esp. 17–21) focus on issues of purity. Two basic distinctions are made (10:10): holy (that which has a special relationship with God) and common (ordinary, profane); clean (normal) and unclean (anomalous, out of place). These distinctions—and all cultures have them—have to do with appropriate boundaries. The spheres of concern are wide-ranging: animals and what goes into the body, for instance, blood from the carrion-eaters and carnivores (11); bodily purity and what comes forth from the body, extended to include clothing and houses—kinds of boundaries (12–15); sacral purity of times, places, persons, acts, and objects associated with the tabernacle, including idolatry (21); and moral purity, including bloodshed and sexual relations (17–18; 20).

Israel integrates these distinctions into the religious sphere. Certain matters are pleasing/displeasing to God because they affect positively or negatively the wholeness and stability, indeed the holiness, of the community—with implications for the creation. The priests are responsible for making these distinctions (10:10); they discern the boundaries set by God, teach them to the people, and preside over rituals of cleansing. These distinctions ought not be translated into moral/immoral or dirty/clean or sinful/righteous. While all sins yield uncleanness, not all impurities are sins. For example, some impurities are associated with that which is natural and necessary (e.g., sex, death), others with sin and evil (e.g., idolatry, homicide, illicit sexual relations).

These laws have occasioned various interpretations. Common suggestions are: the separation of Israel from the (idolatrous) practices of other peoples (see 18:3, 24); hygiene; primitive taboos; issues of life and death (see 17:11; respect for blood is respect for life, as with semen); and a correlation of social order with cosmic order. An anthropological approach has become common (see especially the work of Mary Douglas).[3] This approach emphasizes social order, wholeness, and community identity as factors that shape the community in life-giving ways. Purity concerns may have been informed by several of the above-noted factors, but the texts do not make these matters clear. Their one commonality now is that they are gathered as God's will for Israel; the language of Deuteronomy may also apply to Leviticus: "so that you may live, and that it may go well with you" (Deut 5:33). These statutes are put forth because they have the best interests of the community at heart.

Christians might appropriate these concerns by connecting them with various life situations, including such matters as clothing and food, housing and disease, sexual relationships, and the character of worship and religious leadership. The issue: What best serves the relationship with God and the life, health, stability, and flourishing of the community? The consideration of this question would not commonly yield once-and-for-all responses, so the hard work of interpretation and appropriation must be undertaken anew in every generation. Some modern examples: the Centers for Disease Control, Habitat for Humanity, laws of sanitation, guidelines for the manipulation of blood, the Food and Drug Administration, seminary worship classes, and ordination candidacy committees.

The ritual of the Day of Atonement in chapter 16 is focused both on the cleansing of the people as a whole and of the tabernacle (16:16). Presupposed in this ritual is that sin is not simply to be understood in individual terms; it is a reality that also has a corporate dimension. Thus, the ritual provided a means by which the community as a whole could deal with sin's potential communal destructiveness. To this end, a goat was sent into the wilderness bearing the sins of all the people.

Leviticus 17–26, known as the Holiness Code, is more hortatory and lay-oriented; it centers on behaviors and rituals that promote communal stability in the interrelated spheres of daily life and worship. Key to their force is 19:2, "You shall be holy, for I the LORD your God am holy." This does not mean that holiness is something to strive for; Israel's holiness is a *reality*. The call to "be holy" is a call to be true to the relationship in which the people already stand (Exod 19:6; cf. 1 John 1:7). Basically, this entails being faithful to God in worship *and in life*. Israel's holiness is not simply an internal disposition; holistically, it is to be expressed externally in all spheres of life. What this entailed may be summed up in 19:18 (cf. v. 34), "You shall love your neighbor as yourself."

By virtue of Israel's relationship to a holy God and this calling, and by God's sanctifying action (20:8; 21:8; 22:9), the word *holy* characterizes *all* the people of God (11:44-45; 19:2; 20:7, 26; cf. Num 16:3; Deut 14:2; 26:19), not simply the priests. Yet, the latter seem to have a special holy status ("most holy," Exod 30:29) by virtue of their role with respect to the sanctuary and its service (Lev 21:6-8). This closeness to the tabernacling God entailed an intensification of holiness (places and things associated with worship were also "most holy," Exod 26:33-34; Lev 21:22).

Because the people are genuinely holy, holiness must be defined basically in terms other than unapproachability or "*wholly* other"; it is a relational category wherein one is drawn into relationship with the holy God, with its benefits and responsibilities, without becoming divine. Strict measures associated with holiness exist not to protect God from contamination by the world, nor to protect the world from God (though violation could mean an experience of divine wrath, 10:1-2), but to honor God's character *as God* and to assure a proper relationship with God in the midst of a world of disorder and sin, a serious matter God will not take lightly. Past infidelities loom large over these developments, especially the golden calf debacle (Exod 32:7-10). In the wake of this near disaster, God still graciously chose to dwell among the people; but, given the people's propensity to apostasy, safeguards were instituted so that a recurrence might be prevented.

In sum, the meaning of holiness is focused on distinctiveness and being set apart by virtue of the relationship with the indwelling God and in the service of a mission that is God's but set deeply within the world for the purpose of its sanctification.

At this small, ordered spot in the midst of a wilderness world, in the various rituals, God works toward the objective of a world that once again can be called "very good." Having the priests of the sanctuary go about their appointed courses is like having everything in creation perform its liturgical service—the sun, the trees, human beings. The people of Israel assuming their creation-given responsibilities in daily life are participant with God in making the creation once again correspondent to God's intentions.

The Book of Numbers

Numbers centers on the problems and possibilities of shaping a community identity in tune with God's intentions for the creation. Israel, as a long-oppressed community, had a deeply ingrained identity as "slave"; it does not have the resources to move quickly to a "slaves no more" mentality. God must be at work to enable them to "walk erect" once again (Lev 26:13). The period of wandering is, at least in part, a necessary buffer between liberation and land for the sake of shaping such an identity. This identity does not come easily for Israel or for God; even the most meticulous preparations for the journey are not able to make things go right. One can take the people out of Egypt, but it proves more difficult to take Egypt out of the people. The familiar orderliness of Egypt seems preferable to the insecurities of life lived from one oasis to the next. In other words, the key problem proves not to be the keeping of the law, but an inability to rest back in the arms of the God who has brought freedom and keeps promises.

The book of Numbers, named for its census lists, is the most complex of the Pentateuchal books. Various types of literature are represented—lists, itineraries, various statutes, ritual and priestly prescriptions, poetic oracles, wilderness stories, and even a well-known benediction (6:22-27). Laws are integrated into each stage of the story; they provide for an ongoing ordering of the community as it meets new situations. The positive opening and closing sections of the book enclose a sharply negative picture (10:11–25:18).

Moreover, some Numbers texts border on the bizarre, with talking donkeys, curses from a non-Israelite diviner turned into blessings that have messianic implications, the earth swallowing up people, bronze snakes with healing powers, an almond-producing rod, an execution for picking up sticks on the sabbath, Miriam turning leprous, repulsive instructions for discerning a wife's fidelity, and a judgment on Moses for very obscure reasons. One is tempted to claim that these strange goings-on were constructed to match the incredible response of the community to its salvation. To complicate these matters, God is often depicted in ways that challenge traditional understandings; at times it appears that God's identity is in the process of being shaped, too.

The origin of Numbers is also complex. Most scholars consider it to be a composite of sources (oral and written) from various periods. The book itself speaks of the "Book of the Wars of the LORD" (21:14) and ballads (21:27-30). The Priestly writing, with its interest in worship and priesthood, is most clearly identified (in perhaps several redactions). Other sources (e.g., J and E) are difficult to distinguish; it is best to speak of an older epic tradition. Blocks of texts with three primary locales (Sinai [1:1–10:10], Kadesh [13–20], Moab [22–36]) could reflect a way in which traditions were gathered over time. Beyond this, editorial activity seems unusually common.[4]

The movement through Numbers constitutes a journey toward the fulfillment of the land promise, with all the problems faced along the way in spite of careful preparations. Numbers tracks this journey in three stages, from Sinai (1:1–10:10), through the wilderness (10:11–21:35), to the plains of Moab east of the Jordan (22–36), where the people remain through Deuteronomy.

The strategy of Numbers focuses on two census lists. The book opens with a census of the generation that experienced the Exodus from Egypt and the giving of the law. They prove to be unfaithful, are prohibited by God from entering the land, and die out in the wilderness. The second census (26) records the members of the new generation; as a sign of God's faithfulness to ancestral promises, they will enter the promised land. This new generation is the audience for the book of Deuteronomy.

Looking more closely at the narrative flow, 1:1–10:10 brings the Sinai stage of Israel's story to a close. It describes various preparations for moving through the wilderness to the land of promise; every command of God regarding the organization of the traveling camp is followed to the letter, especially regarding the sanctuary and its leadership. This is a community ordered in all ways appropriate to God's dwelling in the center of the camp (5:3). The Aaronic blessing (6:22-27) is pronounced over the people: "The LORD bless you and keep you; the LORD make his face to shine upon you, and be gracious to you; the LORD lift up his countenance upon you, and give you peace." This benediction is given by God to be spoken over the people during a wilderness journey to be led by God himself (9:15-23). One is given to wonder how anything could go wrong.

The wilderness stories in Numbers (10:11–25:18) are similar in form and content to those in Exod 15–18; once again we hear of manna, rocks producing water, battles with desert tribes, and seemingly nonstop complaints. Yet, Numbers is different. The complaints in Exodus are tolerated, as if in understanding that a long-oppressed people is entitled to grumble. Numbers expresses and assesses them differently, perhaps because of the golden calf apostasy. When faced with the wilderness and the dangers of entering the land, the center no longer holds: obedience to God's command turns to rebellion; trust becomes mistrust; the holy is profaned; order becomes disorder; the future of the people of God is threatened. God's judgment is visited upon them (14:32-33) and, finally, in the wake of apostasy, a golden calf revisited, the old generation dies off in a plague (25:9). Even Moses and Aaron mistrust God and are prohibited from entering the land (20:12); only the faithful scouts, Caleb and Joshua, and the young are allowed to do so (26:63-65).

God's judgmental responses in Numbers are well illustrated in chapter 14. God voices a lament (14:11), echoing those of the people and Moses (11:11-14). God does not remain coolly unaffected. The word of judgment is spoken not with the icy indifference of a judge, but with the mixed sorrow and anger of a lover who has been wounded. That God's lament is repeated in 14:27, interrupting the announcement of judgment, reinforces this understanding.

God responds favorably to Moses and forgives Israel (14:20); but forgiveness, while it ameliorates the effects of sin (they are not annihilated), does not cut off all consequences. Hence, the old generation dies in the wilderness and their children suffer the results of the adults' infidelity (14:33). This reality is true for all acts of forgiveness; the consequences of sin, which can affect the innocent, need ongoing salvific attention (e.g., abusers may be forgiven, but the effects of the abuse do not thereby disappear). Numbers 21:4-9 provides another illustration. Even though the people have repented (and presumably been forgiven), the snakes are not removed nor kept from biting. In other words, the effects of sin continue, but God works on those effects by providing a means (an Egyptian medical technique with which the promise of God is associated) in and through which to heal those who are bitten (cf. the combination of prayer and medicine in 2 Kgs 20:1-7).

God announces the judgment (14:21-25) and details that judgment in moral-order terms ("what goes around comes around"). A key verse is 14:28, "I will do to you the very things I heard you say." In effect: your will be done, not mine. Their desire for death in the wilderness (v. 2) is granted (vv. 32-33); their desire for a return to Egypt (vv. 3-4, a reversal of the Exodus!) is brought close to hand (v. 25); the children who they claim will become booty in the land (v. 3) suffer that fate, but at their own hands (v. 33) rather than in the land (v. 31); they want different leaders (v. 4), and they will get them (v. 30). Judgment is understood to be intrinsic to the evil deed; God does not introduce it into the situation. God does not act arbitrarily but facilitates a consequence that correlates with the deed. One might speak of a wearing down of the divine patience in view of 14:22; the other side of the coin is that persistent negative human conduct will in time take its toll, and God will see to the proper functioning of the moral order.

Integrated with these journey reports are various statutes, focused on purification, the need for which grows out of these experiences (15; 18; 19). They are "perpetual statutes throughout your generations" (e.g., 15:15), so they constitute a hopeful sign. So also do the oracles of the diviner Balaam (22–24), as God blesses the insiders through this outsider. Ironically, these oracles gather the clearest references to the ancestral promises in Numbers (see below); it is almost as if no Israelite, including Moses, has sufficient standing left to bring such a blessing.

In 22:1 the people of God arrive in the plains of Moab, just across the Jordan River from the promised land. They will remain here through the rest of the Pentateuch. After the second census, Num 26–36 presents an entirely positive picture. No deaths, no murmurings, and no rebellions against the leadership or God are in view; it is a time of waiting for the land. Various statutes are woven into the story, especially regarding worship, vows, land apportionment and boundaries, levitical cities, cities of refuge, and inheritance issues. These concerns anticipate a future in the land of promise, where God will (continue to) dwell among the people (35:34); the community is to so order its life that this dwelling place of both God and people will not be polluted.

The issue of who speaks for God becomes an issue during the journey. Challenges to Moses' leadership by the people are intensified in Numbers, when other leaders also take up the argument. The issue is voiced most sharply by Miriam and Aaron: Has God spoken only through Moses? Has he not spoken through us also? (12:2; cf. 16:3). The answer to the first question was given in 11:16-30. God's spirit was shared with seventy elders; they proceed to prophesy, if only once. Moses abruptly puts down those who would try to stop such speaking: "Would that all the LORD's people were prophets!" God's spirit will also rest upon Joshua (27:18) and it even rests upon the outsider Balaam (24:2-4, 15-16). God is not captive to a one-way street into this community; indeed, if need be, God will go around the chosen to get a word through. But Moses does have a special relationship with God and challenges to his role are not countenanced.

God communicates to and through Moses often in Numbers; indeed, 7:89 speaks of Moses' contact with God in an almost routinized way. In 12:8 God himself claims for Moses a unique mouth-to-mouth or face-to-face encounter (see Exod 33:11; Deut 34:10). Moses actually "beholds the form of Yahweh" (as in Exod 24:9-11; cf. 33:21-22; 34:5-6) and lives to tell others about the experience. Given the integrity of God's relationship with Moses, God honors his contribution as an important ingredient for shaping the future. Indeed, in view of such interaction God may move from (preliminary) decisions already made (Num 14:19-20; cf. Exod 32:9-14). But such divine openness to the future will always be in the service of God's unchanging goals for Israel and the creation.

Israel's time in the wilderness is finally shaped by God's extraordinary patience and mercy, and the divine will to stay with Israel in this time of their adolescence as children of God. Coping with "teenagers" is no easy task, even if the parent is God (cf. Hos 6:4). No divine flick of the wrist is capable of straightening them out without compromising their freedom. If God wants a mature child, the possibility of defiance must be risked. Parent and child even do a certain amount of "testing" of one another (see Deut 8:2). But it soon becomes clear that the process of maturation will take longer than a single generation. God will not compromise in holding Israel to high standards, for the sake of the creation.

The Book of Deuteronomy

Deuteronomy is both an ending and a beginning. It recalls the ancestral promises and the Exodus deliverance, retells events experienced by the people at Sinai and in the wilderness, and looks forward to the time in the promised land (and beyond). Deuteronomy provides an interpretive lens through which to view what precedes and what follows.

Deuteronomy ("second law") derives from the Greek translation of a Hebrew phrase in 17:18, "copy of the law." This translation correctly conveys that Deuteronomy (a) is a law that follows upon that given at Sinai (29:1); (b) recasts various stories regarding Sinai and the wanderings as well as laws from Exodus, including the Decalogue; (c) understands that God's law is not a matter given once and for all; it was integral to life before Sinai and develops after Sinai in view of the needs of new times and places; (d) has an authoritative role in how the first law is to be interpreted. These features help explain its association with Moses, which is more a theological claim about its status in the community than a historical judgment (cf. the relationship between the U.S. Constitution and its amendments).

Regarding the origin and formation of Deuteronomy there is both agreement and dispute. Substantial agreement exists in linking (a form of) Deuteronomy with the lawbook found in the temple during a reform in the reign of Josiah (640–609 BCE). Deeply moved by this book in view of the disparity between its contents and Israel's religious practice, Josiah intensifies his reform efforts (see 2 Kgs 22–23). The close correspondence between these efforts and Deuteronomy supports this link (e.g., the suppression of idolatry and the centralization of worship). Another point of agreement is Deuteronomy's relation to the books that follow (Joshua, Judges, 1 and 2 Samuel, 1 and 2 Kings=Dtr, the Deuteronomistic History); the similar style and theological perspective of the final editing of these books indicate a common lineage. Scholars also speak of Deuteronomic editing in Genesis–Numbers (=Tetrateuch), though less agreement exists as to its extent.

These various witnesses suggest that a Deuteronomic School was at work on Israel's traditions during the eighth–sixth centuries BCE. The identity of these leaders is disputed—prophets, scribes, Levites, and officials in Jerusalem have all been suggested. The hortatory style and the interest in spiritual life point toward those charged with the ongoing responsibilities of preaching and teaching. Catechetical interests are also prominent, and a prophetic edge is evident in the strong call to attend to the needs of the disadvantaged. A theological agenda pervades the book; it is an applied theology, concerned to move the hearts and minds of the audience. At heart, the book focuses on the proper relationship between Israel and its God, essential if Israel is to have a future. It is likely that the book should be associated with a group of like-minded individuals, drawn from several leadership groups, who were steeped in Israel's religious traditions and deeply committed to its spiritual health.

Although scholars agree that Deuteronomy developed over a long period of time, less consensus exists regarding details. One plausible scenario: a core of the material is to be tracked back to religious centers in the northern kingdom; after its destruction in 721 BCE, dispossessed leaders fled south with their traditions. There they joined with other sympathetic leaders, and together they were instrumental in the (abortive) reform efforts under Hezekiah (2 Kgs 18:1-8). Forced underground during the reign of the apostate Manasseh (687–642 BCE), they resurfaced under Josiah. But the hopes for reform were dashed with the death of Josiah in 609 BCE and increasing military pressures from the Babylonians, which led to the destruction of Jerusalem in 587 BCE and exile to Babylon. Yet, these traditions continued to be nurtured over the course of these years, for the destruction and the exile seem to be known to the framers of the book (4:25-31; 28–31). So, one might speak of a series of expansions to a basic core of the book (chaps. 5–26?) over the course of several centuries, being brought to completion in the wake of the events of 587 BCE. Members of this school also were at work editing the traditions in Joshua–Kings (Dtr), perhaps producing two editions, one during the time of Josiah and one late in exile (561 BCE is the latest date in 2 Kgs). The opening section of Deuteronomy (1:1–4:40) may have been composed to introduce the entire corpus of Deuteronomy through Kings.

These developments may explain the depth of the warnings of the book and the need for a faithful response; Israel's very survival is at stake.

Until this point the Pentateuch has presented the law as the word of God to Moses (except the Decalogue); in Deuteronomy it is presented as the word of Moses to the generation about to enter the land of promise. Hence, it is a more public word. This elevates the status of Moses, but more basically it lifts up the role of the human in the ongoing task of interpreting the word of God. Even more, it presents a rhetorical strategy for bringing that word of God to *public* expression (see below, "The Sense of the Ending"). Superscriptions set out the addresses, perhaps as many as six (1:1-5; 4:44-49; 6:1; 12:1; 29:1; 33:1).

The first address (1:1–4:40) remembers Israel's journey from Sinai to Transjordan; it gives a realistic picture of a people whose loyalty to God is deeply divided. It concludes with an exhortation on the importance of fidelity in view of both divine command and promise (4:1-40). The entire text is personalized in such a way that every generation can identify with the "you" or the "us/we." The second address (4:44–5:33) makes clear that the new generation stands in fundamental continuity with the old in terms of the divine commands and commitments. The Decalogue (5:1-21) sets the enduring values for all laws that follow (and, by implication, any other laws that might be developed over time). As such, its redactional placement and function are exactly the same as the Decalogue in Exod 20 (see above). The gracious reason for the law is stated clearly: "so that you may live, and that it may go well with you, and that you may live long in the land" (5:33).

Chapters 6–11 are exhortations on the centrality of the first commandment. They are introduced by the *Shema* ("Hear"; 6:4-5), "Hear, O Israel: The LORD is our God, the LORD alone. You shall love the LORD your God with all your heart, and with all your soul, and with all your might." Note the various translation options in the NRSV footnotes. This positive restatement of the first commandment (5:6-7), centers on fidelity to the one and only God. To love with heart, soul, and might engages the entire person in a decisive, passionate, and intense fidelity to this God and to no other. This commandment will definitively shape the telling of Israel's story that follows (Dtr), not least because it is the root of Israel's history of failure. At the same time, it provides Jesus with language to speak of the center of the faith (Luke 10:27).

Chapters 6–11 explore what this fidelity entails from various perspectives, including historical retrospects; they make clear that the heart of the matter for Israel and for God lies with the first commandment. The section climaxes in a key question, "So now, . . . what does the LORD your God require of you?" (10:12; see the similar formulation in Mic 6:8). The rich and powerful response in 10:13-22 sets forth the integral relationship between love of God and love of "stranger" (cf. Lev 19:18, 34; a combination also used by Jesus, Mark 12:28-31), grounded in and motivated by God's saving deeds.

The section 12:1–28:68 contains various statutes that more closely specify the core values of the Decalogue for life in the land of promise. Without attempting to exhaust the matter, they express what God requires regarding love of God and love of neighbor. The statutes are introduced and concluded with matters of worship; the relationship with God is key to all other relationships. Chapter 12 stresses the centralization of Israel's worship life as a strategy for protecting Israel's faithfulness; chapter 26 emphasizes that life in the land is to be centered in a grateful response to God's saving deeds. These chapters bracket a series of laws that touch base with the myriad of life's details, including the character of leadership, various religious and social institutions, the conduct of war, food and clothing, property and animals, and marriage and family life. Woven throughout are special concerns for the first commandment and care for those who are less fortunate (the widow, the orphan, the resident alien, the Levite). The hortatory rhetoric is especially intense when these concerns are touched upon (read 15:1-11). Life with God and life with the other are inextricably interconnected.

This section concludes with blessings and curses that stress the seriousness of Israel's relationship with God and with the other (27–28). The language of the curses is strong, even repulsive (e.g., cannibalism), but those who know something of the history of the twentieth century—from ethnic cleansing to the ravishing of the environment—know that the consequences of human sin can be devastating. What Israelites say and do in the various aspects of their daily lives truly count for something; the future of Israel, indeed the future of the entire creation, is at stake.

The centerpiece of the final sections (29–34) is a second covenant (see below), established with the new generation as a supplement to the Sinai covenant (29–30), followed by various covenant-making provisions (31) and words and acts designed to provide for a future upon the death of Moses (32–34).

The purpose of Deuteronomy is difficult to discern, not least because its genre is not self-evident. *Torah* is the most common self-description, but its use shows that it means more than "law" or "statute," or even "instruction" in its basic sense. In 1:5 and 4:44 Moses is to set forth the *torah*, but what follows is mostly story (1–3) and hortatory address (6–11). Even in chapters 12–26 the word *law* does not adequately express what is presented (read, e.g., 15:1-11). This book would not have constituted a code to be used for legal decisions by Israelite judges or elders. The statutes are more witnesses to the will of God than prescriptions with statutory force. The hortatory rhetoric in particular suggests that these statutes constituted but one source for a more fundamental agenda.

The purpose of Deuteronomy relates to the needs of the new generation. These people not only are to be taught the basics of the tradition, they must take it to heart and live in accordance with it, if they are to move into the future with courage and confidence (Josh 1:7-9). Heeding "the words of this *torah*" is crucial, not only in view of the infidelity of the old generation, but also because of their own sinful propensities (Deut 31:21-29).

In view of this agenda, Deuteronomy could be called a community constitution or a religious education tract or a reform document. Dennis Olson's designation of the book as "catechesis" is helpful; for him it is "a foundational and ongoing teaching document necessitated by the reality of human death and the need to pass the faith on to another generation."[5] Yet, for all the focus on teaching, the book's basic concern is more explicitly religious; the tradition is not simply to be taught but inwardly appropriated. It is not simply a matter of the *fides quae* (the content of the faith), but of the *fides qua* (faith itself). The very relationship with God is at stake; nothing could be more fundamental. As 6:2 puts it, "that you and your children and your children's children, may fear the LORD your God all the days of your life, and keep all his decrees and his commandments." Hence, Deuteronomy is best understood as *spiritual direction*. Such a phrase more adequately describes a book that is so personal in its religious expression and so rich in its spiritual depth. But this spirituality is not simply inward-looking or God-directed; it incorporates a lively concern for a faith that is active in love, especially toward the less advantaged. Moreover, in the face of all that is potentially destructive of this spirituality, all of Israel's individual and institutional resources (judges, kings, priests, prophets, 16:18–18:22) must be readied to protect it.

This purpose is cast in intergenerational terms (6:2-9; cf. 4:9-10; 11:19). Not only are the people to keep these words in their own hearts, they are to transmit them to the next generation; they are to recite them, talk about them in every walk of life, write them down, and display them on their very selves and on their property so that others can see them. Even the questions of children are brought into play (6:20-25; cf. Exod 12:26; 13:14-15): "When your children ask you in time to come, 'What is the meaning of the decrees . . . that the LORD our God has commanded you?' then you shall say to your children, 'We were Pharaoh's slaves in Egypt, but the LORD brought us out of Egypt with a mighty hand . . . to fear the LORD our God.'" The book is not designed simply to transmit a fixed tradition; it is concerned about the *meaning* of that tradition down through the ages.

In addition, Moses' words are to be written down and read every seventh year to the entire community: "Assemble the people—men, women, and children, as well as the aliens residing in your towns—

so that"—and note the religious interests—"they may hear and learn to fear the LORD your God and to observe diligently all the words of this law, and so that their children, who have not known it, may hear and learn to fear the LORD your God" (31:12-13).

In service of this purpose, Moses employs a rhetorical strategy for impressing these materials upon heart and mind (see below). They are presented as orally delivered addresses, not as written documents. The book is directed to "you," to "the heart," "today." The language is relational, personalized for everyone. Its use of vocatives and its calls to hear and heed, to watch and remember, are designed to engage the reader at more than intellectual levels. The "you" is at times singular and at times plural, perhaps as a device to engage readers in both their individual and communal levels of self-understanding.

Leading Themes in Exod 19–Deut 34

1. The Ancestral Promises and Israel's Covenant

Exod 19–40

Israel has been identified as "my [God's] people" throughout the Exodus narrative (esp. chaps. 3–10), even "my (firstborn) son" (4:22-23). These people God "remembers" in 2:24 and 6:4-5, in view of the covenant established with Abraham *and his descendants* (Gen 17:7). The Sinai covenant (Exod 24:1-8) does not establish the God-Israel relationship. As with other major covenants (Noah, Abraham, David), the Sinai covenant is made with those who have already been elected and delivered and have responded in faith and worship. Sinai is a more specific covenant within the Abrahamic covenant; the latter remains in place throughout the narrative (32:13). The focus of the Sinai covenant has to do with vocation (see below).

The common scholarly view that the Sinai covenant is conditional should be reconsidered. This viewpoint is based upon texts such as Exod 19:5, "If you obey my voice and keep my covenant, you shall be my treasured possession." But, what does it mean to "obey my voice and keep my covenant"? The reader has encountered this language before. The formulation in 15:26, "If you will listen carefully . . . do . . . give heed . . . keep," provides a general guideline by which

Israel's relationship with God can be tested (cf. 16:4). This text does not assume that a body of laws exists for Israel, nor does 19:5. Rather, both texts refer to statutes that God may put forward as time goes on, those that are given as a body (chaps. 20–23) and those that emerge in specific life situations (as in 15:25-26; 16:28-29; 18:16, 20). Hence, when laws are given at Sinai they do not exhaust what it means to do the will of God; new laws will certainly be needed for new times and places, and older laws may need to be revised. Sinai fits into a God-Israel relationship in which obedience is *already* an integral component. This makes it clear that to obey the voice of God entails more than obeying the laws given at Sinai. Obedience is a way of exhibiting trust in the God who speaks the word in *any* time or place (for a similar NT perspective, see 1 John 2:3-6).

The phrase *keep my covenant* is not new to the story either; it is integral to the unconditional Abrahamic covenant (Gen 17:9-10), as is "obey my voice" (Gen 22:18; 26:5). To keep covenant *is* to obey God's voice, but with the more specific reference back to Abraham. The only references to covenant in Exodus to this point (2:24; 6:4-5) are Abrahamic, and it is best to so understand 19:5. Israel *as a community* is now to respond as Abraham did. The phrase means being faithful to the relationship with God in which the people stand; that is a responsibility more extensive than obedience to the laws now to be given at Sinai.

The people's response in 19:8, "Everything that the LORD has spoken we will do," ought not be collapsed into the response in 24:3-7. The response of 19:8 is a commitment to obey any words God may command over time; given the personal character of God's language in 19:4-6, the people commit themselves more to God than to specific laws. When the specificity of the Sinai law does come into view, the people respond in terms of their prior promise (24:3-7).

What does "if" mean? There are several possibilities. It could specify a means by which to become God's people; but, as we have seen, their chosen status is already in place. The "if" could be matter-of-fact in nature; that is, obeying the voice of God will have the effect of an ongoing close relationship as a matter of course. It is implied that this closeness could be adversely affected (15:26 speaks of negative effects, but not of loss of status as God's people). This seems a likely interpretation, but another dimension is close at hand. The condition is that an unfaithful people would not be the kind of people God calls them to be, bearing forth God's purposes in the world. For Israel to be vocationally faithful, it must obey God's voice and be loyal to the relationship in which it stands. Israel is to keep covenant for the sake of the world (34:10).

Moses' intercession in 32:13 assumes that, even in the wake of apostasy, the Abrahamic covenant still stands. That God agrees with Moses is clear from the repentance of judgment in 32:14, though it is evident already in God's word about beginning over with Moses (v. 10). God's promise to Abraham is not conditional; even Deuteronomic theology holds to such a perspective (Deut 4:31; 30:1-10; Judg 2:1; 1 Sam 12:22). God's promises will never be made null and void as far as God is concerned. Though a generation that rejects God might not live to see the fulfillment, the promise remains (Lev 26:44-45). God's promise to the community is ever-lasting, though participation in its fulfillment is not guaranteed to every individual within the community. The promise is always there for the believing to cling to, and such persons can be assured that God will ever be at work to fulfill that promise.

Leviticus

Leviticus 26 is key to understanding what has preceded. As in Deut 28, two possible futures are presented. Initially, the positive possibility is stated (vv. 3-12), and this in personal and relational terms. The purpose of "walking in *my* statutes and . . . *my* commandments" is articulated: "I . . . I . . . I will walk among you, and will be your God, and you shall be my people" (26:3-12). God will not simply "dwell" among the people, God will "walk" among them (see Gen 3:8; 5:22-24; 6:9). This mutuality in walking suggests a closeness, even intimacy of relationship. This language of "walking" linked with being God to Israel recalls the ancestral promises (see Gen 17:1, 7; 48:15), as does reference to the ancestral covenant in verses 42-45. Even the potential judgment is articulated in terms of a walking in conflict (26:21-28, 40-41 RSV).

The negative future is outlined at greater length (vv. 14-45). This future is not as clear as it will be in Deut 28–32, but it would be clear for an audience (such as the exiles) that could read some of the details of their own experience on the page. They would understand that these negative possibilities have become a reality for them, and hence the potential for it happening *again* needs to be guarded against. The language is almost more matter-of-fact than threat, though it seeks to instill in readers the seriousness of the covenant relationship. Their response in worship and life will affect every dimension of their individual and communal lives, positively or negatively.

That the ancestral promises remain in view throughout Leviticus can be seen in the references to the land as the context for life with God (e.g., 14:34; 18:3); chapter 26 picks up on many descendants and the ancestral covenant (26:9, 15, 42-45), including the words "I will be your God, and you shall be my people" (26:12, 45). These references show that the covenant is not finally conceived in conditional terms. While the people of God can break the covenant from their side (26:15), God will not break the covenant with them (26:42, 44). Israel is assured that God will not abandon God's people, come what may (26:44-45). This word would assure readers who had enduring questions about their future.

Numbers

The book of Numbers presupposes that God is committed to the ancestral promises. Generally, God has "promised good to Israel" (10:29). Specifically, the promise of land is stressed. As Israel leaves Sinai, the goal is the land that God is "giving" (10:29 and often). Conditions regarding fulfillment of the promise are expressed (14:8), but they affect the future of individuals—even an entire generation—but not finally Israel as such (14:22-24, 30-31). Beyond that, the promises are spoken almost exclusively by Balaam: a great nation with kings (24:7-9, 17-19); blessing (22:12; 23:20; 24:9); to be God to them (15:41; 23:21-23); and many descendants (23:10). Balaam, the outsider, expresses these promises most clearly; for him, God keeps promises (23:19).

Israel's mistrust and apostasy in chapters 11–25 complicate the movement toward fulfillment. The scouts sent to spy out the land of Canaan (13–14) bring back a mixed report. The people, rather than rejoice in the minority report of Caleb and Joshua of "an exceedingly good land" (14:7) and trust that God will see to the promise (14:9), are seduced by the negative report (14:36) and plead to return to Egypt (14:1-4); they even call *Egypt* the "land flowing with milk and honey" (16:13)! Again and again, they look backward rather than forward; they trust the deceptive securities of the past more than God's promised future (11:5; 21:5). Hence, they experience disasters that threaten progress toward the goal, including plagues (11:33), an abortive conquest (13–14), and snake infestation (21:6). Balaam seems to be one of the few who trust where the Exodus from Egypt is heading (23:22-24; 24:8, 17-19).

On the other hand, Num 26–36, with the new generation in place, bespeaks confidence in the promises with the apportionment of land not yet conquered (26:53-56; 33:51-56) and the specification of its boundaries (34:1-15). These and other laws (15; 18; 19), put in place to handle emerging issues, imply that a community will exist to tend to such matters (see 15:2). In spite of Israel's infidelities, land possession is assumed and laws are given for that time. In some sense, the ongoing promulgation of *law* is a witness that the *promise* of land will indeed be fulfilled.

Numbers had begun with preparations for battle (1:3); the land would not be Israel's without a fight. Successful battles occur around the edges of Canaan (21:1-3, 21-32; 31:1–32:42). These initial conquests and the settlements in the Transjordan function as a "down payment" on the fulfillment of the promise. They provide an element of hope; this is the beginning of what shall be. At the same time, the possibility of future loss of the land is hinted at (33:56; 35:33-34), a theme struck already in Lev 26.

Deuteronomy

In Deuteronomy, the people of Israel are one people, chosen by God (Deut 7:6-8; 14:2). The language of election, used for kings (17:15) and priests (18:5), is extended to refer to the people. This election is grounded in God's choice of the ancestors *and their descendants* (4:37; 10:15; Gen 17:1-8). The command placed before Israel to "choose life" (30:19) presupposes Israel's status as God's people; having been chosen, Israel can now choose. The statutes are not understood as a means to establish, preserve, or reestablish the relationship with God.

God makes promises to those whom God chooses. For all of the references to law, Deuteronomy's pages are full of promises. God *swore* these promises to the ancestors (over thirty instances); God puts God's own life on the line for the sake of the promises. The most prominent promise in Deuteronomy is the land. It is set from the beginning (1:8) and reaffirmed at the end (34:4). Everything put forth in the book depends on the fulfillment of this promise; Israel's future with God always comes back to the land.

That the land will be possessed in the near future is a certainty (e.g., 26:3), anticipating the book of Joshua. Yet a loss of the land is just as certain; Israel will prove unfaithful and forfeit it (28:63-64; 29:28). The fall of Jerusalem in 587 BCE and Babylonian exile seem to be in view here. At the same time, beyond judgment, God's promise is that Israel will be restored to the land (30:1-5). So, in effect, the promise of land has a double horizon for Israel in Deuteronomy—a near future and a distant future, with a loss in between.

Deuteronomy's land promise assumes the fulfillment of other ancestral promises—many descendants, nationhood, divine presence, blessing, and relationship (1:10-11; 2:7; 4:20; 7:12-13; 10:22; 13:17; 15:4-6; 26:5, 15-19; 28:9-13; 29:10-13; 30:16). Some of these promises have already been fulfilled (descendants, 1:10-11), but they also extend into the future. The fulfillments of God's promises do not lapse.

For all the importance of the past in Deuteronomy, what is at stake is the identity and character of the community as it moves into the future. Israel must "diligently observe" God's statutes in the land they are about to possess (12:1). What people say and do will make a difference, not only to their own future, but to the future of God. Israel's future will depend finally on God's promise, but that does not relieve Israel from the responsibility of a faithful life. For what is at stake is not only the life and health of Israel, but that of the entire creation.

Covenant in Deuteronomy needs further treatment. The book speaks of two covenants, one at Sinai (5:2) and one in the plains of Moab (29:1), and an early form of Deuteronomy is identified as a "book of the covenant" in 2 Kgs 23:2. The new generation has participated in the former (5:3); the Moab covenant, which is not mentioned elsewhere in the OT, supplements the Sinai covenant.

Structural elements comparable to ancient Near Eastern treaties may be observed in chapters 1–28: historical prologue (1–3), covenant stipulations (12–26), and blessings and curses (27–28).

Also to be noted are the provisions for witnesses, periodic reading, the transference from an oral word to a written word, and its deposition in the ark (31).

Though these connections to ancient Near Eastern treaties are present, they have less substantive import than is commonly suggested. In general, it must be stressed that *covenant is a metaphor*, as such it does not fully describe the relationship between God and people. The covenant is much too personally and relationally construed for treaty or agreement language to do it justice. For example, God is not bound to respond to Israel in strictly legal or contractual terms; God is free to exercise patience and mercy.

Relational categories are the framework within which covenant and law must be conceived. Experience has shown that the law can become an impersonal matter, manifested in a debilitating legalism, a "law unto itself." These texts show that law must not be dissociated from the living and dynamic will of the lawgiver.

The Moabite covenant creates an even greater distance from the Near Eastern treaty; it is essentially a renewal of the *Abrahamic* covenant (29:13; cf. 4:31), and the latter plays a role here not unlike it does in Exod 32:13 in the wake of the golden calf debacle. Deuteronomy recognizes that Israel will fail to keep the Sinai covenant (31:29), but also that God's "sworn oath" (29:12, 14) will not let that failure rule the future (see Lev 26:40-45). Judgment will fall, but this covenant assures the people that "when all these things have happened" (30:1)—judgment, exile, *and* repentance—God will "transform the curse into blessing, the command into promise, and the stipulation into gift."[6] The command that the people circumcise their hearts (10:16) becomes a promise that God will do that; God will enable the people to be obedient and the land will prosper (30:6-10). The move into the future entails settlement in the land, removal from the land, and resettlement in the land, *all* experienced by the "you" addressed by the text.

Chapter 31 provides for a written form of these covenants for the continuing community and its leadership; chapters 32–33 sketch poetically the dynamic between old and new that is at work. The song of Moses in chapter 32 provides a "witness against" the people's failure in the face of God's gracious work in their midst; it is parallel to the law (31:21, 26). Chapter 33 fills out the blessings that will follow upon God's actions announced in 30:1-10. God's people will live within the tension provided by certain failure and judgment and certain promise and restoration.

According to Deuteronomy, every generation (29:14-15) must claim both obligation and promise anew for themselves and hear anew the declaration that they are God's people. They cannot simply rest back on the commitments made by any past generation. The faith cannot be transmitted by genetics (cf. Gen 22:16-18); at the same time, in the face of human failure and beyond judgment, God will see to a future for this people, for God keeps promises.

2. Law, Creation, and Redemption

Israel's law, as with ancient Near Eastern law generally, is most fundamentally associated with creation. This may be observed in the symbiotic relationship between social orders (e.g., family, tribe, nation) and cosmic order. Negatively, disobedience of law has adverse effects in both natural and sociopolitical realms (e.g., Lev 26:19-22, 31-34); positively, obedience is a means by which the divine ordering in creation can be actualized in these same spheres (26:4-10). As such, the law is understood basically in vocational terms. That is, it is grounded in God's work in creation and serves God's purposes of life, stability, and the flourishing of individuals and communities. To this vocation Israel is called, for the sake of the creation.

God's creation has been disrupted by sin and its effects; the divine objective in both redemption and law is the reclamation of creation. In attending to the law, Israel joins God in seeking to keep right what God has put right in redemption, and to extend that rightness into every sphere of life. To that end, God's redemptive work empowers Israel in its vocation and provides paradigms and motivations for obedience (see below).

Israel at Sinai is in effect addressed as humans were on the sixth day of creation. In the law, Israel is given tasks in the tradition of Gen 1:26-28: have dominion over the earth. Mosaic law is a fuller specification of the law for a newly redeemed people, a law implicitly or explicitly commanded in creation (Gen 1:28; 2:16-17; 9:1-7). Law is a God-given means by which God's ordering in creation can be realized once again, integrating cosmic and social orders harmoniously. In Leviticus, this view is supported by links with Gen 1: God's separating in creation and priestly obligation (Gen 1:4-7; Lev 10:10); creation "according to its kind" (Gen 1:20-25; Lev 11:14-22); the concern for "seasons" and Sabbath (Gen 1:14; 2:1-3; Lev 23:2-3; 26:2; even for the land, 25:2-5). Israel's obedience thereby links up with God's ordering work in creation and takes on universal import.

The range of the law's concern in this regard includes worship and the broader life of society and nature. Israel's words and deeds in each sphere are world-preserving and world-restoring activities. They are means by which the people of God can (a) take on the characteristics of that new creation in their own life and (b) participate in the divine efforts to reclaim the creation.[7]

Israel's Worship

The tabernacle and associated worship texts are integrated into this creational view. Jon D. Levenson speaks of "the sanctuary as a world, that is, an ordered, supportive, and obedient environment," corresponding to the depiction of the creation in Gen 1.[8] The tabernacle is a microcosm of creation, God's intended world order writ small in Israel, a beginning in God's mission to bring creation to where it is perfectly reflective of the divine will. The people of God can be assured of the continual divine presence, but it finally moves beyond them to encompass the larger world.

In a recent study of Israel's worship at the tabernacle, Frank Gorman demonstrates its creational import. In worship "human beings are called to become participants in the continual renewal and maintenance of the created order."[9] What happens in liturgy is for the sake of the world; it is a world-making activity. Worship is a God-given way for the people of God to participate in the re-creation of a new world. The issue is not simply Israel as a holy community in itself, but its place among the nations, for "the whole earth is mine" (Exod 19:5). The activity of worship may be local, but its concerns and effects are cosmic.

Sacrifices and offerings are a key aspect of this worship (see Lev 1–7). The lack of explicit theological statements in these texts, however, complicates any attempt to draw out their import; the emphasis is upon implementation. Some basic observations may be made.

Offerings are not magically conceived, as if their efficacy is inherent in the performance of the ritual. God provides the rituals in the first place and *in freedom* grants forgiveness in and through them. Moreover, confession of sin is indispensable to the efficacy of the offerings (Lev 5:5-6; Num 5:7; 1 Sam 7:6); forgiveness is available to one who has faith. These factors show that the common distinction between sacrifice and sacrament is not appropriate for these texts. The gracious role of God throughout makes the phrase *means of grace* applicable to what happens in the sacrifices. These are tangible means through which God acts in a saving way on behalf of the faithful worshiper; sacrifices are sacramentally conceived. We are stuck with the word *sacrifice,* however, because it literally describes aspects of the ritual.

The expiatory aspect of the sacrifices needs further attention. The object of the verb *kipper* ("expiate, make atonement") is sin; it is never God. The action effects forgiveness of sin, not divine appeasement. Leviticus 17:11 states: "For the life of the flesh is in the blood; and I have given it to you for making atonement for your lives on the altar; for, as life, it is the blood that makes atonement." The blood as blood is not expiatory, but the fact that it bears life, and God himself provides this key element in the sacrifice. Again, the God-centeredness of the rite becomes apparent. The offerers are the bearers of a gift from God. Yet, what the offerers bring is not inconsequential (see below).

While it is apparently preferred, it is not necessary for life to be taken for expiation to occur (see Lev 5:11-12), nor is any import given to the act of killing. Hence, by definition, expiation does not involve a penalty. The focus is on the rite as a saving event. Moreover, the language of substitution is not explicitly used in these texts; the animal is not a substitute for the bringer of the offering. (The goat in the Day of Atonement ritual in Lev 16 is not understood in substitutionary terms; it is a symbolic vehicle for dispatching Israel's sins into the depths of the wilderness.)

The links made in Lev 5 between the offering brought and what one could afford to bring are important. The close connection between substance ("wealth") and person suggests that the more wealth one has (in a comprehensive sense), the more "self" there is to give (2 Sam 24:24, "I will not offer burnt offerings to the LORD my

God that cost me nothing"). Thus, in the offering the worshipers submit *themselves* to God. The sacrifice is thus a *tangible sign of faith,* a concrete way in which one offers the self to God; no theory of how the worshiper is related to the animal is involved.

Thus it should come as no surprise that, elsewhere in the OT, sacrifices are not considered necessary for forgiveness (as with the Lord's Supper). Repentance and trust in God are sufficient. This is sharply stated in Ps 51:17; a "broken and contrite heart" is the crucial human element. In 2 Sam 12:13 Nathan pronounces absolution upon David following repentance of his sin with Uriah and Bathsheba, with no accompanying sacrifice.

If any idea captures the essence of the sacrificial ritual, it is God's saving action, which restores the individual and community to life and health in relationship to God and to one another.

Later appropriation of these materials by the New Testament (and the church) relates to the theological convictions that inform practice more than to the practices themselves. This would include the understanding of atonement and the use of visible means in and through which God acts on behalf of the faithful worshiper. Yet some specific practices do need continuing attention in the Christian community (e.g., confession of sin).

The Social Order

Another basic creational/vocational concern for Israel is the social order. The law presupposes that human life falls short of what God intended in creation, with deeply negative effects that fall upon the disadvantaged in particular. The law is a means by which the divine ordering at the cosmic level can be actualized in the social sphere.

The stability of the community and its flourishing is a key concern of the law. In Deuteronomy, for example, provisions are made for rituals and worship (14:1–16:17), institutions with appropriate leadership (16:18–21:14), and marriage and family life (21:15-21; 22:13-30; 24:1-5; 25:5-10). Stability in such societal orders is key to meeting the needs of the disadvantaged. This frames the focus evident in the recurring refrain: the resident alien, the orphan, and the widow (e.g., 24:17-22). For Deuteronomy, the needs of these people stem from the devastation of the North (721 BCE) and the near demise of the South when Israel's armies were decimated by the Assyrians. But in the present text this lively concern for the poor and the needy is generalized; "there will never cease to be some in need on the earth" (15:11). This sets an ongoing vocation for the people of God, who has provided blessings to overcome this reality (15:4).

The laws that seek to protect and nurture the poor and the needy are considered among the oldest in the OT. While also attested in ancient Near Eastern law, their frequency in the Old Testament and the intensity with which they are presented evidence their unparalleled significance for both God and Israel. They are grounded most fundamentally in God's own action on behalf of the Israelites enslaved in Egypt (see Exod 22:21; Deut 10:17-19). Caring for the needy is a theological matter for Israel; these commands come from God, not from "city hall," and the integrity of God's *creation* is at stake in the way in which these people are cared for. One could claim that social justice issues, for all their "liberal" associations, are thereby given a deeply "conservative" cast (cf. the appeal of the prophets to these traditions, e.g., Isa 3:13-15).

The passion with which this concern is presented shows how far Deuteronomy moves beyond a law code. This energy has its roots in older law; see Exod 22:21-27: "You shall not wrong or oppress . . . [or] abuse. . . . If you do . . . I [God] will kill you." The intensity can be seen in Deut 15:1-11, with its strong hortatory language: "do not be hard-hearted or tight-fisted toward your needy neighbor. . . . Willingly lend enough to meet the need. . . . Give liberally and be ungrudging." The law is not simply to be obeyed; an open and generous attitude must inform obedience. This concern is to be shown in very specific ways: food (24:19-22), daily wages (24:14-15), loans and interest (24:10-13; 23:19-20), release from debt repayment (15:1-11), and justice in the courts (24:17-18; 16:18-20). Even more, the needy were to be drawn into the heart of Israel's worship life (16:11-14; 26:11; cf. 5:14). While slavery, inconsistently, remains a part of Israel's life and shows the pressure of economic interests (15:12-18), a humanitarian concern is evident (note the advance over Exod 21:1-11).

Land and Animals

Another basic aspect of the law's creational and vocational concern has to do with the land. Descriptions of "the land of milk and honey" are numerous (e.g., Deut 6:10-11; 7:13-14; 8:7-10). This bounty includes the land itself, iron and copper, water from within the earth and timely rainfall, herds and flocks, grains and vines, and fruit trees. All this is a gift from the Creator, a sacred trust from God. Hence, Israel cannot boast (8:17-18); the people have no "natural right" to use these gifts as they please. Their response is to occur at various levels: confess publicly that God is giver (26:1-11), set apart a tithe of the produce (14:22-29), and tend and nurture these gifts. This tending is to range widely, perhaps grounded in the sabbath rest for the animals (5:14; see Exod 23:12). They are to care for stray or hurt or hungry animals (22:1-4; 25:4; see Lev 25:7), protect mother birds for the sake of producing further young (22:6-7), protect fruit trees when a city is under siege (20:19-20; see Lev 19:23-25), and provide rest for the land (see Exod 23:10-11; Lev 25:2-7).

Though these gifts are in fact available apart from Israel's doing, they will not *remain* available if Israel is not faithful to its relationship with God (Deut 11:16-17; 28:22-24, 38-42, 51; 29:22-27; 32:22-24; see Lev 26:19-20, 32). Moral order may adversely affect cosmic order. Indeed, unfaithfulness not only entails Israel's removal from the land and this abundance; the *land itself* will suffer. These texts make an ecological statement. For example, Deut 11:17 (see Lev 26:19) links infidelity to the absence of rain and an unfruitful land; 28:22-23, 38-42 to drought, blight, insects, and worms; 29:22-27 to a burned-out soil unable to support vegetation. This has been a theme since Gen 3:18, where thorns and thistles grow in the wake of human sin (cf. Hos 4:1-3).

The texts do not make explicit the nature of the connection between such effects and the anger of God (Deut 11:17; 29:23-27; 32:22) or the divine curse (28:15-68), that is, how the divine anger is mediated (28:49-57 speaks of other nations). Yet, the language of the curse "coming upon, pursuing, overtaking" (28:15, 45) suggests an inexorability about sin's consequences. That is, God does not introduce these effects; they grow out of the actions themselves (cf. the plagues in Exod 7–12, here experienced by Israel). Yet, God is not removed from this process (e.g., Deut 28:58-68; see Lev 26:16-33). God sees to the moral order that God built into the creation (this complex reality is conveyed by the fact that some verses speak of God as agent, while others do not). Generally, this vision of disaster is rooted in experience, both that of Israel (Assyrian and Babylonian sieges) and that of other peoples (the curses have parallels in Near Eastern treaty documents). Those with ecological sensitivities will recognize modern parallels here; for example, the link between human behavior and polluted natural resources (with rebounding effects upon human health).

The covenant at Moab and the blessing of Moses (Deut 29–33) envision a new day when the land will again be fruitful and yield its increase (30:9; 33:13-16, 19, 28). The land will participate with the people in the effects of God's new day of blessing and salvation (see Lev 26:34-35, 43; cf. Isa 35:1-10).

Other Nations

God's creation-wide purposes are also evident in the way the nations are drawn into the conversation, especially in Deuteronomy. The God who created human beings (4:32), who is God of heaven and earth (4:36, 39; 10:14), drives out nations before Israel (4:34, 38; 7:21-22). God rules over the nations in such a way that Israel can be chosen from among them (7:6-8). But God's care for these non-chosen ones persists. God gives them lands (2:5, 9, 19), indeed dispossesses peoples to do so; explicit parallels to Israel are drawn (2:12). God is active in the world independent of Israel, working deeds of care and deliverance. In fact, Israel is dependent upon such peoples for its life (2:6) and must be alert to the fact that God can work through them *against* Israel (1:44; 28:48-49).

The outsiders are also given a role as observers and assessors of God's work. In Deut 4:6-8 the nations look at Israel's response to the commandments and conclude that they are "a wise and discerning people" (cf. 26:19). Hence, implicitly, the commandments serve as a witness to God among other peoples. In 29:24-28 the questions and the conclusions of the nations regarding divine judgment are given theological stature: These outsiders will know that the judgment has come because Israel has been unfaithful to God. In 32:26-27 (9:28), God expresses concern about how outsiders might respond to acts of divine judgment. In 4:32-34 other peoples are to be asked whether the activity of Israel's God can be compared to any other. This seems to assume the idea, evident in 29:26 and 32:8-9 (cf. 4:19), that Israel's God in creation had allotted other gods to other nations. Such statements retain a remarkable openness to religious expressions other than Israel's; indeed they claim that Israel's God built such a religious pluralism into the created order of things, while simultaneously insisting that for Israel there is no other God besides Yahweh (32:39).

At the same time, Deuteronomy contains texts such as 7:1-2 (cf. 2:34 and 3:6 with 20:13-14) that are virtually genocidal in their ferocity toward others. While such actions are grounded in a concern about infidelity and extreme danger to the future of Israel (7:4; 20:18), and unfaithful Israel did not remove itself from the line of fire (28:15-68), they remain incomprehensible to most modern religious sensibilities. Perhaps the above reflections on the nations begin already to subvert such ideas internally.[10]

Paradigms and Motivations

The motivational language commonly associated with the laws, especially in Deuteronomy, has to do with a reclamation of creation: long life, peace and stability, healthy and prosperous individuals and communities, and a thriving natural order. Again and again, Israel is to obey "so that you may live, and that it may go well with you, and that you may live long in the land" (5:33; cf. 4:40). God commanded the law "for our lasting good, so as to keep us alive" (6:24). The hortatory nature of the material shows that the concern is not to "lay down the law" or "obey because God said so"; these texts seek to persuade, to inculcate, to instill, and to impress upon both mind and heart. God gives Israel reasons to obey that are linked to a fullness of life and the good order of God's creation. To obey the law is eminently reasonable; any right-thinking person could hardly do otherwise. Even outsiders recognize this (4:6). To obey the law is to trust that God knows what is best for individual and community. Obedience is in *Israel's* own best interests.

Obedience is also in the best interests of *the marginalized and the outsider.* As Deut 10:18-19 puts it: God "loves the strangers, providing them food and clothing. You shall also love the stranger, for you were strangers in the land of Egypt." Israel's obedience is motivated by personal experience with the God who issues the command, and the objective is the well-being of those who have not yet received the effects of God's reclaiming work. Israelites are to extend mercy just as God was merciful to them when they were in such straits. This could be called an ethic of gratitude.

This motivation is important because (among other things) it makes clear that obedience of the law is not a means to right relationship with God. As the introduction to the Decalogue shows (Exod 20:2), these statutes are given to those already redeemed. The law thus does not introduce a new form of slavery; indeed, it is a means by which Israel mediates God's creation-reclaiming work to those still held in one kind of bondage or another.

The language of life and well-being is not reward talk, as if obedience would be so rewarded by God. Rather, such benefits are intrinsically related to obedience, that is, they grow out of the deed (as with negative effects, noted above). To live like this will have such effects; God made the world to work this way. Such effects are not inevitable, of course; life is not that consistent. But, generally speaking, obedience will lead to a fuller life, more in tune with God's intentions in creation.

The Dynamic Character of Israel's Law

A key structural matter in Exodus–Deuteronomy is the interweaving of law and narrative.[11] The law does not stand as an external code but is integrated with Israel's ongoing story. In Exodus, for example, the reader moves from story (19) to law (20:1-17) to story (20:18-21) to law (20:22–23:33) to story (24) to law (25–31) to story (32–34). The following interpretive implications are highlighted by this integration of genres:

—Law is more clearly seen as another gift of God's graciousness for the sake of life and well-being rather than burden;

—Obedience is seen not as a response to the law as law, but as a response to the story of all that God has done;

—The story shows that the law is given to those already redeemed, as a way of doing justice to the relationship with God in which Israel already stands, not as a means to achieve salvation;

—The law is more personally and relationally conceived when part of a story;

—The law is not rigidly fixed but moves with the story—new occasions teach new duties;

—The story gives to the law a vocational character, a promoting and enhancing of the purposes of God for the creation decisively reclaimed by God's narrative deeds;

—The shape that the law takes in Israel's life is to be measured by the shape of the narrative action of God (be merciful, as God has been merciful);

—The basic motivation for obeying the law is drawn from Israel's narrative experience with God rather than from abstract ethical argument or divine imperative;

—That God is subject in both law and narrative provides for a continuity of divine purpose, grounded in the personal will of God.

These implications show that the law is understood not in static terms but as part of a dynamic reality within a living community which, at the end of the Pentateuch, stands ready to move on. Law intersects with life as it is, filled with contingency and change, complexity and ambiguity. Law takes experience into account while remaining constant in its objective: the best life for as many as possible. This means that new laws will be needed and older laws recast or set aside. For example, Deuteronomy reflects later institutions such as prophecy (18:15) and kingship (17:18). Moreover, the admixture of civil, moral, and cultic laws within the texts shows that, unlike a modern tendency, this understanding does not separate life out into such neat categories; the will of God has to do with every sphere of life. So, various types of law from diverse life settings have been integrated into a single fabric. In the service of life, the law is as complex and as dynamic as the God-people-world interrelationship.

This dynamism is also present in the area of worship. In Lev 5:7-13, for example, the wealth of the offerer is taken into account in determining the type of offering. Individual situations affect how the law is to be applied. Such openness to difference witnesses to a dynamic understanding of law.

Another important witness to this understanding is the way in which Deuteronomy recasts the laws (at least nineteen cases) in Exod 21–23. For instance, the laws concerning slaves in Exod 21:1-11 are revised in Deut 15:12-18; note especially 15:17, where one is now to "do the same with regard to your female slave." Such tensions and inconsistencies among the laws are not ironed out or considered a threat to the law's integrity. Rather, old and new remain side by side as a canonical witness to the process of unfolding law. Hence, *development in the law* is just as canonical as individual laws or the body of law as a whole. At the same time, all remain the laws of God—older words from God and newer words from God. Just because laws are from God does not make them immutable, not least because God revises God's own laws; but the retention of both in the canon means that each such word from God is to be considered carefully in moving toward any new formulation. While the law provides a compass for Israel during its journeys, integration with the story means that it does not claim to know absolutely God's will for every future. God will have new words to speak in view of life's ongoing twists and turns, for the purpose of the law is the life, health, and well-being of an ever-changing community and each individual therein. The God who personally interacts with the people throughout their wanderings is the one who gives the law for the sake of the best possible journey.

The Sense of the Ending of the Pentateuch

The way in which a story ends is important for the interpretation of the whole. Indeed, some people read the end of a book first so as to read the whole with a better idea of what the work is trying to do. The ending of the Pentateuch should be considered in terms of both Deuteronomy as a whole and its last chapters. To this end, we seek to discern the rhetorical strategy employed and how readers might experience the book in view of their life situation.

In Deuteronomy, a somewhat idealistic picture of Israel is presented that pushes beyond historical specifics and becomes applicable to *every generation of Israelites.* As 5:3 puts it, "Not with our ancestors did the LORD make this covenant, but *with us,* who are all of us here alive today." Every generation would understand that the "with us" applies to them and that they are the addressees of both the laws and the promises.

This actualizing tendency (making the past real in every present time) is reinforced by the use of the second-person pronoun. The distinction between old and new generations is made (1:35; 2:14), but at the same time it is collapsed. The "you" of the Exodus (4:20) is also the "you" of the land settlement (4:5), and the "you" of the rebellion (1:26) is also the "you" of faithfulness (4:4). All readers would understand themselves as *participants in all phases of this story.* Even more, the "you" includes not only the Israel that lives in the land, but the "you" that is dispossessed from the land (4:25-31) and the "you" that lives through the exile and is restored to the land (30:1)!

To this material may be linked texts associated with worship life. One example is the "place the Lord will choose" (Deut 12:1-28). The place is commonly identified with Jerusalem; yet, the lack of specificity makes it more likely that the identity of the place is left open-ended so that the central sanctuary of any generation would fit. Another example is the Passover (16:1-8), in which the "remembering" effects participation in the Exodus for the "you."

A rhetorical approach also highlights the use of hortatory language. Deuteronomy has even been designated "preached law." This use of language makes clear that it was written to move the readers, to touch not only their minds but their innermost selves. This hortatory character ought not be viewed in isolation from the rest of the Pentateuch. It functions as a particular strategy for impressing upon the reader the importance of hearing *all* that has preceded. Readers are led through the first four books and brought to this point, where the parenetic language now engages them in the fundamental import of what God has been about in their lives, with intense and urgent appeals for present response. To this end, the historical review of chapters 1–3, as well as later retrospects (e.g., chap. 9), catch the reader up in developments that go back through Numbers to Exodus. Earlier hortatory pieces (e.g., Lev 26) prepare for this Deuteronomic strategy. These historical retrospects, combined with future possibilities (e.g., chap. 28) and the enclosure of the law with the promise (4:31; 30:1-5) without relaxing the importance of faithful response, constitute a wide-ranging appeal to both heart and mind.

The ending of Deuteronomy (and here we think of chaps. 29–34) has not often been considered a worthy ending of either Deuteronomy or the Pentateuch.[12] This ending has often been regarded as a series of mixed genres gathered somewhat haphazardly. Indeed, the ending is not a "normal" one; it does not tie things together into a neat package. But what might it mean that the ending contains so many loose ends? For one thing, it creates a sense of uncertainty regarding the future, and it may reflect the situation of readers—exiles—who are at "loose ends" regarding their situation. This kind of ending leaves readers leaning into the future, but wondering what that future might hold.

A comparable appraisal can be made of the content of the ending. The ending defers the fulfillment of the promise; it gives to the Pentateuch the character of an unfinished symphony. The promise is left suspended and the people addressed seem to be dispirited and fearful (31:6, 8). The future is not simply filled with delights; it is fraught with danger. And the danger comes not just from the Canaanites but also from the inner recesses of their own hearts (31:20-29).

The considerable body of law in the Pentateuch, even the ending (Deut 30:11-14), implies that obedience is possible; a community of life and well-being can be created in the land of promise. Human responsibility with respect to such a community is recognized as basic to the shape that the promised future takes. But the same ending subverts that confidence with repeated drumbeats regarding Israel's inclination to infidelity and warnings of consequent disaster (28:15-68; 29:17-28; 30:17-19; 31:16-29; 32:15-35). The people are called to obey, and indeed they often can, but they are also so deeply inclined to disloyalty that they will not finally be able to control their own future or create the order that the law suggests they can. Both law and liturgy will be ongoing "witnesses against" their ability to do so (31:19, 21, 26, 28). Deuteronomy leaves readers wondering what might be in store for this inevitably disobedient people. This creates an ending of no little ambivalence.

The last chapters of Deuteronomy (28–34) have an unusually clear sense of the negative directions Israel's future is likely to take, climaxing with destruction and exile. It is usually concluded that these passages were written in light of the actual experience. This seems likely, but, narratively, they give readers a lens through which they are to interpret the books that follow. These negative futures have not been predetermined from the time of Moses; conditional language punctuates these texts (Lev 26:3-27; Deut 28:1-44, 58-68;

29:18; 30:4, 16-17). Rather, these texts claim that, implicit in the time of Moses, this particular future was a lively possibility.

A few texts, however, make a stronger claim; there *will be* apostasy and judgment (Deut 28:45-57; 31:16-29): "For I know that after my death you will surely act corruptly" (31:29). Such texts are not predictive; rather, they testify to insight into the sinful human condition and its dire effects ("I know well how rebellious and stubborn you are," 31:27, 21; 9:24). This scenario, however, does not go so far as to say that even if Israel were *obedient* this would be its future; this future is still "because" they did not obey (28:45, 47). One key function of Deuteronomy is stated in this connection: "as a witness against you" (31:26); the law will reveal Israel's sin for what it is.

The death of Moses creates an added level of uncertainty. The final verses (34:10-12) recall a glorious past, but it is focused on a person rather than the people. Indeed, Moses is made the subject of words usually reserved for God; it is *Moses* who performed "all the mighty deeds and all the terrifying displays of power" (v. 12; cf. Exod 6:6). Only he has known God "face to face" (v. 10); no prophet holds a candle to him. Joshua is "full of the spirit of wisdom" (34:9), but Joshua is no Moses. Given the loss of Moses, and the propensity of the people to apostasy, this eulogy is not particularly good news. What will they do without Moses and all his mighty deeds? The future does not look so promising. To be left with such an ending is an uneasy, even unnerving experience.

One can observe this disquietude in scholarly assessments of this ending. Scholars have often been moved to create a different ending; they speak of a Hexateuch (or Primary History or Deuteronomistic History). In this way, they get the fulfillment of the promise as the ending, and the story—to their way of thinking— is appropriately rounded off. Is this a way that readers have sought to escape from the unsettling force of the ending?

Yet, the ending does give some basis for hope (29:10-15; 31:1-8; 33:1-29). A genuine sense of expectancy is generated. But it is qualified by the realism of the human condition, so that the people must ground their hope, not in their strength or capacity for obedience, but in the promised presence of God and the certainty of divine faithfulness. Only because God goes with them and keeps promises can they be strong and courageous and be assured that the promises will be fulfilled. And so the basic word at the end of Deuteronomy is: wait on God and hope in God. The way into the promised future is possible only if God is at work, not only in and through this people, but also beyond them and in spite of them.

This sense of an ending, like the word of God more generally, is a two-edged sword. It lifts up the divine promise as basic to Israel's future; but it also makes clear that human fear in the face of uncertainty and death, a transition in leadership, and an inclination to disobedience endangers participation in that promise. The ending is rhetorically designed for a community faced with a situation comparable to the original community on the eve of entry into the land of promise. As such, Deuteronomy's ending is not rhetorically crafted to bring the story to a close; there is a decided open-endedness to the future. But it is still an ending.

The ending of the Pentateuch has parallels with the beginning, providing an inclusio.

The situation of the first human beings standing before God on the morning of creation corresponds to that of the newly redeemed people of God on the eve of the entry into the land. Just as Adam and Eve are created in the image of God and commanded to have dominion in God's creation, so also Israel as God's covenant partner is given responsibilities to further the divine purposes for the life and well-being of the creation. In addition, the prohibition given humankind in Gen 2:16-17, the response to which means life or death, parallels Moses' words to Israel about the commandment (Deut 30:11-20).[13]

In both cases, these commands create a "leaning" toward the future; the human response will shape that future into something different from the present. The commands to have dominion and to "subdue the earth" imply a becoming of creation, that God intends the creation to become something other than what it was at the moment of creation. Within this purpose, God engages the human, the image of God, as cocreator. But, given the violation of the prohibition, God's intentions for the world, while still focused in life and well-being, have become more complex; God now must work within a situation profoundly affected by sin and its evil effects. Yet, God's engagement of the human as cocreator remains in place

(Gen 3:23; 9:1-7; cf. Ps 8); to that end, the law given at Sinai is a fuller particularization of the law given in creation, and that is placed sharply before Israel by Moses (Deut 30:15-20).

The unfaithful response of Adam and Eve to the prohibition resulted in a human condition wherein "every inclination of the thoughts of their hearts was only evil continually" (Gen 6:5; cf. 8:21), and that "inclination" is firmly in place at the end (Deut 31:21, 27). This means that Israel makes its choice (Deut 30:19) from within a situation different from that of their first parents and this reality makes problematic its move into the future. The stories that follow will be deeply colored thereby. At the same time, Deut 30:6-10 envisions a future for Israel when God will give them a new heart, and obedience and faithfulness will follow naturally (see Jer 31:31-34). Hence, the ending of Deuteronomy takes a significant and unparalleled step beyond Eden.

The move from the flood to the post-flood promises is parallel to the disasters of Deut 28 followed by the covenant in chapters 29–32. Despite the fact that the human heart continues to be inclined to evil, and will result in disasters of one kind or another, God chooses to go with the world and Israel (Gen 8:21-22; Deut 29–32). Judgment will not be God's final word for either the world or Israel. The promises are made and, given the divine commitment (Deut 4:31; 30:1-6), will remain intact forever.

Finally, the Mosaic era in some sense constitutes a paradigm for each successive generation of the people of God (see Deut 5:3; 29:14-15). God has chosen Israel, delivered them from bondage, constituted them as a people, and come to dwell in their midst. The vision of Leviticus, with the people of God encamped around the tabernacle, shaped by their deliverance and given instruction for their life as a community, is a pattern for subsequent generations of God's people. Lending support to this notion are the final verses praising Moses, who surpasses all the prophets (Deut 34:10-12). The conclusion of the Pentateuch "designates the Mosaic age as a constitutive and normative narrative."[14]

At the same time, the book of Numbers (especially), with its recurrent testimony to human sin and failure (and God's response thereto), functions to introduce a sharp note of realism into this picture. These realities will intrude again and again into Israel's life, and the books that follow constitute ample testimony to this. While this paradigm remains in the face of such realities (and may inform images of the reign of David, e.g., 2 Sam 7; Ps 72), it does so only as an ideal, something to work and dream toward. The prophets, who are more pessimistic, throw this "dream" onto an eschatological screen (e.g., Jer 31:31-34).

The ending of Deuteronomy sets in place a two-pronged approach to the history of Israel that follows, both curse (28:15-68) and yet the continued articulation of the promises of God. Deuteronomy 4:31 and 30:1-10 (cf. Lev 26:44-45), which have destruction and exile in view, make the strong claim that in spite of Israel's failures God "will not fail you or destroy you or forget the covenant with your fathers which he swore to them" (4:31 RSV), and "from there the LORD your God will gather you, and from there he will bring you back . . . into the land that your ancestors possessed, and you will possess it" (30:4-5).[15]

Notes

1. See J. Milgrom, *Leviticus 1–16* (AB 3; New York: Doubleday, 1991).

2. For details regarding these issues, see R. Nelson, *Raising Up a Faithful Priest: Community and Priesthood in Biblical Theology* (Louisville: Westminster John Knox, 1993).

3. M. Douglas, *Purity and Danger: An Analysis of the Concepts of Pollution and Taboo* (London: Routledge & Kegan Paul, 1966).

4. See J. Milgrom, *The JPS Torah Commentary: Numbers* (Philadelphia: JPS, 1990), xvii-xxi.

5. D. Olson, *Deuteronomy and the Death of Moses: A Theological Reading* (OBT; Minneapolis: Fortress, 1994), 6.

6. Ibid., 128.

7. For details, see T. Fretheim, "The Reclamation of Creation: Redemption and Law in Exodus," *Int* 45 (1991): 354-65.

8. J. Levenson, *Creation and the Persistence of Evil: The Jewish Drama of Divine Omnipotence* (San Francisco: Harper & Row, 1988), 86.

9. F. Gorman, *The Ideology of Ritual: Space, Time, and Status in Priestly Theology* (Sheffield: JSOT, 1990), 230. See also S. Balentine, *The Torah's Vision of Worship* (OBT; Minneapolis: Fortress, 1999).

10. See P. Miller, *Deuteronomy* (IBC; Louisville: Westminster John Knox, 1990), 39-42; T. Fretheim, *Deuteronomic History* (IBT; Nashville: Abingdon, 1983), 68-75.

11. See T. Fretheim, *Exodus* (IBC; Louisville: Westminster John Knox, 1991), 201-7.

12. An exception is D. Olson, *Deuteronomy*.

13. See T. Mann, *Book of the Torah: The Narrative Integrity of the Pentateuch* (Atlanta: John Knox, 1988), 161.

14. J. Blenkinsopp, *The Pentateuch: An Introduction to the First Five Books of the Bible* (New York: Doubleday, 1992), 51.

15. Several segments of this chapter have been drawn from T. Fretheim, *The Pentateuch* (IBT; Nashville: Abingdon, 1996).

Bibliography

Balentine, Samuel. *Leviticus.* IBC. Louisville: Westminister John Knox, 2002.

————. *The Torah's Vision of Worship.* OBT. Minneapolis: Fortress Press, 1999.

Birch, Bruce C. *Let Justice Roll Down: The Old Testament, Ethics, and Christian Life.* Louisville: Westminster John Knox, 1991.

Blenkinsopp, Joseph. *The Pentateuch: An Introduction to the First Five Books of the Bible.* New York: Doubleday, 1992.

Brenner, Athalya, ed. *The Feminist Companion to Exodus–Deuteronomy.* Sheffield: Sheffield Academic, 1994.

————. *Exodus to Deuteronomy: A Feminist Companion to the Bible (Second Series).* Sheffield: Academic Press, 2000.

Brueggemann, Walter. *Deuteronomy.* Abingdon Old Testament Commentaries. Nashville: Abingdon, 2001.

Clines, David. *The Theme of the Pentateuch.* JSOTSup 10. Sheffield: JSOT, 1978.

Douglas, Mary. *Purity and Danger: An Analysis of the Concepts of Pollution and Taboo.* London: Routledge & Kegan Paul, 1966.

Fretheim, Terence E. *The Pentateuch.* IBT. Nashville: Abingdon, 1996.

Gorman, Frank. *The Ideology of Ritual: Space, Time, and Status in the Priestly Theology.* Sheffield: JSOT, 1990.

Levinson, Bernard M. *Deuteronomy and the Hermeneutics of Legal Innovation.* New York and Oxford: Oxford University Press, 1997.

Mann, Thomas W. *The Book of the Torah: The Narrative Integrity of the Pentateuch.* Atlanta: John Knox, 1988.

Miller, Patrick D. *Deuteronomy.* IBC. Louisville: Westminster John Knox, 1990.

Nelson, Richard D. *Deuteronomy: A Commentary.* OTL. Louisville: Westminster John Knox, 2002.

————. *Raising Up a Faithful Priest: Community and Priesthood in Biblical Theology.* Louisville: Westminster John Knox, 1993.

Olson, Dennis. *Deuteronomy and the Death of Moses: A Theological Reading.* OBT. Minneapolis: Fortress, 1994.

————. *Numbers.* IBC. Louisville: Westminster John Knox, 1996.

Patrick, Dale. *Old Testament Law.* Atlanta: John Knox, 1984.

Whybray, R. Norman. *Introduction to the Pentateuch.* Grand Rapids: Eerdmans, 1995.

CHAPTER SIX

"THE PEOPLE OF THE LAND"

Joshua, Judges

From its initial formation as an identifiable, self-aware community, ancient Israel has yearned for and anticipated being settled in the land. According to its normative memory, from its primal interaction with Yahweh, the God who makes Israel possible in the world, Israel has understood that Yahweh's overriding promise to Israel is that Israel will dwell safely in an abundant land, guaranteed by the faithfulness of Yahweh. Indeed, one can say at the outset that Israel in the Old Testament is a land-intoxicated people believing that (a) *land* is indispensable for good communal life and (b) *Yahweh* is a land-giving God. Thus Israel's faith holds *land* and *Yahweh* in intimate connection.

A Long Hope for Land

In our study thus far, we have seen that Israel's most sacred literature, Genesis through Deuteronomy, revolves principally around four themes:

1. *The world as God's creation.* Before Israel comes to its more specific "historical memories," the entire account of Israel's faith is framed by God's governance and guarantee of the whole world:

> In the beginning when God created the heavens and the earth, . . . God blessed them, and God said to them, "Be fruitful and multiply, and fill the earth and subdue it." God saw everything that he had made, and indeed, it was very good. (Gen 1:1, 28, 31)

173

God intends for the entire earth a peaceable, secure, generative existence.

As Israel develops its own faith about the *land of promise,* it is clear that the land is not just real estate or Israel's private property. The land of promise is understood as the full enactment and embodiment of God's will for the earth. Thus the *earth* traditions of creation continue as theological claims for the *land* traditions of Israel.

2. *The promise made to the ancestors* in the book of Genesis. In those treasured narratives, we have seen that Yahweh's recurrent promise to these semi-nomads is that they will receive a good land:

> Go from your country and your kindred and your father's house to the land that I will show you. (Gen 12:1)

> To your descendants I give this land, from the river of Egypt to the great river, the river Euphrates, the land of the Kenites, the Kenizzites, the Kadmonites, the Hittites, the Perizzites, the Rephaim, the Amorites, the Canaanites, the Girgashites, and the Jebusites. (Gen 15:18-21)

> I will make your offspring as numerous as the stars of heaven, and will give to your offspring all these lands. (Gen 26:4)

> The land on which you lie I will give to you and to your offspring; and your offspring shall be like the dust of the earth, and you shall spread abroad to the west and to the east and to the north and to the south. (Gen 28:13-14)

Every generation of ancestors is endlessly assured of the birth of a son who will be an heir to carry the promise of land and eventually to receive the land.

3. *The liberation from Egypt.* This is obviously concerned with Israel's departure from the land of Pharaoh, which is a land of unbearable oppression and abuse. As formulated in Israel's characteristic way, however, the Exodus is not only a *departure* from an unbearable land; it is also an anticipated *entry* into a good land, so that a hoped-for land is an integral part of the Exodus:

> I have come down to deliver them from the Egyptians, and to bring them up out of that land to a good and broad land, a land flowing

with milk and honey, to the country of the Canaanites, the Hittites, the Amorites, the Perizzites, the Hivites, and the Jebusites. (Exod 3:8)

I declare that I will bring you up out of the misery of Egypt, to the land of the Canaanites, the Hittites, the Amorites, the Perizzites, the Hivites, and the Jebusites, a land flowing with milk and honey. (Exod 3:17)

The Exodus will not be fully enacted by Yahweh or fully received by Israel until the new land is assured. And so the concluding Song of Moses anticipates safe settlement:

In your steadfast love you led the people whom you redeemed; you guided them by your strength to your holy abode. . . . You brought them in and planted them on the mountain of your own possession, the place, O LORD, that you made your abode. (Exod 15:13, 17)

4. *The covenant at Sinai.* This binds Israel in radical obedience to Yahweh, in order that the land to which they are going will be alternatively organized according to the purposes of Yahweh. While land is not the principal accent at Sinai, it is unmistakable that the commandments of Sinai pertain to the land where Israel will live according to the holy intentions of Yahweh:

Now . . . if you obey my voice and keep my covenant, you shall be my treasured possession out of all the peoples. Indeed, the whole earth is mine, but you shall be for me a priestly kingdom and a holy nation. (Exod 19:5-6)

I am going to send an angel in front of you, to guard you on the way and to bring you to the place that I have prepared. . . . I will not drive them out from before you in one year, or the land would become desolate and the wild animals would multiply against you. Little by little I will drive them out from before you, until you have increased and possess the land. . . . For I will hand over to you the inhabitants of the land, and you shall drive them out. (Exod 23:20, 29-31)

The entire memory and tradition was apparently codified into a stylized recital (credo), so that all parts of the recital constitute *a hope of land,* and each theme is pressed beyond itself to *the goal of the land* (see, e.g., Deut 6:20-24; 26:5-9; Exod 3:17). We may at the outset observe two factors in this completed tradition that become Israel's primal sacred canon.

First, Israel's faith insistently focused on the *material,* on the real, lived circumstance of life in the world. It is this focus that distinguishes Israel's faith from many other religions that move in the direction of "spiritual" matters removed from lived reality. It is this accent that has taught Israel to pay attention to physical-social-historical existence in the world, so that this faith can never be set apart from the urgent, ambiguous issues of economic and social power. It is, moreover, this accent on the material as the arena of God's importance for Israel that led eventually to the Christian confession of God embodied (incarnated) in Jesus of Nazareth. That is, the subsequent Christian affirmation is possible only in a faith that has always understood that God's engagement with Israel (and with the world) concerns bodily existence in concrete historical communities.

Second, it is to be observed that Israel's narrative faith statement in the Torah is situated *outside the land.* Abraham, Isaac, and Jacob are briefly "sojourners" in the land of promise, but they quickly move out of the land to Egypt. After that, the Israelites are either state slaves in Egypt or desperate wilderness inhabitants. Either way they are not in the land. The Torah, moreover, ends in Deut 34, the final chapter of the narrative text, just outside the land—ready now, finally, to enter the land, receive the promise, and enjoy its well-being.

It is most likely that the final form of the literature of the Torah canon is the product of Israel's sixth-century exile. Given that probability, we may conclude that the Torah canon, with its powerful promises of land, is a faith statement formulated and authorized by exilic Israel in order to sustain the exilic community. Indeed, we may say that *exiles hoping for Yahweh's land of promise* is the characteristic condition of the children of Israel. They are historically landless people living toward the land of promise. It is appropriate that the account of *land entry* in the book of Joshua and *land habitation* in the book of Judges should immediately follow the close of the Torah canon just outside the land.

It is of course true that Israel, in the period of the kings, did possess land. There was a time of being in the land. Thus Israel's memory is always dialectical: *landless* hoping for land/*in the land* but about to lose it. Without land, Israel hopes passionately. With land, Israel possesses precariously.

The Land in Disputatious Reality

The books of Joshua and Judges, as the Old Testament tradition is formulated, are situated in a rather in-between way. In reading them, it is important to notice the position they occupy in the larger narrative presentation of Israel and the transitional function that they seem to perform.

The books of Joshua and Judges are preceded by the five scrolls of the Torah (Pentateuch), as just indicated. Excluding the preliminary materials of the book of Genesis, the Torah materials are essentially the story of Moses and Moses' work in founding the community of Israel at the behest of Yahweh. It is important to recognize that the materials are a *founding document* for Israel. The theological claims made here by Israel and for Israel are its most elemental convictions that persist in every circumstance of faith. These claims arise in part from lived experience but are also in part a confession of faith to which Israel holds passionately, even in the face of experience to the contrary.

When we move beyond the Pentateuch (the first five books), we are moving into a very different literature. Whereas the Pentateuch is organized *in anticipation of the land of promise,* now Israel is prepared to cross the Jordan into the land. It is a common judgment that the books of Joshua, Judges, Samuel, and Kings constitute something of a unified corpus, giving an account of *Israel in the land.* It is a common assumption that all of this material is deeply influenced by the book of Deuteronomy, and so it is called Deuteronomistic History. The connection to Deuteronomy means that all of this material is concerned with the Torah and believes that Torah obedience is the primary condition for entering and keeping the land of promise.

Thus in reading these books, we may suggest a *literature of anticipation of the land* (Genesis–Deuteronomy) and a *literature of possession of the land* (Joshua–Kings). The two together constitute a single presentation of Israel as the people to whom God has given the land of promise.

At the outset of Josh 1, the ideological purity of Mosaic vision is still dominant, for the Torah is featured as the primary resource and criterion for Joshua's mandate in the land:

> Only be strong and very courageous, being careful to act in accordance with all the law that my servant Moses commanded you; do not turn from it to the right hand or to the left, so that you may be successful wherever you go. This book of the law shall not depart out of your mouth; you shall meditate on it day and night, so that you may be careful to act in accordance with all that is written in it. For then you shall make your way prosperous, and then you shall be successful. (Josh 1:7-8)

The mandate is pure theological ideal and is completely unbothered by economic-political-military realities that are yet to come. These verses are presented as God's word to Joshua. After Moses, Israel looked back to the *Torah of Moses* as a focal point of faith.

But actual "entry" into the land turns out not to be as clean and neat as Torah ideology might have suggested. And the reason is that *real land,* unlike theologically *promised land,* is always contested, disputed, and conflictual. That is, there are already other people there who do not yield easily to Israel's theological claim. And therefore to receive the promise, Israel must either engage in military *conflict* with other contestants for the land or *accommodate and compromise.* Either strategy turns out to be a far remove from the simplicity of the Torah promise. Thus it may be suggested that the burden of Joshua and Judges is to adjudicate between the *simple normative claims of the Torah promises* and *the lived ambiguities of life in the world.* Looking back, Israel can rely completely on the Torah promises. Looking forward to Samuel and David, Israel must know that its material setting is endlessly a disputatious one, because the reality on the ground will never concede much to innocent and high ideological claims.

Thus we read this literature of Joshua and Judges as the entry that faith must always make into the complexities of life. It is a journey made by ancient Israel as it formulates its narrative account of its life with Yahweh. It is, moreover, the primary journey that faith must always make as it moves from simple, one-dimensional, childlike claims to the real world, where every such claim is endlessly contested.

Among the Canaanites

Because the story of Israel in Joshua and Judges is on its way to the more secure historical footing of Samuel and Kings, it is unavoidable that scholars should ask *historical questions* of the text: what really happened? It is fair to say that scholars now are much less confident of being able to answer such questions than they were fifty years ago, when there was among us a much greater confidence in the methods and outcomes of positivistic history. Even with such a lessening of confidence, however, it is useful for students of this material to know what the available alternative answers are to historical questions. Much more scholarly attention has been given in this regard to the book of Joshua, so we may focus there, even though the same wonderment and same sorts of answers pertain to the book of Judges. There are conventionally three quite different answers given to the historical questions in the book of Joshua, though the three are by no means mutually exclusive.

1. The older U.S. hypothesis is that the "conquest" of the land of Canaan by Israel under Joshua was a wholesale military onslaught, whereby Israel invaded the land as an effective occupying force and seized much of the land for Israel. This interpretation of the literature was more winsome in an earlier part of the twentieth century when there was more confidence in historical reconstruction on the basis of archaeology. That archaeology shows, so it was claimed, that there was a definite disruption of cultural life in a number of sites that can be identified with biblical places, suggesting a military destruction.

From the outset there have been problems with this hypothesis. Specifically, it was necessary to argue that the city of Ai was confused in the narrative with the city of Bethel (Josh 8:18-29), and it is deeply problematic that there is no recovered evidence to suggest that the site of Jericho was even occupied in the apparent time of Joshua (Josh 6). Beyond these particular problems is the more recent judgment of many scholars that archaeological evidence is mostly not of a character that it may be so readily and specifically correlated with textual references. Very few scholars now have confidence in the capacity of archaeology to suggest such a historical affirmation of biblical texts.

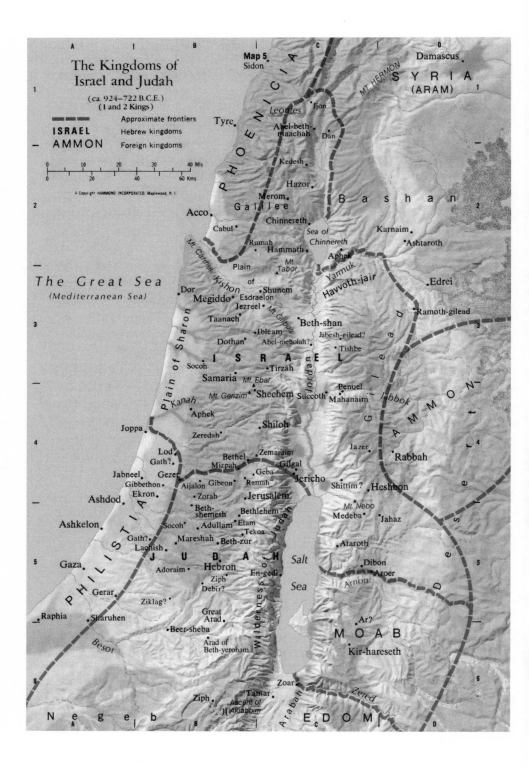

The Kingdoms of
Israel and Judah

(ca. 924–722 B.C.E.)
(1 and 2 Kings)

— — — Approximate frontiers
ISRAEL   Hebrew kingdoms
AMMON   Foreign kingdoms

© Copyright HAMMOND INCORPORATED, Maplewood, N. J.

Map 5

Damascus

SYRIA
(ARAM)

MT. HERMON

PHOENICIA

Sidon

Tyre

Leontes

Ijon

Abel-beth-
maachah

Dan

Kedesh

Hazor

Merom

Galilee

Bashan

Acco

Cabul

Chinnereth

Karnaim

Ashtaroth

Rumah

Sea of
Chinnereth

Hammath

Aphek

Mt. Carmel

Plain

Mt.
Tabor

Yarmuk

Havvoth-jair

Edrei

The Great Sea
(Mediterranean Sea)

Dor

of

Shunem

Megiddo

Esdraelon

Jezreel

Mt. Gilboa

Ramoth-gilead

Taanach

Mt. Kishon

Beth-shan

Dothan

Ibleam

Abel-meholah?

Jabesh-gilead?

Tishbe

Socoh

I S R A E L

Tirzah

Samaria

Mt. Ebal

Penuel

Plain of Sharon

Mt. Gerizim

Shechem

Succoth

Mahanaim

Gilead

Jabbok

Kanah

Aphek

Shiloh

AMMON

Joppa

Zeredah

Jordan

Jazer

Rabbah

Bethel

Zemaraim

Lod

Mizpah

Gilgal

Gath?

Geba

Jericho

Jabneel

Gezer

Aijalon

Gibeon

Ramah

Shittim?

Heshbon

Gibbethon

Zorah

Jerusalem

Ashdod

Ekron

Beth-
shemesh

Bethlehem

Mt. Nebo

Medeba

Jahaz

Ashkelon

Socoh

Adullam

Etam

Gath?

Mareshah

Tekoa

Beth-zur

Lachish

J U D A H

Ataroth

Salt

Dibon

Gaza

Adoraim

Hebron

En-gedi

Aroer

Wilderness of Judah

Sea

Arnon

Gerar

Ziph

Debir?

Ziklag?

Great
Arad

Ar?

Raphia

Sharuhen

M O A B

Beer-sheba

Kir-hareseth

Arad of
Beth-yeroham

Arabah

Zoar

Tamar

Zered

Ziph

Ascent of
)(Akrabbim

Besor

N e g e b

E D O M

2. A second hypothesis offered in German scholarship is that there was no wholesale military invasion, but there was a slow and gradual infiltration of Israelites into the land of Canaan, who settled in the most accessible (least desirable) places and as they consolidated such a presence slowly began to move into more desirable land, and so into some conflict with the inhabitants of the land. This hypothesis has the merit of noticing that in the text Israel, newly in the land, had to contend over time with other occupants of the land and over time reached a variety of different political arrangements, depending upon the relative strength of Israel and the older inhabitants. That is, the hypothesis of total conquest seems to adhere more to the simple ideological claims of Israel, whereas the infiltration hypothesis seems more realistic about the actual circumstance of the land and the competing communities of inhabitants.

3. The third hypothesis is that of a peasant revolt. This hypothesis (which is probably increasingly favored by scholars) may sound strange to the ears of students, especially because it seems so at odds with more popular interpretations of the material. But because it is taken seriously by important and thoughtful scholars and because it utilizes methods of analysis that are currently influential, the student will wisely take some trouble to understand the hypothesis and reflect upon a rereading of the text in light of it.

According to this hypothesis, the conflict over the land in Joshua (and Judges) is a deep conflict *within* the population already in the land. That is, there was no invasion, or perhaps only at the most a "revolutionary cadre" of those who brought news of Yahweh from the Exodus. The conflict within the land was concerned with "the Canaanites." This hypothesis holds, in a widely embraced redefinition, that the term *Canaanite* is not ethnically specific, but is a pejorative, ideological term to refer to those who control the economy, enjoy great concentration of wealth, and occupy the great centers of urban power. Social power in that world is organized into "city-states," whereby an economic-political-military urban center controls and administers the surrounding agricultural land that is worked by peasants. As is the case in any such power arrangement, the control of "urban elites" produces intense peasant resentment among those who work the land but are taxed by the urban government, with the consequence that through taxation the urban elites live well off the work and produce of the peasants. Thus *Canaanite* refers to a class of people who abuse the peasants, so that the story concerns the clash of urban elites ("Canaanites") and resentful peasants ("Israelites").

It is held that peasant resentment is harnessed and mobilized by the impetus of the liberating God of the Exodus, who energizes the peasants to attack and destroy the urban centers of economic monopoly and exploitation and to reorganize the wealth of the community along communitarian lines, thus to overcome the great socioeconomic inequities of the "Canaanite" system of city-states.

The movement of Israel led by Joshua, in this account, is a combination of peasant resentment authorized and mobilized by the claims of Yahweh, who had, according to Torah teaching, already opposed and destroyed the Egyptian oppressor. "Israel," then, consists in peasants who enact the vision of liberation authorized by Yahweh, so that the great "conquests" of the book of Joshua are to be understood as peasant actions of revolution against an oppressive social system.

It is our judgment that this hypothesis has much to commend it, because it situates the narrative of Israel in the real context of contested social power. It is to be recognized at the same time, however, that the hypothesis has not been universally accepted by scholars. It is a useful proposal, but it must remain as an attractive but unproven hypothesis.

A more recent convergence of hypotheses may suggest a *peaceable infiltration* from *within* the land of Canaan itself. The student will do well to consider the force of these several ways of reading the text, to remember that, finally, it is *the text* that must be read and not a hypothesis, and to remember that insofar as historical questions are asked, we cannot do better than hypothesize. But then, that is the case with every historical interpretation. It is best to recall that no hypothesis is neutral, and we have several that in varying degrees warrant attention.

Textual Memories with Ideological Force

The hypothesis of peasant revolt provides access for us to consider the *ideological force* of the books of Joshua and Judges. By *ideology* I mean a forceful advocacy of an interpretive position that is not "innocent" or "objective" but insists that the telling of the past must serve certain interests and champion certain religious and political claims. It is important to see these texts as *advocacy* and not reportage. This does not mean they are untrue, but that truth is always interpretive. We have suggested that if the books of Joshua and Judges are read with reference to Samuel and Kings, we are moving toward historical data. But if the books are kept close to the Pentateuch, and especially to Deuteronomy, then we must pay attention to the ideological force of the books. As already noted, it is widely believed by scholars that the books of Joshua and Judges, together with the books of Samuel and Kings, constitute more or less a single theological perspective, called the Deuteronomistic History. This literary corpus draws upon historical data, but from a distinct theological angle. And in any case, by the end of the twentieth century, many scholarly interpreters have diminished confidence in the ability of historical research to recover "what happened." Consequently, many scholars incline to the view that what is offered as "history" is deeply saturated with ideological weight.

We may pause here to consider *the role of ideology* in a canonical text. There is no doubt of an ideological component in all of the biblical canon, that is, an advocacy making a claim for God and a derivative claim about social reality and social power. But it is perhaps most evident in the book of Joshua, where scholars have paid special attention to it. In its most elemental usage, the term *ideology* means a set of beliefs resulting in a deliberately shaped interpretation of data done knowingly by an interpreting community. That is, where there is ideology, we are moving away from "facticity," so that what "happened" is from the outset filtered through the perspective and interests of the interpreting community. This means that in Joshua and Judges we do not have a factual report on what happened as Israel settled in the land; instead we have an interpretive account of what that land settlement is taken to mean by those who shaped and valued the literature. It can be said that those who ask only historical questions of the text have failed to reckon with the ideological-interpretive character of the text.

Beyond ideology as *intentional interpretation,* two other dimensions of the term may be identified. A second aspect of ideology is that it is a large *sense-making narrative account of reality* upon which a community relies and which it accepts as a normative baseline and does not question. In this sense ideology is not a conclusion drawn from data but a premise from which facts are to be seen and conclusions are to be drawn. It will be evident that the notion of an unquestioned sense-making account of reality moves toward *theology,* that is, toward a faith statement about what the community believes. It is clear that every community that survives through several generations (including ancient Israel) must have such a narrative account that gives coherence to the vagaries of lived experience.

A third aspect of ideology, especially championed by Karl Marx, is that it is an elemental narrative account of reality that *deliberately distorts* reality by presenting biased vested interest as objective, given reality. Marx, moreover, insisted that such distortion is characteristically the work and the achievement of the dominant social class in any community that has the means of twisting the past in order to legitimate certain present power arrangements in society.

At a minimum, we are able to say that the books of Joshua and Judges contain a large ideological component, in that the literature is not a flat factual account of the past, if indeed, such an account is even possible. Thus in the books of Joshua and Judges, we may identify the working of ideology:

—as deliberate *interpretation,*

—as sense-making narrative involving *faith claim and premise,*

—as intentional *distortion* of the past to legitimate present power arrangements.

Whatever we make of this, the recognition of ideology permits an awareness that this literature is not innocent, but is in fact a power play for the control of the community.

We may identify the following factors in the *interpretive-theological-advocating* presentation of Joshua and Judges:

1. Yahweh, the God of social upheaval who emancipated the slaves from Egyptian bondage, is the key player in the settlement of the land and the claim of land for Israel. Yahweh is presented as a powerful force in this narrative of social conflict who engages in a deep struggle with the established social powers in the land and, by implication, with the putative gods of the inhabitants of the land. Thus the land settlement is presented not simply as a military-political dispute, but as a quarrel among the gods concerning who will deter-

mine the future shape of the land. Yahweh is portrayed in these narratives as immensely powerful and determinedly partisan, so that Yahweh is the source and advocate of the rights of Israel to the land. These rights are not otherwise established, but they are legitimated by the holy purposes and promises of Yahweh that intend to put Israelite claims to the land beyond challenge.

2. Yahweh, who legitimates the land settlement, is a God who has the power and the will to bestow *land*. It may well be that behind this presentation of Yahweh as land giver is the well-established land theory that all land, in any such society, belongs to the king. The king is free to deploy and assign and reassign land to various subjects according to the will of the king. Thus since "the whole earth is mine" (Exod 19:5), Yahweh the King is here reassigning land for the benefit of Israel. Indeed it has been Yahweh's intention to reassign the land to Israel since the initial promise to Abraham in Gen 12:1.

In any case, the land is a primal theme in Israel's primal narrative. Israel is on its way to the land at the behest of Yahweh. It is exceedingly important to reflect on what land signifies to Israel in that ancient world. If Israel is composed of either land-hungry semi-nomads or exploited peasants, in either case Israel lives a precarious life, always at the whim and will of a stronger power. Indeed, the community of Israel is likely made up of "Hebrews" (1 Sam 4:6, 9), that is, the lower social class of economically marginal people who always live precarious lives from the grudgingly shared extras of established society. It is no wonder that Israel, as something of a "class movement," should focus on land, for land represents a stabilization and security in the midst of all the threats and vagaries of contested social existence. To have a land that is both secure and legitimate is to have a place in the world beyond threat. Much of the Old Testament, and surely Joshua and Judges, is a reflection on that social possibility in the world. While the *material goal* of Israel's life is a place of safety, security, and well-being, the *ideational legitimacy* for such land is the promise of Yahweh. Israel, like every such land-seeking community, does not want to base its claim to land on the sheer act of violence but on a respected, credible legitimacy that reaches to the intention of the gods.

3. While the land is legitimated by the high resolve of Yahweh and while the land is, according to many of the texts, seized violently, it is crucial to Israel's self-understanding that the land is available to

Israel only as Israel obeys *the Torah* (specifically the teaching of the book of Deuteronomy) and reorders life in the land according to the requirements of Deuteronomic Torah. That is, this is a land revolution that is driven by a social vision with a particular interest.

This emphasis upon Torah is especially explicit in Josh 1:7-8, which we may take as the epitome of the theological-ideological teaching of the whole. The rhetoric of these verses suggests that in fact Israel needs no military equipment but only intense Torah obedience, before which all non-Torah powers will gladly yield. The initial promise of the land settlement in Josh 1:7-8 is matched in the purported liturgical enactment of chapter 24, whereby many non-Israelite inhabitants of the land "sign on" to the Israelite revolution by adhering to Yahweh (24:16-18; see also the Torah accent in 23:6-7). In a solemn treaty-making ceremony, the people swear to serve and obey only Yahweh (24:24). Joshua "makes a covenant" (v. 25) and "wrote these words in the book of the Torah of God" (v. 26). Thus what begins as a program of Torah obedience culminates in an act of Torah loyalty. While "Torah obedience" certainly refers to the commandments of Sinai, it is clear that the *commandments* are vehicles for a relationship of fidelity and trust. Israel's sense of obedience is always *more than* commandments, but it is never *less than* fulfillment of commands.

In a different mode, the oft reiterated formula of the book of Judges consists in a pattern of (a) forgetting Yahweh and worshiping other gods (disregarding the Torah), and (b) crying out to Yahweh, thus returning to loyalty to Yahweh and to Yahweh's Torah. The clear implication of the predominant formula of Judges is that *obedience to Yahweh* is a condition of land possession; conversely, *disobedience to Yahweh's Torah* is a sure way to lose the land. Such a simplistic formulation (which will later be formulated in more imaginative ways by Israel's great prophets) has an elemental theological reference: since the land belongs to Yahweh, Yahweh must be obeyed. Along with this rather *simplistic theological claim*, however, there is also an implied *ethic of considerable rigor,* namely, that prosperity in the land has as a precondition the practice of a just and humane social ethic that attentively shares well-being with all inhabitants. Keeping the land is conditioned not by keeping rules but by organizing social power and social relationships in neighborly ways, for "neighborly ways" constitute much of the substance of Torah obedience. Fidelity toward the neighbor in socioeconomic matters is understood as an enactment of fidelity toward God. This social ethic is detailed in the book of Deuteronomy and explicated in the Prophets, but only suggested here by the general reference to Torah. The Torah reference is an insistence, elemental in Israel, that land cannot be held simply by power that issues in violence; for a genuinely peaceable existence there is a different kind of legitimation that appeals to an identifiable social strategy.

4. While the land is promised by Yahweh and is said to be given by Yahweh as fulfillment of promise, the narrative makes clear that land seizure is indeed a human operation accomplished by *authorized human agents*. The book of Joshua is dominated by the person of Joshua, who leads the aggressive military campaign, who presides over the solemn rituals of land distribution, and who leads Israel's liturgical peacemaking with other inhabitants of the land. Joshua is powerfully legitimated as the heir and successor of Mosaic revolution (Josh 1:1-6).

The picture presented in the book of Judges is much more varied, as there is not one decisive figure but rather a series of local heroes who responded in acute crises. It is likely that these local heroes did not occur in a single sequence as the Judges narrative presents them; more likely this is a collection of popular folk accounts of various local leaders in crisis times and places who acted boldly and courageously on behalf of a portion of the nascent Yahwistic community in the face of more formidable military power. Their function seems to have been, in varying ways, to lead raids against oppressive authorities and, upon their victory, perhaps to exercise provisional, practical leadership, as in the case of Gideon (see Judg 8:22-23). It is evident that such a practice of the defiance of oppressive power fits well with the peasant revolt hypothesis, in that these leaders led resistance movements, perhaps quite short-term, to repel exploitative power. While these "judges" are not provided the full credentialing of Joshua, we are told that they are empowered by Yahweh's spirit, so that they are legitimated and energized by the God of the peasants. This theological-political claim, later on, was important for Israel as it dealt with exile, land loss, and hope for restoration to the land of promise.

These four elements—Yahweh, land, Torah, human agents—are the positive content of the *interpretive-theological-advocating* tale of reality given us in Joshua and Judges. And while one can readily focus on each of these factors, it is clear that the four elements are intimately connected to one another and reinforce one another, so that not any one of them—not even Yahweh—can be taken apart from the others. Together they constitute the telling of the tale of Israel's would-be future in the land.

These positive elements of the tale, however, inevitably carry with them negative counterpoints, namely, the harsh, dismissive attitude toward Israel's enemies, the Canaanites, or better, "the people of the land." Israel's story of the land, much as it is a story of Yahweh's triumphant purposes, is realistic enough to recognize that the seizure of the land was a series of violent confrontations with those who were already in the land, who regarded the land as legitimately their own, who did not easily accept the Yahweh-Israel version of land legitimacy, and who therefore did not willingly cede over their land to the new claimants.

The earlier and rival claimants to the land are a widely variegated people. Joshua 12 provides an extended inventory of conquered peoples, notably "Hittites, Amorites, Canaanites, Perizzites, Hivites, and Jebusites" (Josh 12:8), a list that roughly and nicely echoes Gen 15:19-21. In the book of Judges, moreover, the contestants for the land are variously identified as Moabites, Canaanites, Midianites, and Philistines, among others.

For the theological-ideological purposes of Israel, the identity of the peoples is not especially important. What counts is that they are all opponents of Israel and the God of Israel. Because they did not willingly cede over the land and recognize the superior land-claims of Israel, they are opponents of Yahweh. They cannot withstand the force of Yahweh's people and so are deservedly destroyed. Even though the text identifies many such resistant communities (see Judg 1:1-36), it is convenient, in a reductionist way, to treat all of these opponents "in the land of Canaan" as "Canaanites," that is, those who have not adhered to Yahweh and who did not organize social power in Yahwistic ways. There is no doubt that the Canaanites are treated in a reductionist fashion in the text, condemned along with "Canaanite gods," who are denied legitimacy not only in the text but by much subsequent scholarship that is programmatically sympathetic to Israel. It seems clear that the "Canaanites" and "Israelites" are of common ethnic stock, but the differences are *theological* (holding or not holding to Yahwistic land claims) and derivatively *socioeconomic* (organizing or not organizing social power in more or less communitarian ways).

Given the clear contrast of Israel and "Canaan," however, it is important to notice that Israel is not said to *merit* the land because it is "better":

> It is not because of your righteousness or the uprightness of your heart that you are going in to occupy their land; but because of the wickedness of these nations the LORD your God is dispossessing them before you, in order to fulfill the promise that the LORD made on oath to your ancestors, to Abraham, to Isaac, and to Jacob. (Deut 9:5)

Israel links its reception of the land, albeit by force, to the old enduring promise of God in Genesis. In the end, the land is a *gift* of God.

These theological and socioeconomic distinctions are taken in the literature to be of immense importance, such that savage brutality in the name of the social revolution is readily legitimated, for it is the will of the God of the revolution to destroy:

> For it was the LORD's doing to harden their hearts so that they would come against Israel in battle, in order that they might be utterly destroyed, and might receive no mercy, but be exterminated, just as the LORD had commanded Moses. (Josh 11:20)

A Text with Theological Features

Our purpose in the preceding section is to indicate the way in which interpretive-theological-ideological factors are present in the text that make impossible a flat, historical report. Although our terms—*interpretive, theological, ideological*—overlap and their functions cannot be easily sorted out, we may make some distinctions that will illuminate our reading of Joshua and Judges as sacred scripture.

1. *Theological:* The notion of *theological* is that there is reference to God. And so it is in this literature. Yahweh is presented as the God who makes promises and who keeps them. It is asserted at the end of the land-taking:

> Thus the LORD gave to Israel all the land that he swore to their ances-
> tors that he would give to them. . . . And the LORD gave them rest on
> every side just as he had sworn to their ancestors; . . . for the LORD
> had given all their enemies into their hands. Not one of all the good
> promises that the LORD had made to the house of Israel had failed; all
> came to pass. (Josh 21:43-45)

This God, moreover, will keep promises in stunning ways, in circumstances that are not immediately responsive to Yahweh's intent.
More specifically, Yahweh will make and keep promises to Israel, the
people chosen to receive Yahweh's particular attentiveness.
Yahweh's concrete promise, made and kept to Israel, is a guarantee
of safe, stable, prosperous blessing in a land that can be its very own.

This theological claim has been immensely important to the
community of Israel through the generations, for it has kept alive a
concrete, historical hope for a people that has been characteristically landless and displaced. The same promises have been important, derivatively, for the church that takes these texts as Holy
Scripture. For the most part, however, the faith of the church is not
land-based. (But there are important exceptions to this general
principle. A most prominent case is the way in which European
Christians colonized North America as "God's New Israel," con-
cretely, in an act of land seizure.) For that reason the land claims of
Joshua and Judges have been transposed and spiritualized, so that it
is Jesus who is the land of promise, and communion with God, sacramentally expressed, is the church's sure, safe place. Beyond concrete Jewish appeals to this tradition and transposed Christian
claims out of this tradition, the linkage between the land-giving God
and the land-receiving people has been generative of revolutionary
theology in the contemporary world based in the conviction that
God wants none of God's people to remain landless and precarious,
certainly not in the presence of great landowners who monopolize
land that must be shared. Thus the land promises, along with the
Exodus memory, have been a powerful, elemental source of revolutionary imagination committed to the overthrow of land monopoly
in the interest of land redistribution.

2. *Ideological:* When we take the teaching and advocacies of the
text as *normative,* we may term them *theological.* When we recognize
their function in terms of bias and distortion (to make claims for

land legitimacy in the face of other land claims), we may name them *ideological.* Here we may identify three facets of ideology that deeply pervade these texts:

(a) Other inhabitants of and claimants to the land of promise ("Canaanites") are demonized in flat and wholesale ways. The text is intentional in creating a deep and total either/or between Yahweh and the Canaanite gods and between Israel and the Canaanite population. Indeed such demonizing of the enemy is a characteristic maneuver of propaganda when tension and conflict are acute, for such demonization then becomes the warrant for massive brutality without caution or embarrassment. Thus the anti-Canaanite thrust of these texts proceeds in the claim that the Canaanites are unworthy, have no legitimate claim on the land, and are the enemies of Yahweh whom Yahweh wants destroyed.

It is important to recognize that the ideological impact of the text continues to be effective and generative in a variety of contemporary contexts. Specifically, there is no doubt that the claims of land for the chosen people of Yahweh nourishes and funds the land claims of the contemporary state of Israel; it is, moreover, seen to give warrant for a version of "Greater Israel" in some extreme forms of Zionism that can entertain the elimination of the Palestinian population from the land. To be sure the ancient inhabitants of the land, the Canaanites, are not connected in any historical way to the contemporary Palestinians; in ideological reading, however, the "enemy" of Israel in the land is readily transposed from the one to the other. It is to be recognized that such a utilization of the old tradition is not characteristic of Jewish perspectives on "others," but the tradition lends itself to this reading in an ideological context.

The demonization of the enemy as a stratagem of legitimacy is not unfamiliar to us as we may ponder the ways in which Germans, Japanese, Russians, and North Vietnamese have been variously demonized in order to support the U.S. "war effort," and the way in which, more recently, the several communities in the Balkans have engaged in "ethnic cleansing." It is sobering to recognize, in the Balkan states, for example, that the enemies demonized and "cleansed" are in fact communities of people who in almost every way share a commonality with their enemy.

Closer to home in the U.S., we may also notice that the European "discovery" of North America led to the long-term massacre of Native Americans who already occupied the land. The demonization of Native Americans in popular lore, moreover, is evident in the stereotype of "Cowboys and Indians" offered in endless "Westerns." The U.S. itself has built its national land claim on such wholesale demonization. Such an awareness may help us to appreciate the strategy of demonization in our literature, as it appears that "Canaanites" and "Hebrews" are of a common social, cultural stock.

(b) It follows for such demonization of "the other" that this literature fosters an ideology of violence in the name of Yahweh. The taking of the land was, on the whole, not a peaceable process of negotiation but a violent project aimed at elimination and extremity. That violence, moreover, is rooted, according to the texts concerning the seizure of the land from its earlier occupants, in the violent intentionality of Yahweh, who wills the destruction of inhabitants of the land in order to claim the land for the peasants who carry the promise.

It is difficult to overstate the importance of this ideological claim made for Yahweh. For it means that violence, according to Israel's own text, is legitimated by Yahweh's own mandate, a legitimated violence that has continued to give legitimacy to the violent propensities of derivative communities of faith. It may be argued that such legitimated violence is nothing more than the sociopolitical advocacy of Israel that it dares to assign to Yahweh. Nonetheless, in the text the violence is intentionally and without embarrassment linked to Yahweh's own purposes. Thus the Christian West has a long history of abuse toward those who disagree theologically, as is spectacularly evident in the Crusades and in the Inquisition. Moreover, the several wars of the U.S. have been characteristically conducted with religious rhetoric, so that the wars are characteristically legitimated as actions in the service of Yahweh, whose name is praised in much of the hymnody of the church that is saturated with images of violent militarism. (Only as a small footnote to the Christian exploitation of violence is the same rhetoric operative in the contemporary state of Israel as concerns Israeli claims to the land.)

(c) The demonization of enemies and the legitimation of violence are pervasive themes in these texts. Along with them, more positively, the text also implies a vision of the land that will be reordered according to the purposes of Yahweh as given in the book of Deuteronomy. If Joshua and Judges are intimately linked to the book of Deuteronomy, as seems beyond doubt, and if the literature reflects a peasant revolt, as seems plausible, then it does not surprise us that the books contend for a reordering of the land in a communitarian way with a fuller sharing of resources with all members of the community. The violent assignment is to resist and destroy systems of acquisitiveness that preclude such a society. It is this ideological commitment to an alternative society that is perhaps behind Gideon's refusal of monarchy (Judg 8:22-23).

It should be noticed that ideology as *external policy* (demonization and violence) is in deep conflict with an *internal vision* of communitarian sensibility. Clearly an overt policy of violence and rejection is no viable matrix for a community of sharing. It is this deep contradiction between the brutalizing violence of Yahweh and the Torah provisions of Yahweh for justice that lie at the heart of biblical faith. It is evident that Israel is aware of this contradiction, but it remains pervasive throughout the text in any case.

3. The adjudication of *high theological claim* and *pervasive ideological assumptions* is a tricky task in any case. Those who are adherents of Judaism or Christianity and who take this text as normative will find here a God who is faithful and generous to Israel, committed to well-being for the faithful, and passionate in defense of the claims of the marginated. At the same time, an alert reader cannot fail to see that these high theological claims are shot through with and dependent upon ignoble propensities. There is no easy resolution of this problem, though in any case the first step is to recognize what is before us in the text. It is perhaps a usual strategy among the faithful to take "the good stuff" and ignore or not even notice the embarrassing elements. It is our judgment, however, that high-minded theological affirmation about the God who keeps promises in a material way cannot ever simply disregard what comes with it, so that at best we are left with an uneasy awareness of the compromised foundation upon which such noble claims rest.

One other aspect of this adjudication is worth noticing. It is important not to hold Joshua and Judges to bourgeois standards of a well-ordered society that should be more benignly embraced. Such privileged opposition to violence, that "such things must not be done," is itself an ideological claim in the interest of maintaining the *status quo.* What may seem to us readers in our privilege (and most who read this book will be profoundly privileged) as completely unacceptable violence may not seem so objectionable to the oppressed, marginated, and economically abused who know deep in their bones that such oppression cannot be "right," and cannot be willed by the Creator of heaven and earth. Thus the overthrow of entrenched, abusive power, albeit by violent means, is not as ethically objectionable to the disenfranchised as it is to the safely and prosperously ensconced. This literature may be understood, at least at one level, as the primitive literature of desperate liberation movements who know themselves to be allied with and vouched for by the God of all social transformation. Such revolutionary impetus is not everywhere welcomed in the world and perhaps cannot be finally justified. But it can be appreciated for what it is, without in naïveté insisting that it be what it is not, what it does not intend to be, and what it can never be. There is something to be appreciated in the pervasive affirmation of this literature that the God of the Exodus stands massively against every system of exploitation.

4. Now that we have paid attention to the theological and ideological workings of the text, we may return to ask more soberly about the "history" that may be reflected here, though even that "history" surely has something of ideological force. After the text makes its loud, strident claims for Yahweh's gift of the land, the text must also reckon with lived elements of experience that do not readily conform to the large, loud claims of faith. Specifically, the text itself makes clear that the taking of the land was not clean and wholesale. Indeed, we may say that if the seizure of the land had been as complete as the ideology of Joshua had hoped, then the stories of Judges would not be needed and could not have occurred.

Thus it is clear that on the ground, the process of the land becoming "Israelite" was complex, gradual, and variegated according to local circumstance. In spite of the ideology of elimination of the others, the text makes clear that there were non-Israelites who continued in the land with whom Israel had to come to terms. Most prominent are the narratives of "faithful" Rahab (Josh 2) and of the duping Gibeonites (Josh 9), who are footnotes of exception to the ideology. Moreover, the list of Judg 1:21-36 with its repeated refrain "did not drive out" indicates realism that is reinforced by the acknowledgments of Josh 13:1-7, 13; 16:10; and 17:12-13.

It is evident that the text itself is aware of the incongruity between claim and apparent reality, for it takes steps to comment, explain, and justify the limited implementation of the land seizure. In Judg 2:3, it is asserted that the other nations remain in the land because Israel has been disobedient (see 2:20-23). (By contrast, Exod 23:29-30 offers an alternative reason for the continuation of other peoples, namely, that an empty land would revert to wilderness conditions, so that it is better to give the land over to Israel "little by little.")

With the judgment given in Judg 2:2-3, we begin to see the turn of theological emphasis from the book of Joshua to the book of Judges. Whereas Joshua is almost completely about the gift of the land, Judges begins to reflect on the unwillingness of Israel to adhere to the Torah as condition of the land. That is, the revolution that began in such high-minded passion becomes a sorry compromise already in the first episode in the land (Josh 7–8), a compromise that culminates in Judg 17–21 in disordered barbarism. Having said that, it is possible to see that even the acknowledgment of historical circumstances that do not measure up to ideological claims is put to ideological use. For by the end of Judges, the new recipients of the land are in deep crisis precisely because they themselves fail to live up to the Torah ideology. This turn from gift to judgment makes clear that one cannot sort out ideological and historical elements in the narrative, because even what appears to be a historical acknowledgment can be utilized for a second ideological accent, namely, the land given by *the promise-keeping God* can be taken away by *the Torah-insisting God*.

5. We may now draw a conclusion about the theological-ideological force of this literature that (a) concerns legitimacy in the land, (b) is preoccupied with the expulsion of foreigners, and (c) worries that the land may be lost by excessive accommodation to the social system and practice of the Canaanites. It is thought by many scholars, for a variety of complex reasons, that the ideological intention of this literature is designed for an *exilic community* of Jews in the sixth century who are deported from their own land and who yearn and hope for rehabilitation into the land. That is, the intended canonical locus of the books is far removed from its purported preoccupation with premonarchy, addressing a postmonarchy community. This literature then may serve such a displaced community:

—to assert the legitimacy of claims to the land, claims jeopardized by deportation;

—to warn against "foreigners" with their foreign religious practices seen as a threat to a pure community of faith; and

—to urge careful Torah obedience as the condition for reentry into the land.

Thus the historical specificity of these narratives is considerably removed from their theological intention. The canonical program of the text is to summon and authorize and energize a community about to be reconstituted in the land. In such a context, the problem is not in fact "foreigners," but heterodox religious practice that will endanger the purity of Yahwism, a purity that is taken to be a mark of the emerging community of Judaism.

Rhetoric of Entitlement and Extermination

With this framing of the complex interpretive issues related to these biblical texts, we may now consider more closely the specificities of the text. The book of Joshua is conventionally divided into three parts:

—the seizure of the land (1–12),

—the division of the land (13–19), and

—concluding narratives (20–24).

The story of the seizure of the land (1–12) is framed with the initial authorization of Joshua (chap. 1) and an inventory of conquests that suggests complete defeat (but not extermination) of every enemy (12:7-24). The latter list makes clear the way in which the "Canaanites" had organized social power into a series of city-states.

Chapters 1–5 narrate the preparation for entry and the entry into the land. As indicated, chapter 1 is a theological overture that asserts that (a) Joshua is authorized by Yahweh for the task, and (b) the land enterprise is a Torah project. The other preliminary matter, along with theological justification in chapter 1, is a practical stratagem in chapter 2, namely, reconnaissance of the land about to be entered and the first city to be taken (Jericho). It is remarkable that the first ally for Israel in the new land is a "prostitute" (Rahab), who not only cooperates but also knows of the revolutionary ground from which Israel makes its move about the land:

As soon as we heard it, our hearts melted, and there was no courage left in any of us because of you. The LORD your God is indeed God in heaven above and on earth below. Now then, since I have dealt kindly with you, swear to me by the LORD that you in turn will deal kindly with my family. Give me a sign of good faith. (Josh 2:11-12)

These two beginning points, theological authorization and practical military undertaking, prepare for the actual entry over the Jordan River. It is clear that the narrative of the crossing is presented as a liturgical act that can be replicated in subsequent liturgical activity (Josh 3–4). Moreover, the interpretation of the act, echoing the Exodus testimony of Rahab, makes the act a replication of the Exodus:

For the LORD your God dried up the waters of the Jordan for you until you crossed over, as the LORD your God did to the Red Sea, which he dried up for us until we crossed over, so that all the peoples of the earth may know that the hand of the LORD is mighty, and so that you may fear the LORD your God forever. (4:23-24)

It is clear that the narrative is theologically self-aware; it is not mere reportage, but wants to tie this land project to the Exodus, either as a conclusion to the Exodus or as a parallel. The Exodus-land axis of the narrative exhibits Yahweh as the God who is said to overthrow every *status quo* in the interest of those excluded, who now forcibly push in to the resources of society.

The first acts in the new land are liturgical: circumcision (5:2-7) and Passover (5:10-11). We may notice two other interpretive notes. In 5:1-2 the wholesale character of the coming conquest is anticipated. There are here no exceptions or variations. It is Yahweh who intimidates (see Ps 114). Second, in 5:11-12, Israel may rely no more on miracle bread. In a flash, Israel has arrived as a land-based community with all the wonders and all the risks of that new status. The narrative marks this moment as a genuine turn in Israel's destiny. Israel is now subject to a new set of temptations, those of the land.

Three extended narratives are featured in chapters 6:1–10:15. The first of these in chapter 6 reports on Rahab, whom we have already encountered in chapter 2. In this narrative, she is spared (6:25), since she had already acted faithfully toward Israel (2:12).

Thus she is an important exception at the outset to the general rule of extermination of all non-Israelites. In the second narrative, Achan, an Israelite, brings defeat upon his people because he has coveted and withheld from his own community (7:20-21). As a consequence, he is executed, even though he is an Israelite. These first two narratives together are a study in contrasts: Rahab, the non-Israelite, is spared for fidelity; Achan, the Israelite, is executed for infidelity. In seeing these two stories together, one can see a tension in the self-understanding of Israel in the text. The surface ideology consists in life for Israelites and death for foreigners. In the practice of these two narratives, however, a quite different criterion is employed, whereby the faithful foreigner is spared and the exploitative Israelite is not. Thus the issue of covenantal fidelity, whether by a foreigner or by an Israelite, preempts the first set of criteria.

The figure of Rahab in the narrative is an especially important and interesting one. She is a representative figure of the way in which "Canaanites" were occasionally included in the Israelite world, even receiving steadfast love from Israel. Her role indicates that the sharp distinction between "Canaanites" and "Israelites" was not always maintained. Indeed the difference between the two is only one of theological loyalty, not at all linked to any ethnic or cultural identity. She is of interest beyond that because she is a woman in a man's culture. As a woman she acts with courage and freedom and so plays the decisive role in the narrative. It is clear in the storytelling memory of ancient Israel that women could indeed be agents of their own history. The significance of Rahab in the tradition is evidenced by the fact that she reappears in Christian tradition as a model for faith. In Heb 11:31 she is cited as an example of faith and in Jas 2:25 she enacts "works" that signify faith.

The third narrative concerns the Gibeonites, yet another community of foreigners (9:1–10:15). In this narrative the Gibeonites are fearful before the threat of Israel. By a deceptive stratagem they trick Israel into making a treaty with them. As a consequence Joshua "makes peace" with them, even if it is a *shalom* between a master and a servant (9:15; 10:1). The thrust of the narrative is that even though the treaty is gained dishonestly, it must be honored. Joshua is therefore committed to protecting the Gibeonites, even though they are among the foreigners otherwise scheduled for extermination.

The narratives of Rahab and the Gibeonites are perhaps a deliberate pair in the text. Both turn out to be exceptions to the rule of extermination of foreigners, thus making clear that the rule of extermination is not absolute. In both cases, Joshua and Israel are bound to act in protective fidelity toward a foreigner, and so to save them from the general policy. It is instructive that in both these cases, the foreigner appeals to an affirmation of Yahweh, in both cases aware of Yahweh's awesome intention for the land and seeking exception from the general policy. We have seen the affirmation of Rahab (2:11). It is matched by a Gibeonite assertion:

> Because it was told to your servants for a certainty that the LORD your God had commanded his servant Moses to give you all the land, and to destroy all the inhabitants of the land before you; so we were in great fear for our lives because of you, and did this thing. (9:24)

These two cases show that non-Israelites can come to respectful terms with Yahweh, and on the basis of such an acknowledgment inhabitants of the land are saved. The narrative indicates the extent to which the ideological absoluteness must be handled through a process of attentive negotiation.

The narratives of the seizure of the land conclude in 10:16–12:24 with a summary report of the conquest. One is struck in these verses by the ferocious character of the conquest, repeatedly ending in wholesale destruction, as in the following phrases:

- great slaughter on them, until they were wiped out (10:20);
- put them to death (10:26);
- utterly destroyed every person (10:28);
- he left no one remaining in it (10:30);
- struck it with the edge of the sword, and every person in it (10:32);
- every person in it he utterly destroyed (10:35);
- utterly destroyed every person in it (10:39);
- utterly destroyed all that breathed (10:40).

The rhetoric is relentless. This summary account is a sharp, perhaps intentional contrast with the narrative accounts of Rahab and the Gibeonites. This collection of concluding reports is interrupted in 11:1-15 concerning the great fortress city of Hazor. But the conclusion is the same as the preceding; none escaped (11:11, 14). After the Hazor narrative, moreover, the same harsh notes conclude the summary of 11:16-22, with an acknowledgment of the exception: "There was not a town that made peace with the Israelites, except the Hivites, the inhabitants of Gibeon" (11:19). The wholesale quality of the onslaught is reinforced by chapter 12 with its concluding list of thirty-one kings. In verses 1, 6, and 7, the NRSV uses the translation "defeat," but the Hebrew term is much more harsh, better rendered "smite" or "strike," thus implying execution. The conquest is complete. We are left to ponder the odd role and presence of the narratives concerning Rahab and the Gibeonites. There are hints that Israel's relationship to outsiders is not as one-dimensional as first glance may suggest.

The middle part of the book of Joshua concerns the division of the land (chaps. 13–19). This material, in deliberate and symmetrical fashion, assigns to each tribe an allotment of guaranteed territory, so that the land promise is made specific and concrete for each social unit in Israel. Scholars have long debated the boundaries that are drawn for the several tribes. More conservative scholars regard these boundaries as the situation of early, premonarchic Israel. But most scholars believe that the layout is too symmetrical to reflect actual geographical reality. More plausibly the list is a fictive presentation from the exilic community of Israel that yearns for a restoration to the land and that imagines how it will be when all is reordered and safely assured by the promises of Yahweh. Thus Joshua's imagined division of the land takes place within the context of Yahweh's large and reliable land promises. An even more idealized account of land allotment, perhaps to serve a parallel purpose, is upheld in Ezek 47:13–48:35.

We may notice three particulars in this extended portion of text. First, it is acknowledged that "the nations" are not all expelled from the land according to the ideology of total conquest. Israel will have to learn to live with and among the nations. Two texts are of interest in this regard. The opening paragraph of 13:1-7 likely functions as a transition from "conquest" (1–12) to "division" (13–19). These verses acknowledge on many fronts that other peoples still occupy the land. Most interesting is the assertion of verses 6-7 that what is left of the conquest will be Yahweh's own work; Joshua is to leave off the work of conquest to concentrate on land division (see also 13:13; 15:63; 16:10; 17:12-13).

The brief note of 17:16-18 is evidence of a "class" distinction in dispute over the land. The "Canaanites" are said to control the technology that permits high-powered militarism, a technology Israel does not possess (see 1 Sam 13:19-22). Such a statement coheres with the notion that "Canaanite" refers to the urban elites who monopolize power, whereas "Israelites" have no access to such power. Thus a primary reason that other peoples still hold the land is superior military technology. The assurance of verse 18 is that Israel—perhaps at the behest of Yahweh—will eventually prevail.

Second, it belongs to standard Israelite formulation concerning land allotment that the tribe of Levi, a priestly tribe, is given no land, for Yahweh is its "portion" (13:33; 14:3-4; 18:7; see also 21:1-42). This recurring notion indicates that at least the idealized form of land allotment is still represented as a sacral act that defers to the priests. This understanding will be important when Israel reflects upon the ritual purity of the land (see Ezek 48:8-14; Josh 22:19-20).

The third, more curious note is the special provision made for Caleb (14:6-15; 15:13-19). This narrative account in the midst of stylized lists is worthy of notice. Caleb is featured in Num 13:30–14:10, along with Joshua, as a man of faith and courage who trusted Yahweh in the face of intimidating circumstances. Indeed,

My servant Caleb, because he has a different spirit and has followed me wholeheartedly, I will bring into the land into which he went, and his descendants shall possess it. (Num 14:24; see Num 26:65; 32:12; Deut 1:36)

The reference suggests that Caleb is entitled to special land as a consequence of his profound faith. The narrative notice is a reminder that land, in the end, requires great faith. The alternative to such faith is anxiety that produces compromise and accommodation and eventually disobedience, propensities already anticipated in the fearful colleagues of Caleb and Joshua in Num 13:27-28, 31-33. In the end, so the tradition attests, the way of compromise and disobedience leads to land loss.

The final section of the book (chaps. 20–24) consists in a miscellaneous collection of materials reporting on unfinished business, including a provision for "cities of refuge" (20:1-9), provision for the Levites (21:1-42), and completion of the relationships among the tribes (22:1-34).

The Structure and Number of the Clans

The Clan of Reuben:

A. The descendants: Reuben

Hanoch (Hanochites)   Pallu (Palluites)   Hezron (Hezronites)   Carmi (Carmites)

Eliab

Nemuel   Dathan   Abiram

B. The number: 43,730 (as compared to 46,500 in Numbers 1)

The Clan of Simeon:

A. The descendants: Simeon

Nemuel (Nemuelites)   Jamin (Jaminites)   Jachin (Jachinites)   Zerah (Zerahites)   Shaul (Shaulites)

B. The number: 22,200 (as compared to 59,300 in Numbers 1)

The Clan of Gad:

A. The descendants: Gad

Zephon (Zephonites)   Haggi (Haggites)   Shuni (Shunites)   Ozni (Oznites)   Eri (Erites)   Arad (Arodites)   Areli (Arelites)

B. The number: 40,500 (as compared to 45,650 in Numbers 1)

The Clan of Judah:

A. The descendants: Judah

Er   Onan   Shelah (Shelanites)   Perez (Perezites)   Zerah (Zerahites)

Hezron (Hezronites)   Hamul (Hamulites)

B. The number: 76,500 (as compared to 74,600 in Numbers 1)

The Clan of Issachar:

A. The descendants: Issachar

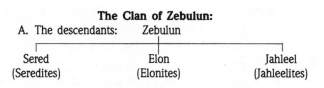

Tola	Puvah	Jashub	Shimron
(Tolaites)	(Punites)	(Jashubites)	(Shimronites)

B. The number: 64,300 (as compared to 54,400 in Numbers 1)

The Clan of Zebulun:

A. The descendants: Zebulun

Sered	Elon	Jahleel
(Seredites)	(Elonites)	(Jahleelites)

B. The number: 60,500 (as compared to 57,400 in Numbers 1)

The Clan of Joseph:

A. Manasseh (vv. 29-34)

1. The descendants:

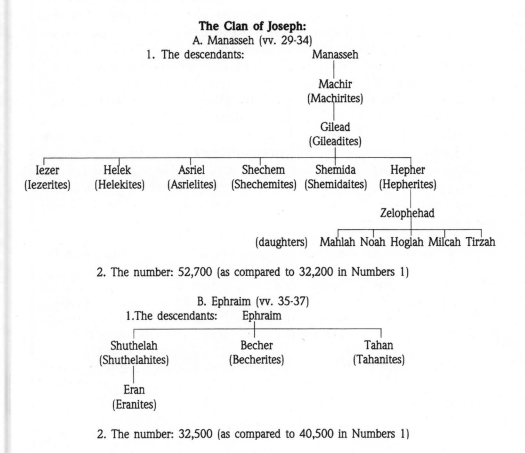

Manasseh

Machir
(Machirites)

Gilead
(Gileadites)

Iezer	Helek	Asriel	Shechem	Shemida	Hepher
(Iezerites)	(Helekites)	(Asrielites)	(Shechemites)	(Shemidaites)	(Hepherites)

Zelophehad

(daughters)   Mahlah Noah Hoglah Milcah Tirzah

2. The number: 52,700 (as compared to 32,200 in Numbers 1)

B. Ephraim (vv. 35-37)

1. The descendants: Ephraim

Shuthelah	Becher	Tahan
(Shuthelahites)	(Becherites)	(Tahanites)
Eran		
(Eranites)		

2. The number: 32,500 (as compared to 40,500 in Numbers 1)

We may notice three items in particular. First, in 21:43-45, the narrative ends with a sweeping conclusion, asserting that all of Yahweh's promises to Israel have now been fulfilled: "Not one of all the good promises that the LORD had made to the house of Israel had failed; all came to pass" (v. 45). Some scholars have suggested that these verses are designed to look back to the initial land promise of Gen 12:1, thus completing a tale of promise and fulfillment. The reception of the land is regarded as a gift of Yahweh, who now makes possible a safe, stable community in the land, without threat or anxiety.

Second, the address of Joshua to Israel (23:2-16), now settled in the land, is a quite intentional piece of land theology that is a counterpart to 1:2-9. Both speeches by Joshua to Israel focus upon the land, and both speeches mention land in relation to the Torah. We can, however, notice that the two speeches have quite different emphases. In 1:2-9, the speech is an invitation to courage and an assurance that Torah obedience is the only "weapon" needed for the land. *Obedience* to Yahweh's Torah makes land reception and maintenance possible. It is important to keep in mind that "obedience" has to do with a certain quality of life that is rooted in an elemental relationship of love, loyalty, and gratitude.

By contrast, 23:2-16 is not an assurance but a warning. It is as though the tradition has now become aware that as Israel has settled into a safe land, it has come to think of itself as self-sufficient, no longer in need of Yahweh, no longer dependent on Yahweh, but free to live autonomously. The urging of Joshua is for Torah obedience:

> Therefore be very steadfast to observe and do all that is written in the book of the law of Moses, turning aside from it neither to the right nor to the left, so that you may not be mixed with these nations left here among you, or make mention of the names of their gods, or swear by them, or serve them, or bow yourselves down to them, but hold fast to the LORD your God, as you have done to this day. (23:6-8)

Israel's temptation is to compromise its Yahwistic identity, to traffic ("mix") with the other peoples and their gods. The speech concludes with a serious threat:

> If you transgress the covenant of the LORD your God, which he enjoined on you, and go and serve other gods and bow down to them,

then the anger of the LORD will be kindled against you, and you shall perish quickly from the good land that he has given to you. (v. 16)

Disobedience will cause land loss. Failure in Torah obedience will lead to the retaking of the land by the Canaanites.

It is likely that this material, like much of the book of Joshua, is from a perspective of the sixth-century exile. The exile is land loss, pure and simple. From the perspective of the Torah tradition, moreover, it is Torah violation that causes exile. Reading the text intelligently requires us to keep in view the long history of Israel that is clearly on the horizon of this text. In any case, the imperative of verse 6 and the warning of verse 16 prepare us for what is to come next in the book of Judges, namely, the crisis of seduction and disobedience.

Third, the meeting assembled in Josh 24 is regarded by scholars as a great summary statement of all that has gone before in the tradition of Israel. We may identify the following elements in the text:

1. Verses 2-13 are a narrative recital that summarizes the normative lore of Israel from Abraham forward. Israel's present identity depends upon keeping its past immediately available in the present tense.

2. The meeting at Shechem is a negotiation whereby inhabitants of the land are invited into the community of Israel (vv. 14-15). This negotiation requires a clear decision for Yahweh, but the mood is quite in contrast to the ideology of extermination in the earlier part of the book. Israel will not live in a clean, unambiguous environment, but must always find a way for faith amid seductive alternatives.

3. The decision to be made here, and always again to be made, is to "put away the foreign gods" (v. 23) and enter into a covenant of obedience to Yahweh's Torah (vv. 25-26). The linkage between land and Torah is reasserted.

4. Joshua dies (vv. 29-30). The period of the great takeover and settlement is ended. Israel now faces a dangerous time without great leadership.

The book of Joshua begins in a death (1:1). It ends in a death (24:29-30). Between these deaths Israel begins in a buoyant assurance from Joshua. It ends in a stern warning and threat from that same Joshua. The tradition understands that the land that is an enormous gift is also an endless seduction.

The Book of Judges as a Theological Vision

In the book of Joshua we have seen that the land-Torah vision moved from *assurance* to *warning*. The book of Judges is preoccupied with the latter theme, namely, that departure from Yahweh jeopardizes the land. The book of Judges, in its central part, is upon the surface a collection of folktales about various heroes who have in clever and courageous ways enhanced the freedom and well-being of Israel (3:7–16:31). These tales are means whereby a community of story hearers can celebrate its own identity, can name the times and places and persons who have outthought and outfoxed stronger, oppressive powers, and can mark the oppressor peoples who abused but who finally proved inept and were defeated.[1] It is clear, however, that these hero tales have been formulated for a didactic purpose, to reiterate the starchy warning of Josh 23:16 that violation of Yahweh will risk the land.

That central section of the book of Judges, comprising folktales as testimony to Torah faith, is framed by a beginning and an ending. The beginning section provides continuity with the book of Joshua (Judg 1:1–3:6). The preponderant theme in this section, echoing the realism of Josh 13:1-7, is a candid acknowledgment that other peoples are still in the land, that Israel was unable to drive them out, and that Israel must come to terms with that political-geographical reality (1:19, 21, 27, 29, 30, 31-32, 33, 34). The totalizing land ideology of early Joshua has not yet been implemented. This acknowledgment is offered simply as a statement of political-military reality without any didactic implication. Israel must live in the real world, whether this is the Canaanite world of the thirteenth century or, as seems likely, the belated world of sixth-century exiles.

That predominant theme of "did not drive out" is surrounded by two other accents that reach all the way from unembarrassed military brutality to a first presentation of the didactic theology that will dominate the book of Judges. The unembarrassed military brutality is narrated in the opening verses in 1:5-7. These verses reflect the deep resentment, indeed hatred, of an oppressed people toward the oppressor, people who take drastic vengeance on the object of their hatred. The object here is "Adonibezek." They gave him back in kind, forcing him, with toes and thumbs cut off, to pick up crumbs from the table. The unbearably cruel picture offers a humiliated king who, without digits or dexterity, can only pick up crumbs with his mouth, face to the ground. The conquering Israelites—perhaps abused peasants—were so filled with hate that they implemented the violence learned from their overlords. The faith of Israel in the Old Testament is shot through with brutalizing violence learned through suffering.

At the other extreme, the presence of other peoples in the land, contradicting the ideology of total conquest, provides occasion for Torah instruction. The tradition takes the opportunity to give theological justification for the continuation of other peoples in the land. The reasons given for their continuation in the land are these:

—Israel has not obeyed (listened), so they are continuing traps to seduce Israel (2:2-3). The phrase "not obey" (*shema'*) refers to Torah obedience.

—Israel has not obeyed (listened; 2:20).

—They are there to test Israel, to find out if Israel is serious about the Torah (2:22-23; 3:1-7).

All of these statements are a focus on Israel's *disobedience* to Yahweh's Torah.

It is asserted that Joshua's generation was faithful to Yahweh (2:6-10). But the next generation was not (2:11-19). The rhetoric of Judges regularly speaks of "following other gods," so that Israel's departure from Torah is a wrong choice of gods. But that religious choice is not to be understood thinly, because the choice of gods always brings with it a decision about *socioeconomic-political practice.* Allegiance to Yahweh brings with it an embrace of communitarian covenantalism, that is, an economy that practices neighborliness between haves and have-nots. Conversely, embracing of other gods entails "Canaanite" socioeconomic-political practices, that is, the utilization of social power for self against neighbor. It is important to recognize that the faith in Yahweh here championed by the text and (allegedly) rejected by the people consists in an entire way of organizing social power and social relationships, even if the tradition voices these matters simply as religious choices.

These introductory verses focus upon Israel's disobedience, because settlement in the land brought with it the seductions of power and autonomy (see Deut 8). It is such departure from Torah that causes new waves of oppression and that evokes in turn a return to Yahweh, who saves.

This theological interpretation of Israel's history clearly voiced in 2:11-19 is the dominant didactic tendency in the central part of the book, 3:7–16:31. This material consists in a series of hero tales, seemingly in no particular order, that bespeak bravery and defiance of oppressors in the service of Yahweh and to the enhancement of Israel. In reading this material attention should be paid to the delicate interface between *imaginative narrative freedom* and *stylized didactic theological claim*. The two forces in the text do not easily fit together. But the combination of the two explicates the conviction of Israel that its lived narrative is permeated with powerful Yahwistic reality.

The brief narrative of Othniel provides a clear outline of the theology that dominates the larger narrative in four main points (3:7-11; see Josh 15:13-19; Judg 1:11-15):

—Israel *forgets* Yahweh (v. 7; see Deut 8:11, 19 on the theme);

—Yahweh *sells* Israel into oppression (v. 8);

—Israel *cries out* in petition to Yahweh (v. 9*a*);

—Yahweh raises up a deliverer who, as a "judge," becomes the hero of the story of rescue (vv. 9*b*-11).

Everything in Israel turns on its commitment to Yahweh, and by extrapolation, on the social practice of a Yahwistic ethic. It is to be recognized, however, that the book of Judges has a quite peculiar notion of *hero* not at all congruent with the conventional "hero myth." These heroes are odd, so that their achievements are all to be seen as miracles of God. Thus Ehud is a left-handed "misfit," Deborah is a woman, Gideon is a cowardly weakling, and Samson is a blind prisoner—an odd lot through which God acts for Israel!

The accounts of Ehud (3:12-30), Deborah and Barak (4:1-24), Gideon (6:1–8:35), Jephthah (11:1-40), and Samson (13:1–16:31) each feature an entertaining and subtle narrative that is made into a carrier of the determined Torah theology of this tradition. As one reads in these narratives, the interface of the two accents should be noticed in their great, imaginative variation.

Here we shall consider only the great poem of Judg 5, commonly called the Song of Deborah. In chapter 4, Deborah and Barak are the subjects of a hero tale that is closely parallel to the other hero tales that constitute the core of the book of Judges. It is remarkable that in the case of these two heroes, as for no other, the narrative account is paralleled by an extended poem. This poem, a victory song, is commonly regarded as one of the oldest, most powerful, and most artistic in the poetry of ancient Israel. It is the sort of poem that an oppressed people might delight to recite, as it tells about the defeat of a despised, oppressive power.

After the introductory verses, 2-3, identifying Yahweh as the celebrated subject of the poem, the poem characterizes the dramatic, overpowering entry of Yahweh as a vigorous warrior who comes from Sinai in the midst of a huge rainstorm (vv. 4-5). Verses 6-11 tell of the wondrous prosperity of the peasantry that becomes dominant in the land, which intimidates and disrupts common commerce (vv. 6-7a). This newly found dominance happened because of the leadership of Deborah, "mother in Israel," and because there was the embrace of a "new God" who gave power and energy to the peasants.

Of the two central characters in this combination of narrative and poem, there is no doubt that Deborah is the key actor, the one who looms large in Israel's memory. This poem in Judg 5 is conventionally designated as "The Song of Deborah." The victory poem shows the way in which this remarkable woman acted with bravery and energetic military leadership to accomplish a victory attributed to Yahweh. Alongside Deborah, it is worth noting that Jael, wife of Heber, is also a key actor in the victory of Yahweh (Judg 5:24-27). The two women together, Deborah and Jael, evidence the openness of Israelite memory and Israelite society in its early stages to the decisive role played by women in the most public affairs of the community.

The victory song tells, of course, of battle. The battle is presented as a great confrontation with the Canaanites of such scope that it might have concerned all the tribes of Israel. The great confrontation was apparently in the area of Megiddo, a prominent place for classic showdowns. We might imagine that the telling of the story of the great battle is for that culture not unlike the movie *Gettysburg*, which makes ancient defining memory available in the present tense. The poem proceeds in four scenes:

1. The poem speaks of the mustering and mobilizing of the tribes for battle (vv. 12-18, 22-23). The song first characterizes the summons of Deborah and Barak into the crisis, and then the mobilization of the several tribes. The poem is attentive to the different political positions of the several tribes, for this was a quite loose confederation that did not act in easy concert. Each tribe responded to the crisis according to its sense of its own interest, not unlike the way in which the powers of Europe responded differently to the recent

Bosnian crisis. The rhetoric communicates vigor and passion and momentum for an army on the move. Verse 22 treats us to the sounds of the horses charging into battle.

2. The lead warrior, Yahweh, is the vigorous partisan of Israel (v. 23). This is none other than the Creator of heaven and earth. The one who comes in a rainstorm (vv. 4-5) is the one who will mobilize large players in the creation stories, including rain, on behalf of Israel (see Josh 10:12-13). Israel has the sense of all of creation being mobilized on its behalf, so that in verse 21*b*, the warriors of Israel draw courage and energy from their cosmic allies.

3. In verses 24-27, the cosmic battle is focused, as a camera might zoom in, on a quite special scene. The action is in the tent of Jael, wife of Heber, a member of Israel now renowned for her courage. The poem tells how she duped the Canaanite general, Sisera, by a fake offer of hospitality. And when he had fallen asleep in her falsely reassuring tent, she beat him to death. The death scene in verse 27 is brief, but artistically exaggerated, so that the series of verbs makes the staggering work of dying as dramatic and drawn out as any elongated, violent death on television. Jael for this one great act is celebrated forever in Israel, a modest "tent-dwelling woman" overpowering a great Canaanite general—the stuff of self-congratulations in a peasant community.

4. The final scene of the poem (vv. 28-30) stands in stark contrast to the preceding. Here we witness a cadre of the wives of Canaanite military leaders. They are watching and waiting anxiously for the return of their men from battle. They wonder why they delay in coming home. They imagine that the generals dally over gambling and women, as military men might. These women are about to learn of the devastating defeat at Israelite hands. These grief-stricken women are contrasted with the buoyant, daring Jael. The poet knows, and all Israel knows, that the Canaanites are not coming home from battle. Because Israel has prevailed!

Indeed, in characteristic war rhetoric, verse 31 imagines that the enemies of Israel are the enemies of God. The victory is the large, sweeping claim that Yahweh's intention for Israel is bound to succeed. The land will be "ours" and the enemy will fail. This poetry, which is likely earlier than any of the prose narratives, is unchecked by Torah theology. It is the voice of emancipated Israel, utterly sure of Yahweh. This confidence in Yahweh is feebly echoed at the end of the Samson narrative, the last of the great "judges": "Lord GOD, remember me and strengthen me only this once, O God, so that with this one act of revenge I may pay back the Philistines for my two eyes" (16:28). Samson performs his show of strength. It is, however, a sorry business, for he dies with his enemies. The arrangement of the narrative, culminating with Samson and then going on to the sordidness of chapters 17–21, suggests that zeal for Yahweh has, by this time, been so compromised and accommodated that the capacity of the judges to cope with the threats posed to Israel is feeble and ineffective. Disobedience, cumulatively narrated through these stories, has taken its heavy toll.

The conclusion of the book of Judges narrates the failure of the era of the Judges (17–21). Two stories are told, one an account of the practice of idolatry (17–18), the other a narrative about barbaric social relations (19–21). These odd stories are framed by the repeated refrain:

In those days there was no king in Israel; all the people did what was right in their own eyes. (17:6; 18:1; 19:1; 21:25)

The stories tell about a land now in the grip of chaotic social relationships. The formula "no king" apparently refers to civil government and is an anticipation of the rise of monarchy to follow, an emergence narrated in 1 Samuel. It could also be that the "no king" formula is subtly understood as the failure of Torah governance and the disregard of the God of the Torah as the true King in Israel. In any case, the grand vision that propelled the entry into the land in the book of Joshua has come to a sorry end. It is evident that in tension with the claims of Torah faith, these stories imply a powerful advocacy for the coming monarchy as Israel's only hope. Without a reliable, stable institution of monarchy, Israel is destined to social chaos. The claim is not primarily descriptive, but an assertion made in the dispute over the "true" character of Israel.

In Judg 18:9-10, five men from the tribe of Dan in an odd tale of land assert:

"Come, let us go up against them; for we have seen the land, and it is very good. Will you do nothing? Do not be slow to go, but enter in and possess the land. When you go, you will come to an unsuspecting

211

people. The land is broad—God has indeed given it into your hands—a place where there is no lack of anything on earth."

This rhetoric is reminiscent of the urging of Caleb and Joshua:

> "The land that we went through as spies is an exceedingly good land. If the LORD is pleased with us, he will bring us into this land and give it to us, a land that flows with milk and honey." (Num 14:7-8; see Num 13:17; 14:9)

Except that the great anticipation of land in Numbers and Joshua is now chastened and weakened by idolatry. The great assurance at the beginning has now become a sorry condemnation. The Torah requirement is more than the new inhabitants of the land can sustain. The land of promise has become the land of an enormous problem, a problem in Israel writ large in exile (see 2 Kgs 23:26-27).

Conclusion

At the core of the Old Testament is a pondering of the land. Indeed Israel can never move far from the land, precisely because the God of promise is a God who cares about material existence and social well-being:

> There is an inseparable link between God's People, Law and Land. Without this "materialism" Judaism could not have made its fundamental contribution to Christianity, nor could it continue to bear its full witness to the world. How far from understanding the human texture of God's working are all these mysticisms and spiritualisms which attract so many today![2]

—*The land is gift,* for Yahweh intends those without land to receive a safe place in which to live;
—*The land is summons,* for those who live in the land must respond to the gift of the land;
—*The land is seduction,* for the safety of land is an invitation to trust the land as property and not as gift.
It is clear that the books of Joshua and Judges celebrate the capacity of Yahweh to work a revolutionary newness in the life of the world.

It is equally clear in these texts that Israel's memory and hope of land are saturated with violence in which even Yahweh is implicated.

A study of this literature may help us consider the strange measure of violence that continues to haunt Israel and, derivatively, Christian culture. The ideology of the land of promise shows up in all kinds of imperialisms, never more compellingly than in U.S. political history, which from the outset took North America to be a land of promise for Europeans, willing to displace Native Americans by violence, even as the Canaanites were routed. Belatedly and in a much lesser way, the same ideology feeds the militarism of contemporary Israel. And beyond the large history of violence in the U.S. and the recent ideology of Israel, we may observe that the great quarrels of our time, as in every time, are about land: the Basques in Spain, the Balkans, Northern Ireland, Israel and the Palestinians.

In its ancient time Israel all too readily and uncritically embraced that totalizing ideology. There is, now as then, the counterinsistence of Torah obedience as a way to organize the land alternatively. But the requirements of Torah are in practice a lean insistence in the face of an ideology of land possession. The end of such a perspective, so Israel learned, is displacement and dislocation exile:

> O land, land, land,
>   hear the word of the LORD! (Jer 22:29)

Israel hopes, against exile, in the God of all land promises, a hope beyond the exile that is itself the fruit of not listening:

> For surely I know the plans I have for you, says the LORD, plans for your welfare and not for harm, to give you a future with hope. Then when you call upon me and come and pray to me, I will hear you. When you search for me, you will find me; if you seek me with all your heart, I will let you find me, says the LORD, and I will restore your fortunes and gather you from all the nations and all the places where I have driven you, says the LORD, and I will bring you back to the place from which I sent you into exile. (Jer 29:11-14)

Notes

1. See J. C. Scott, *Weapons of the Weak* (New Haven: Yale University Press, 1987).

2. Amos Wilder, quoted in W. D. Davies, *The Territorial Dimension of Judaism* (Quantum Books 23; Berkeley: University of California Press, 1982), 138.

Bibliography

Butler, Trent C. *Joshua*. WBC. Waco: Word, 1983.

Carroll, Robert P. "The Myth of the Empty Land." *Semeia* 59 (1992): 79-93.

Davies, W. D. *The Territorial Dimension of Judaism*. Quantum Books 23. Berkeley: University of California Press, 1982.

Exum, J. Cheryl. "The Centre Cannot Hold: Thematic and Textual Instabilities in Judges." *CBQ* 52 (1990): 410-31.

Gnuse, Robert. "Israelite Settlement of Canaan: A Peaceful, Internal Process." Part 1, *BTB* 21 (1991): 56-66. Part 2, *BTB* 21 (1991): 109-17.

Gunn, David M. "Colonialism and the Vagaries of Scripture: Te Kooti in Canaan." In *God in the Fray: A Tribute to Walter Brueggemann,* edited by Tod Linafelt and Timothy K. Beal. Minneapolis: Fortress (1998), 127-42.

Hawk, L. Daniel. *Every Promise Fulfilled: Contesting Plots in Joshua*. Literary Currents in Biblical Interpretation. Louisville: Westminster John Knox, 1991.

Mitchell, Gordon. *Together in the Land: A Reading of the Book of Joshua*. JSOTSup 134. Sheffield: Sheffield Academic, 1993.

O'Brien, Conor Cruise. *God's Land: Reflections on Religion and Nationalism*. Cambridge: Harvard University Press, 1988.

Polzin, Robert. *Moses and the Deuteronomist: Deuteronomy, Joshua, Judges*. A Literary Study of the Deuteronomic History. New York: Seabury, 1980.

Prior, Michael. *Bible and Colonialism: A Moral Critique*. Sheffield: Sheffield Academic Press, 1997.

―――. *Zionism and the State of Israel: Moral Inquiry*. London: Routledge, 1999.

Schwartz, Regina M. *The Curse of Cain: The Violent Legacy of Monotheism*. Chicago: University of Chicago Press, 1997.

Scott, James C. *Weapons of the Weak*. New Haven: Yale University Press, 1987.

Stone, Lawson G. "Ethical and Apologetic Tendencies in the Redaction of the Book of Joshua." *CBQ* 53 (1991): 25-36.

Webb, Barry G. *The Book of the Judges: An Integrated Reading*. JSOTSup 46. Sheffield: Sheffield Academic, 1987.

Whitelam, Keith W. *Invention of Ancient Israel: The Silencing of Palestinian History*. London: Routledge, 1997.

Yee, Gale A., ed. *Judges and Method: New Approaches in Biblical Studies*. Minneapolis: Fortress, 1995.

CHAPTER SEVEN

THE RISE OF THE MONARCHY
1 Samuel, 2 Samuel, 1 Kgs 1–11, Selected Psalms

The opening chapters of the book of 1 Samuel introduce a period of social transformation in Israel. The time of the judges has ended and the period of kingship begins. In an ongoing narrative dominated by its central characters (Samuel, Saul, David, and Solomon), Israel moves through a period of crisis that ends with the reluctant participation of the prophet Samuel in the establishment of an Israelite kingship around 1000 BCE. The shaky transitional rule of Saul is displaced by the unifying leadership of David, who establishes a secure kingdom and passes the throne to his son Solomon. Solomon's reign takes on the trappings of many of the surrounding kingdoms and achieves considerable influence, but his rule also sows the seeds of dissension that lead to the division of the kingdom in 922 BCE. Although the books of 1 and 2 Samuel and 1 Kgs 1–11 give us information on the historical and sociopolitical realities that led to this reshaping moment in Israel's history, they are most concerned to provide a theological perspective on these transition events. How is the covenant community of the people of God to understand itself when it must accommodate to a kingship that borrows much of its trappings from surrounding Canaanite culture? How is the reign of earthly kings to be understood in light of the sovereignty of God? How is the activity of God seen in these transforming events? Why was Saul rejected, David affirmed, and Solomon judged? We will first set this period in geopolitical perspective but then turn our attention to the theological perspectives of the texts and traditions of these books in an effort to understand what this reshaping period came to mean for Israel's understanding of its life in relation to God.

The Crisis of Israel and the Transition to Kingship

The opening chapters of 1 Samuel gradually reveal an Israel in crisis. The crisis is both internal and external and will provide the final push toward the formation of a centralized form of governance and leadership in Israel. The biblical traditions as we now have them understand this new institution as a kingship, although its beginnings under Saul may have been little more than a chiefdom.[1]

The *internal pressures* toward kingship reach a crisis point in the biblical story with the corruption of the sons of Eli, the priest at Shiloh, where the Ark of the Covenant was kept and the religious traditions of Israel were preserved (1 Sam 2:11-17). Eli seems powerless to change their behavior (1 Sam 2:22-25). Further, we are told that the "word of the LORD was rare in those days" (1 Sam 3:1). In the period prior to this time (the book of Judges) the ongoing institutions of leadership that crossed tribal lines in Israel had been largely religious in character, involved in ritual observance (priesthood) and interpreting of the covenant law (judges, perhaps seers or interpreter's of God's word). Periodic military threats allowed for the raising up of charismatic military leaders to bring deliverance from the threat, but this office did not become institutionalized beyond the crisis, and never involved all of Israel's tribal groups.

Recent sociological and anthropological methods, applied to the data of the biblical text and of archaeological materials, suggest that there were growing pressures on the tribal groups of early Israel toward centralization even before the events of 1 Samuel.[2] These probably included increased population, incorporation of diverse cultural groups, and the agricultural limitations of the hill country. Recent studies of economic factors in this period suggest that there was a growing accumulation of wealth that needed to be defended. This would have produced pressure toward cooperative patterns of centralized governance and defense. Certainly there are indications of support in tribal Israel for kingship at an earlier stage. Gideon is invited to accept kingship after his victory over Midian: "Rule over us, you and your son and your grandson" (Judg 8:22). He refuses by affirming that "the LORD will rule over you" (8:23), but his son Abimelech tries to establish a kingship based at Shechem (Judg 9), which meets a disastrous end. The final chapters of Judges (17–21) reflect violent conflicts between tribal groups and suggest there is no authority to give unity, governance, and moral guidance in such times. "In those days there was no king in Israel; all the people did what was right in their own eyes" (Judg 17:6; 21:25).

The crisis of Israel and the transition to kingship is also the result of *external pressure*. This came in the form of the Philistines. In the tribal period reflected in the book of Judges, Israel had faced military threats from enemies before, and leadership had been raised up to lead coalitions of tribes to victory and relief from the threat. A single battle or campaign was sufficient to end the threat from an aggressive and ambitious neighbor or a hostile group preying on the weak. The Philistines represented a threat of a different order.

The Philistines established themselves on the Mediterranean coastal plain at the beginning of the twelfth century BCE as part of a general migration out of the Aegean of Sea Peoples attempting to settle coastal territories throughout the eastern Mediterranean. These Sea Peoples had tried to enter Egypt and were turned back, as wall paintings and inscriptions at Medinet Habu record. Pharaoh Rameses III allowed them to settle on the coastal plain to the southwest of Israelite tribal territory, where they formed a coalition of five chief cities: Gaza, Ashkelon, Ashdod, Ekron, and Gath. The Philistines, as this group of Sea Peoples were called, generally replaced the ruling class of Canaanite populations already in that region. They were well organized militarily, utilizing both professional standing armies and the hiring of mercenary troops. They had a strong economic base on the coastal plain and possessed iron weapons.

Toward the end of the eleventh century BCE, conflicts broke out between the Philistines and the southern tribes of Judah and Dan. The Philistines wished to expand their territory and sphere of influence. These conflicts are reflected in the stories of Samson (Judg 13–16). Eventually the tribe of Dan is forced to relocate in the far north of Israelite territory (Judg 17–18), and Judah seems, at least for a time, to have regarded the Philistines as their rulers (Judg 15:11).

This threat becomes more serious in the opening chapters of 1 Samuel. The Philistines appear to have embarked on military campaigns aimed at establishing their sovereignty over all of the Israelite central hill country. As we shall see, 1 Sam 4–6 records a major defeat of Israel at the hands of the Philistines. The Ark of the Covenant was captured, the city of Shiloh and its sanctuary destroyed, the hill country occupied by Philistine garrisons, and iron working monopolized so Israel could not make weapons (1 Sam 13:19-22). The attempt of tribal levies to meet the threat was swept away. Israel could submit to absorption into a Philistine empire or they could develop new forms of military and social leadership capable of meeting the more sustained threat represented by the Philistines.

At the opening of 1 Samuel we are in a time of growing pressure and support for new institutions of centralized governance and military leadership, and the primary model of the surrounding peoples is kingship. "We are determined to have a king over us, so that we also may be like other nations, and that our king may govern us and go out before us and fight our battles" (1 Sam 8:19*b*-20). Further, the institutions of religious leadership associated with Israel's identity as God's covenant people have become corrupt and self-serving (1 Sam 2:11-17, 22-25). By the end of the books of Samuel we have two new offices in Israel to meet this leadership crisis: the mediators of God's word, the prophets, and God's anointed ones, the kings.

Theological Perspectives on Kingship

The internal and external crises of Israel sketched above can be described in historical and socioeconomic terms, but 1 Samuel sees these crises primarily in theological perspective. God will not tolerate the faithlessness of the house of Eli (1 Sam 2:25*b*, 27-36). God will not tolerate the victory of the Philistines over God's own people (1 Sam 5:1–7:1). God will not tolerate the absence of the word of the Lord in Israel (1 Sam 3:19–4:1*a*). If there is to be a new future for Israel then God will raise up kings and prophets. But this affirmation is not made without some evidence of theological tension and ambiguity in Israel.

The Sovereignty of God

To understand the establishment of monarchy in Israel as not only a sociopolitical transformation but a theological transformation as well, we must give brief attention to the concept of the sovereignty of God. The notion of Yahweh as divine ruler appears much earlier in the biblical story. For example, it is God as sovereign Creator whose image we bear in our humanity and whose dominion we exercise as representatives of divine rule (Gen 1:26-29). The victory of Yahweh as divine warrior over an oppressive Pharaoh to bring Israel out of bondage in Egypt is celebrated by the proclamation of divine rule in Exod 15:18, "[Yahweh] will reign forever and ever." The imagery of Yahweh's rule as divine sovereign continues to be important in the ongoing story of Israel, as references from the Prophets and the enthronement psalms make clear. There are two distinct foci to the claim that Yahweh reigns as sovereign: God is sovereign over the cosmos, and God is sovereign over God's own people, Israel.

The clearest affirmations of Yahweh as *sovereign over all creation* are found in the enthronement psalms. These liturgies proclaim that Yahweh is King. Yahweh's sovereignty is manifest in ascendancy over all other gods, and rooted in divine rule over all creation as its originator. To create the cosmos and become its ruler Yahweh overcame the forces of chaos (appearing as "the flood," "Rahab," "waters"), a common motif in other ancient Near Eastern creation traditions.

> For the LORD is a great God,
> and a great King above all gods.
> In his hand are the depths of the earth;
> the heights of the mountains are his also.
> The sea is his, for he made it,
> and the dry land, which his hands have formed. (Ps 95:3-5)

> Let the heavens praise your wonders, O LORD,
> your faithfulness in the assembly of the holy ones.
> For who in the skies can be compared to the LORD?
> Who among the heavenly beings is like the LORD,
> a God feared in the council of the holy ones. . . .
> You rule the raging of the sea;
> when its waves rise, you still them.

You crushed Rahab like a carcass;
>   you scattered your enemies with your mighty arm.
> The heavens are yours, the earth also is yours;
>   the world and all that is in it—you have founded them. . . .
> For the LORD is yet our shield;
>   the Holy One of Israel is yet our king.
> (Ps 89:5-7*a*, 9-11, 18 [author's translation of v. 18])

The LORD is king, he is robed in majesty;
>   the LORD is robed, he is girded with strength.
> He has established the world; it shall never be moved;
>   your throne is established from of old;
>   you are from everlasting.
> The floods have lifted up, O LORD,
>   the floods have lifted up their voice;
>   the floods lift up their roaring.
> More majestic than the thunders of mighty waters,
>   more majestic than the waves of the sea,
>   majestic on high is the LORD! (Ps 93:1-4)

God's reign over all creation has moral implications for relationships among the nations. God's sovereignty is not morally and theologically neutral.

> Righteousness and justice are the foundation of your [God's] throne;
>   steadfast love and faithfulness go before you. (Ps 89:14; cf. Ps 97:2)

> Say among the nations, "The LORD is king!
>   The world is firmly established; it shall never be moved.
>   He will judge the peoples with equity." . . .
> He will judge the world with righteousness,
>   and the peoples with his truth. (Ps 96:10, 13*b*)

This portrait of God as sovereign Creator is foundational to the opening affirmation of God in the Bible in Gen 1. God in power and majesty imposes the order of creation on the chaotic waters and gives "dominion" to human beings created in God's own image as representatives of divine sovereignty over creation. The royal term "dominion" is not a reference to inherent human privilege to do with the earth what we wish. It is a commission to represent the sovereignty of the Creator as those in the "image of God."

God is also affirmed in the biblical tradition as *sovereign over Israel*; God is Ruler of a particular people in history. This understanding of God as King develops early in Israelite tradition in connection with the Exodus-Sinai traditions. The Song of the Sea celebrates Yahweh's victory over Pharaoh and deliverance of Israel with an affirmation of God's reign and God's royal abode (Exod 15:17-18). The sovereignty of the Creator God over all the nations is now related to kingship over Israel, and the victory over chaos is related to deliverance from oppression in history.

> The LORD their God is with them,
>   acclaimed as a king among them.
> God, who brings them out of Egypt,
>   is like the horns of a wild ox for them. (Num 23:21*b*-22)

God's rule and its moral bias to justice and righteousness will now be experienced in particular as a part of Israel's history.

> The LORD is king; let the peoples tremble!
>   He sits enthroned upon the cherubim. . . .
> Mighty King, lover of justice,
>   you have established equity;
> you have executed justice
>   and righteousness in Jacob. . . .
> Moses and Aaron were among his priests,
>   Samuel also was among those who called on his name.
> (Ps 99:1, 4, 6)

In light of these traditions it is understandable that Gideon would respond to the notion that he and his sons should be kings in Israel by saying, in effect, "We already have a king!" (Judg 8:22-23). Until the time of Samuel the view that earthly kingship would be in conflict with the idea of Yahweh's kingship seems to have held sway. The crises in Samuel's time, described above, began to tip the balance, but not without serious theological implications and accommodations.

The Literary Traditions of the Books of Samuel

The story of the establishment of kingship, from the tentative beginnings with Saul through the establishment of a secure state under David and a brief period of empire under Solomon, appears in the books of Samuel and the first eleven chapters of 1 Kings. But these narratives are not themselves neutral and disinterested tellings of the story. Neither do these narratives represent a single telling of the story. Almost all scholars agree that the present shape of these narratives reflects both the ambiguities and tensions of the time when these transitions to kingship first occurred in Israel and the reassessment of these events theologically at later crucial points in Israel's life. Thus, some brief comments on the *theological viewpoints of the literary traditions* are necessary.[3]

Especially in the narratives on the beginning of Saul's kingship there are differing theological assessments of the monarchy. Some materials clearly disapprove and find kingship sinful (e.g., 1 Sam 8 and 12). Other episodes are decidedly positive about Saul and his kingship, and see the saving work of God in these events (e.g., 9:1–10:16; 11:1-15). In earlier scholarship it was customary to find here a pro-kingship source and an anti-kingship source (the former judged as early and the latter as late). This effort has largely been abandoned. It seems likely that these traditions to some degree reflect the ambiguity and tension over kingship at the time it was established. There was no doubt support and opposition for this development. Collections of narratives for particular segments of the story of this period seem to have developed. Most scholars agree on finding a History of the Rise of David in 1 Sam 16:1–2 Sam 5:10, a Court History of David (sometimes called the Succession Narrative) in 2 Sam 9–20 and 1 Kgs 1–2, and a narrative on the Reign of Solomon in 1 Kgs 3–11. But these stories and collections with differing evaluations of kingship have been artistically woven into larger ongoing narratives by later persons or groups who also reflect their experience of kings at later points in Israel's history. Some scholars would see evidence of a Prophetic Edition of this story emphasizing the role of the prophets in anointing kings, holding them accountable to God's will, and ultimately rejecting them (Saul) or confirming them (David). Almost all scholars would see the Deuteronomistic Historian giving 1 and 2 Samuel, 1 Kgs 1–11 its final artistic shape as part of a great history work stretching from Joshua through 2 Kings and reflecting the experience of Babylonian exile and the final failure of kingship. This Deuteronomistic telling of the story of Israel's kings in the context of exile gives final shape to the text of the books of Samuel and Kings. The exile experience of the failure of kingship sometimes gives an urgency and poignancy to the Deuteronomistic retelling of the story of Israel's early kings.

Each of these retellings of the story of kingship and unified kingdom in Israel has its own perspective on these events and attempts to find meaning in these stories for their own experience as God's people. When we move through the narratives as they are now shaped, we will be interested from time to time in the vested interests of these various retellings as they become evident in the text. We must be aware that the voice of the storyteller is almost never a disinterested and neutral voice, but in the end we must encounter the story as it is now shaped and handed on through generations of the community of faith to make claim on our interests. Each segment of the story is dominated in turn by one of four figures: Samuel, Saul, David, and Solomon.

Samuel: Crisis and Transition (1 Sam 1–7)

We have already discussed the internal and external crises pressuring Israel toward the reshaping of its life in this period. These come to light in the opening chapters of 1 Samuel, but significantly the story of this time in Israel's life does not begin with a grand sketching of great issues. It begins with the desperation of a childless woman named Hannah. In 1 Sam 1, Hannah is one of two wives of Elkanah. Although she has the love of Elkanah, she is taunted by his other wife, Peninnah, and burdened by the stigma attached to childlessness for women of her time. On a pilgrimage to the sanctuary at Shiloh she boldly prays to God for a child and vows the dedication of such a child to the service of Yahweh. She is observed by the priest Eli, who thinks her drunk but ends by blessing her petition. "[Yahweh] remembered her" (1:19); she conceives and bears a child whom she names Samuel. When the child is weaned he is brought to the priest Eli to be raised in the service of Yahweh at Shiloh.

At key points in the final portion of Hannah's story the gift of the child is described in relation to the Hebrew verb *sha'al* "asked, lent" (vv. 20, 27-28), and this is the root of the name Saul. Samuel, of course, is to become God's prophet, and his life will be inextricably intertwined with that of Saul, Israel's first king.

Hannah's story is no doubt intended as representative of Israel's story in the chapters ahead. As we shall see, Israel, too, is facing an uncertain future. God's remembering of the plight of a childless woman like Hannah gives hope that God will remember and provide for Israel's future. We are placed on notice that in the coming stories of prophets and kings, battles and politics, the real story is of God's grace. Israel's future will be the gift of God and not simply of its own making. The movement of God's grace toward Israel's future with kings will begin with Hannah and her son, Samuel. Indeed, Hannah's name itself means "grace" in Hebrew.

Hannah's song in 2:1-10 is a hymn of thanksgiving, perhaps drawn from wider doxological traditions in Israel (see Ps 113), but placed here in the mouth of Hannah as not simply mother of Samuel but as mother of Israel. It moves from the lifting high of the horn ("strength") of Hannah (2:1a) to the lifting up of the horn ("power") of God's anointed one, the king (2:10b). Samuel's birth, an act of God's grace, is tied to the birth of kingship in Israel as an act of God's grace. The fortunes of Israel will look bleak in the chapters immediately ahead, but Hannah's song celebrates the reversals of power that God makes possible: weakness made strength; the lowly made exalted; the hungry filled; the poor made rich; the barren given children (2:4-8a). Indeed, these reversals made possible in God's power are a major theme of the books of Samuel. In 2 Sam 22 (almost identical to Ps 18), David sings a song of thanksgiving that touches on many of the same themes as Hannah's song. The books of Samuel are bracketed by the singing of Hannah and David, in anticipation and grateful acknowledgment of the power of God to overcome the obstacles to Israel's future. Hannah's singing becomes the pattern for Mary's singing in the Magnificat (Luke 1:46-55). Once again a woman sings in celebration of a birth enabled by the power of God's grace. Once again the song looks to a coming anointed one (*Messiah,* from the Hebrew for "anoint"). Both songs see the power of God as transforming power in behalf of the weak and powerless. Both sing of new power arrangements and potentialities that God can make possible for Israel and for the church. For Israel this will eventually be embodied in David; for the church this will be embodied in the son of David, Jesus.

Only after learning of God's grace through the distress of Hannah are we introduced to the distress of Israel. The sons of Eli have become corrupt, taking from the sacrifices for their own gain and engaging in immoral practices; Eli is powerless to stop them (2:12-17, 22-25). God cannot tolerate such faithlessness, and God's judgment on the house of Eli is pronounced in 2:27-36 (probably from the Deuteronomistic Historian, who can see the fulfillment of this fate). Eli's sons, Hophni and Phinehas, will die on the same day as a sign of this judgment. The house of Eli will die by the sword (Saul kills them all at Nob in 1 Sam 22:6-23). Only one will escape (Abiathar), and he will end in grief (he is banished by Solomon in 1 Kgs 2:26-27). God will raise up a new faithful priest (Zadok, made the priestly family of Solomon's temple, 1 Kgs 2:35).

Throughout the narration of the corruption and fate of the house of Eli runs a constant thread affirming the boy Samuel as the harbinger of God's new future for Israel. "The boy Samuel continued to grow both in stature and in favor with the LORD and with the people" (2:26; see also 2:11, 18, 21*b*; 3:1*a*; compare Luke 2:52). First Samuel 3 begins by noting that "the word of the LORD was rare in those days" (3:1*b*), and then tells a story of the divine word coming to Samuel while yet a boy. It is a word of judgment that Samuel must bring to his own mentor, Eli. It is a story of poignant contrasts. Eli, who is pious but compromised, cannot be a part of Israel's future, but it is he who recognizes Yahweh in Samuel's experience. Samuel, inexperienced and naive as just a boy, is the beginning of Israel's future. The chapter ends with priesthood discredited, but with Samuel raised to leadership as "trustworthy prophet of Yahweh" and a channel of God's word to all Israel (3:19–4:1*a*).

Our introduction to Israel's internal crisis gives way to an account of external threat, the Philistines. For the moment, Samuel recedes into the background while we are forced to face the seriousness of Israel's circumstances. It is nothing less than the survival of Israel that is at stake. The perspective of the narratives that tell this story in 1 Sam 4–6 is that nothing less than the power of God can save Israel, so human agency plays little role in the drama that unfolds here. The chapters are usually called the Ark Narrative and are thought by some to belong with 2 Sam 6, where the ark is brought to Jerusalem (this is by no means certain).[4] It is the Ark of the

Covenant that stands at the center of these episodes. The ark was the sacred symbol of God's presence in the midst of Israel, kept at the sanctuary in Shiloh. It was a gilded box containing treasures from Israel's past, but most significantly topped by winged cherubim above whom God was said to be invisibly enthroned. The ark was a kind of throne pedestal for God, the King. The making of the ark is described in Exod 37:1-9.

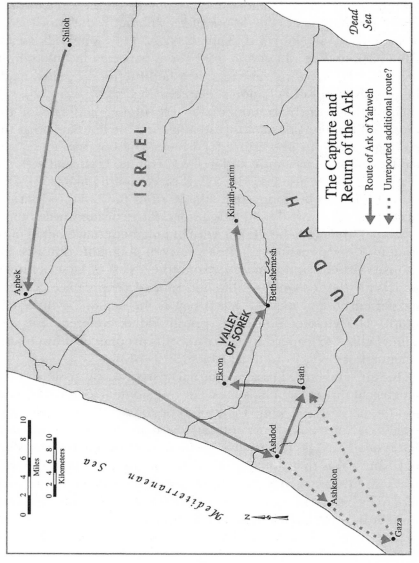

First Samuel 4 tells the disastrous story of a Philistine campaign to occupy the central hill country of Israel. In two battles Israel is decisively defeated, in spite of trying to summon a wider tribal levy to meet the threat. Most tragically the Ark of the Covenant is brought into the field to ensure God's presence in the second battle, and it is captured and carried off to Philistine territory. The sons of Eli, who carried the ark to battle, are killed in fulfillment of the earlier prophecy, and on hearing news of this Eli himself falls over dead. It is the beginning of the end for the house of Eli. We know from other references that the Philistines went on to occupy the land by the placement of garrisons throughout the country and the monopolizing of iron working to prevent the making of weapons (see 1 Sam 13–14). References by Jeremiah suggest that Shiloh was destroyed at this time as well (Jer 7:12; 26:6, 9). Political autonomy and religious identity for Israel are in danger of being swallowed up permanently by this enemy.

The central theological questions of the Ark Narrative are "Why has God let this happen?" and "What future can Israel possibly have in such circumstances?" These are not only important questions arising out of the events of Philistine conquest in the time of Samuel but important questions for later Babylonian exiles who have again lost the ark and its sanctuary, and for whom the Deuteronomistic historian is now retelling this story. This connection may be made explicit in the naming of the child Ichabod in 4:21: "The glory has *gone into exile* from Israel" (author's translation).

In its present placement after 1 Sam 1–3, the answer to the first question is that God has let this happen as judgment on the faithless leadership of Israel. The Ark Narrative itself says nothing about the sin of Eli's house but simply narrates the deaths of Eli and his sons, and the reader makes the connection with the corruption of the Elides. It takes chapters 5 and 6 to answer the second question.

In 1 Sam 5 and 6 the message is clear that God is the source of hope in seemingly hopeless circumstances. In chapter 5 the tables are turned. The ark is placed in the temple of Dagon, the Philistine god, as a sign of subjection. In the morning the statue of Dagon lies on its face; on the second morning Dagon lies with head and hands cut off. It only seemed that Yahweh was defeated, but now the "hand of the LORD" is "heavy" against the Philistines (5:6, 7, 9, 11), who are struck with a plague, and Dagon lies without hands, powerless to do

227

anything. In the face of this plague, the Philistines decide to send the ark home on a cart drawn by milk cows with offerings to appease the wrath of Israel's God (1 Sam 6). The power of God manifest in the ark is dangerous even to those Israelites who greet its return, and it is lodged at Kiriath-jearim where it will remain forgotten until the time of David (6:19–7:2).

It is significant that at the beginning of the books of Samuel is placed a story where human leadership plays no role at all in the course of events, for most of the books of Samuel and Kings are dominated by powerful and charismatic personalities. We are reminded by the Ark Narrative that salvation ultimately comes as the gift of God. When the drama of royal power gets under way, it will be well to remember this reminder that Yahweh is the real power behind these events and stories.

In 1 Sam 7 the internal and external crises of Israel come together. To meet the internal need for faithful and authentic leadership, God has raised up the prophet Samuel as the agent of *God's word*. To meet the external need to demonstrate where true power lies, Yahweh humiliated the Philistines and their god Dagon through the power of *God's hand*. Now, both Samuel and the Philistines appear in chapter 7. Samuel leads the people of Israel in turning away from idolatry (7:3-4) and in praying before Yahweh (7:5-6). When the Philistines attack at the time of this assembly, Samuel cries to the Lord and the Philistines are thrown into confusion by the thunder of Yahweh and routed by the Israelites (7:7-11).

The pattern here is much like what we have seen earlier in the book of Judges. In fact, three times in this chapter Samuel is said to have "judged" Israel (vv. 6, 15, 16). The pattern shows Israel turning from idolatry, God raising up a faithful leader, victory being won by the power of God to panic the enemy, and a period of peace lasting the lifetime of Samuel. The notice of peace from the Philistine threat (vv. 13-14) states that they did not again enter the territory of Israel for the lifetime of Samuel. This, of course, does not accord with many further references to conflict with the Philistines during the time of Saul and David.

The picture of Samuel here is an idealized one. He has already appeared as the prophet of God's word. Now he is charismatic deliverer like the judges of earlier times. Further, he is pictured in 7:15-17 as traveling a judicial circuit to administer the covenant law, and as building an altar (a priestly role). In a time of threat and dissolution Samuel is seen as standing in the breach, exerting leadership on several fronts, and almost single-handedly maintaining existence and identity for Israel. The suggestion of the narrative at this point is that God has raised up faithful leadership capable of meeting both the internal and the external crises of Israel. What need does Israel have for a king? The request for a king from the elders of Israel in chapter 8 is really unnecessary. Whereas Samuel cried to Yahweh and Yahweh answered (7:9), Samuel's warning in chapter 8 suggests that those who have chosen a king may someday cry to Yahweh and Yahweh will not answer (8:18). This may, in particular, be a portion of the storytelling addressed to exiles who have trusted kings instead of Yahweh. The episode in 1 Sam 7 may suggest to such exiles that they can still cry out and Yahweh will answer if their trust is in God (and God's prophets?) and not in the institutions of human power. As we shall see, even kings might be redeemed if their trust is in Yahweh rather than in their own power. As we head into a time of kingship in Israel, 1 Sam 7 is a final reminder that true security is always with Yahweh.

Chronology for the United Monarchy*

1020 BCE   Beginning of Saul's reign

1000   Death of Saul; David king at Hebron

993   David king of all Israel

961   David's death; Solomon becomes king

922   Death of Solomon; division of kingdom

*Chronology is uncertain; dates are approximate

Saul: The Threat, the Promise, and the Tragedy of Kingship (1 Sam 8–15)

In 1 Sam 8 the elders of Israel approach the prophet Samuel with a request to give them a king. Saul is not yet on the scene. Our first encounter with kingship in Israel is with the problems it poses and the dangers it represents as these are voiced in Samuel's response to the people's request.

Except for an allusion to the corruption of Samuel's sons, his successors as judge in Israel (8:1-3, 5), there is no mention of crisis in Israel as a justification for raising the issue of kingship. The Philistines are not mentioned, and the request of the elders has little to do with the problem of Samuel's sons. The focus is on kingship as a challenge to Israel's religious tradition as God's covenant people, and we are not yet allowed to consider pragmatic justifications for turning to kingship.

The *threat of kingship* is seen first in the people's request for a king "like other nations" (8:5, 20). Israel's life as God's covenant people set them apart from the nations. The patterns of covenant loyalty and obedience represented a model of alternative community in the world. It is the distinctiveness of Israel's covenant calling and the danger of accommodation to the cultural patterns of the surrounding nations that is at stake in this transition moment. The issues of distinctiveness and accommodation will appear over again in many forms throughout the story of Israel's kings. Even after Samuel's warning of the dangers (8:11-18), the people insist, "No! but we are determined to have a king over us, so that we also may be like other nations, and that our king may govern us and go out before us and fight our battles" (8:19-20).

The theological threat of kingship is also presented as a challenge to the sovereignty of God. Samuel, who is displeased and rather petulant throughout this encounter, prays to Yahweh, and Yahweh responds, "They have not rejected you, but they have rejected me from being king over them" (8:7b). Yahweh suggests that the people's behavior is part of a pattern of idolatry since they left Egypt. Kingship, as the abandonment of God's rule, is equated with apostasy. Loyalty to an earthly king would displace loyalty owed to God alone. Yet, surprisingly, Yahweh tells Samuel to listen to the people's voice, but he is to warn them of the "ways of the king" (8:9).

The speech of Samuel describing the practices of kings is dominated by the verb *take* (8:11-18). Kings operate by the grasping that comes from power. Covenant community operates by the gift of relationship to God, from which loyalty and obedience flow. Royal power takes for its own needs. Many think the practices reflected in Samuel's warning show knowledge of the actual practices under

Solomon when much of Samuel's picture becomes reality. The most devastating warning comes at the end: "And you shall be his slaves. And in that day you will cry out because of your king, whom you have chosen for yourselves; but the LORD will not answer you in that day" (8:17b-18). It will be a reversal of the Exodus, when the people cried out and God delivered them (Exod 2:23-24). This slavery will be of the people's own choosing. The choice of a king runs the risk of negating the covenant community for which God delivered them.

God goes further in instruction to Samuel, "Listen to their voice and make for *them* a king" (8:22, author's translation and emphasis). If there is to be a king, it will come through the designation of God's prophet. But this first experiment is on the people's terms. God will not abandon them in this experiment, but eventually, when the kingship of Saul has failed, God will insist on kingship on divine terms. In later sending Samuel to anoint David, God says, "I have provided for *myself* a king among his [Jesse's] sons" (16:1). Indeed, Samuel first rejects Saul by looking forward to David as "a man after his [God's] own heart" (13:14).

Perhaps reflecting the divided mind of Israel over the matter of kingship, Samuel's warning is followed in 1 Sam 9:1–10:16 by a story filled with the *promise of kingship.* Saul enters the story as a young man sent to seek the lost donkeys of his father. In a story of considerable charm and rich detail, the reader listens as God reveals to Samuel that God has sent this inexperienced young man as the one who will "save my people from the hand of the Philistines; for I have seen the suffering of my people, because their outcry has come to me" (9:16). The role to be given Saul could hardly be more positive. It is to be God's deliverer in language reminiscent of the Exodus deliverance.

Samuel is to anoint him as *nagid,* a term translated as "ruler" or "prince." Some believe this term indicates a role as military commander rather than as king, but this seems unlikely since the whole episode is referred to in 10:16 as "the matter of the kingship." The term may indicate a royal-designate who has not yet acceded to the throne. Saul and his young companion naively seek out Samuel as a seer to help find the lost donkeys, only to become part of the large drama God has set in motion. Saul is made honored guest at a banquet, and in the morning Samuel anoints him and commissions him to "reign over the people of the LORD and . . . save them from the

231

hand of their enemies all around" (10:1). Samuel promises confirming signs, the most important of which is narrated in detail. As Saul encounters a band of ecstatic prophets God gives him "another heart" and he is seized by the "spirit of God" and prophesies with them (10:9-13). Saul is transformed by God's spirit for the sake of the task given to him.

Saul is now God's anointed one and the recipient of God's spirit. In 10:17-27, although there is a brief reference to the theme of the rejection of God (v. 19), Saul is designated by lot, and presented by Samuel to the people as "the one whom the LORD has chosen" (v. 24a). The people acclaim Saul as king (v. 24b). It now remains for Saul to demonstrate the power of God's spirit and vindicate the acclamation of the people. The episode in 1 Sam 11 serves this purpose as word reaches Saul that the people of Jabesh-gilead are besieged by the Ammonites. In the style of the stories of Judges, the spirit comes mightily upon Saul (11:6), and he leads the tribal levies to the relief of Jabesh-gilead. Again the people acclaim him king (11:14-15) in what may have been a parallel account of Saul's kingship but is now styled a renewal (v. 14) of kingship. Some had earlier expressed doubts about Saul, perhaps about kingship in general, by asking "How can this man save us?" (10:27). Now the question of whether Saul can save has been answered in the affirmative.

In the present form of the story, 1 Sam 9–11 represents a positive response to the questions raised about kingship in 1 Sam 8, but it is a conditional response. What appears in these positive chapters is an emergent theology of God's anointed one (Hebrew *mašiaḥ* or Messiah). Kings are to be allowed in Israel, but they must be designated by God and anointed by God's prophet. They will be empowered by God's spirit and affirmed by the people. They will demonstrate the power of the spirit in mighty deeds. What remains ahead, for Saul or any of God's anointed kings, is a career that must be measured by obedience to God's covenant and monitored by God's prophet. In such a theology of God's anointed it is clear that kings in Israel will not be self-justifying centers of authority, rivaling God's ultimate sovereignty. They rule subject to God's designation and accountability. In the books of Samuel, this theology of kingship is used to answer the question of why Saul failed but David succeeded. Saul will be called to account by the prophet Samuel for disobedience and rejected. David, like Saul, will be anointed by a prophet, receive God's spirit, be publicly presented in the service of Saul, perform a mighty deed in the killing of Goliath, and ultimately pursue a career that is judged faithful. Instead of rejection, David and his dynasty will be confirmed in kingship by the prophet Nathan. Because of the prominent role of the prophet in this pattern, many believe that 1 Samuel reflects a prophetic editor shaping and combining diverse traditions into the present pattern. This pattern now makes clear that kings in Israel reign through the empowerment of God's spirit and their ultimate authority rests in God, who can withdraw that spirit, as Saul will learn to his grief.

The great speech of Samuel in 1 Sam 12 occupies a key position between the stories of Saul's accession to kingship and his career as king. Such great speeches at key points in Israel's story are a mark of the Deuteronomistic History and divide it into epochs (e.g., Josh 24; 2 Sam 7). This one bridges the tension between threat and promise that kingship introduced into Israel's story. Following a vindication of his own leadership (vv. 1-5), and a recitation of God's faithfulness to Israel (vv. 6-11), Samuel declares that the kingship arose in disobedience and rejection of God's rule (v. 12). He speaks of the king both as the one "you have chosen" and as the one "the LORD has set . . . over you" (v. 13). The people acknowledge and confess their sin: "We have added to all our sins the evil of demanding a king for ourselves" (v. 19). But despite its origins in disobedience, kingship can serve God's purposes and the people's well-being: "If both you and the king who reigns over you will follow the LORD your God, it will be well" (v. 14). However, there is still danger. "If you still do wickedly, you shall be swept away, both you and your king" (v. 25). The danger for Saul becomes reality in the immediate context when he is rejected for disobedience to God's word (cf. esp. 1 Sam 15). In the longer flow of Israel's story this warning may already reflect the Deuteronomist's experience of Babylonian exile.

It is not a coincidence that kings and prophets appear at the same point in Israel's story. Samuel makes clear that alongside Israel's kings there will be a role for Israel's prophets. "Moreover as for me, far be it from me that I should sin against the LORD by ceasing to pray for you; and I will instruct you in the good and the right way" (12:23). The intercession and guidance of the prophets will help ensure covenant faithfulness in this new age of Israel's kings. What unfolds from this point forward in the books of Samuel and Kings is Israel's experience of life under this model. What had been largely a story of God and people becomes a more complex story of God, king, prophet, and people. (The role of priest was a defined leadership office in respect to cultic matters prior to this time, but even its character will be redefined by the building of Solomon's temple.)

In 1 Sam 13–15, three episodes chronicle the failure of Saul's kingship as rapidly as the three episodes in chapters 9–11 celebrated Saul's rise to the throne. In these chapters and on through the stories of David's rise until Saul's own tragic suicide (1 Sam 31), Saul's story models the *tragedy of kingship*—the unhappy consequences that flow from failure to conduct the affairs of the kingdom in harmony with God's covenant.

In 1 Sam 13:7-15 Saul becomes impatient at a deteriorating military situation with the Philistines and conducts a prebattle sacrifice that was to wait for Samuel's arrival. When Samuel arrives he condemns Saul's action and rejects him from the possibility of dynasty in Israel. In 1 Sam 14:1-46 Saul's son Jonathan heroically initiates an action against the Philistines that becomes the occasion for a great Israelite victory. Saul is slow to take advantage of the opportunity. He seeks ritual assurance before taking action. He makes an ill-advised oath trying to guarantee victory, and he is willing to take the life of his own son for inadvertently violating this oath, but he is prevented by the people. Saul's leadership seems uncertain and hesitant. He is outwardly pious but is unable to act in trust that God's purposes will go forward. In 1 Sam 15 Saul is commanded by the prophet Samuel to conduct a campaign against the Amalekites and put them to the ban (the ritual destruction of an enemy and their possessions). Saul returns with the Amalekite king as a prisoner and the best of the cattle as booty. For this disobedience Samuel declares that God has rejected Saul as king and the kingdom is torn from his grasp.

In 15:11 God regrets making Saul king. The experiment with Saul is over. Kingship on the people's terms has failed in the disobedience of Saul. A cycle of rejection has been completed. The people had "rejected" God as king over them (8:7); Saul had "rejected" God's word and God had "rejected" Saul as king (15:23*b*).

We are torn over the fate of Saul. Particularly at this point, his story is told as that of a tragic man who meant well for Israel. It is easy to be sympathetic to Saul, especially when Samuel seems so petulant, and we are not sympathetic to the ordinances of holy war that Saul has violated. Samuel is not a disinterested, innocent theological voice here. He represents an ideological commitment to the older tribal system in Israel, and therefore stands in opposition to the new future God may bring. The clash between Samuel and Saul is a conflict of older and emerging views on how God is at work in Israel. Nevertheless, Saul is not simply a victim. What is also at stake here is the danger of autonomous political authority extending its influence into the realm of religious institutions and violating covenant commands for its own political purposes. God's focus in 1 Samuel is Israel's future and not Saul's. The episodes of 1 Sam 13–15 expose Saul's weaknesses. He is the people's king, and the course of kingship is not going well. There is a danger that Israel's future is to be "swept away" with its king (12:25). God's regret signals a divine decision that Saul cannot be the direction of Israel's future. Already in the two rejection stories David begins to appear as Israel's future. It is David who is the "man after God's own heart" sought out to rule after Saul in 13:14, and it is David who is the "neighbor of yours, who is better than you" and will receive the kingdom torn from Saul's grasp (15:28). God will establish the kingship on a new footing with David. Saul was the people's king (8:22) and that experiment of kingship depended on obedience (12:14-15, 25). David would be God's king (16:1), and Davidic kingship would rest on God's unconditional commitment and God's faithfulness to that commitment. David, too, will be a sinner, and he will suffer consequences for his sin; but God's faithfulness will allow the dynasty of David to endure (see later discussion of 2 Sam 7). Indeed, David and his dynasty become a symbol of hope in God's faithfulness, even when earthly kingdoms seem to have perished and only the eschatological hope of a coming anointed one (a Messiah) endures. David is the true heart of the story of Israelite kingdom and it is to his story that we must turn.

David: The Man After God's Own Heart
(1 Sam 16–2 Sam 24)

The biblical tradition is endlessly fascinated with David. Clues to his arrival on the scene are scattered throughout 1 Samuel long before he appears. Subsequent kings are measured against his story. He is linked with the poetry of the Psalter, and his story is idealized and told again by the Chronicler (1 Chron 11–29).

It is clear in 1 Samuel that as soon as David appears, even though Saul still physically occupies the throne, the story is David's story. Scholars have long recognized a collection of materials on the *Rise of David* that stretches from 1 Sam 16:1 to 2 Sam 5:10. At the beginning of this long collection we can recognize a pattern of episodes similar to Saul's story. David is also anointed by the prophet Samuel (16:1-13) and "the spirit of the LORD came mightily upon David from that day forward" (v. 13). Saul's possession by God's spirit seemed to be more episodic. David makes a public appearance in the court of Saul (16:14-23), but he cannot yet be publicly acclaimed king since Saul still occupies the throne. David does a mighty deed in killing Goliath and bringing deliverance to Israel (17). What follows then are detailed narratives on David's rise to the kingship and his actions as king. Instead of rejection David is eventually confirmed in the kingship by the prophet Nathan and given a dynastic promise (2 Sam 7). David becomes the model of success as God's anointed one.

Sadly, David's reception of God's spirit is followed immediately by a notice of the departure of the spirit of Yahweh from Saul, and further, "an evil spirit from the LORD tormented him" (16:14). Just as Yahweh's spirit marked the presence of God with Saul, so too the evil spirit marked the alienation of Saul from God. The concept here is not a divine determination of Saul's behavior. Some think the word translated as "evil" here would be better translated as "troubling." The coming of this "troubling" spirit was an occasional matter, seeming to signal times of depression, panic, and loss of control by Saul. Ironically, David's music could dispel these moments (16:23). There is no suggestion that this spirit is the determiner of Saul's actions in general. The story of David's rise is unfortunately a story of Saul's decline. Saul could not be Israel's future as king, but he still had the freedom to be a man of integrity. Unfortunately, this is not the path Saul chose. David's early successes as a military commander anger rather than please Saul. He is consumed with insane jealousy and plots to have David killed (1 Sam 18–19). When David is forced to become a fugitive, Saul pursues him, wasting the energies of the kingdom, which should have been used against the

Philistines. Saul turns on his son (20:30) and his own men (22:7-8). In a moment of insanity he orders the massacre of the priests at Nob for imagined support of David (22:6-23). A pathetic, broken man, Saul finally takes his own life on Mt. Gilboa after witnessing the defeat of his army and the deaths of his sons at the hands of the Philistines (1 Sam 31).

David is the rising counterpoint to Saul's fall. Over and again we are told that "the LORD was with David" (17:37; 18:12, 14, 28; 20:13; 2 Sam 5:10). It is clear that David represents God's future for Israel. The stories of these chapters on the rise of David (1 Sam 16:1–2 Sam 5:10) are a unique mixture of theological assurance and sociopolitical honesty about the actions and events that took David to the throne. David appears as genuinely pious, praying to God for guidance and recognizing his own subordination to divine will, yet trusting in God's acceptance of his own freedom to claim the future. The collection of traditions on David's rise are probably intended to exonerate him from claims that he came to power by illegitimate means. The stories carefully show him as respectful of Saul, even sparing his life (chaps. 24 and 26). Even though he served the Philistines, he used his position to aid the people of Judah and did not take arms against Israel (chaps. 27, 29). He mourned the deaths of Saul and Jonathan and was guiltless in the deaths of Ishbosheth and Abner (2 Sam 1–4). He was a capable military commander and an astute politician and acted accordingly, but he was also the "man after God's own heart" and acknowledged the role of divine providence in his life (see, e.g., 1 Sam 23).

An element of David's story is his identification with the marginal and dispossessed. God's choice for Israel's future is an eighth son of a little-known Bethlehemite (Saul seemed to be from a prosperous and well-known family). He cannot afford a dowry for the king's daughter (18:23). As a fugitive he attracts to himself the economic and political outcasts of Israel, who become his entourage (22:1-2). In these early stories David is celebrated, but not idealized. He is courageous, resourceful, loyal to friends, ambitious, and a bit rough-hewn. He does what he must to survive. Not a bad choice for the future of a people who were once slaves in Egypt.

In 2 Sam 5–8 we move from David's rise to David as king. These are texts that tell us something of the *Davidic kingdom* and the development of a *royal theology*. In these chapters David becomes king over South and North, consolidates and expands the kingdom, and establishes a true royal state for the first time in Israel. There are indications in the Saul stories that he aspired to full kingship. He had a small capital at Gibeah. He appointed some permanent royal officers, such as Abner, who commanded his army. He hoped for dynasty through the succession of his son Jonathan to the throne (1 Sam 20:31). Nevertheless, many historians of this period believe that Saul achieved little more than a chiefdom with influence largely limited to his own tribe of Benjamin and some of the immediately surrounding Israelite territory. It remained for David to establish true kingship in Israel.

The final chapters of the rise of David material (2 Sam 2:1–5:10) detail the complex series of events following the death of Saul that brought David at last to the throne. Of greatest significance in this narrative sequence is the fact that David becomes king first over the tribe of Judah at Hebron (2 Sam 2:1-4*a*), which is his own tribe and the place where he has built a base of influence while seeming to serve the Philistines. In the North, Saul's general, Abner, tries to maintain Saul's son Ishbosheth as king, but finally abandons this effort in order to support David, only to be murdered in a personal vendetta by David's general, Joab (2 Sam 3:6-39). Subsequently, Ishbosheth is assassinated and his head brought to David (4:1-12). David publicly mourns Abner and has Ishbosheth's assassins executed to avoid personal responsibility for these deaths, and his efforts are apparently successful. The elders of Israel, the remnants of Saul's northern kingdom, come to David and make him their king as well (5:1-5). David in effect now occupies two thrones and possesses a much broader base in united Israel than Saul ever did. Significant victories over the Philistines (5:17-25) establish secure borders for the development of a true kingdom—a nation. David extends the borders of this small kingdom (8:1-14) and establishes economic ties with the Phoenician city of Tyre (5:11). If Saul was little more than a tribal chief, David certainly moves toward true kingship. The picture of his activities and accomplishments is one of kingdom building, and David is shown as politically astute and militarily formidable in establishing his kingdom. Yet, throughout the narrative we are reminded of Yahweh's ultimate role in David's successes. The story of his rise ends in 5:10: "David became greater and greater, for the LORD, the God of hosts, was with him." His military success is marked by the notice in 8:14*b* that "the LORD gave victory to David wherever he went." The role of divine providence is not simply one shared by the narrator with the reader; David is also aware that he has been gifted by God's grace: "David then perceived that the LORD had established him king over Israel, and that he had exalted his kingdom for the sake of his people Israel" (5:12).

Two of David's actions are of special significance, both theologically and politically. David was faced with the problem of locating his capital. He could not afford to show favoritism to either the Judean or the Israelite groups that had made him king. In 2 Sam 5:6-10 we are told that David captured the Jebusite city of Jerusalem by stealth and made it his capital. Jerusalem was located on the boundary between Judah and Benjamin and was now the literal city of David, belonging to none of the Israelite tribal groups. It has been suggested by many scholars that with Jerusalem David gained not only a politically neutral capital but an urban Canaanite (Jebusite) center with many of the scribes, tradesmen, architects, and managers necessary to establishing a full-scale monarchy and its attendant bureaucracy.[5] Village-based and tribal Israel did not possess populations with these skills in any abundance. David found a nucleus for his needs in Jerusalem, but eventually incorporated all of the other Canaanite cities within his borders into the kingdom.

With no other existing models David, and Solomon after him, largely models the institutional structures of kingship after existing monarchies in the Canaanite city-states and small kingdoms of the region. These cultural borrowings, however, come with their own ideologies. The danger is that this adoption of institutions and practices alien to Israel would drive out those things distinctive to Israel and its Yahwistic faith. This was no doubt the danger feared by those who opposed monarchy in any form for Israel. It was this clash of new ways and older traditions that had also led to the conflicts between Samuel and Saul that resulted in Saul's rejection.

David took a second dramatic action at the beginning of his kingship to resolve this tension and preserve a role for Yahwistic faith in this newly emergent Israelite monarchy. In 2 Sam 6 David launched a successful search for the Ark of the Covenant, which had been

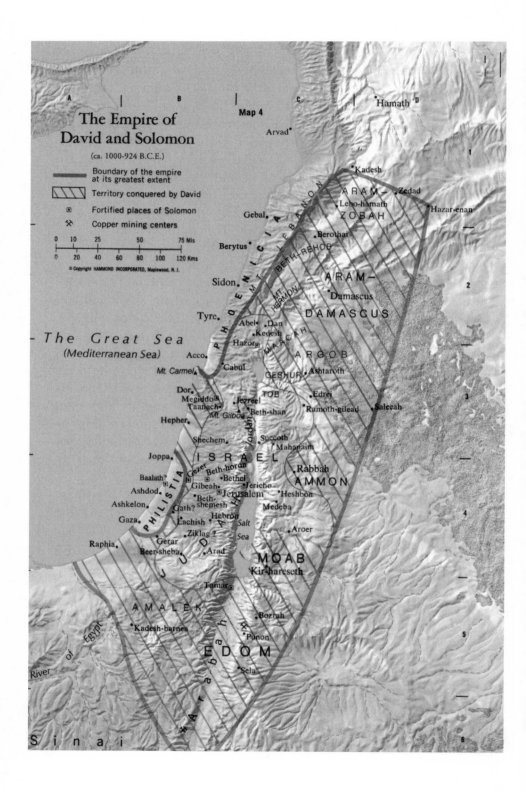

The Empire of
David and Solomon

(ca. 1000-924 B.C.E.)

Boundary of the empire
at its greatest extent

Territory conquered by David

Fortified places of Solomon

Copper mining centers

0	10	25	50	75 Mis
0	20	40	60	80	100	120 Kms

© Copyright HAMMOND INCORPORATED, Maplewood, N.J.

Map 4

Hamath

Arvad

Kadesh

ARAM-
ZOBAH

Zedad

Leho-hamath

Hazar-enan

Gebal

Berytus

Berothai

Sidon

ARAM-
DAMASCUS

Damascus

Tyre

Abel

Dan

Kedesh

Hazor

ARGOB

Acco

Cabul

GESHUR

Ashtaroth

The Great Sea
(Mediterranean Sea)

Mt. Carmel

Dor

Megiddo

Taanach

Mt. Gilboa

Jezreel

Beth-shan

TOB

Edrei

Ramoth-gilead

Salecah

Hepher

Shechem

Succoth

Mahanaim

Joppa

ISRAEL

Baalath?

Gezer

Beth-horon

Bethel

Rabbah

AMMON

Ashdod

Gibeah

Jericho

Heshbon

Ashkelon

Beth-
shemesh

Jerusalem

Gath?

Medeba

Gaza

Lachish

Hebron

Salt
Sea

Aroer

Raphia

Gerar

Ziklag?

Arad

Beer-sheba

JUDAH

MOAB

Kir-hareseth

Tamar

AMALEK

Bozrah

Kadesh-barnea

Punon

EDOM

Sela

Sinai

lodged in obscurity at Kiriath-jearim since the great Philistine defeat of Israel recorded in 1 Sam 4–6. David brought the ark to Jerusalem in a celebratory procession and danced before the ark himself. He lodged it in a shrine in Jerusalem, now making his capital also the central sanctuary of Yahwistic covenant faith. Instead of the antagonism that brought Saul to grief, David was now the patron of the older covenant traditions. David raises the possibility that kingship can serve this covenant faith rather than displace it.

This connection with the ark signals the development of a Davidic or royal theology in Israel, an effort to understand the development of Davidic dynasty as a further expression of Israel's Yahwistic covenant faith.

Psalm 132 may show this emergent Davidic theology at an early stage. This psalm remembers and celebrates David's search for the ark and his concern that it find an appropriate resting place (vv. 1-7). It then goes on to celebrate the "sure oath" that Yahweh swore to David. This oath involves the promise of ongoing dynasty to David and the choice of Zion as God's dwelling place. Davidic dynasty and the temple on Mt. Zion (which Solomon builds) are to be new signs of God's grace toward Israel. In Ps 132:11-12 there is, however, a conditional element:

> "One of the sons of your body
>   I will set on your throne.
> If your sons keep my covenant
>   and my decrees that I shall teach them,
> their sons also, forevermore,
>   shall sit on your throne."

The kings of the Davidic dynasty are to be the servants of the covenant and its instruction.

This Davidic theology is more fully presented in the dynastic oracle given by the prophet Nathan to David in 2 Sam 7. This complex but centrally important text shows evidence of development long after the time of David, so it reflects both emergent and fully developed royal ideology in Israel. The central feature of this is the understanding that God has made an unconditional promise (some use the term *covenant*) of eternal dynasty to David. The conditional "if" of Ps 132:12 is gone. The tension between conditional and unconditional promise is a struggle at the heart of Israel's life. We will see this issue reflected again in the preaching of judgment to later Israel and in the theological crisis represented by exile. Is God's promise ended with disobedience or does it endure in spite of disobedience? Psalm 132 and 2 Samuel 7 represent differing poles in this theological tension within Israel's experience of Davidic dynasty.

David desires to build a house for Yahweh (7:1-2) since he himself has a fine house of cedar and the ark is lodged in a tent. This chapter plays on the multiple meanings of the word *house*. Here *house* can mean "temple" or "palace." Through the prophet Nathan, God responds that David will not be the one to build such a house for Yahweh. Further, God has never needed such a house but has been content with a tent sanctuary, a tabernacle (7:5-7). The text here reflects the tension in Israel between the freedom of God expressed in the mobility of ark and tent, and the fixity (even the possession) of God represented in a temple. Temples were associated with Canaanite religion, and this text may reflect opposition to the adoption of such Canaanite practices.

The prophet Nathan announces that God does not desire a house, but instead promises to build a house for David (7:11). Here *house* is used to mean "dynasty." The son who reigns after David will build a "house/temple" for the Lord (7:13). This is obviously a reference to Solomon. His sons, David's descendants, will reign forever. There are no conditions expressed. If disobedient the descendants of David may be chastised, but God will not take steadfast love away from them as with Saul (7:14-15). "Your house and your kingdom shall be made sure forever before me; your throne shall be established forever" (7:16). Unlike Ps 132, 2 Sam 7 holds that kingship is an eternal, unconditional promise, and the chapter probably represents a later stage of development in the royal theology.

Those who see only self-serving political interest here may see in 2 Sam 7 the attempt of earthly power to justify itself by appeal to divine authority. This remarkable text cannot, however, be so easily caricatured. In the notion of divine unconditional promise lies an understanding of divine providence that refuses to be deterred by the sins of individual kings or their potentially self-serving royal ideologies. God's promise implies a divine future for kingdom in Israel that will not be limited by human sin. Sin will have its consequences, but the promise will not be revoked. This makes the Davidic theology a powerful new witness to God's grace in behalf of Israel. In fact, this promise will outlast the Judean political throne, which ends with exile, and will find expression in Jewish messianism. Trust in the promise given by this text kindles hope that one is always coming in the line of David who can bring hope in the midst of hopelessness and the kingdom of life among the kingdoms of death. The early Christian church saw in Jesus Christ one who came in the line of David to demonstrate God's faithfulness to this promise that the kingdom will always come.

The narratives of 2 Sam 9–20 have long been recognized by scholars as a separate source document.[6] Some have included 1 Kgs 1–2 and labeled this chronicle the Succession Narrative for its major emphasis on who will succeed to the throne of David. It is Solomon who finally is chosen in 1 Kgs 1–2. Others would see succession as only one concern and call this material the Court History of David with its emphasis on happenings in the royal court and the royal family. Many of these scholars would leave 1 Kgs 1–2 separate as the start of Solomon's story. The miscellaneous materials in 2 Sam 21–24 are often called "appendices to the books of Samuel," but they may be more than simply afterthoughts, and we will want to look at these chapters more closely after we have considered the stories of the Succession Narrative/Court History. In these stories we see a more personal side of David and gain a fuller understanding of his human weaknesses. The picture is not of royal power but of human vulnerability. This picture is painted with uncommon literary artistry and psychological insight in these chapters. In the judgment of many, this portion of 2 Samuel represents a considerable cultural achievement as it moves beyond reportage and narration to literature of uncommon sensitivity to human possibilities and vulnerabilities.

Both 2 Sam 9 and 10 show David as king acting with loyalty (*ḥesed*), a quality of steadfast commitment often associated with covenant. In chapter 9 he shows this loyalty to Mephibosheth, the son of Jonathan, who is brought to court and given an honored place there to fulfill the vow of loyalty David made to his friend Jonathan, Saul's son, whom he loved (1 Sam 20; 2 Sam 1). In chapter 10 he acts with loyalty toward the Ammonites only to have his envoys humiliated. This leads to war with Ammon and with the Aramaeans who come to Ammon's aid, but the outcome is a victory for David and Israel.

Both of these episodes seem to set the stage for the story of David, Bathsheba, and Uriah in 2 Sam 11, an episode where it is not David but Uriah who acts loyally, and we see a darker side of David's character.

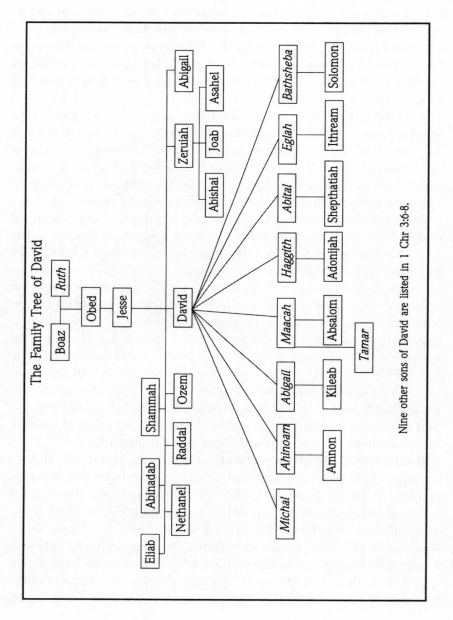

The Family Tree of David

Nine other sons of David are listed in 1 Chr 3:6-8.

In 2 Sam 11 David uses royal power first to "take" Bathsheba, another man's wife, and then to murder her husband, Uriah, to cover up his misdeed. Bathsheba was pregnant; and it was Uriah, summoned from David's own army on the battlefront, who loyally refused to break his battle vows and sleep with his wife. He is sent back to the battle and to his death. This violent use of royal power to defend royal privilege reflects the "taking" by kings of which the prophet Samuel warned (1 Sam 8:11-18). This time the prophet is Nathan, and he comes to David with a tale of a rich man who took and slaughtered a poor man's only lamb. When David judges that such a man deserves to die, Nathan responds, "You are the man!" (2 Sam 12:1-7). David receives this indictment as just and responds in repentance. Nevertheless, Nathan's oracle of judgment is the announcement of violence in David's family even as he has done violence in the family of Uriah and of Israel.

The stories of 2 Sam 13–20 are tales of family tragedy. David's son Amnon rapes his half sister Tamar and is killed for it in revenge by Tamar's brother Absalom. Absalom is banished for this act but later restored through the intervention of a wise woman from Tekoa. Seeds of bitterness have been planted, however, and Absalom leads a rebellion against David, even forcing David into a humiliating retreat from Jerusalem. The rebellion is put down, and David's general, Joab, kills Absalom. David is grief-stricken over his son in spite of the rebellion and withdraws into his grief, neglecting the affairs of the kingdom until he is forced back to his duties by Joab. Even after this victory David is forced to put down a revolt by a man named Sheba.

In our final view of David, he is on his deathbed (1 Kgs 1–2). He is old and ineffectual. Parties within the court lobby for his decision on a successor, and through the persuasion of Nathan and Bathsheba, Solomon (the son of Bathsheba) is designated.

When David finally dies it is not a heroic moment. We have seen too much of the man behind the heroic images of his rise and the royal ideology of the kingdom. But the final episode of this man's life is oddly powerful in part because we have seen the vulnerability of David the man. He was not so different from us after all. If we had only the hero of the people and the monarch of the state, the portrait would be strangely unfinished. It is remarkable that the community has preserved this human side of the David portrait. Later generations find it uncomfortable and idealize it (the Chronicler). But the humanness of David brings home what has been said at various quiet moments throughout the books of Samuel.

David did not of his own accord bring a new future to Israel. David was God's new future for Israel. Further, God's providence worked in and through David in spite of his weaknesses. David Gunn has traced a pattern of gift and grasp throughout the David story. When David was most attuned to the giving and receiving of gift all went well. When he attempted to grasp through his own power (as with Bathsheba), disaster followed. The kingdom, as God's gift, can be a source of God's grace for Israel. The kingdom, as power to be grasped, can lead Israel and its king to be "swept away" as Samuel warned and exile eventually demonstrates.[7] Walter Brueggemann has found an emphasis throughout the David stories on God's willingness to risk human freedom and responsibility while yet pursuing the divine purposes through these "trusted creatures." He even finds purposeful echoes of this aspect of the David story in the stories of human freedom, responsibility, and sin in the episodes of the primeval history in Genesis, which may have received shape shortly after the time of David.[8] A heroic David demonstrates such freedom and giftedness at its best, but the David of the Succession Narrative/Court History shows all too well the temptation of every human to sinful grasping and its painful consequences. David's portrait is a full human portrait in these stories.

Although the story of Solomon and his brief period of Israelite empire is yet ahead of us, his story is, as we will see, fatally flawed. It is David's story that captures the imagination of the ongoing tradition and reverberates with new meaning for each generation. It is from David's story that a *royal ideal* emerges, against which the conduct of earthly rulers is measured and, when earthly rulers fail, from which the hope for the return of God's anointed one (messiah) arises.

Already in the books of Samuel the attachment of the appendices in 2 Sam 21–24 seems to be an attempt to conclude David's story with narratives, lists, and songs that both review David's career and look beyond it. The narratives and lists touch on themes of political intrigue and Davidic cunning, warrior exploits and Davidic leadership. But at the heart of these familiar themes of the David story lie two songs that cast David as the prototype of God's righteous king

(22:1-51; 23:1-7). Together with the Song of Hannah in 1 Sam 2, these songs bracket the books of Samuel and make clear God's working through these events to raise up the poor and oppressed and to bring down the proud and the powerful—to establish a reign of justice and righteousness. David is the seed of God's planting to bring this hope to flower in Israel.

> The God of Israel has spoken,
>   the Rock of Israel has said to me:
> One who rules over people justly,
>   ruling in the fear of God,
> is like the light of morning,
>   like the sun rising on a cloudless morning,
>   gleaming from the rain on the grassy land. (2 Sam 23:3-4)

This royal ideal is seen in the royal psalms, where not only is God's kingship celebrated but earthly kings are called to embody the reign of God.

> Give the king your justice, O God,
>   and your righteousness to a king's son.
> May he judge your people with righteousness,
>   and your poor with justice. . . .
> May he defend the cause of the poor of the people,
>   give deliverance to the needy,
>   and crush the oppressor. (Ps 72:1-2, 4; see also Ps 101:1-8)

This royal ideal remained alive and influential in Israel even when the royal reality of sinful Israelite and Judean kings sought to subvert the covenant tradition of Yahwistic faith. It can be seen in the prophets' hope for an anointed one (a messiah) who would truly return righteous rule to the people (see, e.g., Isa 11:1-9, where this ideal royal figure comes from the "stump of Jesse" and ushers in an age of peace). When exile seems to end the line of earthly Davidic kings this becomes an eschatological hope for God's ultimate return of a righteous and just kingdom under messianic rule. In an age of diverse messianic expectations, the early church saw Jesus Christ as the fulfillment of this hope for messianic kingdom, although his was not an earthly throne. It was an important aspect of the tradition that Jesus was said to be born in the line of David.

David's own story is idealized in its retelling by the historian of 1 Chronicles. The rough edges of David's story are smoothed, and his role in the religious life of Israel is enhanced. The model of leadership in the community is that of representative of God in political and liturgical realms.

But the story of Israel's united kingdom is not complete. Solomon takes the stage, but his is not to be a piece of the witness to emergent royal ideal in Israel and beyond. His story, for all its glitter, is the first episode in the chronicles of a royal reality that failed to live up to the royal ideal. The royal reality of Solomon's reign is one marked by growing distance from the people, little discernible prophetic influence, and the growing influence of Canaan and Egypt on Israelite political and religious life.

Solomon: Empire and Fracture (1 Kgs 1–11)

Solomon is something of a Jekyll/Hyde figure in biblical literature. It is the ruthless, violent side of Solomon that emerges first in the story (1 Kgs 1–2). When David names Solomon as his successor and dies, Solomon consolidates his power with a ruthless purge of his opposition. He has his half brother and rival Adonijah killed, along with his influential supporters, including David's general, Joab. David's priest Abiathar is banished.

Abruptly, in 1 Kgs 3:3-15, we hear that "Solomon loved the LORD, walking in the statutes of his father David" (v. 3*a*), and we see a pious Solomon praying to the Lord at Gibeon. In a vision God offers Solomon his choice of a divine gift. Solomon chooses "an understanding mind to govern your people, able to discern between good and evil; for who can govern this your great people?" (v. 9). God is pleased by this request and grants Solomon the gift of wisdom and additionally grants him wealth and honor. This encounter is immediately followed by the episode of the two women claiming the same child, a case Solomon settles in a manner that demonstrates his practical wisdom (3:16-28).

By the end of Solomon's story the image has changed again—back to the dark side of the Solomonic tradition. Chapter 11 details Solomon's complicity in idolatry and attributes the division of the kingdom to his sin. Solomon had seven hundred wives and three

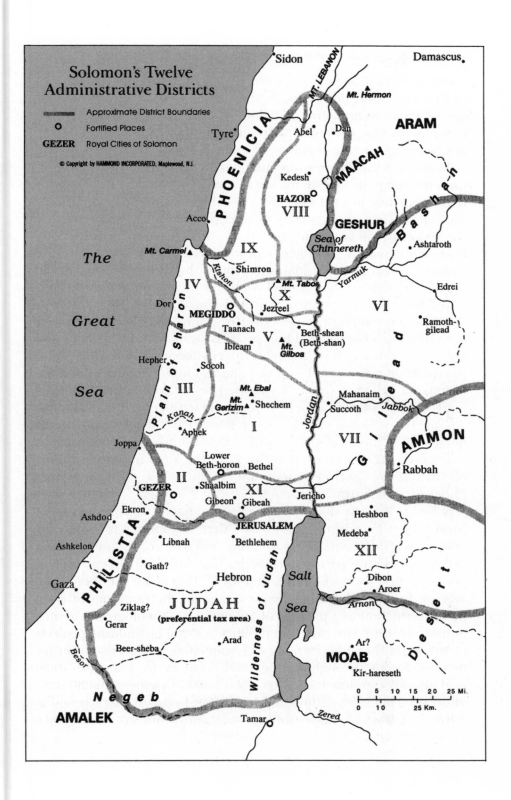

Solomon's Twelve Administrative Districts

- Approximate District Boundaries
- ○ Fortified Places
- **GEZER** Royal Cities of Solomon

© Copyright by HAMMOND INCORPORATED, Maplewood, N.J.

Sidon

Damascus

MT. LEBANON

Mt. Hermon

ARAM

Tyre

Abel

Dan

MAACAH

Kedesh

HAZOR
VIII ○

GESHUR

Acco

IX

Sea of Chinnereth

Bashan

Ashtaroth

The

Mt. Carmel ▲

Shimron

Kishon

IV

Mt. Tabor ▲

X

Yarmuk

VI

Edrei

Great

Dor

MEGIDDO ○

Jezreel

Taanach

V

Beth-shean (Beth-shan)

Ramoth-gilead

Ibleam

Mt. Gilboa ▲

Hepher

Socoh

Gilead

Sea

Plain of Sharon

III

Kanah

Mt. Ebal ▲

Mt. Gerizim ▲ Shechem

Mahanaim

Succoth

Jabbok

VII

AMMON

Joppa

Aphek

I

Jordan

Rabbah

Lower Beth-horon ○

Bethel

II

GEZER ○

Shaalbim

XI

Jericho

Ashdod

Ekron

Gibeon

Gibeah

Heshbon

Ashkelon

Libnah

JERUSALEM ○

Bethlehem

Medeba

XII

Gaza

PHILISTIA

Gath?

Hebron

Wilderness of Judah

Salt Sea

Dibon

Aroer

Ziklag?

JUDAH
(preferential tax area)

Arnon

Ar?

Gerar

Arad

MOAB

Beer-sheba

Besor

Kir-hareseth

Negeb

AMALEK

Tamar

Zered

Desert

0 5 10 15 20 25 Mi.

0   10   25 Km.

hundred concubines, a measure of his influence in the ancient world since these were largely marriages used to seal treaties or agreements. A measure of Solomon's stature was that his first recorded marriage was to a pharaoh's daughter (3:1-2), a notice that also accounts for the evidence of many Egyptian influences during Solomon's reign. These wives and concubines were allowed to bring their foreign gods with them, and Solomon not only built shrines for these gods but himself became a worshiper at many of them (see esp. 11:4-8). For this apostasy God angrily reveals to Solomon that the kingdom will be "torn" from the hand of his son (vv. 9-13). The language is similar to Samuel's pronouncement of God's rejection to Saul (1 Sam 15:28). Judah will remain, but the rest of Israel will never be under the rule of the Davidic line again. Solomon has journeyed from pious humility to rejected idolater.

In the intervening chapters (4–10) we find detailed descriptions of Solomonic policies, building projects, administrative details, and Solomon's growing reputation for international wisdom. Here again the tradition can be read with two minds. On the one hand, the traditions on Solomon's reign have often been taken as evidence of a kind of golden age in Israel—a time of magnificence and influence among the nations. On the other hand, careful attention to the details of Solomonic policy and activity shows a dismantling of covenantal practices rooted in the Yahwistic Sinai tradition in favor of institutions and practices largely modeled on Canaanite/Phoenician or Egyptian practices.

Solomon's court does indeed take on magnificent trappings of royal power. First Kings 4:22-23 says that "Solomon's provision for one day was thirty cors of choice flour, and sixty cors of meal, ten fat oxen, and twenty pasture-fed cattle, one hundred sheep, besides deer, gazelles, roebucks and fatted fowl." This is not the diet of the average Israelite. A further major witness to the trappings of royal power is the building projects of Solomon. Archaeological evidence tends to confirm the extensive military and public building projects of Solomon. He builds fortresses, chariot cities, and garrisons for his defense forces throughout the land. Notices in 4:26 and 10:26 attribute to Solomon 1,400 chariots, 12,000 horsemen, 40,000 stalls of horses. He builds shrines and houses for his many wives as well as public buildings of a variety of types (e.g., governor's residences; see 7:1-12; 9:15-19).

All of this requires funding, and a good deal of Solomon's administrative policies have to do with generating economic resources. For his more modest needs, David acquired resources by expanding the borders of his kingdom. This is no longer possible for Solomon. In fact, during his lifetime territories revolt or withdraw from the Israelite kingdom and Solomon is apparently powerless to do anything about it: Edom (11:14-22); Syria (11:23-25). Solomon institutes heavy taxation on the territories of the kingdom. In order to develop an efficient tax system he creates twelve royal districts responsible for the provisions of the court one month out of each year (4:7-27). Each is given an appointed royal governor, and its boundaries are drawn without regard to tribal territories, thus undermining traditional tribal patterns of authority and governance in favor of a strictly hierarchical royal system. The tribe of Judah, Solomon's own, is exempt from this twelve-district system. Solomon also institutes a forced-labor policy (sometimes called the corvée) that is a tax in the form of free labor for the state. Able-bodied men are taken on a three-month rotation from the tribes to work on Solomon's various building projects (5:13-14). When Rehoboam sends the administrator of the forced-labor details as his representative to meet with the northern tribes, he is so hated that they stone him to death (12:18).

What happens under Solomon's administrative policies is that the concern for equitable distribution of economic resources reflected in the covenant law codes is displaced by an economics of privilege that begins to create sharp class divisions of wealthy and poor within Israel. The redivision of tribal territories signals the beginning of forced shifts in land tenure and inheritance that move land out of the realm of continuous family inheritance and initiate the accumulation of land by royal retainers and wealthy elite classes associated with royal power structures. The eventual outcome of these economic shifts that begin under Solomon can be seen particularly in the economic practices condemned by the prophets at a later point in Israel's story.

Political power has displaced the emphasis on justice in the covenant law codes. The weak and the poor no longer have real access to the precincts of royal decision making. Significantly the people play no role in the elevation of Solomon to kingship as they did for Saul and David. Solomon comes to power completely as a product of politics inside the royal court. His policies clearly weigh heavily on the common people because rebellions break out toward the end of Solomon's reign (11:14-40). One of these is led by Jeroboam, who escapes Solomon's hand to return after his death and lead the northern tribes in a demand to Solomon's son for justice and lightening of Solomon's burdensome policies. When this is refused Jeroboam leads the northern tribes to form a new northern kingdom. Israel is permanently divided by the Solomonic politics of oppression (1 Kgs 12).

In the materials on Solomon, the building of the temple in Jerusalem is given considerable attention (5:1–6:37; 7:13–8:66). This is a measure of the importance of the temple in ongoing Israelite tradition. But the temple is an ambiguous achievement on the part of Solomon. In many ways it represents the danger of the domestication of the radically free God of Israel's covenant tradition. The temple is built with forced labor (9:15), and it adjoins the royal palace. Although the building of the palace is given only twelve verses (7:1-12), it took thirteen years to build, while the temple took only seven. The palace was much larger than the temple—2,700 square feet for the temple (6:2), compared to 11,250 square feet for the palace (7:2). The temple seems almost an attachment to the royal palace. The models for the temple are generally agreed to be Canaanite/Phoenician since similar floor plans have been found at numerous locations. The very notion of a permanent dwelling place is in tension with the notion of Israel's tent tabernacle. Solomon's temple introduces the temptation to think of a God domesticated in behalf of the royal interests. This notion is not helped by Solomon's appointment of Zadok and his descendants as the permanent priesthood of the temple in Jerusalem. Zadok is rewarded for his support of Solomon at the time of his accession, while Abiathar, David's other priest, is banished (interestingly to Anathoth, the hometown of Jeremiah, who preached his most famous sermon against reliance on the temple, Jer 7; 26).

God's dwelling place on Zion does eventually find a positive place in Israel's royal theology (as we saw in Ps 132). The psalms as liturgical material reflect a role for the temple as a place where the traditions of God's saving grace in Israel are remembered and celebrated, both in the common, daily, liturgical practices and on special festival occasions. The temple is thought of as God's dwelling place, and the presence of God is mediated there through priest and

Solomon's Temple

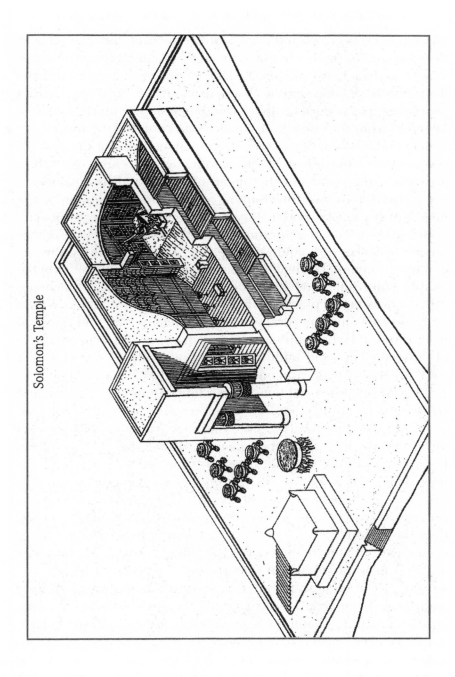

sacrifice. The prophets Jeremiah and Ezekiel both warn Israel later that this cannot be construed to mean that God has become a possession of Israel. We will see in later chapters that exile and the destruction of the temple lead, after the return to rebuild Jerusalem, to a restored role for the temple in the midst of Israel's life apart from the ambiguities of its connection to kingship.

Solomon led Israel to a place of prominence among the nations, both in terms of wealth and political influence. First Kings 10, with its account of the visit from the queen of Sheba and its detailing of royal expeditions and the resulting wealth, shows Solomon at the height of his secular power. But it is clear that Solomon's policies have laid the foundation for the kingdom's collapse and have undermined concerns for equity and justice central to the Yahwistic covenant tradition. Further, his idolatry and the entanglements of the temple with royal power suggest ongoing areas of struggle between the realities of royal practice, which are in conflict with the covenant faith of Israel, and the royal ideal, which begins with and develops from David. It is the prophets who will champion these perspectives of covenant faith and faithful kingship over against this praxis of royal power, privilege, and nationalized (domesticated) religion.

What happened to Solomon's wisdom? Didn't he ask for and receive the gift of wisdom for the governance of the people? One answer to this question is to note that the giving of a gift does not mean that the gift cannot be squandered. In 1 Kgs 9:1-9 Solomon has a second vision. God does not seem pleased with Solomon this time. The vision is a stern warning on the consequences of straying from the path of covenant obedience. The restatement of the promise to David seems closer to the conditional statement of Ps 132 than the unconditional statement of 2 Sam 7. Israel and her kings can be cut off, and the house (temple) that Solomon has built can be left a heap of rubble. In the context of Solomon's story it is a warning, followed in short order by the texts on Solomon's idolatry and its consequences. In the longer view of the Deuteronomistic Historian, writing to and for Babylonian exiles, it is a grim explanation of the very fate they have experienced (cf. 2 Kgs 17:7-8; 21:11-15).

But the question concerning Solomon's wisdom can also be answered by pointing to the manner in which Solomon used his gift of wisdom. By and large he does not seem to have used it for matters of practical governance. He does, however, become renowned for his encyclopedic knowledge, his telling of proverbs, and his trading of observations with wise teachers (4:29-34; the queen of Sheba also comes to experience and test his reputation for such wisdom, 10:1-10). These texts reflect the beginning under Solomon of Israelite participation in an international tradition of wise teaching and proverbial wisdom that is known and associated with royal courts in both Mesopotamia and Egypt. Solomon is perhaps more concerned to build an international reputation for mastery of such wisdom than to rule wisely. Solomon's reputation for wisdom is such that Israel's own later-developing wisdom traditions are attributed to Solomon. He is said to be the author of both Proverbs and Ecclesiastes, although both books bear the marks of much later composition. He is also said to have authored even the apocryphal book of the Wisdom of Solomon, which was written in Greek in the first century BCE. Solomon should probably be considered the patron and founder of the Israelite tradition rather than the author of it all, much as David's name is associated with so many of the psalms. In a strange way Solomon's fostering of such wisdom traditions in Israel is more enduring than any of the power or magnificence he garnered for himself as a ruler.

The period of a unified Israelite kingdom is at an end. In Saul kingship experienced an abortive birth. Under David we glimpsed the promise of kingship. With Solomon the promise of kingship was broken. All of the themes of royal ideal and royal reality, covenant faithfulness and covenant disobedience in a time of Israelite kingdom, are introduced in the stories of these three kings. In a time of shattered Israelite unity we must now watch these themes played in many variations as kings, prophets, and people move down a road that tragically will lead to oblivion for the northern kingdom and exile for the southern kingdom. It may be that the searching questions of exile gave the impetus for a Deuteronomistic retelling of the stories of Israel's first kings, thereby preserving these traditions for future generations.

Notes

1. See James W. Flanagan, "Chiefs in Israel," JSOT 20 (1981): 47-73.
2. See Frank S. Frick, *The Formation of the State in Ancient Israel: A Survey of Methods and Theories* (SWBA 4; Sheffield: JSOT Press, 1985).

3. See the fuller discussion of various hypotheses on the complex literary history of the books of Samuel in Bruce C. Birch, "The First and Second Books of Samuel: Introduction, Commentary, and Reflection," *NIB*, vol. 2 (Nashville: Abingdon, 1998), 951-58; and R. P. Gordon, *1 and 2 Samuel* (OTG; Sheffield: JSOT Press, 1984), 14-20.

4. The fullest discussion of issues related to an ark narrative can be found in Patrick D. Miller, Jr. and J. J. M. Roberts, *The Hand of the Lord: A Reassessment of the "Ark Narrative" of 1 Samuel* (Baltimore: Johns Hopkins University Press, 1977). John T. Willis, in "Samuel versus Eli: 1 Sam 1-7," *TZ* 35 (1979): 201-12, has also made a convincing argument for the present cohesive relationship of 1 Sam 1-7 as a unit, whether the ark narrative existed independently or not.

5. See Norman K. Gottwald, *The Tribes of Yahweh: A Sociology of the Religion of Liberated Israel, 1250-1050 BCE* (Maryknoll, N.Y.: Orbis, 1979), 571; and George E. Mendenhall, "The Monarchy," *Int* 29 (1975): 160.

6. See the discussion of recent hypotheses in Birch, "The First and Second Books of Samuel," 1269-71; and P. Kyle McCarter, *II Samuel* (AB 9; Garden City, N.Y.: Doubleday, 1980), 4-16.

7. D. M. Gunn, *The Story of King David: Genre and Interpretation* (JSOTSup 6; Sheffield: JSOT Press, 1978).

8. Walter Brueggemann, "The Trusted Creature," *CBQ* 31 (1969): 484-501.

Bibliography

Commentaries

Anderson, Arnold A. *2 Samuel*. WBC 11. Waco: Word, 1989.

Birch, Bruce C. "The First and Second Books of Samuel: Introduction, Commentary, and Reflection," *NIB*, vol. 2. Nashville: Abingdon, 1998.

Brueggemann, Walter. *First and Second Samuel*. IBC. Louisville: Westminster John Knox, 1990.

Klein, Ralph W. *1 Samuel*. WBC 10. Waco: Word Books, 1983.

McCarter, P. Kyle, ed. *I Samuel*. AB 8. Garden City, N.Y.: Doubleday, 1980.

————. *II Samuel*. AB 9. Garden City, N.Y.: Doubleday, 1984.

Other Studies

Birch, Bruce C. *The Rise of the Israelite Monarchy: The Growth and Development of I Samuel 7–15*. SBLDS 27. Missoula, Mont.: Scholars Press, 1976.

Brueggemann, Walter. *David's Truth in Israel's Imagination and Memory*. Philadelphia: Fortress, 1985.

————. *Power, Providence, and Personality: Biblical Insight into Life and Ministry*. Louisville: Westminster John Knox, 1990.

Gunn, David M. *The Fate of King Saul*. JSOTSup 14. Sheffield: JSOT, 1980.

————. *The Story of King David*. JSOTSup 6. Sheffield: JSOT, 1978.

Miller, Patrick D., Jr., and J. J. M. Roberts. *The Hand of the Lord: A Reassessment of the "Ark Narrative" of 1 Samuel*. JHNES. Baltimore: Johns Hopkins University Press, 1977.

Rad, Gerhard von. "The Beginning of History Writing in Ancient Israel." *The Problem of the Hexateuch and Other Essays*. New York: McGraw-Hill, 1966 (German original, 1944).

CHAPTER EIGHT

KINGS AND PROPHETS IN THE DIVIDED KINGDOM

1 Kgs 12–2 Kgs 13, Selected Psalms

U nfortunately, Israel did not have an Abraham Lincoln. If such a person had lived at the time Israel became a divided country, its history might have been different. When the American South seceded from the Union over the issue of slavery, the personality and policies of Lincoln were instrumental in keeping the country intact. In Israel's history, the North seceded from the South, but slavery (in a different form) was still involved. No Lincolnesque personalities emerged, however, who could resolve the dilemma of division, either politically or militarily. Divided, Israel fell. First there were two (in 922 BCE), then there was one (721 BCE), and finally there were none (587 BCE).

Amid all the military and political maneuvering of this period of time, the texts claim that the most acute issue for Israel was a spiritual sickness that slowly but surely consumed the heart of its people. And so, in 1 Kgs 12–2 Kgs 13, the texts sketch a coherent history of the divided kingdoms, but they are interested most fundamentally in religious and theological matters. To this end, major portions of the narrative focus on the word and work of God through the prophets, especially Elijah and Elisha.

Because of this overarching religious concern, in this chapter we consider, first of all, a key theological issue that informs and undergirds the narrative and in view of which this tumultuous segment of the history of Israel is interpreted by the books of Kings (and other books in the Deuteronomistic History). We will then turn to a sketch of the history of this period.

Apostasy Shapes Israel's History

What is the apostasy of which the books of Kings and Israel's prophets speak so sharply and so often? Or, to use the question of 1 Kgs 9:8-9 (written in light of the destruction of Jerusalem; cf. Deut 29:24), "Why has the LORD done such a thing to this land and to this house?" The reply gets to the point quickly: "Because they have forsaken the LORD their God . . . and embraced other gods, worshiping them and serving them."

The influence of Canaanite religion played a significant role in these developments. Our knowledge of this religion has been much advanced by archaeological discoveries of documents, especially from Ugarit (Ras Shamra) on the Syrian coast, dating from the middle of the second millennium BCE. This religion had a powerful impact on the Israelites, particularly during the period of the divided kingdoms. According to the books of Kings, this religion gained entry into Israel's life especially under the program and policies of Jeroboam, the first king of the northern kingdom (Israel). But it was under Ahab and Jezebel that a virulent form of Canaanite religion was practiced that threatened the very future of Yahwism in both North and South (see below).

Canaanite religion was polytheistic. Chief among the deities was El, the high god of the Canaanite pantheon, whose consort was Asherah (she is also associated with Baal, 1 Kgs 16:32-33; 18:19) and who presided over the council of the gods. Most well known to Old Testament readers among these deities is Baal, whose consorts included Anat (and Astarte). Their mating was believed responsible for overcoming the powers of death and enabling a renewal of life, especially evidenced in the rains and the fertility of the soil (an important reality for those living in Canaan). Every year this drama was reenacted and the people participated in the associated rituals, which were often of a sexual nature.

Canaanite religion influenced Israel's religion in both negative and positive ways. Positively, names and metaphors for Yahweh were appropriated (e.g., the various El names; storm imagery such as "rider of the clouds"). Important rituals and festivals were also adapted, as well as theological themes (e.g., Yahweh as one who defeats chaos, is the source of fertility, and has power over death and life, including resurrection). Negatively, these considerable similarities may have been a key factor that led to a blending of Baal and Yahweh themes and practices. The reasoning may well have gone like this: Why not revere Yahweh, while at the same time honoring the god responsible for the fertility of the land and the life cycles? Such a syncretistic theology and associated idolatrous worship practices became increasingly common and deeply compromised Israel's commitment to Yahweh.

Early prophets, especially Elijah, enter into this crisis for Israel's faith and life, reject the syncretistic tendencies, and insist that Israel is called to worship Yahweh alone. First Kings 18, which describes the struggle of Elijah with the prophets of Baal (see below), is a key source for understanding the negative impact of Baalism on Israelite life and the prophetic program relating thereto. Various narratives in Kings, as we shall see, rhetorically engage this struggle for the allegiance of the people of God to Yahweh in the face of a virile opposition. The prophet Elijah states the issue squarely: "How long will you go limping with two different opinions? If the LORD is God, follow him; but if Baal, then follow him" (1 Kgs 18:21).

The focus of Israel's apostasy is unfaithfulness to God, manifested fundamentally in the worship of other gods. The issue is the first commandment (Deut 5:7-10; 6:5). The problem at its heart is thus a matter of faith and unfaith, and not (dis)obedience of an external code. The failure to keep the commandments is understood to be symptomatic of a more pervasive problem, namely, Israel's disloyalty to God and its refusal to heed the prophetic call for repentance. In 2 Kgs 17:7-18, a theological statement that explains the factors at work in Israel's fall to Assyria, all the specific sins cited as contributing to this debacle have to do with the service of other gods (see also 1 Kgs 11:4-11; 2 Kgs 23:4-25). The first commandment is also the focus of what it means to "forsake" the covenant (Deut 29:25-26; 1 Kgs 11:9-11; 2 Kgs 17:15, 35-38). Moreover, idolatry is the force of the repeated assertion in the Deuteronomistic History regarding "the sin of Jeroboam" (see below). This recurrent evaluation of Israel's kings focuses on the idolatrous practices that drew the people away from Yahweh (e.g., 1 Kgs 15:30-34; 16:19-31; 2 Kgs 17:21-22).

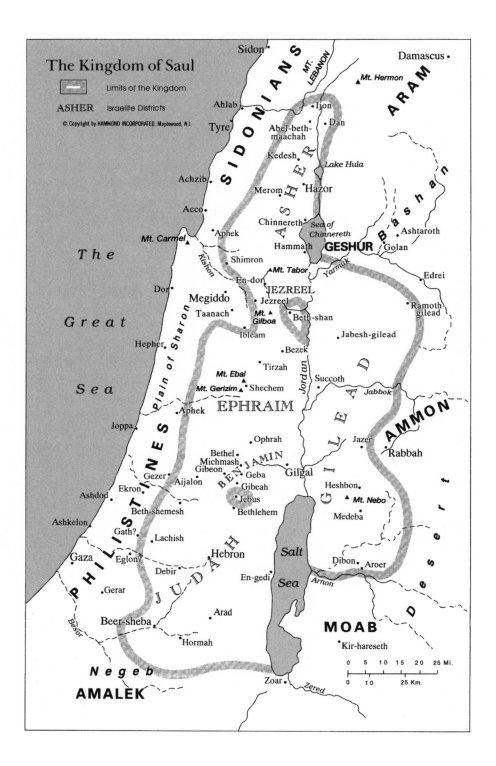

The Kingdom of Saul

☐ Limits of the Kingdom

ASHER Israelite Districts

© Copyright by HAMMOND INCORPORATED, Maplewood, N.J.

Sidon

Damascus

Mt. Hermon

ARAM

S I D O N I A N S

Mt. LEBANON

Ahlab

Ijon

Tyre

Abel-beth-maachah

Dan

Kedesh

Lake Hula

A S H E R

Achzib

Merom

Hazor

B a s h a n

Acco

Chinnereth

Sea of Chinnereth

Ashtaroth

Aphek

Mt. Carmel

Hammath

GESHUR

Golan

The

Shimron

Mt. Tabor

Yarmuk

Edrei

Kishon

En-dor

Dor

Megiddo

JEZREEL

Jezreel

Ramoth-gilead

Great

Taanach

Mt. Gilboa

Beth-shan

Hepher

Ibleam

Jabesh-gilead

Bezek

Sea

Tirzah

Jordan

Succoth

G I L E A D

Mt. Ebal

Plain of Sharon

Mt. Gerizim

Shechem

Jabbok

Aphek

EPHRAIM

Joppa

Ophrah

Jazer

AMMON

Bethel

Rabbah

Michmash

B E N J A M I N

Gezer

Gibeon

Geba

Gilgal

Heshbon

Aijalon

Gibeah

Ekron

Jebus

Mt. Nebo

Ashdod

Beth-shemesh

Bethlehem

Medeba

Ashkelon

Gath?

Lachish

J U D A H

Hebron

Salt

Dibon

Aroer

Gaza

Eglon?

Debir

En-gedi

Sea

Arnon

D e s e r t

Gerar

Arad

MOAB

Besor

Beer-sheba

Hormah

Kir-hareseth

0   5   10 15   20   25 Mi.

N e g e b

Zoar

Zered

0   10   25 Km.

AMALEK

PHILISTINES

A Kingdom Divided

The division between the North (Israel) and the South (Judah) upon the death of Solomon had its roots deep within Israel's pre-monarchical history. The ten northern tribes (dominated by Ephraim) and the two southern tribes (dominated by Judah) had somewhat different histories and religious commitments. When King Saul died, those divisions broke out into the open, and it took David seven years to unify the country. Solomon managed to maintain this fragile unity, but his oppressive policies and syncretistic encouragements alienated many people, particularly in the North. The luxurious life of the court and extensive building programs placed a heavy tax burden on the people, and many were forced into labor gangs to carry out Solomon's projects.

This oppressive situation deteriorated to such an extent that the prophet Ahijah encouraged a northern leader (Jeroboam) to revolt (1 Kgs 11). Although Jeroboam's revolt failed initially, he renewed his efforts on behalf of northern tribes with Solomon's son Rehoboam. Though Rehoboam rejected Jeroboam's appeal for reform, the northern tribes successfully seceded from Judah and crowned Jeroboam king (1 Kgs 12). Jeroboam established his political capital at Shechem, later moving it to Tirzah. Somewhat later, in 870 BCE, King Omri built a permanent capital at Samaria.

Jeroboam: Theological Issues

Jeroboam established two religious capitals, at Bethel and Dan (in the far South and far North), seeking to break any continuing allegiance to Jerusalem. At each shrine, he set up golden calves (actually bulls). These objects were apparently not intended to be idolatrous, but rather pedestals on which the invisible Yahweh was thought to stand (and hence parallel to the Ark of the Covenant in the Jerusalem temple). This was, however, a dangerous move, given the connections of the bull (a symbol of fertility) to the Canaanite god Baal. That danger was soon realized as Baalized worship practices had an increasing impact on Israel's life (already in 14:15). In view of this later development, the narrative in 1 Kgs 12–14 is critical of Jeroboam's action in uncompromising terms, sharply stated by the prophet Ahijah (1 Kgs 14:6-16). Jeroboam's action was idolatrous and stood in the tradition of the golden calf of Exod 32 (cf. 1 Kgs 12:28 with Exod 32:4; see also Hos 8:5-6; 10:5-6). As noted above, the books of Kings pass a theological judgment on subsequent kings in terms of how they related to Jeroboam's religious program (over twenty times; first in 1 Kgs 15:26; finally in 2 Kgs 17:22-23). The assumption is that Jeroboam's successors could have reversed this state of affairs, but none of them did, and it no doubt became more difficult to do as time passed.

These negative developments in Jeroboam's reign may make the reader wonder about the prophetic word spoken to him in 1 Kgs 11:26-39. Did God's word set him up for a fall? Two factors should be taken into account in considering this question.

One, what Jeroboam does counts with God. Though God's powerful word to Jeroboam through the prophet Ahijah fills this scene, the word *rebel* stands at the beginning (11:27) and has important content. God's word is spoken to one who has already rebelled against Solomon's policies; God works in and through what Jeroboam is doing. This divine way of working was just made clear regarding Solomon's adversaries, Hadad and Rezon, who are rebellious figures *before* God raises them up (see 11:14-25). What Jeroboam has done and will do counts in charting a future course, not simply what God does or what God's prophet says. Both Jeroboam and God/God's word are effective agents. Specifically, Jeroboam's faithfulness or lack thereof is seen to be crucial for the course that future takes (11:38).

Two, the future that God's word gives to Jeroboam in verse 38 is a genuine possibility. God holds out high hopes for Jeroboam and his reign, comparing him to David. God uses important theological language for this word to Jeroboam (11:35-38). God will "give" him the kingdom and he shall reign; God "will be with" Jeroboam and "build" him an enduring dynasty. God sees his potential, that he has the strength to resist the oppressive forces at work under Solomon and Rehoboam. God raises him up as, in effect, a savior figure (see 2 Kgs 13:5).

The realization of God's desires for Jeroboam has not been divinely predetermined or foreknown in any absolute sense. The text gives us no reason to believe that God is being deceptive here, as if God knows for sure that this future will not come to pass but lays it out anyway. God's stated desire for his kingship is genuine, and the conditions stated are actual conditions (11:38; see also God's "if" and "if not" in 9:1-9).[1] In fact, 1 Kgs 12:15, 24 indicates that God is at work to fulfill the prophet's word. God no doubt knows that a negative future is a real possibility, but this positive word to Jeroboam is *also* a genuine possibility, for *both* Jeroboam and God. God here treats Jeroboam *with integrity* in the outline of possible futures. God's will for him is clear; at the same time, Jeroboam's (dis)loyalty will make a difference regarding the shape of his future and that of Israel.

More generally, God cares about the future of the North as much as the South. God's chosen people extend across both kingdoms, as will be evident in the narratives that follow. And, notably, no indication is given that the northern tribes should not continue to regard the Mosaic covenant and its obligations, as well as the Jerusalem temple, as central to their faith. As it turns out, the "sin of Jeroboam" flies in the face of these divine concerns and a sharply negative future becomes a reality. God's will for Jeroboam is not realized, not because God has failed, but because Jeroboam has. Jeroboam's sins are of such a magnitude that they successfully resist the will of God for him and his dynasty. The only other interpretive option for understanding Jeroboam is to view the litany of his sins in 12:28-32 as the will of God. But, the will of God is evident in the narrator's *condemnation* of his actions as idolatrous. Jeroboam, who started out as a savior, ends up as such a sinner that the last state of affairs for Israel is worse than the first. God's hopes for him are dashed and God's will for Israel is frustrated.

All of Jeroboam's sins are connected to worship in some way. There are no signs that he violated the principles of justice for the oppressed, upon which his rebellion was grounded (with God's approval). From both political and ethical perspectives, Jeroboam's work is commended. Jeroboam's religious violations, however, which are used to serve personal and political ends (a universal way of using religion), subvert the positive political agenda. Political liberation cannot stand by itself if the worship of God is not in order. This issue is the opposite of the problem often addressed by later prophets, where the worship is appropriate but justice is absent (Amos 5:21-24; Isa 1:10-15). Neither worship nor justice can go it alone; both are necessary for Israel's life and well-being.

Chronology of the Kings of the Divided Monarchy*

Judah	Israel
Rehoboam (922–915 BCE)	Jeroboam I (922–901 BCE)
	Abijam (915–913)
Asa (915–873)	Nadab (901–900)
	Baasha (900–877)
	Elah (877–876)
	Zimri (876)
Jehoshaphat (873–849)	Omri (876–869)
	Ahab (869–850)
	Ahaziah (850–849)
Jehoram (849–843)	Jehoram (849–843/2)
Ahaziah (843/2)	
Athaliah (843–837)	
Jehoash (837–800)	Jehu (843/2–815)
	Jehoahaz (815–802)
	Joash (802–786)
Azariah/Uzziah (783–742)	Jeroboam II (786–746)
	Zechariah (746–745)
	Shallum (745)
Jotham (742–735)	Menahem (745–737)
	Pekahiah (737–736)
	Pekah (736–732)
Ahaz (735–715)	Hoshea (732–724)
	Fall of Samaria (722/1 BCE)
Hezekiah (715–687/6)	
Manasseh (687/6–642)	
Amon (642–609)	
Jehoahaz (609)	
Jehoiakim (609–598)	
Jehoiachin (598/7)	
Babylonian conquest of Jerusalem and first deportation (597 BCE)	
Zedekiah (597–587/6)	
Destruction of Jerusalem and second deportation (587/6 BCE)	

*Dates following the kings' names are approximate years of their rule.

The Divided Kingdoms: A Narrative Rhythm

From Jeroboam (and Rehoboam) on, the narrator works through the history of the two kingdoms in synchronistic fashion, first one and then the other, with overlaps and resumptions as necessary.[2] This reveals an understanding that North and South, while divided, are both part of the story of the one people of God. Major "interruptions" (e.g., the Elijah stories) and transitional materials are interwoven in this rhythmic retelling.

Introductory and concluding résumés for each reign, typically structured (e.g., 14:21-24, 29-31; 15:1-8, 25-32), punctuate the narrative. The repeated evaluation of the royal regimes is cast in religious terms regardless of political and military success. Apostasy becomes a dominant theme; faithfulness to God is what counts over the long haul. The repeated drumming of this cadence interprets this history, but it also provides readers with a word of warning and a call for reform. The narrator is not fundamentally concerned with historiographical matters, reconstructing the past for the sake of writing history. The concern is to bring a word of God to the readers and to learn from the past in such a way as to chart a course for the community's future. When the prophets become involved, the story is expanded and theological interpretation is more in play. Finally, what God is about in this story drives the narrative and determines what is important to consider.

The variation in the regnal summaries and in related comments about specific kings evidences a less rigid analysis and a more subtle theology at work in these texts than might at first appear. Despite the appearance of reducing these kings to a formula, defeat is not always linked to sin, nor is prosperity necessarily linked to faithfulness to God. For example, God acts on behalf of *faithless* Israel in 2 Kgs 13–14. Jeroboam II is "evil," but recovers Solomon's empire (2 Kgs 14:23-27); Jehoahaz is "evil," but his prayers are answered (13:4-5). God's compassion and promises continue to shape Israel's life in the midst of its evil ways (see 2 Kgs 13:23). In Judah, Azariah/Uzziah is judged by God for his sins (15:5)—though he reigns for fifty-two years. Amaziah is a good king who scrupulously obeys the law (14:6), but he is bested in battle by an evil king of Israel and is assassinated.

These promissory and "inconsistent" texts are often considered intrusive or surprising. But in such theological comment the narrator qualifies his own somewhat mechanical royal summaries. The summaries give the basic direction of a reign and its more long-range impact, but the narrator has no precise retributive sense of the relationship between good and bad kings and what happens to them individually. Both divine and human activity upset any mechanistic understandings of these summaries. God is at work, pursuing the divine designs, making people accountable, and pursuing well-being for all, but no dogma of retribution is evident.

One claim of these summaries seems incontestable. Because God is at work in all aspects of life—social, economic, political, and military—issues of moral accountability will regularly surface. Leaders will be held accountable by God, often through other human beings, for *all* aspects of their work within the community. To pass such theological judgments is to be true to the way in which God evaluates life in the world. God will not be evicted from the public arena, for God's purposes for life are at stake in those precincts far removed from churchly buildings and confessions.

The narrator often cites a source for further reading (and perhaps for checking accuracy)—the book of the annals of the kings of Israel/Judah (e.g., 1 Kgs 14:19, 29). The title suggests a more "historical" source than Kings, with its overriding theological interests, proves to be. Some additional details are provided in 2 Chr 10–36, but the Chronicler passes over the northern apostates. The chronological framework of the two hundred years of the divided monarchy presents problems that have not yet been resolved.

The Divided Kingdoms: A Downward Spiral

A comparison of the two kingdoms is helpful in understanding the history that follows. The kingdom of the ten northern tribes had a total of nine dynasties (and nineteen kings) in its two-hundred-year history. Internal political instability was nurtured by ongoing differences among northerners regarding the issue of dynastic versus prophetically designated kings. During this period, the southern tribes (Judah, with Benjamin) had only one dynasty (and twelve kings), that of David. This dynasty had been prophetically designated as divinely chosen and grounded in everlasting promises (2 Sam 7).

The reader should not underestimate the power and symbolic value of this perduring Davidic dynasty and the associated covenant, even with all of the royal failures. One can observe to some extent how these images functioned for the Davidic monarchy in the so-called royal psalms, which were used in kingly rituals over the course of the Davidic monarchy. They include coronation hymns and liturgies (2; 72; 101; 110; 132), petitions and prayers of thanksgiving (18; 20–21; 89; 144), and a royal wedding song (45). Later messianic hopes would draw much of their imagery and energy from this royal tradition, especially the divine promises. The Davidic kings failed again and again, and their reigns betrayed the ideal of these psalms. But the prophets would pick up on these themes and project them into the future: someday a king would arise who would truly mediate the rule of God (e.g., Isa 7; 9; 11). The prophetic claim is that royal failure could not undo the promises of God. The Christian claim is that those promises are fully and finally realized in Jesus the Christ. But this fulfillment represents a shift in the divine strategy for the realization of the promises, for the crown Jesus would wear was made of thorns. The King of the Jews would reign from a tree.

Undergirded by these perpetually reiterated royal themes, Judah was more stable politically than Israel. In other ways, Israel appeared to have the advantage, but it was illusory. Geographically, Israel was three times larger than Judah, but with more extensive and less-well-protected boundaries. Israel also had more fertile land and natural resources, but its wealth in time led to a more stratified society, with increasing gaps between rich and poor. With twice the population of Judah, Israel was a less homogeneous people, including many Canaanites, and this made for a mixed religious allegiance among its populace. Given these realities, Israel's initial religious conservatism proved to be precarious over time, and Israel succumbed more quickly to the spell of outside religious influences than did Judah. A victor-to-victim pattern often characterizes the North, as a relentless spiral downward consumes king after king, with only occasional respites on the way to doom. An apostasy-reform rhythm is common in the South, as the Jerusalem temple and the Davidic dynasty provide greater stability over time. But Judah is finally judged to be just as guilty as Israel in violating the relationship with God (cf. Jer 3:6-11). And its fall was just as great.

This division also meant periodic civil war between North and South for several decades, a conflict from which no clear winner emerged. This strife weakened both states, a situation that allowed Egypt to wreak havoc for a time, crippling Judah in particular (1 Kgs 14:25-26). Intermittent conflict with Aram (Syria) and Moab troubled later generations, especially in Israel (1 Kgs 20; 22; 2 Kgs 3; 5–16), and the rise of Assyria in the eighth century would eventually lead to the destruction of the North (721 BCE) and the near fall of the South (701 BCE).

During much of their divided history, the two kingdoms were second-rate powers in the ancient Near East, as the Solomonic empire lost much of its extent and luster under mostly inept and corrupt rulers. There were some periods of relative peace and prosperity, especially under Jeroboam II in the North (786–746 BCE) and Azariah/Uzziah in the South (783–742 BCE), but such stable conditions were fleeting. In the paragraphs that follow we trace briefly the history of each kingdom up to these more prosperous times for both North and South. The books of Kings focus on the history of the North (1 Kgs 12–2 Kgs 17). Some attention is given to the South, but not much detail (2 Chr 10–36, which speaks only of the South, provides further information).

In the North, after a period of civil war and instability, King Omri (876–869 BCE) was able to steady the relationship with Judah and entered into alliances with surrounding nations, putting Israel on the commercial map. One such alliance, with serious repercussions for Israel, was sealed by the marriage of Ahab, son of Omri, and Jezebel, daughter of the king of Sidon. While the reign of Ahab (869–850 BCE) was externally successful, the narrator's interest is focused in a sustained way on pernicious religious developments associated with this royal family (1 Kgs 16:29–22:40). Ahab and Jezebel authorized the worship of Baal in Israel and encouraged associated religious practices, often with zeal. Their conflict with prophetic figures over idolatry and syncretistic religious practice shows the extent to which Yahwism's future was threatened.

King Jehu (842–815 BCE), with the help of the prophet Elisha, purged the country of this dynasty and many of the Baal worshipers. His dynasty would remain in place for about a century (see his mixed review in 2 Kgs 10:28-31). The prophets who backed Jehu's purge probably reasoned that Israel's existence was at stake, but the misplaced zeal and graphic violence (later condemned in Hos 1:4) finally did not resolve the issues of the heart. Jehu's efforts were not sustained by his successors, and Baal worship emerged later in even more vigorous forms. Moreover, Jehu weakened the country in its ability to resist foreign incursions. When he paid tribute to hold off an expansive Assyria, Syria (under Hazael) was so offended that it reduced Israel to a shadow of its former self. Yet, later, Assyria's defeat of Syria enabled Israel to enjoy several decades of prosperity under Jeroboam II.

In the South, idolatrous practices begin to make inroads as well. Reforming activities under kings Asa and Jehoshaphat are reported (1 Kgs 15; 22; cf. 2 Chr 14–15; 17–20), but they have only temporary effects, not least because Jehoshaphat married his son (Jehoram) to Athaliah, the daughter of Ahab. Athaliah introduces pagan elements into Judah's worship life and seeks to make the religion of Baal official in Judah. Upon the death of Jehoram she seizes the throne and puts to death all members of the Davidic line, save one— Jehoram's grandson Je(ho)ash. Her six-year reign (842–837 BCE) was brought to an end by a coalition of religious and political leaders; they put her to death and reestablished the Davidic monarchy in the person of Jehoash (2 Kgs 11; 2 Chr 22–23). The narrator draws a brief but vivid picture of the end of an era: "So all the people of the land rejoiced; and the city [Jerusalem] was quiet" (2 Kgs 11:20). Jehoash (837–800 BCE) instituted important religious reforms (2 Kgs 12:1-16) and helped prepare the way for a somewhat sustained time of peace and prosperity under Azariah/Uzziah.

The Beginnings of Prophecy in Israel

In contemporary speech the word *prophet* is often misunderstood. For many people, a prophet is one who foretells the future and/or who speaks out on issues of social justice. While these elements may indeed often be found in prophetic speech, prophecy is a complex phenomenon that evolved over the centuries; a single definition of *prophet* will not serve the Bible reader well. Later discussions of prophecy in this volume will fill out the picture.

The origins of prophecy in Israel are not altogether clear. Prophets were not unique to Israel in the ancient world; prophets are attested among Israel's neighbors, including the Canaanites (see 1 Kgs 18). The people of Israel would thus have been familiar with such individuals in the larger culture. Israelite prophecy developed in interaction with already existing rhetorical strategies and roles of non-Israelite prophets. At the same time, individual Israelite prophets had a self-understanding that they were specially called spokespersons for Israel's God in a way that no others were. They believed this to be the case whether the source of their speech was ascribed to the Spirit (more characteristic of early prophets, e.g., 1 Kgs 22:24) or visions (Amos 1:1) or the word of God (e.g., Jer 1:2).

Prophecy in Israel takes root in the period of the judges. Persons such as Abraham, Moses, and Miriam are occasionally called prophets, but that naming is a theological judgment made by later generations that detected significant continuity between these figures and the later prophets. One may also discern links between the prophets and the judges of early Israel, who assumed religious, political, and military responsibilities (e.g., Gideon, Deborah). The Spirit of the Lord came upon such individuals to empower them for word and action in crisis situations in Israel's life. One could, in fact, define a prophet in remarkably similar ways, though their actions were usually quite different.

In the eleventh century, under the Philistine threat to Israel's life, Israel's leadership proved inadequate. The people demanded a king to solve the crisis. Perhaps because of significant opposition to kingship, a division of the responsibilities of the judges was developed under Samuel and Saul. The military/political tasks would be taken up by a *nāgîd* ("prince"; Saul was the first), while the responsibility for discerning and announcing the word of the Lord would be given to a prophetic figure (*nābî*; other words for these individuals are used at times, with little or no distinction in meaning, such as *seer, visionary,* and *man of God*). The prophet's role would be to legitimate the king's appointment and to function in an ongoing way as the king's counsel and conscience, an important counterbalancing function.

The degree to which prophecy was an "office," and the prophets a professional class, remains uncertain. The phrase *sons of the prophets* (1 Kgs 20:35) and the relationship between Elijah and his successor, Elisha (apparently a unique relationship), suggest something on the order of prophetic schools or communities. The prophets were not the isolated eccentrics or radicals that popular tradition has often made them out to be. Generally speaking, earlier prophets worked more with individual leaders (usually kings), while later prophets, though they also often interacted with kings, addressed the entire people of Israel. This shift in prophecy from a predominantly individual to a community orientation appears to coincide with the beginning of written prophecy (Amos, in the mid-eighth century). Only after this shift does the word regarding the future judgment or salvation of the entire people of God come clearly into view. When their words were fulfilled, it was a key factor in the preservation of the prophets' words.

Samuel became Israel's first prophet, though he functions in other capacities as well. Samuel's links to priestly circles are one indication that prophets were (usually?) associated with Israel's life of worship (cf. Ezekiel in a later period). From the beginning of the monarchy, prophets were also regularly associated with the royal court, in both North and South, functioning in both critical and affirming ways. This is most clearly seen in Nathan's relationship to David; Nathan both announces the covenant with the Davidic line (2 Sam 7) and denounces David in the Uriah-Bathsheba affair (2 Sam 12). One can also see this dual role in Ahijah; as noted, he became a key figure at the point of the division of the kingdom (1 Kgs 11–14).

Israel's kings, however, began to act as kings are wont to do. They became increasingly reluctant to listen to criticism and sought to assume absolute power for themselves. In response, the prophet's relationship to the king became more complex and tension-filled. Some prophets were unqualifiedly supportive of the king; others were sharply critical. The prophet Micaiah plays the latter role in 1 Kgs 22, and increasingly this more critical stance becomes the primary prophetic role in relationship to the royal office. Conflict among the prophets would intensify in the centuries to follow and led to a sharp distinction between true prophets and false. Criteria for distinguishing between true and false were never able to be precisely developed, however (see Deut 13:1-5; 18:9-22; Jer 23; 28); only

271

later generations were able to discern the identity of the true prophets and collected their stories and words. As has been noted, an especially serious conflict between prophet and king emerged in the North in the relationship between the prophet Elijah and Ahab and Jezebel.

Elijah and Elisha

Much of 1 Kgs 17–2 Kgs 10 focuses on the ministry of Elijah and on that of his successor, Elisha. Most scholars agree that these narratives circulated independent from their present context in an earlier form (perhaps both oral and written). They were drawn into this larger story by Deuteronomic editors—with minimal revision, sufficient to fit them into their larger story of Israel's apostate kings.

Elijah and His Time

Elijah was called to be a prophet during the reigns of the northern king Ahab (869–850 BCE) and his son Ahaziah (850–849 BCE). This royal house generated a time of deep crisis for Israel, though this was not externally apparent. Under Omri, Ahab's father, Israel had once again been put on the map of the world of nations, and for several decades was successful in its military and commercial undertakings. Ahab ruled during a time of relative peace and prosperity. But, as often proved to be the case in the course of Israel's history, external success masked an internal rottenness. Israel had succumbed to the idolatries associated with Baal worship, became engaged in the violent persecution of the worshipers of Yahweh, and promoted oppressive policies toward the less fortunate (see 1 Kgs 21). In the tradition of several of his predecessors, Elijah criticizes the regime on these various fronts with a sharp and specific word from God. He serves as royal critic and general "troubler of Israel" (1 Kgs 18:17).

The stylized notices of the kings in 1 Kgs 15–16 are "interrupted" at 17:1 by a return to narratives. The change in style signals a change in content; Elijah is an interruption. Elijah is a towering figure, a new Moses, who bursts upon the scene from outside normal channels (Gilead is east of the Jordan, away from the centers of power) and confronts the power structures in uncompromising terms. The spirited stories about Elijah focus on his confrontation with Baal and his advocates; they follow the report of Ahab's introduction of idolatrous practices (1 Kgs 16:31-33). Elijah's zeal for Yahweh more than matches the zeal for Baal on the parts of Ahab and Jezebel. These stories claim that no compromise on this issue is possible; Yahweh and Baal cannot coexist in an easy syncretism.

But Elijah's journey is not depicted simply in heroic terms; a deep questioning of self, of vocation, and of God also characterizes his journey. No doubt because of this complexity, Elijah lives deeply embedded in Israel's memory, so much so that the last words of the Old Testament (Mal 4:5-6) are expectant of his return to usher in the day of the Lord. At the same time, these chapters in Kings are not simply a story about a prophet's life; they are also a story about the divine life and the interaction between prophet and God. God's future with this people is on the line, and neither God nor prophet remains unaffected by that struggle.

Elisha and His Time

Elisha is active during the reigns of Jehoram, Jehu, Jehoahaz, and Jehoash (849–786 BCE). Elisha is Elijah's appointed successor, but he serves a somewhat different role. Several elements in the Elisha story mirror those of his predecessor, particularly his miracle-working activities. The latter seem designed to enhance the prophet's reputation as a mediator of divine word and deed (cf. 2 Kgs 4:1-7 with 1 Kgs 17:8-16). But Elisha is even more engaged in activities associated with political and military crises. These include affairs of state, such as entering into intrigue regarding the threats to Israel's well-being posed by the Moabites (2 Kgs 3) and Aramaeans (2 Kgs 6–8), even intruding into the affairs of Syrian rule (see 8:7-15). Elisha also engaged issues internal to Israel's political life, promoting the activities of Jehu in bringing down the rule of Ahab's dynasty and assassinating Jehoram, Jezebel, and associated Baal worshipers (2 Kgs 9–10).

Elisha represents the word and work of a God who is active in every sphere of life, not just the religious. Despite appearances to the contrary, God works through the prophet in giving shape to Israel's history amid the swirl of these events. The reader might wonder about God's connections with such intrigue and violence. But

273

God chooses to work through means such as these and with what is available. God does not perfect people before God decides to work in and through them. Hence, violence will be associated with the work of God in the world.

Generally, these narratives in 1–2 Kings are designed to serve several purposes: to condemn the policies and practices of the evil rulers of Israel; to oppose the idolatrous worship of Baal; to enhance the role of the prophets in charting Israel through these dangerous times; and to magnify the God of Israel. Implicit throughout is the recognition that this sorrowful tale of idolatry and judgment is not simply past history. The narratives stand as a strong word to all subsequent generations regarding the central importance of the first commandment in Israel's life and worship and the dangers of syncretism and apostasy.

We take a closer look at several of the stories about Elijah and Elisha that speak narratively to these purposes. The most fundamental witness of these stories is that *Israel's* God makes true life possible in every sphere.

1 Kgs 17—Miracles of Life in the Midst of Death

The opposition to Baal is sharply pronounced in these stories, especially the notion that Baal controlled life and death, whether in the human or natural order. The witness of these stories is that life and death are in the hands of Israel's God, not Baal. At the same time, in each story, God, through the word (17:4, 9, 16, 24), mediates life through various creatures: nonhumans; a poor widow; the prophet himself. Regardless of their place in God's good creation, God's effective word is at work through them to serve life.

In the first story (17:1-7), Israel's God is acclaimed as the Creator, who sees to the cycle of the dry/rainy seasons and who works through nonhuman creatures (ravens) to provide food and water to the faithful. This theme continues in chapter 18, where the conflict between Yahweh and Baal comes to a head. In the second story (17:8-16), Elijah is commanded to go to Zarephath, near the capital of Baal worship (Sidon; see 16:31), to demonstrate in the very center of the opposition that true life depends upon the God of Israel. God acts on behalf of the poor (those neglected by the political power structures) to provide food and works through even such lowly persons to care for the faithful. Here the prophet is dependent upon such a lowly one for his basic needs.

The third story (17:17-24; cf. the similar story of Elisha in 2 Kgs 4:18-37) continues with the same characters in the same opposition-filled setting. This time the issue of life and death is more sharply raised. Israel's God is the God of life, not simply in the world of nature or in the provision of life-giving food and water, but even at the point where physical death has intruded upon human life. Here the prophet himself, like the ravens and the poor widow, is portrayed as the one who mediates the power of God for life by raising the widow's son from the dead. He uses an existing healing ritual, which combines stretching his body over the boy (to communicate some of his own life to the boy) and a further prayer to God to restore his life (this time with an imperative). Note that prayer alone is not considered sufficient (for a comparable combination, see 2 Kgs 20:1-7). God responds to the prophet; in fact, God "listened" to Elijah.

The climactic note in the story lies not in the restoration as such but in the testimony of the woman (17:24; see also 18:39). In the movement from the woman's accusation to her affirmation, a public witness is made to this God and God's prophet by a resident within Baal's own land. God and his effective witness have entered into enemy territory and have begun to conquer the powers of death *from within*—no military, political, or ecclesiastical activity here—through seemingly small gestures, feeble words, and the witness of a lowly woman. One small healing act here and there, and more testifying women like her, and the word about this life-giving God will get around. This witness sets the stage for the major confrontations of Elijah with the powers that be in chapter 18.

These miracle stories (the similar stories of Elisha in 2 Kgs 4–5 are also in view here) shift the readers' focus away from larger societal issues to the needs of individuals—both rich and poor. Royal persons and policies are hardly in view; they do not finally define reality. Apostasy and its effects have not taken over God's world. These stories speak most fundamentally about God's will for life that continues amid all that makes for wrath and death in Israel. Needs are being met; life is being given and restored; God the Creator is still at work for good.

Note that the needs met are not narrowly religious or spiritual—true also of the miracles of Jesus, which these stories anticipate and help interpret. They are concerned with quite mundane matters that have to do with enough food, safe food, freedom from debt that can break up families, sickness, and death. They recognize that suffering is real, that pain is an everyday experience for wealthy and poor, even for the faithful. The people of God are not exempted from the pains and sorrows of life. As Ps 23:5 puts it, "You prepare a table before me *in the presence of* my enemies." These are not escapist stories, designed to take readers out of the world; rather, they put life back into place according to God's creational design.

Remarkably, these prophetic deeds are not presented in terms of a divine disruption of God's creation. Indeed, they are seen in more matter-of-fact terms; as such, the stories testify that God's good creation is *properly* at work in the midst of those who would disrupt it. The stories are remarkably unconcerned to explain how these deeds take place, except to make clear that God works through already existing means in each case. The Creator has placed within this world human beings with compassion and remarkable gifts who can bring life and well-being to those in need. Each of these stories involves human activity; a prophet enters into the lives of others and seeks to ameliorate their life situations. Moreover, the prophet uses a variety of creational resources. His work is not a creation out of nothing, but the expansion and development of already existing gifts of God's creation. The links to contemporary life entail discerning the gifts the Creator has already given that can enable such life-giving surprises in our own time—for example, medical research and the skills of surgeons and counselors. While the texts are not interested in promoting methods by which miracles might be brought about, they invite the reader to imagine creational resources not yet tapped.

The witness of these texts, finally, is that God's will for life working through human beings and other created realities is living and real even in the worst of times. They make clear that there are possibilities for life and healing in God's world that go beyond our present calculations and understandings, and they give us hope that God's working in this world through people like ourselves may indeed make miracles happen.

Such stories do not necessarily stand over against modern views of reality. Modern physics (quantum mechanics, chaos theory) has helped us see that this world is not a closed system of cause and effect; the loose, if complex, causal weave allows for "play" within God's design that makes novelty, freshness, surprise, and serendipity possible (see Job 38–41). Even more, such a world makes it possible for God to be at work *within* the interplay of natural law and the loose weave. God's creation is not fixed and static, but full of surprises and new possibilities. Historians still have their work to do in sorting out issues of probability as to whether these particular miracles occurred, but they cannot with integrity begin by saying they *could* not happen.

1 Kgs 18—Yahweh Alone Is God

This chapter is set during a time of severe drought throughout the land of Israel; it provides the occasion for a confrontation between Yahweh and Baal: who would be able to break the drought and provide the rains needed for fields and flocks? Baal was supposedly the "expert" in such areas; but Elijah enters into the heart of Baal's very domain, and goes for the jugular. Elijah's strategy is to set up a challenge between himself (and Yahweh) and four hundred fifty prophets of Baal to resolve the matter. The prophets of Baal resort to a variety of ecstatic behaviors and rituals, hoping thereby to prompt action on the part of Baal. But nothing happens. Elijah's response (vv. 27-29) is filled with satire, mocking such efforts as futile: Baal must be asleep or meditating or on a journey; or perhaps he is going to the bathroom.

Elijah proceeds with his own strategy. He builds an altar and prepares a sacrifice. He pours water (symbolizing the end of the drought) over the altar, and calls upon Yahweh to demonstrate who is truly God. The "fire of the LORD" falls from heaven and consumes the burnt offering and the entire sacrificial structure. The people respond with a confession that Yahweh is God, seize the prophets of Baal at Elijah's command, and Elijah single-handedly kills them all. The drought is broken, demonstrating that Yahweh, not Baal, is the God of life and fertility.

The violence in evidence here should not be explained away, but neither should it be considered necessarily just. Once again, God does not act alone; but God works in and through that which is available, with human beings as they are, with all of their flaws and foibles. Again, God does not perfect people before deciding to work through them. Moreover, this divine action does not necessarily confer a positive value on the specific human means through which God chooses to work, nor does that divine involvement allow one to say that the end necessarily justifies the means. In any case, God's actions in the event ought not be reduced to human proportions.

The reader might be tempted to suggest that this story is most basically concerned to demonstrate God's transcendent power. But such language can be misleading. The problem with Baal (as with idols generally, see Ps 115:3-8; Jer 10:5) is not that he is distant and removed (though he does that well), but that he does not speak or feel or act or care: "There was no voice, no answer, and no response" (18:26, 29). The concern here is more to protect Yahweh's immanence than divine transcendence. Yahweh listens to Elijah's prayers and responds to them.

One might also be tempted to think that this story, in contrasting Yahweh with idols, emphasizes Yahweh's freedom. But more to the point here is the concern for God's commitment, which by definition entails a self-limitation of freedom. God has promised to send rain (18:1); God honors the relationship with the prophet; God remembers commitments made to Abraham, Isaac, and Israel (18:36) by responding to that particular formulation in the prophetic prayer. God has named this people Israel (18:31; all twelve tribes), has called them God's own, and acts in faithfulness to that relationship.

The concern of the text is not simply to show that Yahweh alone is God, as important as that is. The concern is also to reveal something about the basic character of this God. Yahweh is one who is active in human affairs, who listens, speaks, and acts, and who honors commitments made to chosen representatives and to the people with whom a special relationship has been established. It is precisely *this kind of God* who is the only God for Israel. Even more, it is this kind of God who is the only God, period. Yahweh is the only God for Israel, and divided allegiances are as unfaithful as abandonment of Yahweh altogether.

This story ought not be used to suggest that God cannot lose in any contest. To be consistent, such a perspective would have to claim that there was no loss for God in the apostasies of Jeroboam or Ahab or anyone else in this spiraling downfall of Israel. The alternative is for apostasy to be considered the will of God. And, if that is so, God has no business being angry at what happens. The apostasy we encounter in these texts means that the will of God is resistible. And if resisted, that is a loss for God and the occasion for divine grief (see Ps 78:40; Eph 4:30).

We should speak in a more qualified way and say that in *this* particular contest God *does* not lose. But the divine action is not unrelated to prior human activity, and that human action is not irrelevant to God's action. The list is considerable: Elijah's boldness in standing before Ahab and all the false prophets; his conviction that Baal is nothing and Yahweh is God and his speaking and acting on that conviction; the care and confidence with which he sets the scene in terms of a perfectly executed sacrificial act; his prayer with its fine historical sense and proper communal motivations, to which God listens (cf. 17:22); and his ritual actions to prepare for the coming of the rain. These human activities count; they make a difference to the situation and to God. The possibilities for God in this contested moment are sharply enhanced by the prophet's words and deeds.

1 Kgs 19—A Personal Crisis for the Prophet

This chapter centers on the prophetic commission that issues from an encounter with God (vv. 15-18) and Elijah's fulfillment of the succession of Elisha (vv. 19-21). Second Kings 2 continues the issue of Elisha's succession, at which point Elisha actually picks up the mantle of Elijah and becomes his successor.

In 18:22 Elijah had complained to God that he was the only prophet left who had not bowed the knee to Baal. He was the only true "man of God" left in town. This complaint of Elijah is evident in 19:16 as God promises him that Elisha will be his successor, and that he is not as alone as he may think; some seven thousand Israelites remain faithful to God (19:18).

Threatened by Ahab and Jezebel, Elijah flees for his life, heading south toward Mt. Horeb, the traditional site of divine revelation. On the way he relives some of Israel's experiences in the wilderness; he complains because of his failures and expresses a wish for death (ironic, given his flight from death at royal hands). But God again (cf. 17:1-16) provides for life in the midst of death. Having arrived at Horeb, God repeatedly (vv. 9, 13) rebukes Elijah as to what he is doing in *this* place. Elijah, perhaps expecting divine commiseration and focusing on himself, has the same reply (vv. 10, 14, author's translation): "I've been working my head off to no effect; all Israelites have proved unfaithful, and now my life is in danger." It is as if he had heard nothing between the questions. And in fact, while there had been a lot of noise (earthquake, wind, and fire—signs of the storm god Baal but not realities "in" which the God of Israel is to be found), no real communication had taken place. After the noise there was only the "sound of silence."

When Elijah simply repeats his reply, God responds (vv. 15-18, author's translation): "Get out of the doldrums, quit the pity party, much work remains to be done, and here are a few starters; besides, you are not alone" (see also 18:3-4). No new word was available to Elijah from Mt. Horeb (Elijah was no Moses); it was essentially the same old word. Nor is Elijah given special protection; he is given only some new tasks and the promise of help to carry out his responsibilities. Hazael and Jehu will be instruments of God's purposes, and a successor prophet will be raised up to continue his work. And remember the seven thousand.

God's commands to anoint two kings are not actually carried out by Elijah, but by Elisha and one of Elisha's followers (2 Kgs 8:7-15; 9:1-13). The purpose for making Hazael king of Aram (2 Kgs 10:32-33) is to cut back Israel's territory and mediate God's judgment on Israel for its idolatry (as God will later use the Assyrians and the Babylonians). The second case (2 Kgs 9:1-13) also relates to divine judgment as Jehu puts an end to Ahab's dynasty and initiates reforms that begin to turn back the inroads of Baal on Israel's life. In both cases, once again, God becomes involved in violent human activities, whereby judgment is mediated through a foreign people upon Israel for its unfaithfulness. The one command that Elijah does carry out provides for prophetic continuity in the person of Elisha (1 Kgs 19:19-21). Such a concern for succession is not the usual way in which prophets are raised up in Israel. Succession is the means God uses in this instance because of the concerns expressed by Elijah and the severity of the crisis for Yahwism in Israel at this time. This crisis calls for continuity in having a "man of God" on the scene who can address the issues forthrightly. This stress on continuity shows that the calling of the prophet as spokesperson of God is the central concern of this narrative.

Elisha (a very rich man) is not eager to pick up Elijah's mantle and begs for a delay to say his good-byes. Whether Elijah rebukes him is unclear; he appears to tell Elisha to return to what he was doing as if the call had not occurred. Elisha is too indecisive to serve the calling Elijah has in mind. But when Elisha returns home he slaughters the oxen with which he had been working the fields (rather than, say, selling them) and provides a feast for the community; he is given a second chance (unlike in Luke 9:61-62). Elisha's act is a sign that he has made the decision, and that it is irrevocable; he no longer has a vocation to which he can return. Having burned all his bridges, he leaves the farm and follows Elijah, becoming his servant.

Elisha actually becomes fully his successor in 2 Kgs 2. The basic concern of that story is not Elijah's "ascent" into heaven. Rather, the story establishes Elisha's faithfulness and authority for the narratives that follow. This point is achieved not simply through links to Elijah but also through elaborate intertextual references to the stories of Moses and Joshua. Some assessment of these stories in terms of symbolic narrative may help us see how the narrator accomplishes this here and elsewhere in the Elijah and Elisha cycle.

On Symbolic Narrative

The modern reader should not interpret these texts in a narrowly historical way, as if they were fundamentally concerned to reconstruct the history of Israel. They do tell a story about the past, and they frame that telling with a chronological schematic. But to consider them straightforward historical accounts is as reductionistic as to dismiss them or diminish them to fantasy, fairy tale, or morality play.

One helpful way in which to think about many of these texts is in terms of symbolic narrative. This designation moves in two primary directions. One, the characters are presented as types of certain persons, roles, or behaviors. For example, while Ahaziah plays a minor historical role in 2 Kgs 1, he also portrays a typical apostate, embodies the sickness of Israel, and typifies the struggle between the adherents of Yahweh and Baal for the soul of God's elect. He is portrayed in larger-than-life terms. Something similar could be said about Elijah and Elisha. They emerge at a time when the future of Yahwism in Israel is deeply threatened. That the word of God was able to be heard and accomplished through them in such a time could, finally, be described only in less than ordinary terms. That Elijah was taken by God by means other than death expresses not only divine approval of his extraordinary ministry and the power of Israel's God to overcome death, but the continuity in the ministries of these two prophets. In some inexplicable way Elijah lives on in the ministry of Elisha; Elisha is Elijah one more time, larger than life.

Two, significant levels of intertextuality are present in the narrative, that is, direct and indirect allusions to other texts and traditions (especially those of Moses and Joshua). By such linkages, the reader is invited to move imaginatively into other worlds that the tradition presents and connect them with the text at hand. Such intertextual work by the narrator implies a significant level of interpretation regarding the meaning of the matter under discussion. This means that the reader should not interpret in an overly literal way the wondrous events that occur, mediated by the word or deed of these prophets or other human and nonhuman realities. The wonders enhance the authority of the prophetic word and are emblematic of God's commitments to the ministry of these prophets and of God's own remarkable actions in and through them.

A mysterious, elusive quality pervades these narratives. The narrator does not "explain" what occurs, or spell out the details, or even connect God closely with the wondrous events. In 2 Kgs 2, for example, only in verse 1 does the *narrator* explicitly make God the subject of what occurs. Virtually every word and action is given symbolic value. The import of these twists and turns can be discerned only by considerable intertextual work, and even then full interpretations do not become available.

It is important to note that the narrator does not linger on the "miraculous," but presents each occasion in almost matter-of-fact terms. "The wonders themselves seem only little more than ordinary in this understated world."[3] The narrator does not pause to savor the marvel of it all or express awe or wonder at what happens (even in 2 Kgs 2:12). The reader is thereby pushed away from focusing on the spectacular in itself and asked to discern the theological and religious import of what is being stated. The center of that concern could be summarized in this way: In the face of numerous and powerful adversaries, God has not left himself without a mediator of the word of God and a faithful witness to God's purposes in Israel and the world. This, finally, is the real "miracle."

The Word of God Shapes Israel's History

One of the commonly noted perspectives of the Deuteronomistic History is that God's word spoken by prophets shapes Israel's history.[4] This word takes the form of both promise and judgment; instructional and hortatory language is used to convey both (e.g., 1 Kgs 8; 2 Kgs 17). The use of this kind of language (by an author who lived after the fall of Jerusalem) entails a claim that Israel has a future beyond any experienced disaster—because of the kind of God to whom they are related.

1. With respect to God's word of *judgment*, many texts can be cited wherein the prophetic word spoken is fulfilled later in the history (cf. Josh 6:26 with 1 Kgs 16:34; 1 Sam 2:31 with 1 Kgs 2:27). Such words of judgment are understood to have had a powerful effect on the course of Israel's history. Generally speaking, the prophets claim that Israel's apostasy constitutes the most basic reason for that judgment: the country's division and, finally, the destruction of both kingdoms by foreign armies (first the Assyrians, then the Babylonians). Earlier in this chapter we explored the nature of this apostasy.

Yet, to speak of fulfillment is not to tell the only story about prophetic words of judgment. Now and again, the judgment word of God spoken through the prophets is not (literally) fulfilled.

Isaiah, for example, announces to Hezekiah that he will die and not recover. Yet, in response to Hezekiah's prayer the prophetic word is reversed through a direct word from God (2 Kgs 20:1-6). Similarly, when Ahab repentantly responds to God's word through Elijah, God delays the fulfillment of the word (1 Kgs 21:27-29; cf. 2 Chr 12:1-12). Or, God's word to Elijah in 1 Kgs 19:15-18 is only partially fulfilled in the ministry of Elijah; aspects of this word remain for others to accomplish (2 Kgs 9–10). In addition, God's ongoing merciful interaction with the people affects the course of Israel's history, even in the face of contrary prophetic words (cf. 2 Kgs 13:23).

The fact that *some* prophetic words are not (literally) fulfilled means that, in *every* such case, the future is understood to remain open until fulfillment actually occurs. Israel's future is not absolutely determined by the prophet's word. In other words, prophetic words of judgment do not function mechanistically, as if the word were some autonomous power beyond the reach of God's continuing attention. Even more, this "play" that exists during the time between the word and its (potential) fulfillment gives room for the promise to be at work, even in the midst of judgment. Indeed, finally, God *uses* judgment, not as an end in itself, but as a refining fire for salvific purposes—in the service of the word of promise. Unlike love, wrath is not a divine attribute (if there were no sin, there would be no wrath) but a contingent response to Israel's sin. God's wrath is always "provoked" by sinful activity (1 Kgs 14:9, 15, and often).

2. The Deuteronomistic History specifies the word of *promise* as an unconditional word, either to David or to the people of Israel (Deut 4:31; Judg 2:1; 1 Sam 12:22; 2 Sam 7:16; 2 Kgs 13:23). The ongoing fulfillment of that promise in Israel's history is noted (1 Kgs 8:20, 56), and that word has been fulfilled by God's own hand (1 Kgs 8:15, 24; cf. 2 Sam 7:25), not by some power that the word itself possesses. But even when fulfillment occurs, a literal interpretation may not be in view. For example, the strong words of Josh 23:14 (cf. 11:23; 21:43-45; 1 Kgs 8:56) that every word of God regarding the land has been fulfilled stands in tension with other notices that territory remains to be taken (cf. Josh 15:63; 23:4-13; Judg 1). The word of promise did come to pass, but not with the literal precision one might expect from the word as originally spoken.

A comparable perspective on the fulfillment of words of divine promise is present in the Davidic texts. The promise of 2 Sam 7:16 appears to be conditioned in the word to Solomon in 1 Kgs 9:5-7 (cf. 2:3-4). It becomes clear in the subsequent narrative, however, that this condition is limited in its scope. The fundamental Davidic promise is reiterated by the prophet Ahijah, albeit in more restrictive terms (1 Kgs 11:11-13, 32-38). This promise continues to be articulated, in times of both apostasy (1 Kgs 15:4-6; 2 Kgs 8:19) and faithfulness (2 Kgs 18:3-7).

At the end of the history, however, the word of judgment on Judah is expressed in unequivocal terms (2 Kgs 23:26-27), and the fulfillment of the promise is stated in more ambiguous language in the reference to the release of the Davidic king Jehoiachin (2 Kgs 25:27-30). Yet, the promise to David articulated in earlier texts is never set aside and hence must have been thought to remain in force. The ambiguity in the narrative portrayal corresponds to Israel's *experience,* wherein the promise is clouded by the disastrous events. But the promise remains for the believing to cling to, even through the most devastating fires of judgment, and divine forgiveness remains available to a repentant people (1 Kgs 8:46-53). This repentance, however, is not generated by the people, but is a reality that God works within them (1 Kgs 8:57-58).

This tension carries forward the ambiguities present at the end of Deuteronomy, wherein the promise is articulated clearly (30:1-10), but only within the context of certain apostasy and judgment (28:45-57; 31:16-29). Yet, even for Deuteronomy, the promise takes priority in its thinking about Israel's future (Deut 30:4-5; cf. 4:31; Lev 26:40-45). Indeed, God's promise includes a unilateral circumcising action on Israel's heart so that the people will unfailingly obey the first commandment (30:6; note that the command to circumcise the heart in Deut 10:16 here becomes promise). The priority of the promise is such that, in effect, God himself will see to the obedience to God's own law. These themes of judgment and promise are both poetically represented in Deut 32–33, but promise retains the climactic position with its strong concluding word in 33:26-29. Deuteronomy and the Deuteronomistic History seem finally to value Davidic promise over obedience to Sinaitic law. In the end, it is God who will see to both, but only on the far side of a devastating judgment.

Generally, it may be said that God's word of promise through the prophets will not fail; as far as God is concerned, the promise will never be made null and void. The promise is finally dependent only on the faithfulness of God. This promise can be relied on, though a rebellious generation may not live to see the fulfillment, and those who remain alive can claim the promises only through a refining fire. The prophetic word of disaster and death does not become a word of eternal death or annihilation. No word of final rejection is pronounced or announced.

Israel's history is lived out within a tension of judgment and promise, but it is important to state clearly that no inherent theological contradiction exists between God's death-dealing judgment and the divine promise. God's move through death to life is a prominent biblical theme. The word of promise finally proves decisive for the continuing existence of Israel beyond the apostasy and consequent judgments.

The book of Lamentations, written in the wake of the fall of Jerusalem in 587 BCE, is not unlike the books of Kings in this regard. Trust in a God of love and faithfulness is sharply attested in the midst of an experience of uncompromising devastation (3:22-33). Trust in this kind of God resounds clearly, even though it stands together with the ambiguity of the Kings-like ending of Lam 5:20-22. Hope for the future depends solely on this God.

Another source for such a tension-filled understanding is Book III of the Psalter (Pss 73–89). Several of these psalms clearly reflect the uncertainties associated with the destruction of Jerusalem (74; 77; 79; 89) and interweave community lament with signs of hope and trust in the God of the promise. Additional laments and prayers for restoration from oppression by enemies (73; 80; 83; 85–86; 88), as well as claims regarding Israel's own stubbornness and God's judgment (78; 81–82), are interwoven with confident psalms of Zion (76; 84; 87). Finally, Ps 89 ends this book of the Psalter with a deep and questioning lament, with the future of the people of God stated in ambiguous terms. At the same time, Ps 89 continues to affirm the unconditional promises to David. These promises are finally inviolable and everlasting, grounded in the very Godness of God, who will not lie. Despite every appearance to the contrary, Israel continues to lay claim to these promises before the throne of the very God who seems to have broken them (vv. 3-4, 18-37; cf. 2 Sam 7:13-16).[5]

Notes

1. For the argument that these texts do not claim absolute foreknowledge for God, see T. Fretheim, *The Suffering of God: An Old Testament Perspective* (Philadelphia: Fortress, 1984), 45-59.

2. For detail and ancient Near Eastern parallels, see B. Long, *1 Kings, with an Introduction to Historical Literature* (FOTL 9; Grand Rapids: Eerdmans, 1984), 159-64.

3. B. Long, *2 Kings* (FOTL 10; Grand Rapids: Eerdmans, 1991), 34.

4. Cf. G. von Rad, "The Deuteronomic Theology of History in I and II Kings," in *The Problem of the Hexateuch and Other Essays* (New York: McGraw-Hill, 1966), 205-21.

5. Several paragraphs in this chapter have been drawn from T. Fretheim, *First and Second Kings* (Louisville: Westminister John Knox, 1999). Used by permission of Westminster John Knox Press.

Bibliography

Brenner, Athalya. *A Feminist Companion to Samuel and Kings.* Sheffield: Sheffield Academic, 1994.

Brueggemann, Walter. *1 & 2 Kings.* Smyth & Helwys Bible Commentary. Macon: Smyth & Helwys, 2000.

Fretheim, Terence. *First and Second Kings.* Louisville: Westminster John Knox, 1999.

Long, Burke O. *1 Kings, with an Introduction to Historical Literature. 2 Kings.* FOTL 9–10. Grand Rapids: Eerdmans, 1984, 1991.

Nelson, Richard D. *First and Second Kings.* IBC. Louisville: John Knox, 1987.

Petersen, David L. *The Prophetic Literature: An Introduction.* Louisville: Westminster John Knox, 2002.

Provan, Iain W. *1 and 2 Kings.* Peabody, Mass.: Hendrickson, 1995.

Rice, Gene. *1 Kings: Nations Under God.* ITC. Grand Rapids: Eerdmans, 1990.

For bibliography on the Deuteronomistic History, see the conclusion of chapter 6.

CHAPTER NINE

PROPHECY AND REFORM: FROM JEROBOAM TO JOSIAH

2 Kgs 14–25, Amos, Hosea, Micah, Isa 1–39,
Deuteronomy, Zephaniah

The eighth and seventh centuries BCE saw the destruction of the northern kingdom and the subjugation of the southern kingdom by the Neo-Assyrian Empire. Moreover, these two centuries witnessed a major change in the ancient Near Eastern power structure, the defeat of the Assyrians by the Babylonians, though the Assyrian Empire was ascendant during most of this time.

The Old Testament attests these events in two basic kinds of literature, both of which are theologically charged. On the one hand, the major histories, 2 Kings and 2 Chronicles, cover the span in systematic fashion—king by king in annalistic style. On the other hand, books attributed to various prophets offer a focused gaze at one or another moment during which the prophet was active. Although prophets per se are mentioned in summary fashion in Kings (e.g., "Yet the LORD warned Israel and Judah by every prophet and every seer" [2 Kgs 17:13]), only Isaiah (and Jonah—see 2 Kgs 14:25) are mentioned by name, at least of those prophets for whom we have books. Others like Micaiah ben Imlah (1 Kgs 22) are known to us only in the Deuteronomistic History. Important though Amos, Hosea, and Micah might seem to us, we find no evidence of them in either Kings or Chronicles. This fact suggests that the biblical witness offers diverse angles of vision on these events: those of two different historians and those from various prophets. As we will see, each literature displays intense, though not identical, theological preoccupations.

The Eighth and Seventh Centuries

The eighth and seventh centuries might be called the ascent and descent of the Neo-Assyrian Empire. (Scholars often speak of Old, Middle, and Neo-Assyrian periods.) Whereas in the ninth century, biblical narratives refer primarily to the relatively small cities and states of Syria-Palestine (e.g., Moab, 2 Kgs 3; Aram, 2 Kgs 5), the map broadens in the eighth century. In the early part of that century, both Judah (under Amaziah and Uzziah) and Israel (under Jeroboam) were able to secure their territories against earlier foes. But by the middle part of that century, the biblical text reports that Tiglath-Pileser III (also known in the Bible as "Pul") had attacked Israel (2 Kgs 15). Such incursions by the Neo-Assyrian Empire were consistent with their imperial strategies, and they would continue until the Neo-Assyrian Empire expired. However, as we will see, Israel's historians (and prophets) understood such actions to be part of God's intentions regarding Israel (so, e.g., 2 Kgs 17:7). What the Neo-Assyrians might deem to be a campaign designed to punish a disobedient vassal or to secure certain economic goods was judged by the biblical historians to be God's punishment on Israel for worshiping other gods.

Both biblical histories talk about this period by referring to those who were on the throne and by offering an evaluation of their reigns. The formulaic evaluations were uniformly based on the religious behavior of the king, not on his political, military, or economic prowess. For most kings, the historian adjudges, "He did what was evil in the sight of the LORD" (e.g., 2 Kgs 21:2). All northern kings receive these negative judgments, even though some, such as Jeroboam II, must have been capable rulers (see 2 Kgs 14:25). A few of the southern kings received relatively good press—"He did what was right in the sight of the LORD"—a judgment offered about both Amaziah (14:3) and his son, Azariah (15:3). But even these individuals are condemned for permitting certain ritual activities, e.g., the offerings and sacrifices on high places (2 Kgs 15:4).

From the perspective of political and/or military history, there were some epochal moments during these two centuries: the so-called Syro-Ephraimitic crisis (735–732 BCE), the destruction of Samaria (721 BCE), the assault on Jerusalem by Sennacherib (701

BCE), Manasseh's long reign (687–642 BCE), the defeat of Nineveh (612 BCE), and the death of Josiah on the battlefield (609 BCE). Each period receives intense scrutiny from biblical historians and/or prophets and, hence, requires some comment in this volume.

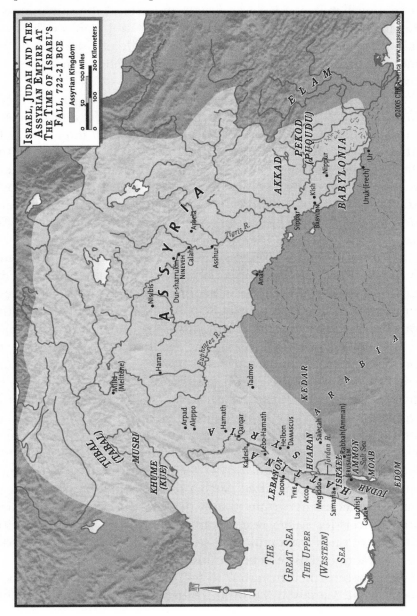

1. The Syro-Ephraimitic crisis pitted Israel in league with Damascus against Judah. The southern state responded by asking for Assyrian assistance against the coalition at their northern borders. Such swirling loyalties offered the opportunity for interesting geopolitical analysis. However, Isaiah understood the situation as a theological test for Israel—whether those in Judah would trust Yahweh or trust in political alliances. His angle of vision was different from that of the biblical historian, who provided a more neutral assessment of Ahaz's solicitation of Assyrian aid (2 Kgs 16).

2. The destruction of Samaria and the defeat of the northern kingdom in 721 may be viewed as due to both radical internal instability—six kings in twenty-five years—and Assyrian imperial goals. However, whether in the eyes of Hosea or in the eyes of the Deuteronomistic Historian, the real cause was religious impropriety, worshiping a god (Baal) other than Yahweh (see 2 Kgs 17:7-18 for a straightforward explanation by the Deuteronomistic Historian). Moreover, both these literatures affirm that Yahweh, and not Assyria (or Assyrian gods), was responsible for Israel's destruction.

3. During Hezekiah's reign (715–687 BCE), Judah suffered assault by the Neo-Assyrians under Sennacherib's leadership. These events are chronicled in Neo-Assyrian sources and presented in two very similar versions in the Bible (Isa 36–39 and 2 Kgs 18–20). As with the Syro-Ephraimitic crisis, Judah sought assistance from another major power, now Egypt (2 Kgs 18:21). But this time, at least according to the biblical historian, the Neo-Assyrians explicitly claimed that Israel's God was on their side (2 Kgs 18:25). When confronted by such a remarkable claim, Hezekiah sought counsel from the prophet Isaiah. Isaiah responded (2 Kgs 19:6-7) by stating that Judah should wait for Yahweh to act on Israel's behalf, which in due course happens. According to 2 Kgs 19:35-37, "the messenger of the LORD" attacked the Neo-Assyrian forces, decimating the army and hence causing the siege to be lifted. Such a remarkable lifting of the siege may be reflected in certain psalms that attest to the ways in which God protects Jerusalem (e.g., Ps 48). What for Isaiah was a specific moment of relief from military assault appears to have become part of a far more extensive belief in this divinely protected city.

4. Manasseh ruled from 687 to 642 BCE. This reign is, in itself, a major event. Manasseh was on the Judahite throne longer than any

other member of the Davidic line, including David himself. One can only imagine the challenges he faced in trying to maintain Judah's identity in the face of vigorous internal and external challenges. This son of Hezekiah and Hephzibah, however, receives no good word from the biblical historians (2 Chr 33:11-13 presents a scene favorable to Manasseh; this scene does not exist in Kings). Dynastic stability apparently meant nothing to the Deuteronomist, who focused instead on what he deemed to be errant religious practices (2 Kgs 21:3-7). Manasseh's improprieties—rebuilding shrines that Hezekiah had destroyed and support of Canaanite religious practices—were so offensive that the Deuteronomist offers them as *the* reason Jerusalem will be destroyed and Judah defeated. The biblical historian's judgments about religion far outweighed any sentiments he might have had about political longevity as a value.

5. Near the end of the seventh century BCE, major changes were occurring in Mesopotamia. The dominant force, Neo-Assyria, was facing challenges it would be unable to meet successfully. There were the Neo-Babylonians to the south, but the Neo-Assyrians confronted others as well, that is, Arameans, Lydians, and Medes. This transition in power from one to another empire did not happen immediately. One pivotal date is the defeat of Nineveh, a capital of the Neo-Assyrian Empire, which fell in 612 BCE. One searches Kings and Chronicles in vain for comment about this momentous transition. In contrast, however, prophetic literature does provide perspective on the downfall of Nineveh. Even as early as the book of Isaiah, Assyria stood under critique (10:13-19). But it is the little book of Nahum that offers a remarkable focus on the Neo-Assyrian capital, Nineveh. After an opening acrostic psalm, Nahum provides a graphic picture of Nineveh being destroyed. To be sure, Yahweh had used Nineveh to punish Israel (Isa 10). But Assyria had overstepped its bounds and acted with radical violence and without acknowledging that it was an instrument of Yahweh. Hence, Nineveh, symbolizing the Neo-Assyrian Empire, was to be destroyed. Judah no doubt delighted in this news. However, such applause might be viewed with some irony, since the Neo-Babylonians, who would decimate Nineveh, would also be the agent of God's punishment against Jerusalem.

6. The death of King Josiah is bound up in the imperial changes just mentioned, but it symbolized more for Israel than mere ancient Near Eastern politics. As we will see momentarily, Josiah was deemed to be an unusually righteous king. A prophetess, Huldah, when responding to a query from the king, reported to Josiah the following oracle: "Therefore, I will gather you to your ancestors, and you shall be gathered to your grave in peace" (2 Kgs 22:20). This peaceful fate would be "just," meaning that Josiah had acted in accord with the norms honored by the Deuteronomistic Historian and would have expected blessings rather than curses, to use covenant vocabulary. However, such was not to be the case. Instead, the biblical historian reports that Josiah was killed by Egyptian forces. The Egyptians and the Assyrians planned to attack the Babylonians, and Josiah had apparently intercepted the Egyptians on their way to that battle. His death in that encounter runs counter to the promise uttered by Huldah.

It would be easy to talk about this eventuality as a false prophecy. However, given some of the theological perspectives we have already discerned, it may be better to say that by engaging the Egyptian troops, Josiah made a fateful mistake, one which ran counter to God's intentions for both the Neo-Assyrians and the Neo-Babylonians. The time of the former was past, the time of the latter just arriving. Hence, Josiah's fate, apparently unjust on personal terms, might be understood in a wider theological context. The death of the righteous Josiah and some of the issues it raises also foreshadow the destruction of Jerusalem, which will be razed in less than twenty-five years from the date of Josiah's death.

Hezekiah and Josiah

Two Judahite kings receive special notice in the biblical histories: Hezekiah and Josiah. About the former, we are told: "He trusted in the LORD the God of Israel; so that there was no one like him among all the kings of Judah after him, or among those who were before him" (2 Kgs 18:5). (Interestingly, the Chronicler has an even more positive view of Hezekiah than does the author of Kings.) The Deuteronomistic Historian offers a similar judgment about Josiah: "Before him there was no king like him, who turned to the LORD with all his heart, with all his soul, and with all his might, according to all the law of Moses; nor did any like him arise after him" (2 Kgs 23:25). (The alert reader will note that these descriptions stand in tension, which suggests that one version of this history may have been completed before Josiah acceded to the throne.)

The biblical historians offer some reasons for these glowing appraisals. Both kings are remembered as having acted on behalf of the true worship of Israel's God. Those who study the history and religion of ancient Israel often refer to the "reforms" of Hezekiah and Josiah. By so doing, they focus attention on what might be described as religious activities attributed to Hezekiah and Josiah. Hezekiah, we are told, "removed the high places, broke down the pillars, and cut down the [asherah]. . . . He kept the commandments that the LORD commanded Moses. . . . He rebelled against the king of Assyria and would not serve him. . . . He attacked the Philistines as far as Gaza" (2 Kgs 18:4-8). The first two sets of actions apparently involve the destruction of religious shrines outside Jerusalem. Whether they were devoted to Yahweh or to other gods is not made clear.

Since the historian links such actions to adherence to "Mosaic" admonitions, we should understand Hezekiah's work as reform rather than revolution, the more so since the book of Deuteronomy identifies precisely those things that Hezekiah challenged:

high places——Deut 7:5; 12:2
pillars————Deut 7:5; 12:3
asherah————Deut 7:5; 12:3

Such actions may, therefore, be construed as religiously conservative, affirming a "good, old-time" religion.

This religious reform instigated by Hezekiah was consistent with the other two kinds of activity attributed to him, rebellion and assault. According to the book of Kings, Hezekiah rebelled against his vassal status, in effect declaring his independence from the Assyrians. Moreover, he went on the attack, moving against Israel's traditional enemies to the west, the Philistines, who were also vassals of the Assyrians. The picture of Hezekiah's activities in Chronicles is painted on a larger canvas. There is more said about ritual matters, such as the cleansing of the temple and the celebration of Passover on a massive scale. This Passover included worshipers not only from Judah, but from Israel as well—from as far north as Dan (2 Chr 30:1-5). This note is striking, as is the claim that high places in Ephraim and Manasseh were destroyed (31:1). According to Chronicles, Hezekiah appears to be incorporating elements of the northern or Israelite population, soon after the defeat of that nation in 721 BCE.

About Hezekiah's reforms at least two things must be said. First, they appear linked to political agendas. It would have made sense for Judah to expand its sphere of influence soon after the demise of the northern kingdom. The destruction of regional shrines was one way Hezekiah could justify his move into the area previously ruled by Israel, now nominally a district of the Neo-Assyrian Empire. (There is also some warrant for thinking that Hezekiah's actions occurred about the time that Sargon died and that Sennacherib acceded to the throne, i.e., his religious and political reforms responded to events in the Neo-Assyrian Empire.) Second, though Isaiah appears in the stories about Hezekiah (see 2 Kgs 19), the reforms of Hezekiah were not instigated by prophets. One might even go so far as to say that the kings, not the prophets active at this time, were the reformers. Such a claim recognizes that reforms require power, usually political power, which prophets did not routinely possess.

Josiah, too, is remembered as a good king because of reform activities. Unlike the situation with Hezekiah, we are told about the putative reason for these reforms. Repair work was being undertaken on the temple in Jerusalem. During the course of this work, a "book of the law" was found inside the temple and was brought to Josiah. After Josiah had the book read out loud, he consulted with the prophetess Huldah, who affirmed the import of the book. As a result, Josiah undertook a series of reforms. First Kings 23 provides a lengthy list of all the acts he undertook, for instance, tearing down regional shrines, cleansing the Jerusalem temple, deposing idolatrous priests, removing idols from shrines. Josiah even sponsors a centralized Passover, as had Hezekiah according to the Chronicler. And as with Hezekiah, there is a "northern" dynamic. First Kings 23:19 reports that Josiah destroyed shrines in the towns of Samaria, far beyond the normal range of Judahite control.

In Chronicles, Josiah's reforms are described differently from the version in Kings. Perhaps the major difference is the beginning point. Whereas the book of Kings reports activity commencing in 621, Chronicles starts the story in 627, with religious reforms even in the North (in the towns of Manasseh, Ephraim, Simeon, and Naphtali). Then the Chronicler recounts the story of the book and a second stage of the reform commences.

In both reforms, the kings seem to be responding to events beyond Israel's borders; their religious reforms are part of larger national strategies. Their stories are essentially hopeful, suggesting that with proper political and religious leadership, the people of God could reform their behavior and act in conformity with the covenant. Such sanguinity was, however, tempered even in the biblical narratives. First, the story of good King Hezekiah concludes with an unpleasant episode in which he inappropriately reveals information about Judah's financial and military condition to Mesopotamian officials. Moreover, Hezekiah is, finally, depicted as primarily interested in his own welfare (2 Kgs 20:19). And, as we have seen, the situation with Josiah was even more dire. He died ignominiously on the battlefield, a fate different from that one would have expected, based on his reforms, and different from that predicted by Huldah. In sum, reform was possible, but not regular, and even one of the two great reformers died not long after his reform efforts. Royal reformers there were, but the effects of these reforms were limited and not long-lasting.

Deuteronomy

In both Hezekiah's and Josiah's reforms, the acts of religious purification seem to be linked with the book of Deuteronomy. That book of Torah prescribes a way of life for the community to which kings could appeal. But how does this book work theologically and why is it the source of these reforms?

Deuteronomy is a complicated book. At its heart is a law code (chaps. 12–26); some would call it a constitution. Just as Moses delivers the law, or *torah* (which might better be translated as "instruction"), so, too, he delivers lengthy speeches to the people about that law. Before the so-called Deuteronomic law code, there are two major introductions, 1:1–4:43 and 4:44–11:32. The second introduction is particularly important, since it offers a version of the Ten Commandments (Deut 5:6-21; cf. Exod 20:2-17), the *Shema*, "Hear, O Israel: The LORD is our God, the LORD alone" (Deut 6:4), and a number of speeches—one might even call them sermons—in which

Moses admonishes the people about the importance and meaning of this Torah. Then, after Moses has promulgated the laws, the book reports the making of a covenant (chaps. 27–30) in Moab before Moses dies and Israel prepares to enter the land.

The Deuteronomic law code could have served as the basis of the reform under King Josiah. Most scholars agree that the book discovered in the temple ("the book of the torah"—2 Kgs 22:8) was probably some form of the book of Deuteronomy. Deuteronomy does insist on the veneration of Yahweh alone at one central place, in Josiah's time of course Jerusalem, and polemicizes much of that which Josiah destroyed: idolatrous priests, the asherah, male cult prostitutes, the high places, among them. One could, however, say that Josiah focuses only on the ritual aspects of that which is stipulated and/or prohibited in Deuteronomy. That book deals with far more than ritual matters. In fact, one theological hallmark of Deuteronomy is its comprehensive quality. To be God's people, Yahwists were called to a style of life that involved economic, political, social, even military as well as religious prescriptions.

Israel remembered the book of Deuteronomy in a number of ways. The name itself belongs to the Septuagint and means "Second Law," the first law presumably being that revealed to Moses at Sinai and preserved in Exodus and Leviticus (so Deut 29:1). Even more apt is the description given in 2 Kgs 23:21, "this book of the covenant." Deuteronomy is *the* covenant book par excellence. Deuteronomy 26:16–30:20 is replete with rituals and affirmations that belonged to the ratification of covenants in Israel and throughout the ancient Near East. The blessings (28:1-14) and curses (28:15-46) graphically articulate the two ways that God lays before Israel. Quite simply, the people can choose life or death.

The prominence of stipulations—the Deuteronomic law code—might give the impression that the Deuteronomist represents a religion of overly refined and arid legalism. Such could not be further from the case, as the following text makes clear:

> You shall love the LORD your God with all your heart, and with all your soul, and with all your might. Keep these words that I am commanding you today in your heart. Recite them to your children and talk about them when you are at home and when you are away, when you lie down and when you rise. (Deut 6:5-7)

The covenant relationship represents a religion of the heart and family, quite simply, a person's entire being. Further, those who wrote Deuteronomy understood Israelites to be capable of living in a covenant relationship: "Surely, this commandment that I am commanding you today is not too hard for you" (Deut 30:11). The book of Deuteronomy depicts Yahweh as a God who has chosen Israel to be a special people (Deut 26:18-19). And within the covenant context, that relationship involves specific responsibilities for Israel. As we shall see, many of the prophets will offer judgments about whether or not Israel had lived up to those expectations.

The word *today* occurs with extraordinary prominence in Deuteronomy (see, e.g., 8:1; 11:2; 26:17, 18; 30:15). This word signifies what we would call a contemporizing motif in the book. Whenever Israelites in later times heard or read this book, they were put, rhetorically and theologically, in the position of thinking about these "words" (see Deut 1:1) as directly relevant to them "today." Such a contemporizing strategy is also attested in Deut 6:20-25: "When your children ask you in time to come, 'What is the meaning of the decrees and the statutes and the ordinances that the LORD our God has commanded you?' then you shall say to your children . . ." The book is designed both to elicit precisely such questions and to offer the raw theological material out of which ensuing generations can create answers. Such a contemporizing dynamic helps explain why Deuteronomy—and neither Exodus nor Leviticus—would serve as the basis for reforms, whether under Hezekiah or Josiah. It was a book designed to challenge later generations, not simply to function as an archive of earlier laws.

Eighth- and Seventh-century Prophetic Literature

Soon after the beginning of the eighth century BCE (800–700), a small number of individuals arose whose words have been preserved in biblical books labeled by the names of those individuals. We know them as prophets, a word that derives from a Greek verb meaning "to foresee or prognosticate." As we shall see, although Israel's prophets talked about the future, they did far more than that.

Several of these prophets were active prior to the reforms of Hezekiah: Amos, Hosea, Micah, and Isaiah. Zephaniah may predate

Josiah's reforms, but not by much. Nahum would have come soon thereafter, followed in a matter of decades by Habakkuk, Jeremiah, and Ezekiel—the last two of which witnessed the destruction of Jerusalem and the exile of many Judahites. The rest of the prophetic books date to the exilic or post-exilic periods.

Biblical scholars have invested considerable effort in attempting to understand these individuals and the books attributed to them. Hence, before addressing the books individually, some comments about prophets and prophetic literature are in order.

Prophets

We have had occasion earlier in this volume to refer to individuals known as prophets. Nathan and Gad were active during the reign of David, and Elijah and Elisha were noteworthy figures in Israel during the ninth century. One might describe the first two as court prophets, since they were apparently located at and presumably supported by the royal court. To term an individual as a court prophet is not a pejorative act. Though active at the court, both Nathan and Gad offered remarkably critical words to the king. Elijah and Elisha seem quite different from their prophetic forebears. Elisha is often labeled a "man of God," a phrase also applied to Elijah (2 Kgs 1:9). Both men acted in decidedly powerful, even magical ways; for example, Elijah by providing an unending source of olive oil for a Phoenician widow (1 Kgs 17:8-16), Elisha by making an ax head float (2 Kgs 6:1-7).

Such variation among what these individuals generally conceived as prophets did makes one draw back and ask: What is a prophet? One way to answer this question is to use a general term drawn from the study of religion, namely, an *intermediary*. Such a term is more neutral than is the word *prophet*, with its implications of foreseeing. Intermediaries stand between the worlds of the gods and humans, the worlds of the sacred and the profane. And they do this in diverse ways. They can personify the sacred power of the Deity (Elijah in 2 Kgs 1), they can utter words on behalf of the Deity to humans (Hos 4:1), they can utter words on behalf of humans to the Deity (Amos 7:2), they can see things in the world of the sacred that other humans cannot see (Zech 3), or they can participate in deliberations of the divine council (Isa 6). They can even offer their own words as prophets (Jer 28:7-9). Moreover, they are remembered as communicating—whether speaking, writing, or acting—that which they had received from the world of the Deity. In some ways, they are like priests, another kind of religious specialist who mediated between the worlds of the sacred and the profane. (A few prophets belonged to priestly families: Jeremiah, Ezekiel, and Zechariah for certain.) However, unlike priests, prophets did not have to be born into a special lineage nor did they have to meet special purity requirements in order to do their job. (Isaiah may be an exception to the latter criterion.)

Prophets are not attested at all times in all cultures. Put another way, certain social and political conditions were necessary as prerequisites to prophetic behavior. In Israel, prophets were particularly prominent during what we call the monarchic period, though, of course, there were exceptions.

Times of crisis or radical social change seemed to elicit prophetic responses. One could say that much of the prophetic literature in the Old Testament reflects the pressures of either the Neo-Assyrian or Neo-Babylonian Empires on Syria-Palestine. Israel attests that God is responding to these crises through the prophets. Although God was remembered as providing no new Torah (cf. the noteworthy exception in Ezek 43:12), the prophets proclaimed and interpreted their understandings of Torah requirements for different generations of Israelites, especially at critical moments in its history.

In the world of the ancient Near East, other cultures knew prophets. Archaeologists have discovered an archive attesting prophetic activity long before Israel existed. In the city of Mari, on the upper Euphrates River, prophets of various types were active in the eighteenth century BCE. As did those in Israel, they spoke to the royal house and nation about political and military matters. Another archaeological find, this one in Jordan (at Deir 'Alla), has produced a fragmentary text that describes the work of a Balaam son of Beor, almost certainly the same individual (not an Israelite) attested in Num 22–24. This person was remembered both biblically and extrabiblically as a "seer," someone who had visions that explored the fate of the people whom he addressed.

Variety, then, seems to have been a hallmark of prophets as intermediaries, both inside and outside of Israel. However, beginning with Amos, in the eighth century, many of these intermediaries in Israel are known as *nebî'îm*. *Nabi'* is a word regularly translated as "prophet" in English, but it probably means "one called." These individuals are attested by books that share some important literary similarities, which we shall examine shortly.

The prophet as *nabi'* offers an important hint about the way in which ancient Israelites understood the religious authority of these individuals. One does not have the sense that an individual volunteered to be a prophet. Rather there is a report of vocation, of a call or commission to be a prophet. Amos claims that he was told by God to leave his job as a shepherd and to "go, prophesy to my people Israel" (Amos 7:14). Jeremiah 1 attests that the Deity designated Jeremiah as a prophet to the nations, even prior to his birth. Ezekiel 2 states that the Deity said to this prophet, "Mortal, I am sending you to the people of Israel." Prophets are rather like royal heralds, sent by the Deity and commissioned to do particular tasks.

As agents of the Deity, the prophets had remarkable rhetorical authority. When the prophet spoke, it was as if God were speaking. On occasion, we encounter so-called prophetic speech, namely, a text in which the prophet talks about God, such as Amos 1:2: "The LORD roars from Zion, and utters his voice from Jerusalem." However, even more prominent in prophetic literature is divine speech, those instances in which the prophet speaks directly on behalf of the Deity, for example, Amos 1:3-4: "I will not revoke the punishment . . . I will send a fire on the house of Hazael." The "I" is Yahweh, not Amos. Here the prophet is, quite literally, the mouthpiece of Yahweh. It is no accident, therefore, that some of the prophetic books begin with the phrase "The word of the LORD" (Hos 1:1; Joel 1:1; Mic 1:1).

Prophetic Literature

Some discussions of prophetic literature distinguish so-called classical from preclassical prophets. This distinction has less to do with notions of classical literature than with the simple fact that, beginning with prophets active in the eighth century BCE, the Old Testament includes individual books attesting their activities. There is no book of Elisha, though there was clearly a collection of compelling stories told about him (2 Kgs 8:4), and there is a book of Amos. This difference in character of literature from or about prophets, however, calls for an explanation. Why did individually attributed books emerge, beginning in this period? There is no standard answer. Perhaps the most straightforward is that the literature was preserved in order to see if what prophets from Amos's time on had said would stand the test of time, particularly those who had predicted the downfall of the northern kingdom, most notably Hosea and Amos. Such a test by time was consistent with the test of true prophecy provided in the book of Deuteronomy ("If a prophet speaks in the name of the LORD but the thing does not take place or prove true, it is a word that the LORD has not spoken" [Deut 18:22]). Moreover, once these prophets had been vindicated by the events of 721 BCE, even more Judahites may have paid attention when Jeremiah and Ezekiel and others pronounced doom on Jerusalem. Such paying of attention probably resulted in the collection of and reflection upon the words and deeds of these prophets, in sum, the formation of prophetic literature into books.

Prophetic literature was formed. When reading the book of Amos, one is struck by the various smaller collections that make up the larger whole: oracles against foreign nations, vision reports, little doxologies, oracles against Israel. Or in Isaiah, some of the woe oracles have been placed together (chap. 5) just as have the oracles against the nations (chaps. 13–23).

Within these books and the small collections that make them up, it is possible to identify two different rhetorical modes: the prophet speaking on behalf of God and the prophet speaking as God. In the latter, God speaks in the first person, just as the Deity has elsewhere in the Old Testament, for instance, Exod 20:2. Amos 5:21-24 provides a classic example:

> I hate, I despise your festivals,
>   and I take no delight in your solemn assemblies.
> Even though you offer me your burnt offerings and grain offerings,
>   I will not accept them;
> and the offerings of well-being of your fatted animals
>   I will not look upon.
> Take away from me the noise of your songs;
>   I will not listen to the melody of your harps.
> But let justice roll down like waters,
>   and righteousness like an ever-flowing stream.

The prophetic text presents discourse directly from God. Just as the Pentateuch attests that God spoke to Moses, prophetic texts such as these affirm that God speaks directly to Israel during the monarchic period. We may term this sort of discourse as divine speech.

Amos 5:6-7 presents another form of discourse, one in which the Deity is spoken about by the prophet:

> Seek the LORD and live,
>> or he will break out against the house of Joseph like fire,
>> and it will devour Bethel, with no one to quench it.
> Ah, you that turn justice to wormwood,
>> and bring righteousness to the ground!

Here, in what we may call prophetic speech, the voice of the prophet is more overtly present. The message may be similar—both *justice* and *righteousness* are present in these two texts—but one might imagine that the words of the prophet as prophet were easier to challenge than was a divine oracle. And challenged they were. Amos's words "Jeroboam shall die by the sword" (7:11) were viewed by those in the northern kingdom as treason. Despite whatever authority he might have had as a prophet, he was forbidden from offering such judgments in that nation. One should, therefore, always be alert to the rhetorical force of the speeches attributed to the prophets.

Throughout much of the twentieth century, people who read prophetic literature focused on the individual speeches or narratives that make up the prophetic books. They discovered that such speeches often share a number of formal features. Amos 1–2 offers an instructive set of examples. Each of the speeches is introduced by the phrase "Thus says the LORD," which is followed by a formulaic statement about three or four transgressions, which are then specified in some way. Then there is language about punishment. The same basic pattern is repeated throughout these chapters, and occurs not only elsewhere in Amos but in other prophetic books as well.

Such highly structured forms of literature make it appear that prophets were appropriating forms of speaking from the larger society. Their choice of such forms was no doubt informed by theological perspectives. Some forms of discourse were more appropriate than others. For example, what we might call legal language is remarkably prominent in prophetic literature. There are legal challenges, such as Mic 6:1-2, which eventuate in lawsuits. There are lists of indictments, as in Amos 2:6-8. There is language of legal punishment. This sort of language is so prominent that some have called prophets God's prosecuting attorneys.

From a theological perspective, this legal language derives from the "legal" agreement between God and the people, namely, the covenant(s) attested in the Pentateuch, especially the so-called Mosaic or Sinai covenant. Israel's story affirms that God chose Israel for a special relationship, one that involved Israel's accepting certain obligations, what some have described as covenant stipulations. It is possible to read the prophetic literature as a testimony to that covenant relationship and as a hardheaded reminder that if the stipulations are ignored, then the covenant curses (see, e.g., Deut 28) will ensue.

From this covenant perspective, the prophets are theologically conservative, even radical, in the strict sense of that term. They challenge Israel to reflect upon their covenantal roots and to acknowledge the dire consequences of Israelite life lived apart from that theological grounding.

All such attempts to speak in general terms about prophets and prophetic literature run into at least two problems, the first of which we have already mentioned, namely, there are different kinds of prophets. Different kinds of prophets, active in different historical periods and social contexts, proclaimed quite different messages—from words of judgment to words of comfort, from words for Israel to words for Judah. So, it is difficult, if not impossible, to distill a general prophetic theology from the prophetic literature.

Second, much of what the prophets were about is attested in remarkable poetry. Poetry is not discursive literature, which presents a self-evident theme or meaning. Rather, Hebrew poetry, with its various forms of parallelism as a constitutive hallmark, includes, as does poetry in many languages, a remarkable number of figures of speech. It is dense language. Hosea 13:3 provides a good example. In this verse, Hosea is commenting about the fate of those who venerate silver idols. Based on the visceral destruction described elsewhere in the book (e.g., 13:7-8), one might think that the prophet will identify a terrible fate for those idolaters. The text reads:

Therefore they shall be like the morning mist
  or like the dew that goes away early,
like chaff that swirls from the threshing floor
  or like smoke from a window.

At the outset, we are not certain to whom or what the "they" refers. The previous clause, literally, "calves they kiss," would allow either the calf idols or the people who kiss them to be the subject of these similes. Since the pronoun referring to the people appears last in that clause, one could argue that the people are the more likely subject. And then, similes, not the "real-world" language of politics and military action, dominate these lines. Two related sets of similes are present. The first involves water in the atmosphere, the second dust particles in the air. If the people are the subject of the similes, the first set suggests that they will simply vanish quickly, as does mist or dew. The second set of similes has more to do with vanishing as such, like pieces of grain husk that are lifted away by the wind. Fragments of grain, like smoke, will never return; they are gone forever.

Graphic though these four lines of poetry may be, they do not allow the reader easily to abstract a "doctrine" of punishment, or even know what the punishment will be. We are not even sure who or what is being punished. Although the prophet clearly thinks something will happen either to the idols or to the people, it would be difficult to determine exactly what it is that will happen. Something will vanish, more cannot be said. In sum, prophetic poetry provides some inherent limitations to what we can discover about an individual prophet's "message."

Before turning to the individual prophetic books that we will discuss in this chapter, it seems appropriate to identify some of the primary theological issues present in that literature. As we will have occasion to mention, particularly with regard to Isaiah ben Amoz, the theological traditions present in prophetic literature are attested elsewhere in the Old Testament. In particular, the notion that God lives in a covenant relationship is evident in many prophetic books. The affirmation that Yahweh has ordained kingship as the polity for Israel is also a given in virtually all books.

Still, one may abstract a scenario that is characteristic of much theological reflection in the prophetic literature. First, most prophets identify specific ways in which God's people have violated the covenant relationship, whether by worshiping other gods or by engaging in unethical behavior. Typical also is the next step, namely, proclaiming that such violations will lead to destruction, whether at God's hand or by enemy troops. That much—indictment and sentence—one might expect from someone articulating the logic of covenant stipulation and curse as found in the book of Exodus or Deuteronomy. However, most prophetic books take a further step, namely, reflecting about a time after punishment.[1] One must admit at the outset that such texts have been viewed by some scholars as stemming from hands later than the prophet's to which they have been attributed. However, among both prophets and those who created prophetic literature, there was a conviction that out of the divinely ordained past there would come a future in which some of God's people would continue to exist.

We now turn to books attributed to prophets who were active during the eighth and seventh centuries. We pursue them in "rough" historical order. The particular angle of vision is afforded by the critical theological issues at work in each book.

Amos

The book of Amos provides some tantalizing hints about the prophet's biography. He must have been a fairly well-to-do sheepherder in Judah before he worked as a prophet in Israel, though his agricultural background is probably less significant than his regional affiliation. As a Judahite, he would have been heir to the important traditions concerning Yahweh's "house" or temple in Jerusalem. Moreover, there is another "house," the Davidic lineage, that was constitutive for religious and political thinking in this small country (cf. 1 Sam 7 for an elegant reflection on these two notions of *house*). At the end of the book of Amos, we find mention of the Davidic house (Amos 9:11). Moreover, the first poetic lines of Amos (1:2) depict Yahweh as a God who speaks from Jerusalem. Such affirmations would, perforce, play well in Judah, but far less so in Israel. And therein lies one of the critical theological issues posed by the book of Amos. What transnational religious traditions undergird this "missionary" to the northern kingdom?

Amos responds to this question in various ways.[2] The most impressive treatment occurs at the very beginning of the book, where we find no less than six oracles addressing nations other than Judah and Israel. When reading these six oracles, one does well to focus on the indictments—namely, 1:3, 6, 9, 11, 13; 2:1—for it is in these places that Amos identifies what wrongs these nations have performed. There is a common denominator—violating basic norms of human community, particularly in the context of warfare. One could say that verses 3 and 13 of chapter 1 reflect violence against noncombatants in warfare. Verses 6 and 9, with their use of *entire*, betray attempts at genocide. Verse 11 depicts fratricide and 2:1 the violation of basic rights for proper burial of the dead. Genocide, fratricide, noncombatant immunity, and appropriate burial involve norms far beyond ancient Israel's covenant with God, in fact they are rarely, if at all, mentioned in Old Testament covenant texts. These indictments attest to "universal" or natural moral norms that this prophet of Yahweh can use to call nations to account. And, in answer to the question at the end of the last paragraph, if God can indict other Syro-Palestinian states, God can, through this Judahite prophet, indict Israel as well.

These so-called oracles against the nations are not the only place in which God's international range of activity is attested. Amos 9:7 draws a direct analogy between Israel's Exodus from Egypt and other migrations, namely, those of the Philistines and Arameans. Or, the final doxology, Amos 9:9 (on which see below), places God's action toward Israel as occurring "among all the nations." Such a note makes sense, especially when those who rule from Samaria are understood as "the notables of the first of the nations" (6:1). After being so labeled, these people are asked, "Are you better than these kingdoms?" that is, Calneh, Hamath, and Gath (6:2). Amos even calls nations—Ashdod and Egypt—as witnesses to the "oppressions" that are being practiced in Samaria (3:9). In sum, even though Jeremiah is explicitly commissioned as "a prophet to the nations," a revised form of that title would be appropriate for Amos: "a prophet with an international perspective and task."

Even though Amos could speak a prophetic word to any nation, he was commissioned to address primarily Israel (7:15). The book offers a clear theological warrant for that task. When addressing Israel, the Deity comments, "You only have I known of all the families of the earth" (3:2). Despite the many exoduses that Yahweh has enabled (9:7), God has had a special relation with only one people, which probably means the forebears of what are now two nations, Israel and Judah. The verb *to know* bears many connotations in the Old Testament. However, both in the larger ancient Near Eastern context and in the Old Testament, that verb can mean to be in a covenant relationship with someone else. So, this poetry probably alludes to the covenant relationship that God established with Israel at Sinai. Covenant, not exodus, is of singular importance here.

As we saw earlier (chap. 5), God's covenant with Israel created obligations. Israel was expected to behave in certain ways, as those were articulated in the so-called covenant stipulations. These stipulations involved concrete action in legal, economic, and religious life. Moreover, such obligations could be described in summary form. Amos addresses both issues.

The book of Amos includes several classic references to the covenant norms of justice and righteousness. If *righteousness* represents the principle of benevolence, the will to act beneficently toward another person, then *justice* involves the norm of distributing such good intentions toward many in the society, not just a few. Justice and righteousness figure prominently in Amos poetry:

Let justice roll down like waters,
    and righteousness like an everflowing stream. (5:24)

You that turn justice to wormwood,
    and bring righteousness to the ground! (5:7)

Further, if the covenant stipulations involve specific behaviors, the book of Amos attests to particular misdeeds. These occur in the religious sphere (2:8; 4:4; 5:21-24), economic sphere (2:6; 5:11; 8:5), and legal sphere (5:15, by implication). (In his indictment of religious perfidy, Amos may be advocating the notion that Yahweh could be worshiped only in Jerusalem.) If the covenant involves concern for specific classes of disadvantaged individuals (in Deuteronomy, the widow and orphan), that is expressed in Amos as a regard for the poor or the needy (2:6; 4:1; 5:12; 8:4). Finally, there is a minor topic in the book of Amos (5:25-27; 8:13-14) that foreshadows much in later prophetic books: the veneration of deities other than Yahweh. In sum, Amos indicts the northern kingdom for violating God's covenant, but with special attention to social justice issues.

The book of Amos presents several different ways in which Israel might think about or respond to this indictment. First, Amos apparently challenges the people to abandon such behavior. Several admonitions begin with the imperative verb *Seek!* "Seek me and live" (5:4); "Seek the LORD and live" (5:6); "Seek good and not evil" (5:14). Such rhetoric clearly implies that the final die has not been cast. And yet, any easy optimism needs to be tempered by another imperative verb: "Prepare to meet your God, O Israel!" (4:12). The actual encounter with the Deity, if and when Israel seeks and finds Yahweh, may be a dire event.

Amos encounters the world of the Deity in five visions, which graphically convey the looming disaster. On two occasions, he envisions destruction to which he can react (7:1-6). When he sees a locust plague and a cosmic fire, he intercedes, saying, "O Lord GOD, cease, I beg you! How can Jacob stand? He is so small!" However, in the ensuing visions, no such intercession occurs. Two wordplay visions (7:7-9; 8:1-3) trick Amos into uttering something banal: "a plumb line," "a basket of summer fruit," whereupon the Deity explains that what Amos has seen really signifies death and destruction. Then, in a final and macabre vision (9:1-4), Amos "sees" the Deity standing on an altar, directing the destruction of the temple and summarily announcing that he will kill the remnant. No one will be able to escape.

Admonitory language—"seek the Lord"—pales when compared with the number of occasions on which Amos proclaims Yahweh's coming judgment on Israel. One may say at least two things about such punishment. First, God will act directly. Amos 3:14-15 emphasizes that "I" will punish by cutting off, tearing down. Similarly 5:17 states that "I" will pass through the midst. Or in 2:13, "I" will press down. Second, there is an irony in the punishment because the people themselves are seeking a day of Yahweh (5:18). But this hoped-for day will be a day of darkness, not light. This motif or tradition about a day of Yahweh (see also 3:14) will appear as a significant feature of other prophetic books (cf. Zeph 1:14-16; Zech 14).

The book of Amos offers at least two perspectives beyond God's indictment and judgment of Israel. First, there are three hymnic fragments embedded in the book: 4:13; 5:8-9; 9:5-6. Each section describes God using language typical of hymns in the Psalms. As described in these five verses, God is a Creator, responsible for the cosmic order and still able to affect it, as well as a warrior. In addition, God "reveals his thoughts to mortals" (4:13). One might say that this is precisely what a prophet like Amos has done throughout the book, namely, offered vision reports and sayings that convey an understanding of the world from the Deity's perspective. And instead of being a lamentable situation—this hymnic language is not typical of lament psalms—these verses praise the God of justice and power who has revealed his will to humans. The God of justice is a God to be worshiped.

The concluding poem in the book offers a hope beyond the crisis, an expectation undergirded by royal traditions. The book of Amos conceives the Davidic house as a building that can be repaired and that will allow Judah to reexercise its imperial rule over other states in that region. And then the poetry turns to the imagery of fertility, which was often associated throughout the ancient Near East with the successful reign of a king. Amos 9:11-15 emphasizes that this future will eventuate only as a result of God's direct action—"I will raise up, I will restore, I will plant"—just as only God could destroy.

Hosea

According to the book's superscription, Hosea was active in roughly the same period as Amos, the middle part of the eighth century. But Hosea is as different from Amos as was Israel from Judah. This judgment holds whether one is talking about literary style or theological perspective. Even the language is different, as one might expect since Hosea is the only clear Old Testament example of Hebrew that would represent the northern dialect spoken in Israel.

One may read the book of Hosea as comprising two distinct but related parts: chapters 1–3 and 4–14. Both offer comparable themes, but they reach them in utterly different ways. Hosea 1–3 makes up an envelope. The two outside portions report prophetic symbolic actions, biographic and autobiographic respectively. By contrast, the interior portion comprises poetry that explores, in both positive and negative terms, the issues raised in these symbolic action reports.

The very first verse of the initial symbolic action report makes clear that the relationship between Hosea and Gomer is, in some sense, to be understood as a symbol for God's relationship to Israel. However, the more explicit meaning of the report stems from the names of the children born to Gomer and Hosea: Jezreel, Lo-ruhamah ("Not pitied"), and Lo-ammi ("Not my people"). Together, these names signify both indictment and sentence upon Israel. Jezreel represents the violent behavior of the northern ruling house. As a result, Yahweh will reverse one standard way of affirming the covenant relationship, "You are my people, I am your God." Israel will no longer receive God's "pity."

The second symbolic action account also details a relationship between Hosea and a woman, though this time she has no name. Moreover, there are no children. The significance of this report focuses on the relationship between Hosea and the woman. Again, the initial thrust seems to be negative, namely, the woman is to live without a sexual relationship (3:3), a situation that symbolizes the fate of Israel, which is to be without essential political and religious structures (3:4).

That the prophet might convey such judgments is not surprising. After all, Amos had uttered comparable perspectives. However, both symbolic action reports conclude with a view beyond judgment to a better future. Hosea 1:10-11 envisions a time when Israel will be restored, when the judgments symbolized by the names of the children will be reversed. Similarly, Hos 3:5 anticipates a return from exile. These concluding sections to the symbolic action reports have often been viewed as additions, reflecting experiences of later times. But, in the book of Hosea, there may be another theological dynamic at work, one attested in chapter 2 as well.

Hosea 2 begins with the imagery present in chapter 1, discourse with and about the children of Hosea and Gomer. However, by verse 5, primary attention has shifted to the woman, who symbolizes Israel. From verse 6 to verse 13, the poetry presents various punitive acts that the Deity will undertake, for instance, "I will hedge up her way with thorns" (Hos 2:6). This metaphor of the Deity as a husband who shames and punishes his wife, Israel, occurs in later prophetic literature, where it had become even more violent (e.g., Ezek 23). Unfortunately, this metaphor, both in ancient and modern times, has been used as a warrant for spousal abuse.

Unlike Hos 1, chapter 2 gives one the sense that, underlying the negativity, there is a hope that the relationship might be restored: "Then she shall say, 'I will go and return to my first husband'" (Hos 2:7). Later in the chapter, the Deity states expressly, "I will now allure her. . . . There she shall respond as in the days of her youth" (v. 15) and "I will take you for my wife forever" (v. 19).

The language of human courtship and marriage dominates here, not of children as in chapter 1, not of sexuality as in chapter 3. And this system of metaphors for exploring the relationship of God to Israel seems to disallow the notion of an absolute end to the relationship. These chapters permit the possibility of divorce, but do not see this as the necessary conclusion. Why?

One answer involves the theological controversy reflected in the book of Hosea, the conflict between Yahweh and Baal. That Israelites venerated this powerful Canaanite deity is clear; see, for instance, Hos 2:8, 13, 17. Hosea charges that what Israel thought Baal had provided—wine, grain, oil—had in fact been created by Yahweh (2:8). Yahweh, not Baal, was the author of agricultural and human fertility.

But here is where Hosea enters challenging theological terrain. Canaanite religion celebrated the regular agricultural cycle; one could count on the return of the spring rains, one could count on the grape and grain harvests. Hence, if Yahweh is to be as reliable as Baal, something Hosea advocated, then Yahweh too must undergird the natural and reliable cycles. Just as Baal was the husband of the land, so too must be Yahweh. And if so, what sense does it make for Yahweh to say, "I will take back the wine or grain"? Similarly, Baal was worshiped as the lord of the people, the guarantor of human fertility. And so too must be Yahweh. Hence, the idea that Yahweh would or must court Israel, even after his indictment and sentence of the people, may in some sense be necessary, given the god with whom Yahweh was competing. Just as the annual agricultural cycle is permanent and unending, so too is the connection between the Deity and the people. Hence, language about divorce always stands in a charged dynamic with the hope, even necessity, for reconciliation. Only the death of one of the spouses might preclude such hope.

Hosea 4–14 explore these same issues—indictment, sentence, and hope—in various poems. Many indictments remain the same, such as worship of gods other than Yahweh. However, political intrigue, improper foreign alliances, and unethical behavior by priests and other leaders are added to the mix. The very first oracle of this section strikes a note, part of which could have been uttered by Amos:

> Swearing, lying, and murder,
>   and stealing and adultery break out;
>   bloodshed follows bloodshed. (4:2)

It is as if one is listening to a recitation of the Ten Commandments. Hosea, like Amos, critiqued Israel for not living up to the covenant stipulations, of which these commandments serve as an exemplary summary. But Hosea's take on the issue is distinctive in the following verse:

> Therefore the entire earth shrivels
>   all who live in it wither;
> the wild animals together with the birds of the air,
>   even the fish of the sea are perishing. (4:3, author's translation)

Whereas Amos tended to focus on specific nations within the international order, Hosea is concerned about the fertility of the land and the impact of human error on the ecological order. If Baal was lord of all life, Yahweh was even more so. If Baal was lord of the rain, then Yahweh could pose a devastating challenge by proclaiming that the earth—land and sea—would suffer radical dessication.

Unlike Hos 1–3, the book's latter chapters offer explicit language of exile and death. Those earlier chapters had talked about isolation, the end of a relationship. The rhetoric in the latter chapters is far more vivid. One finds here the language of real-world politics, as in 9:3. The prophet clearly foresees the reality of exile for Israel. His audience could have anticipated such a fate since the exiling of population groups was a standard practice of the Neo-Assyrian Empire. More radical is the prominent language in which Yahweh speaks, in the first person, about the devastation he will wreak (e.g., 9:16; 10:10; 13:9).

Hosea's most powerful language appears in figures of speech:

> I will become like a lion to them,
>   like a leopard I will lurk beside the way.
> I will fall upon them like a bear robbed of her cubs,

and will tear open the covering of their heart;
there I will devour them like a lion,
    as a wild animal would mangle them. (13:7-8)

This is a far cry from the language of isolation in chapters 2–3.
Hosea here proclaims that Israel will suffer a violent death. And yet,
even in these chapters, one hears the voice of the Deity asking if he
can indeed act in such a violent way toward the people.

Hosea 11:8-9 presents one of the most poignant speeches:

How can I give you up, Ephraim?
    How can I hand you over, O Israel?
How can I make you like Admah?
    How can I treat you like Zeboiim?
My heart recoils within me;
    my compassion grows warm and tender.
I will not execute my fierce anger;
    I will not again destroy Ephraim;
for I am God and no mortal,
    the Holy One in your midst,
    and I will not come in wrath.

There is a certain irony in this speech, because Hosea's God expresses
powerful human emotions that seem to affect the decisions that the
Deity makes. Hosea presents us with a Deity torn by indecision—in
love, but capable of violence toward the beloved.

Finally, the acts of destruction and exile won out. Israel was
defeated by the Neo-Assyrians in 721 BCE. A major portion of the
population was taken into exile. We never hear about them again.
Some remained in the land hitherto known as Israel, which would
now become a province in the Neo-Assyrian Empire. Still others
moved to Judah. It is this group that preserved the words of Hosea
and created an early form of the prophetic book, which, as we shall
see, influenced later prophetic theological perspectives, particularly
those of Jeremiah.

Micah

Of the four books normally attributed to the eighth century BCE,
Micah has the least clearly defined theological identity. The reasons

315

for this situation are several: (1) at many points Micah sounds like an Amos who is now addressing Judah instead of Israel; (2) some of the issues raised by Micah were also broached by Isaiah (they even share one oracle of salvation—Mic 4:1-3/Isa 2:2-4); and (3) much of the book, especially in chapters 4–7, has been attributed to later authors and editors. Most scholars who wrestle with this book emphasize Micah's place of origin, rural Judah, not his theological distinctiveness. But the two are related. As we will see with Isaiah, it was possible for a prophet in Judah to be heavily influenced, if not dominated, by major national religious-political traditions, namely, the importance of Yahweh's residence on Zion, and the significance of the Davidic lineage. But what about those in Judah who lived at some distance from the capital? (Amos's Tekoa was closer to Jerusalem than was Micah's Moresheth-gath, which probably lay some twenty-five miles southwest of Jerusalem, on the edge of the coastal plain.)

Micah's message *is* derivative, and therein lies part of the theological dynamic in this book. Micah claims explicitly that what can happen one place can happen in another; what happened in Israel can happen in Judah. He uses this principle as both a theological strategy and a rhetorical ploy. Micah 1:5 exemplifies the theological strategy:

> All this is for the transgression of Jacob
>   and for the sins of the house of Israel.
> What is the transgression of Jacob?
>   Is it not Samaria?
> And what is the high place of Judah?
>   Is it not Jerusalem?

If one may presume that Micah is speaking to a Judah in the period after 721 BCE, there is a prophetic track record about the fate of Israel, namely, what Amos (and Hosea) had proclaimed had been verified by historical events. Amos had offered indictments and a sentence of destruction. Micah seems to know about Amos's work— his book even commences, as did Amos's, with a God emerging from the temple in Jerusalem and with an ensuing theophany, in which the natural order reacts violently to the presence of the Deity. For Amos, Samaria could symbolize all that was wrong with the northern kingdom (3:9; 4:1). Micah took this image and transferred it to Jerusalem (as had Amos on one occasion, Amos 6:1). In principle, then, what the prophets had said about the northern kingdom could be said about the southern kingdom as well. Earlier prophetic words could be rethought and redirected to new audiences.

Micah presents an example of how such rhetoric might work:

> Hear this, you rulers of the house of Jacob
>> and chiefs of the house of Israel,
> who abhor justice
>> and pervert all equity,
> who build Zion with blood
>> and Jerusalem with wrong! (Mic 3:9-10)

Earlier, Jacob and Israel were ways in which Amos could refer to the northern kingdom (e.g., Amos 6:8; 7:10). Perhaps those who heard Micah's words had access to what Amos had said. Were this the case, those who encountered the first two lines would have thought Micah was referring to the northern kingdom. Such is not the case, however, as the rest of the poem makes clear. Language about the house of Jacob could refer to Zion/Jerusalem as well. Prophetic words and traditions can be oriented in new ways as the occasion demands. What happened to the North will now happen in the South. Micah refined such discourse to the South by using at several places the imperative verbs of the lawsuit, as in Mic 1:2; 6:1. In the first instance, all people are summoned; in the latter, only Israel, which, according to Micah, means all the people of Yahweh.

The indictments present in Micah do sound like those in Amos—misappropriation of land and other inherited goods rank high on the list (2:2). Moreover, he focuses on the leading groups: "heads," "rulers," "prophets," "chiefs," "priests," "seers," "diviners" (all in chap. 3; cf. 7:1-7). The sentence will be drastic, involving military destruction and deportation.

> Zion shall be plowed as a field;
> Jerusalem shall become a heap of ruins. (3:12)

Proportionately, there is more language about a time beyond disaster than there is in Amos or Hosea. Micah 2:12-13; 4:1–5:15; and 7:8-20 offer various perspectives on a future that involves a move back to the land from exile, focus on Zion and Davidic leadership, the notion of a remnant (5:7-8), and the destruction of Israel's enemies.

In sum, the book of Micah redirects prophetic words from Israel to Judah. Despite its relatively small size, it encompasses notions ranging from God's radical destruction (3:12) to restoration (2:12-13). Most important, it demonstrates that one's location—geographic and social—affects profoundly what one says theologically.

Isaiah

The book of Isaiah presents special problems since it is clear that the book reflects literature written long after the time of Isaiah ben Amoz. (Chapters 40–55—called Second Isaiah or Deutero-Isaiah—are routinely dated to the mid-sixth century; chaps. 56–66—called Third Isaiah or Trito-Isaiah—to the late sixth or early fifth century; chaps. 24–27 to sometime in the Persian period.) As a result, scholars have offered numerous theories by means of which to explain the formation of the book. Though no consensus has been achieved, many would argue that the book of Isaiah, that is, the book in its canonical form, dates to the Persian period, and was of special importance to the Yahwistic community attempting to understand its place and the place of Jerusalem at this time. Still, there are sections that predate the disaster of Judah's defeat and exile (chaps. 2–11 and 28–32 contain most of this material). Moreover, later sections in the book represent strong continuities with what might be dated to the pre-exilic period. Hence we now turn to focus on those earlier materials, which grew into such a powerful prophetic expression.

For much of the latter half of the twentieth century, the work of Gerhard von Rad influenced significantly the ways in which people thought about theological issues in the book of Isaiah. Von Rad maintained that Isaiah was influenced by two primary traditions important in Judah: the tradition about Zion as the impregnable residence of Yahweh and the tradition about the Davidic king as emblem of righteous and everlasting rule.[3] Von Rad was surely correct in his judgments, and yet they need to be placed within a larger theological context.

Isaiah offers an imperial vision, one in which Yahweh, "the LORD of Hosts," is the sovereign of the universe (see, e.g., Isa 3:1; 10:16, 33). This prophet is convinced that God has a plan, which, when properly perceived, allows humans to understand both domestic affairs and international politics.

> This is the plan that is planned
>   concerning the whole earth;
> and this is the hand that is stretched out
>   over all the nations.
> For the LORD of Hosts has planned,
>   and who will annul it?
> His hand is stretched out,
>   and who will turn it back?
>   (14:26-27; see also 30:1)

Earlier prophets to be sure, for example, Amos, had understood that Yahweh affected the fates of various nations. And Micah even spoke about "the thoughts of the LORD" (Mic 4:12). But Isaiah is the first to suggest that there is a comprehensive and comprehendible plan that involves all creation.

Such a claim surely grows, at least theologically, out of the call narrative of Isaiah (Isa 6). Here, in an autobiographical chronicle, Isaiah, after experiencing the presence of the Deity as one of radical holiness, participates in the deliberations of the divine council. It was in precisely such a place that the fates of peoples and nations, including Israel, were decided (cf. 1 Kgs 22:19-23). As a prophet, Isaiah was privy to divinely ordained plans for all humanity. Moreover, he was charged with proclaiming what he knew.

In programmatic terms, Isaiah offered indictments, as had other prophets. One hears echoes of Amos and Micah when Isaiah charges the leaders of Judah with "grinding the face of the poor" or "crushing my people" (Isa 3:15; cf. 5:8-23). And it is indeed those in power against whom Isaiah proclaims such invective:

> Ah, you who make iniquitous decrees,
>   who write oppressive statutes,
> to turn aside the needy from justice
>   and to rob the poor of my people of their right,
> that widows may be your spoil,
>   and that you may make the orphans your prey! (10:1-2)

Then, too, Isaiah speaks words of judgment; Judah will be punished for such injustices. Often, this response focuses on those who have perpetrated such evil: "the nobility of Jerusalem and her multitude go down," but all will suffer; "people are bowed down, everyone is brought low" (5:14-15). When a national cataclysm occurs, no one is safe.

Isaiah did understand Judah to be experiencing a divinely wrought cataclysm in the form of attack by Neo-Assyrian forces. The following words probably reflect the destruction caused by a campaign of Sennacherib:

> Your country lies desolate,
>   your cities are burned with fire;
> in your very presence
>   aliens devour your land;
>   it is desolate, as overthrown by foreigners. (1:7)

However, despite such destruction, there is reason to think Isaiah thought Jerusalem would be saved from Assyrian destruction. The so-called Zion tradition, as exemplified in Isa 29:5-6, expresses the expectation that, in spite of an awesome military attack, God will save the city of divine residence, something Judah apparently experienced with the lifting of Sennacherib's siege ca. 701 BCE (see Isa 36–37). In some measure, the punishment is more that of chastening (cf. the language of "more beatings," Isa 1:5) than of cosmic destruction. Such punishment may exceed God's original intent because of the terrible violence wrought by the Assyrians, but then they too will be subject to radical punishment (Isa 10:5-19; 31:8-9). Nonetheless, Judah had suffered military disaster, and Isaiah understood it to have been a divine response to social injustice throughout the land—part of the divine plan.

The so-called Syro-Ephraimitic crisis was another and earlier defining moment for Isaiah, another time when he had affirmed the notion of a divine plan. Chapters 7–8 zero in on this critical moment ca. 735 BCE. Ahaz was on the throne in Judah. Nations to the north and east—Israel and Aram—were set to attack Judah, in part because Ahaz had refused to join with them in a military coalition against the Neo-Assyrians. Ahaz, probably under assault from other armies as well, was desperate. He thought his only hope lay in securing aid from the Neo-Assyrians. Isaiah confronted him and offered a divine oracle, assuring him that the threat from Israel and Aram would end soon (Isa 7:7-9). Such was the divine plan. However, if Ahaz acted counter to that plan by making an alliance with the Neo-Assyrians, then Judah would ultimately suffer attack by those very forces.

Isaiah's words were corroborated. Ahaz made such a treaty (see 2 Kgs 16:7-9), which resulted in the decimation of both Israel and Aram by Tiglath-Pileser. However, within a matter of decades, Sennacherib was conducting military campaigns against Judah. Isaiah explained such attacks as punishment both for unethical behavior and for disregard of God's international plan.

Isaiah understood Yahweh to have formulated a domestic plan as well. Here again, Isaiah moves in a direction different from that of his prophetic forebears. Isaiah speaks about a specific political order, one in which there are a king and princes. It is an order that existed in his own time and it is an order for which he had high hopes. To be sure, Isaiah had experienced leaders who did not act according to God's plan, most notably Ahaz and the princes (and others) who had acted with disregard for the people's welfare. Still, there are a number of texts that express a profound hope for effective leadership from the king.

Isaiah 32:1-8 talks about the splendid rule that both king and princes will effect. Its hallmarks are justice and righteousness (v. 1), vocabulary and values important to other prophets. Their rule will be a boon to all in their land. They will have plans that result in "noble things" (v. 8). Isaiah believed that such a king would come from the line of David (11:1), would be empowered by God's spirit—as had been both judges and David in prior times—and would administer justice and provide for peace in the created order. And Isaiah thought such a king would rule in the near future. "For a child has been born for us, a son given to us" (Isa 9:6) is poetry sung by those in the divine council. They were aware that a human king had been adopted as God's son (see Ps 2) on the day of that king's coronation. (Most probably, Isaiah thought Hezekiah would be this king.) These three texts (32:1-8; 11:1-9; 9:2-7) create a powerfully hopeful picture of a righteous king on the Judahite throne—and all three texts use the vocabulary of justice and righteousness.

Isaiah, however, never experienced the reign of such a king. Hezekiah, as Isa 36–39 reports, was a far better ruler than Ahaz had been. But the peace, fertility, and security that Isaiah had foreseen remained a hope rather than a reality. Further, Isaiah's theological affirmations about place and person—Zion and David—stood in some tension with his conviction about the judgment that would come upon Judah and Jerusalem. One could use the vocabulary of ideology and theology to express this dialectic. Without the hoped-for king, according to Isaiah's logic, God's judgment was virtually inevitable, especially if God's holiness was continually offended.

Zephaniah

After a relatively long period of prophetic quiet (Isaiah of Jerusalem's last oracle probably dates from early in the seventh century), we hear next from Zephaniah. The book's superscription places him during the reign of King Josiah (640–609 BCE). Scholars have routinely noted that many of the charges that Zephaniah levels at Judah and Jerusalem are addressed in the reforms of Josiah. Hence, to place Zephaniah's literature in the period immediately preceding those reforms seems reasonable.

If it is licit to speak about a prophetic literary tradition in ancient Israel, the connections between Zephaniah and Amos can provide exemplary evidence. Although the book of Zephaniah is only about half the size of Amos, it includes many of the basic features in Amos: oracles against foreign nations (2:4-15), oracles of indictment and judgment against God's people (1:2-18), admonitions (2:1-3), and language of promise (3:9-20). And there is more; Zephaniah expands upon a motif struck by Amos, the day of the Lord as a cataclysm.

The ways in which Zephaniah articulates his understanding of the day of the Lord should strike one, at first reading, as problematic. The first two verses (1:2-3) of the initial poem depict the undoing of the created order. The prophet proclaims an ecological catastrophe, a vision of extermination. To be sure, the language of violence against humans regularly appears in prophetic rhetoric. However, these verses step up the intensity of destruction such that all life will be extinguished. (One often finds the term *apocalyptic* used to describe such a notion.)

How can Israel's God admit to such a holocaust for all that lives? There may be no easy answer to such a question, though the facile response would be that the prophet speaks in hyperbole, and does not really mean literally that God will kill everything that breathes. A reading that more readily struggles with the text must recognize that these two verses are rooted in the language of Gen 1–2, Israel's stories of creation. The logic seems to be: what God has created, God can remove—all life (Zeph 1:2-3) and even the earth itself (1:18). The created order was established for certain reasons, and if they are being violated, then the world no longer deserves to exist.

The book of Zephaniah, which here resonates with other traditions in the Hebrew Bible, does not think life, as such, is sacred. God is sacred. And if humans, especially those who are supposed to worship this God, venerate another deity, then their disregard for Yahweh's exclusive status in Israel creates such a level of impurity in the world that all life has become contaminated and hence stands under a sentence of death. Still, the predominant judgment in Zephaniah falls particularly upon those who may be judged for having acted improperly—officials, kings' sons, idolatrous priests.

In the book of Zephaniah, people and place loom large. God will bring home those who have been removed from the land (3:20). The general language of restored fortunes, used by Amos (9:14), reappears in Zeph 3:20. However, whereas Amos spoke of the house of David, Zephaniah focuses on the city that David conquered, Zion—the holy mountain (3:11). But there is no explicit reference to a rebuilt temple. Instead of a special building there will be a special people, "humble and lowly . . . the remnant of Israel" and without "a deceitful tongue" (3:12-13). It almost sounds as if Zephaniah is referring to a special group of those who venerate Yahweh, a sect. Moreover, beyond the borders of Israel there shall be many peoples of "pure speech" (3:9), presumably a reference to some sort of religious conversion (cf. Isa 56:6 or Zech 14:16-18). (The presence of oral/verbal imagery is particularly interesting in Zephaniah.)

With Zephaniah, we reach the end of those prophetic books, beginning with Amos, that have addressed Israel under threat from the Neo-Assyrian Empire. Major international changes were at work that would lead to a new force, the Neo-Babylonians, who would be viewed both as God's avenger upon Assyria and as God's agents of final punishment against Judah.

Conclusion

So, one may read the books of the prophets and the reforms associated with Hezekiah and Josiah as part of a story in which a few kings are reported to have undertaken important religious reforms. And yet, the economic, social, and political issues broached by the prophets, particularly those involving violations of Israel's covenant ethos, seem not to have been addressed by these imperial initiatives.[4] The kings, not the prophets, were the reformers, and only in discrete ritual and political areas. As a result, during the period under discussion, Israel as a nation was annihilated and Judah became a vassal to the Neo-Assyrian Empire. The magnificence of monarchy in Israel had been lost. Radical questions were being posed about the nature of the relationship between Yahweh and the communities that venerated this Deity. Were covenant curses inevitable? What theological traditions would help explain the demise of Judah? What were the religious grounds for hope? Moreover, the prophetic books that derive from the eighth- and seventh-century prophets contained important theological affirmations, such as the importance of a righteous king, that enabled later Israelites to formulate responses to these critical questions.

Notes

1. See C. Westermann, *Prophetic Oracles of Salvation in the Old Testament* (Louisville: Westminster John Knox, 1991).
2. Scholars debate vigorously the formation of the book attributed to Amos. Some (e.g., Jeremias) argue that very little may be assigned to Amos. Others claim virtually all the book stems from Amos. Mays provides a mediating position.
3. G. von Rad, *Old Testament Theology*, vol. 2 (New York: Harper & Row, 1965), 155-75.
4. Cf. Blenkinsopp's argument that Micah may have influenced the book of Deuteronomy, *A History of Prophecy in Israel*, rev. ed. (Louisville: Westminster John Knox, 1996), 120.

Bibliography

Berlin, Adele. *Zephaniah*. AB 25A. New York: Doubleday, 1994.

Blenkinsopp, Joseph. *A History of Prophecy in Israel*. Rev. ed. Louisville: Westminster John Knox, 1996.

Jeremias, Jörg. *Amos*. OTL. Louisville: Westminster John Knox, 1998.

Mays, James L. *Amos: A Commentary*. OTL. Philadelphia: Westminster, 1969.

———. *Hosea: A Commentary*. OTL. Philadelphia: Westminster, 1969.

————. *Micah: A Commentary.* OTL. Philadelphia: Westminster, 1976.

Miller, Patrick D. *Deuteronomy.* IBC. Louisville: Westminster John Knox, 1990.

Petersen, David L. *The Prophetic Literature: An Introduction.* Louisville: Westminster John Knox, 2002.

Rad, Gerhard von. *Old Testament Theology,* vol. 2. New York: Harper & Row, 1965.

Wolff, Hans W. *Hosea: A Commentary on the Book of the Prophet Hosea.* Hermeneia. Philadelphia: Fortress, 1974.

————. *Joel and Amos.* Hermeneia. Philadelphia: Fortress, 1977.

————. *Micah: A Commentary.* Minneapolis: Augsburg, 1990.

CHAPTER TEN

COLLAPSE/EXILE/HOPE

Jeremiah, Lamentations, Nahum,
Habakkuk, Ezekiel, Isa 40–55

In the sixth century BCE, there occurred a deep and irreversible disruption in the life of ancient Israel. This fissure became decisive for the faith of Israel as it is voiced in the Old Testament. The disruption is indeed a concrete, describable sociopolitical event, and it cannot be understood without attention to the specificities of political history. That event, however, became decisive and definitive for Israel's faith, not simply because of its inescapable concreteness but also because Israel found in this event the workings of the inscrutable sovereign God upon whom it had staked its life. Thus, in understanding this awesome and definitive moment in Israel's faith, it is imperative that we give attention at the same time to the identifiable concreteness of political occurrences and to theological, interpretive dimensions of this happening that are seen by Israel to be intrinsic to the events themselves.

The Geopolitical World of Judah

It is of course the case that the lived, public experience through which the Old Testament articulates the faith of Israel is never the lived, public experience of Israel in a geographical or political vacuum. At every moment of its life, Israel had to reckon with its social environment, which was richly peopled with other communities that were at various times allies and positive resources or threats and challenges to Israel. Given that general reality, however, it is in the moment of Israel's history that now concerns us that the peopled

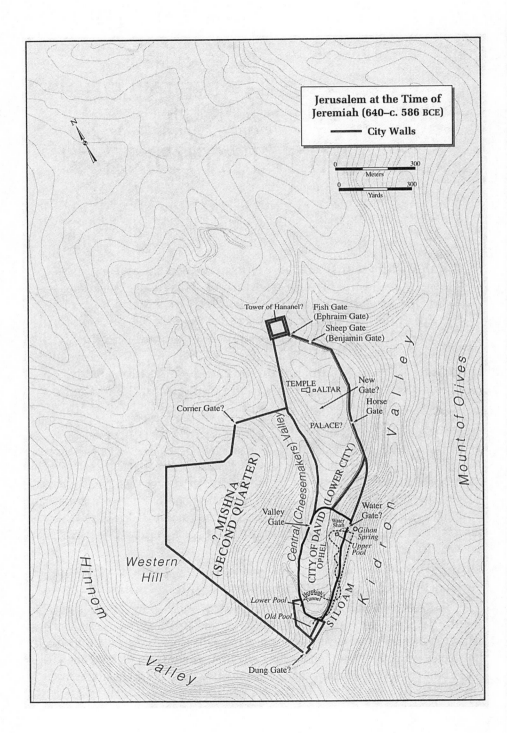

Jerusalem at the Time of Jeremiah (640–c. 586 BCE)

——— City Walls

0 ——— 300
Meters

0 ——— 300
Yards

N

Tower of Hananel?

Fish Gate (Ephraim Gate)

Sheep Gate (Benjamin Gate)

TEMPLE ▫ALTAR

New Gate?

Horse Gate

Corner Gate?

PALACE?

Central (Cheesemakers) Valley

(LOWER CITY)

?MISHNA (SECOND QUARTER)

Valley Gate

Water Gate?

Water Shaft

Gihon Spring

CITY OF DAVID

OPHEL

Upper Pool

Western Hill

Hinnom Valley

Hezekiah's Tunnel

SILOAM

Kidron Valley

Mount of Olives

Lower Pool

Old Pool

Dung Gate?

environment of Israel becomes crucially important for our understanding of the Old Testament. It is in this period in particular that the horizon of Israel's faith, of necessity, becomes boldly international, as it had not been before.

The geopolitical situation of the ancient kingdom of Judah (like the geopolitical situation of the contemporary state of Israel) dictates that Judah shall be endlessly at risk between the strong and durable powers of the South (always Egypt), and of the North (for our period of study, in sequence Assyria, Babylon, and Persia; and for contemporary Israel, Syria, Iraq, and Iran). Indeed, Judah, for all its extravagant Davidic rhetoric, is most of the time a client state, whereby Judah lives under the influence and at the behest of one major power or another. For the most part, Judah did not have the resources or the capabilities to chart an independent political or military course. In any case, even when it sought to do so, it was with extreme vulnerability.

The period of our consideration in this chapter focuses almost completely upon the fate of Judah during the time of the Babylonian Empire (605–540 BCE). In order to situate the Judean crisis properly in the time of Babylonian hegemony, however, we must pay some attention to the Assyrian Empire as the predecessor power to Babylon in the North and to Persia as the successor power in the North. (We may notice that during all of our period of consideration, Egypt, as a counterweight to Mesopotamian power, went through a series of reassertions of power, but none that were decisive for Judah. Egypt is always there, providing an alternative scenario for Judah. In the main, however, it is the powers of the North that must dominate our attention.)

The most important geopolitical fact for our subject is that during the seventh and sixth centuries, the Near East, the environment of Judah, witnessed an extraordinary political upheaval with the rise and fall of superpowers. While a student of the Old Testament does not need to know this material in great detail, the broad outline of events is indispensable for an informed reading of these books.

1. The disappearance of the Assyrian Empire was a defining fact for Judah in the seventh century. The Assyrian Empire, with its capital city of Nineveh, had dominated the politics and economics of the ancient Near East since 745 and the rise of Tiglath-Pileser III. It

had preoccupied the attention of the fragile kingdoms of Israel and Judah and had caused the final termination of the northern kingdom of Israel in 722. Assyria was viewed by these endlessly threatened peoples as a force capable of enormous brutality. We know, already in the book of Isaiah, that Assyria under Sennacherib had over time threatened the city of Jerusalem and had come twice in assault against it.

The Assyrians, however, in the seventh century came upon evil days. In 663 BCE Assyria, in its aggressive military expansionism, had extended its military control across the Fertile Crescent into Egypt, as far as Thebes. For a moment, it enjoyed complete domination of its entire geopolitical horizon. Within a fifty-year period, however, the Assyrian capital of Nineveh had been destroyed, and the empire of Assyria was no more. The fall of the capital city and of the empire was a remarkable turn of affairs, one that surely captured the imagination of Judah, a turn that provided breathing space for the kingdom of Judah from constant jeopardy.

2. The demise of Assyrian power created a brief power vacuum in the Near East, during which time Judah's King Josiah (639–609) asserted some Judean independence, seeking to recover some lost territories of the old Kingdom of David in the North. Judean reassertion and renaissance, however, were short-lived. The power vacuum created by the fall of Assyria did not last long. After 626, Nabopollassar began to assert Babylonian independence from Assyria and to establish the city and the kingdom of Babylon as the coming force in international politics. By 605, Assyrian power had completely vanished. It remained only for Nebuchadnezzar, son of Nabopollassar, to complete the establishment of Babylonian dominance by the decisive defeat of Egypt, which he did at the battle of Carchemesh in 605. This battle may thus be taken as the point from which to reckon the beginning of the hegemony of Babylon, under the determined and effective leadership of Nebuchadnezzar.

Having defeated Egypt, it does not surprise us that Nebuchadnezzar took pains to secure his flank exposed toward Egypt, thus requiring that Judah come firmly into the sphere of Babylonian policy and influence. The leadership of the Davidic dynasty in Jerusalem was able to practice no sustained policy in this dangerous, volatile situation, for at times it submitted to Babylonian demands (which of course included taxation), and at times, with appeals to Egypt, it resisted Babylonian requirements.

As a consequence of such uncertain compliance, Nebuchadnezzar and his general, Nebuzaradan, forcibly intruded into Judah and Jerusalem three times, in 598, 587, and 581. These incursions were part of a larger Babylonian policy of defusing and precluding rebellion in conquered territories by the systematic deportation of leading citizens from their home territory to alien territory. The result was that the departed leadership could thus constitute no threat, and the home territories, without such leadership, could not mount any serious rebellion. Thus Babylonian policy was to form docile, compliant colonies.

From the perspective of Judah, however, these deportations constituted a theological reality. Because the ones deported were characteristically leaders and opinion makers in the community of Judah, it was inevitable that those who were deported came to be thought of—at least in their own rhetoric, which became the dominant rhetoric of Judah—as the whole community, and so the deportation came to be termed "the exile" of Judah, even though it did not include, by any means, all Judeans.

The small group of Judeans deported to Babylon proved to be an assertive, imaginative, generative community that seized the initiative in constructing the image and self-understanding of all Israel. They did so, moreover, to cast themselves—the "exiles"—as heroes and as the legitimate heirs to and carriers of the old memories of Israel. It is for this reason that many contemporary scholars view the notion of "exile" as an ideological construct of this minority community in the service of its own legitimacy. One can of course see the matter of vested interest in such an imaginative enterprise without denying the historicity of the deported community. One of the outcomes of such a generative construction is that the population of Judeans who remained in the land and avoided deportation is largely "written out" of Israel's normative history. The deportation, which decisively marked Israel's faith in this period, was, in the first instance, simply an instrument of the Babylonian policy of "pacification" of restless, occupied territories.

The dominating power of Babylon lasted only a few years beyond the reign of Nebuchadnezzar, which ended in 562, so that in a certain sense the Babylonian Empire is quite personally the empire of Nebuchadnezzar. The Babylonian Empire, which had decisively impinged upon Judah's life, ended in 540, only two decades after the death of Nebuchadnezzar. The empire was not so much defeated or destroyed as it ran out of steam. Its exhaustion is marked by a series of weak leaders and an irreversible loss of moral authority and religious legitimacy among its own people. It faded in 540 as rapidly as it had appeared in 615–605.

3. The power of Babylon was dislodged and displaced by the rise of Persia, a non-Semitic power from the East, led by Cyrus. The Persians, in what was a prudent administrative decision, reversed the Babylonian policy of deportation and permitted the deportees to return home, thus gambling that such generosity produced more cooperative subjects. In the case of the Jews (as the returnees to Jerusalem were now called), the gamble worked, for the Jews came to regard the Persians as a benign power. Persian power, with its enormous expanse, endured with great effectiveness until its power-ending conflict with the Greeks under Alexander.

This brief recital of
—the disappearance of *Assyrian* power,
—the abrupt rise and equally abrupt fall of *Babylonian* power, and
—the rise of *Persian* power
constitutes the backdrop of our study of the Old Testament in the midst and in response to this unparalleled disruption. Judah was required to understand and live its life and its faith in relation to, in the presence of, and at the behest of these greater powers. But it is the disruption (deportation, exile) itself that is the focus of our study. The Old Testament is preoccupied with the question "What does it mean for the faith of Israel that this community, which takes itself to be the beloved partner of Yahweh, is so vulnerable to the vagaries of international politics and so helpless in the face of brutalizing power?"

A Biblical Rendering of Geopolitics

Knowledge of geopolitics, however, is only an access point to our study, for the biblical literature produced in this period of crisis is not interested in geopolitics per se or in historical reportage on the

332

rise and fall of the great powers. The biblical literature purposes, rather, to offer a peculiar and intense interpretation of these events that in part arises from the events themselves and in part is imposed upon the events, but which faithful Israel regards as intrinsic to the events themselves.

It would be possible to understand this dramatic scenario of geopolitics as a case of *Realpolitik*, wherein it is self-evident that "might makes right." Perhaps in our own intensely secularized context, moreover, that is our first interpretive inclination. However, biblical texts emerging from and reflective of this geopolitical scenario have no such view of events. Rather the texts insist upon a quite different interpretive angle arising from a normative account of history that has Yahweh, the God of ancient Israel, as the key character and decisive agent in the public processes of history. Yahweh, in such a view, is not a theological "add-on" to *Realpolitik*, but is the initiator and definer of what happens in the visible world of public power. This claim, moreover, pertains not only to the Israelite community, which names the name of Yahweh; it applies with equal decisiveness to all the other powers of the world, who do not know the name of Yahweh.

This ground assumption of the cruciality of Yahweh has two important derivative implications for the Old Testament literature situated in this crisis. First, the cruciality of Yahweh means that Israel, the peculiar people of Yahweh, is understood as a central participant in all that happens in Near Eastern politics. This is a claim that is as remarkable as it is uncompromising in the literature, because in any account of *Realpolitik*, Israel would be at most a bit player, if mentioned at all. Second, the cruciality of Yahweh for understanding geopolitics requires the affirmation of Yahweh's righteous, sovereign will as crucial in the public process. The operation of this righteous, sovereign will not only includes the insistence of coherence (i.e., that it all makes sense as a single pattern and purpose). It also asserts an ethical dimension, monitored by Yahweh, so that issues of justice and righteousness are seen to be operative in the public process. It is evident that insistence upon (a) Yahweh as the key agent in the public process, (b) coherence of the entire process, (c) Israel as a key actor, and (d) ethics as an effective dimension of public activity produces a very different sense of what is happening and what it means when it happens. As students of these venturesome texts, we are permitted to marvel at this courageous and highly imaginative angle of vision, a vision that flies in the face of what must have been "common sense," that is, *Realpolitik,* to the major imperial players of that time. Our study of a series of biblical texts will note how this peculiar vision of public history reshapes all of reality—historical, political, military, economic, and theological.

The Collapse of Judah

In 587, in the second incursion of Nebuchadnezzar's armies into Judah (the first being in 598), everything valued by the citizens of Jerusalem was terminated in a harsh way:

—*the Davidic dynasty* was nullified and the king ignobly taken away,

—*the city of Jerusalem,* locus of Yahweh's promise to Israel, was razed, and

—*the temple,* place of Yahweh's assured presence, was devastated.

All that was visible and institutional, all that seemed theologically guaranteed by Yahweh's faithfulness, all that gave symbolic certitude and coherence, all that was linked to significance, identity, and security, was gone. Judah as an identifiable state was swept away, victim of imperial ruthlessness. As an inevitable consequence, Judah's most trusted theological convictions were placed in acute jeopardy. And all of this at the devastating hands of the Babylonians.

The destruction of 587 is the pivot point in our study of "collapse and hope." In order to understand this moment of profound loss and displacement, however, we may go back a bit into the events preceding this moment. We have seen that Assyria reached its zenith of power in 663 and disappeared in 612, all in the short span of fifty years. The demise of the Assyrian Empire was indeed welcome to the Judeans, for the crushing brutality of that empire was too long on the horizon of Judah. The collapse of Assyria is duly celebrated in one of the oddest books of the Old Testament, the book of the prophet *Nahum.* This short, poetic collection, dated somewhere in the wake of the demise of Nineveh, expresses unrestrained glee at the failure of the hated city of Nineveh. The poetry has no concern for or sympathy with those now savaged in Nineveh, for they only get their rightful punishment for their long practice of uncaring brutality. The poem belongs to a long tradition of "war piety," which readily assumes "God is on our side" and vividly describes (anticipates?) invasion and devastation of a hated enemy. Thus the poem is a tightly disciplined, eloquent piece of rhetoric that celebrates victory over a despised oppressor. It is to be noted that the name "Nahum" is the Hebrew term *nhm,* which often means "comfort." This defeat of Assyria was indeed a "comfort" to Judah.

This lyric of hate, retaliation, and vengeance, completely devoid of compassion, might strike one at first as awkward and embarrassing in the Bible. But that is the case only if we have a romantic view of imperial aggression and a correspondingly unreal notion of faith, a view that does not notice the enduring and erosive effects of brutality and its evocation of hostility. Thus we may judge the poem of Nahum in two positive ways.

First, the book of Nahum is the poetry of profound resentment voiced in a community so long threatened and endangered that when release from the threat comes, there is no limit to the relief that permits all of the stored-up hostility to be expressed. The poetry is not unlike the venom poured out on the Marcos government in Manila, when the peasant masses stormed the opulent palace, or when the mobs in Bucharest moved to terminate the bloody ways of the entourage of Ceausescu. The Bible is realistic about the way hurt will produce a literature that must be voiced, and none too soon.

Second, this celebrative hate is, however, not merely an expression of human vengeance. It is most important that the poetry of Nahum is profoundly Yahwistic. It is Yahweh who is "slow to anger but great in power" (1:3). It is Yahweh who has "commanded concerning you" (1:14). Thus the fall of Nineveh is a theological event, taking place in the history of Yahweh in the world. The fall of Nineveh not only gives release to Judah but reasserts and reestablishes the rule of Yahweh over the nations, a rule that will punish the oppressor and protect Yahweh's own people:

> The LORD is good,
>   a stronghold in a day of trouble;
> he protects those who take refuge in him,
>   even in a rushing flood.
> He will make a full end of his adversaries,
>   and will pursue his enemies into darkness. (1:7-8)

Thus the fall of Nineveh at the same time signifies Yahweh's sure rule over the nations and Judah's chance for well-being and safety.

This astonishing turn in history, causing the end of a great and brutal power that seemed assured to perpetuity, must have been for Judah a great vindication and a confirmation of its sense of specialness in a history governed by Yahweh. That is, relief from the Assyrian threat created space for Judean reassertion and affirmation, space taken up by the reform of Josiah (2 Kgs 22–23) and the modest expansionist efforts of the Jerusalem government. (On the reform of Josiah, see chap. 9.) The fall of Assyria seemed evidence of Judah's guarantee by Yahweh in the historical process.

If, however, some in Judah counted too heavily upon the Assyrian fall as affirmation, it was a gross miscalculation, because the real threat of the movement was not in fact the Assyrians, but the emerging Babylonians, who finally did in Jerusalem what the Assyrians were never able to do. The Babylonian threat against Jerusalem, constant from 605 onward, must have created a deep and endless anxiety in Jerusalem. That anxiety is reflected in the vacillating royal policies under the sons and successors of King Josiah. The crown could not decide whether to resist Babylon with Egyptian support or to submit to Babylon. In the end, Babylon, exhausted with the vacillation and soft loyalty of its client state, lost patience. In 598, the armies of Babylon carried away the boy-king Jehoiachin (grandson of Josiah) into exile (2 Kgs 24:12). In 587, moreover, they took away yet another king, Zedekiah, son of Josiah and uncle of Jehoiachin (2 Kgs 25:1-7).

Our concern, however, is not with royal history or with imperial policy. So far as the Bible is concerned, this period is dominated by two figures who are far away from the circles of royal power and influence. Jeremiah and Ezekiel, around each of whom gathered literature that became a biblical book, tell us the most about how Judah responded in faith and anguish to the events of 587, which irreversibly reshaped Israel's life, faith, and memory. In very rough outline, each of these prophets-poets-pastors worked in the period of collapse and then continued as a powerful presence in the exile after the collapse. In both cases, moreover, it is clear that the prophetic person continued to be a generative force in the exilic community into the next generation, even after their deaths, as their remembered words were reused, expanded, and interpreted in a variety of ways. We will deal with the literature of Jeremiah and Ezekiel in two quite distinct sections, first concerning the pre-587 judgment of Jerusalem, and second, concerning the post-587 offer of hope to exiles.

The book of Jeremiah, as we have it, represents the culmination of a long editorial, interpretive process. That process began in the work of a remarkably sensitive, imaginative, eloquent prophetic personality and culminated in a convinced theological vision that is informed by the tradition of the book of Deuteronomy and is deeply derivative of the prophetic traditions of Hosea (see chap. 9). While there are important differences between the eloquent personal testimony at the outset and the framing theological vision of the completed book, there is a coherence to it all. We may treat the whole by reference to "Jeremiah," which we take to include the entire interpretive process that produced the canonical book of Jeremiah.

The tradition of Jeremiah is deeply rooted in the old memories of Moses, as they are mediated in the teaching of Deuteronomy (see the discussion of Deuteronomy in chaps. 5 and 9). That old Mosaic memory understood that Israel, as theological community, was in covenant with Yahweh since Sinai and was subject to the commands of Yahweh there, and that therefore Judah's destiny in the world depended upon obedience to Yahweh's covenant commandments. When Israel obeyed Yahweh's commands, it prospered. When Israel disobeyed, it suffered. To be sure, the rhetoric of Deuteronomy presents a tight connection of *deed* and *outcome*. It becomes clear, however, that Israel's theological traditions handled this matter with great interpretive flexibility. In the end, the covenant concerns a deep, demanding, and intimate relationship that is more open and complicated than any flat formula.

The lyrical, poetic texts of Jeremiah, commonly assigned to the prophetic personality, are not at all didactic. They do not scold or coerce, or ask Israel to do anything. They are, rather, the utterances of a poet who was acutely sensitive to the pain and failure of his community, and who saw in penetrating ways the failed core of Judah's life, which could not be covered over by the facade of royal self-deception. This poetry, with enormously inventive imagery, seeks to help the community of Jerusalem to see what it refuses to see, but

337

what it must see if it is to reposition and revision its life in terms of its commitment to and reliance upon Yahweh.

The book of Jeremiah, in its now thematized form, begins with what purports to be the "call of Jeremiah" by Yahweh to be a prophet, to speak Yahweh's word in the midst of Israel, to utter the truth of Yahweh in a social setting that refuses to see the truth of its own self-destructiveness (1:4-10). Put succinctly, the negative thrust of the word entrusted to the prophet is "to pluck up and to pull down, to destroy and to overthrow" (1:10). (The two positive verbs, "plant and build," become enormously important in the subsequent hope of exilic Judaism. They refer to the restoration of Jerusalem; see p. 360.) That is, the word to be uttered by the prophet is to assert that Yahweh has already begun to terminate Judah, because Judah has proved to be an unreliable, unresponsive, disobedient covenant partner to Yahweh, and Yahweh will not finally tolerate such a partner. We should not miss the radicality of this assertion. There is nothing here of *Realpolitik* or of Babylonian expansionism. The root cause of destruction, in this tradition, is Yahweh's sovereign decision to abandon Judah to its own chosen destruction.

This theme, expressed in the four verbs of destruction (1:10), becomes a recurring motif across the book of Jeremiah (18:7-9; 24:6; 31:28; 45:4). The book of Jeremiah is offered as an assertion that Yahweh is the agent of Judah's termination. Judah's history has a powerful theological dimension. At the center of its life is this sovereign who will tolerate no such depth of infidelity, and who can decree even the nullification of Yahweh's own beloved people.

The poetry of the book of Jeremiah enunciates this theme of coming devastation under a variety of imaginative and inventive images. It is as though a master of eloquence utilizes all of his gifts to communicate what the populace and the royal leadership are completely unwilling and unable to recognize. A student of Jeremiah will do well to read aloud and to notice the daring and powerful images in the service of this decree of devastation. Here we may mention only two such images, though there are many more.

In 2:2-3 and 3:1-5, the poet presents Yahweh as the affronted husband and Israel as the faithless wife. (It is to be recognized, given our contemporary sensitivities, that this imagery is powerfully patriarchal and sexist, featuring, characteristically, the "woman" as the offender, and not noticing the abusive conduct of the "man." Such an awareness, however, does not vitiate the power of the imagery, in terms of communicating the message of Israel's fickleness and consequent jeopardy.) The poetry in this scenario remembers a "honeymoon period" of well-being, when Israel was deeply responsive to husband Yahweh (2:2-3). But then there was fickleness, refusal to follow (2:5), and "forsaking" (2:13, 17, 19). In that ancient world of patriarchy, moreover, a fickle wife who goes after "other lovers" (3:1) makes restoration of the relationship impossible. The poet is not speaking of sexual offenses as such, but employs such imagery as a metaphor for unfaithfulness, in order to show why the relationship must be terminated. One can detect, in the development of the imagery, wistfulness and yearning upon the part of "the husband," but the affront is so great as to prevent reconciliation.

The presentation of Yahweh and Israel under the rubric of husband-wife is an especially poignant one, for it gives access to emotional interactions of commitment and betrayal that are far more elemental, far more powerful, and far more wondrous than any contractual, legal relationships. At the same time, however, the imagery that casts Yahweh as the male partner in the relationship reflects a patriarchal assumption that permeates much of the Old Testament. That same usage, moreover, feeds patriarchal assumptions even in contemporary church usage, and consequently, invites abusive power relations between men and women, the male partner characteristically cast in God-like dominance. Thus the imagery is at the same time poignant and illuminating, but also a carrier of toxic power.

A second image taken up to communicate the hopelessness of Israel is sickness. Israel is said to be terminally ill. Yahweh may seek to heal, but this illness is beyond healing:

For the hurt of my poor people I am hurt,
    I mourn, and dismay has taken hold of me.
Is there no balm in Gilead?
    Is there no physician there?
Why then has the health of my poor people
    not been restored?
                    (8:21-22; cf. 30:12-13)

In this imagery, Israel is beyond hope or recall.

These images remove the issue of Judah's future from the world of *Realpolitik,* and indeed away from commandments and juridical categories, to the most elemental crisis of betrayed relationship and the failure of the human body. The poet seeks to go "underneath" everything that is visible in society, to take his listeners inside the vexed life of Yahweh, to show that for Yahweh, who is inordinately sensitive and caring, the conduct and attitude of Judah have made life for Yahweh completely unbearable.

But of course, the poet does not completely avoid public reality. Along with intimate bodily and familial imagery, the writer also uses remarkable poetic daring to imagine the immediacy of military danger from an invasion that is yet to come. Thus the poetry describes the coming invasion "out of the north" (1:14) of people with great horses and chariots (4:13-18) who will come and devour all that Judah is and has (5:17), until the enemy penetrates even into the tent where one is sleeping (4:19-22). This rhetoric of invasion is escalated to make the threat and danger into a cosmic threat, the ending of all of creation (4:23-26). It is as though the poet, with uncommon sensitivity, can see the outcome of the foolish, phony, self-deceiving choices of Judah. Judah, however, is numbed into self-deception and self-assurance. And so the poet must use extreme and extravagant rhetorical measures to penetrate the numbness about the nullification. Judah is in a permanent state of denial about its true condition. That, however, will not stop the deep trouble to come.

The poet draws closer to the jugular. In his well-known "temple sermon," the poet imagines the destruction of the temple in Jerusalem, which had become an engine of corruption and self-indulgence (7:8-15), so that disregard of Yahweh's commands is not even on the horizon of the community. The temple sermon is one of the most important texts in articulating the deep prophetic critique of the temple establishment. The text asserts that the temple is no guarantee for the security of Jerusalem, as was widely believed, and anticipates the destruction of the temple. It is this public assault on the temple establishment that provoked the trial of Jeremiah (26:7-19). That text leaves the impression that Jeremiah could have been executed as a traitor had it not been for the precedent of the prophet Micah, who had a century earlier also anticipated the failure and destruction of Jerusalem (Jer 26:17-19; Mic 3:12). The entire passage evidences the deep tensions in Israel's faith and the high public stakes in theological advocacy. In like fashion, the poet pronounces a devastating and humiliating judgment upon the king, Jehoiakim, who has not practiced justice (22:13-19). And he anticipates a devastating and pathos-shaped rejection of the boy-king Jehoiachin (22:29-30). In parallel fashion he denounces the prophets who have become phony endorsers of the status quo (23:9-22), and in the end issues a wholesale condemnation of narcoticized leadership, which serves only the numbing of the community:

> From the least to the greatest of them,
>   everyone is greedy for unjust gain;
> and from prophet to priest,
>   everyone deals falsely.
> They have treated the wound of my people carelessly,
>   saying, "Peace, peace,"
>   when there is no peace.
> They acted shamefully, they committed abomination;
>   yet they were not ashamed,
>   they did not know how to blush.
> Therefore they shall fall among those who fall;
>   at the time that I punish them, they shall be overthrown,
>   says the LORD. (6:13-15)

Along with the utterance of Jeremiah, the book of Jeremiah also gives reports on what apparently happened to him as a result of his abrasive utterance. We may mention only three matters. First, it is reported that he was on trial for his life, because he had publicly criticized the civil religion of the ruling establishment (26:10-19). He escaped harsh punishment only by the remarkable intervention of those with long memories and keen theological sensitivity. Second, uncredentialed as he was, he was sought out as a counselor to kings in their distress, when all the proper channels of "intelligence" had been found inadequate (37:17-21). His counsel to the king, against the nationalistic Yahwism of the ruling establishment, was to urge submission to Babylon as the will of Yahweh. And third, because of his pro-Babylonian posture, he was regarded as a traitor and ended in considerable abuse, because his verdicts on the public process collided with the prevailing official views (38:4).

341

It is clear that the legacy of the person of Jeremiah was a powerful and treasured one and that it became the disputed property of an ongoing political interest group that emerged after the collapse of Jerusalem. Formally that group, which took care of, shaped, and developed the book of Jeremiah, is informed by the theology of Deuteronomy. Practically, that group is especially identified with the family of Shaphan, apparently a very influential and prominent family in the politics of Jerusalem (see 26:24; 36:11-19). That family moved easily in royal circles but stood some distance from the royal policies, which it regarded as foolish and destructive. In addition to Shaphan and his offspring, Jeremiah's tradition is connected to two sons of Neriah, Baruch (36:4-32) and Seraiah (51:59-64), apparently a second scribal family of some importance.

It was apparently the work of this continuing political group to take up the remembered words of Jeremiah and to fashion them into a political-theological opinion that would prove durable into the exile that Jeremiah had anticipated. The study of this process of reinterpretation of prophetic words is important, not only because it suggests how prophetic utterance became prophetic book but because it may also illuminate the way prophetic words have a continuing and powerful "afterlife" among those who keep listening. In this interpretive process, we may identify, among others, three motifs that proved important to Judah's self-understanding in exile.

1. While the poetry had anticipated a foe from the North (1:14) and had described a coming, invading army, that foe is not anywhere identified in the poetry. Given geopolitical realities, perhaps Babylon is intended in the poetic utterance, but that is not made explicit. The subsequent interpretive community makes what is hinted at explicit. The invading army is indeed the Babylonian army of Nebuchadnezzar, so that Yahwistic claim and geopolitical reality are fully equated. Indeed, this tradition has Yahweh say, "Nebuchadnezzar . . . my servant" (25:9; 27:6). The feared and hated ruler of Babylon, who is about to dismantle Jerusalem, is understood as an instrument of Yahweh's purpose, so that the Babylonian destruction of Jerusalem is taken as Yahweh's own work of terminating Judah. This is an incredible affirmation about the public political process. Thus Yahweh wills the end of Judah, the termination of its public life and identity, and initiates that action in history.

2. This subsequent interpretive community takes up Jeremiah's remarkable poetry and fashions it into instruction. Now it is urged and hoped that Israel might repent (18:8; 23:22; 25:3; 26:3; 36:3), reengage Torah obedience, and so avert disaster. This urging to repent might appear to be an invitation to avert the coming catastrophe of 587 by serious obedience. If, however, this interpretive extrapolation is later, as seems likely, then the repentance ostensibly aimed at the Jerusalem populace is in fact a later appeal to the community in exile. In either case, this interpretation moves beyond the words of the poet to help shape emerging Judaism as a community of serious and intentional obedience.

3. This subsequent interpretive community is active in its own interest in the midst of exile. With the deportation of 598 (52:28; 2 Kgs 24:8-17) and the later one in 587 (52:29, 2 Kgs 25:1-21), there were competing communities of Jews in exile. With the loss of the dynasty, moreover, there was immense energy given, in the rival communities, to establish one community as the "true community" that could give "correct" interpretation of the past and assure authority for the future. (The maneuver is not unlike Charles de Gaulle's claiming during World War II to be "true France.") The community active in the tradition of Jeremiah insisted that it was the wave of exiles from 598 who were "true Judah" (i.e., the "good figs" of 24:4-7), in contrast to the alternative communities in exile or in the land (the "bad figs" of 24:8-10). Thus the book of Jeremiah begins, in its editorial development, to look beyond the deportation and to struggle with issues of truth and power as concern the shape of the future. Indeed, that it pondered the future at all is itself remarkable, and runs beyond the horizon of the poet Jeremiah, who anticipated no future for Israel.

There is one other factor in the "collapse tradition" of Jeremiah to which particular attention should be paid. In a series of prayers addressed to Yahweh (commonly called "confessions"; see Jer 11:18-23; 12:1-6; 15:10-21; 17:14-18; 18:18-23; 20:7-18), the poet prays to Yahweh out of hurt, grief, anger, and a sense of acute danger. The poet bids for help from Yahweh and petitions Yahweh to act in vengeance against those who have threatened the prophet. This series, if indeed it is a series, ends in a shrill cry of despair (20:14-18).

It is not at all clear what to make of these prayers. Even as their wording and form are relatively clear, the intent, purpose, and function of them in the book of Jeremiah is not obvious. It may be, as has been commonly assumed, that they are the cries of a faithful servant of Yahweh who enjoys intense access to Yahweh, daring to speak intimately to Yahweh about the risks and costs of faithfulness. It has been alternatively suggested that these prayers, though presented as personal prayers, in their present form and location are the voice of jeopardized Israel, now seeking the support and advocacy of Yahweh in a circumstance of acute danger. Interpretation is not easy. It may be enough, provisionally, to see that these prayers introduce into the tradition of Jeremiah a dimension of pathos, hurt, anger, and need. That is, the force of Jeremiah cannot be reduced to a conventional theology of blessing and curse. The human reality vis-à-vis Yahweh, in a dangerous world of *Realpolitik,* is much more ragged and unsettled than that. And so these prayers refuse any reductionist view of history. As we shall see, this voice of pathos becomes crucial as the tradition of Jeremiah moves beyond collapse to hope.

The tradition of Jeremiah is disordered and not smoothly edited. For that reason, it is exceedingly difficult to read. But for the same reason, it is endlessly suggestive. What does emerge, even when the details are unclear and unsettled, is testimony to an awesome ending in the midst of history, an ending of everything trusted in Jerusalem, and everything that had been promised by Yahweh. This tradition, moreover, will not allow that the sheer force of "history" has overwhelmed Yahweh's intention. On the contrary, the powers of ending are precisely at the behest of Yahweh (and not Nebuchadnezzar), who in sovereignty finally will cast off beloved Israel as a hopeless project. It is no wonder, given such an unutterable reality, that the tradition of Jeremiah can speak such reality only in fits and starts, disjointed but fully unflinching. Deportation as death comes next, because Yahweh will not be mocked.

The last years of the kingdom of Judah, before the deportation of 598 and the decisive termination of 587, were a time of profound historical upheaval and of theological instability and uncertainty, which evoked the daring, disjunctive rhetoric of the tradition of Jeremiah. In a world seemingly out of control, questions about the rule of Yahweh in the historical process and about the justice of

Yahweh's governance were difficult and inescapable. Such questions were bound to occur to serious folk. The quandaries faced by serious people of faith in the midst of upheaval are reflected in the small corpus of *the book of Habakkuk,* who in the canon of biblical literature is a lesser figure than is Jeremiah. The book of Habakkuk is dated somewhere in this period (with its reference to the Babylonians in 1:6), but scholars are not agreed on the dating with any precision.

The rhetoric of this little book concerns the wild, destructive power of evil in the world of Judah, perhaps wickedness within the community of Judah or perhaps the massive evil perpetrated by the Assyrians (1:2-4). In either case, the Babylonians are dispatched by Yahweh in response to the evil, Babylonians who come with massive and ruthless power (1:5-11). But of course, the Babylonians are indeed penultimate, for this literature does not suggest that Babylonian power, even if dispatched by Yahweh, is the permanent resolution of the historical process. For this superpower, like every superpower before and after, becomes arrogant and destructive. Particular attention should be paid to Hab 2:4:

> Look at the proud!
> > Their spirit is not right in them,
> > but the righteous live by their faith.

This text powerfully contrasts the "proud" enemy and the faithful in Israel, who will be safe because they trust Yahweh. This verse later became important in Paul's understanding of the Christian gospel (Rom 1:17; Gal 3:11; see also Heb 10:38) and subsequently became an important marker in Martin Luther's theology of grace. In its original and derivative uses, it affirms that *trust in God* is the source of true well-being and security. Thus after affirming the Yahwistic function of Babylon, the series of woe-oracles in 2:6-19 apparently are threats against Babylon, for its arrogance, violence, and self-aggrandizement.

The odd verse concluding chapter 2 marks a turn in the book of Habakkuk:

> But the LORD is in his holy temple;
> > let all the earth keep silence before him! (2:20)

This verse seems to suggest that until this point in the poetry of Habakkuk, nothing has been gained in regard to justice. Israel can only silently wait for the vigorous intervention of Yahweh that will happen in chapter 3. Now attention is no longer on Babylon or on any other historical agent or event. The following chapter is a vision and anticipation of Yahweh's own powerful coming to work devastation upon the exploitative powers. The voice of this text does not doubt that, in the end, soon or late, Yahweh will right the historical process in the face of every discomfort. The concluding phrasing of the chapter (vv. 16-19) articulates a resolution of all trouble in confident waiting and hoping for Yahweh. Thus:

> I wait quietly for the day of calamity
>> to come upon the people who attack us.
> Though the fig tree does not blossom,
>> and no fruit is on the vines;
> though the produce of the olive fails
>> and the fields yield no food;
> though the flock is cut off from the fold
>> and there is no herd in the stalls,
> yet I will rejoice in the LORD;
>> I will exult in the God of my salvation.
> GOD, the Lord, is my strength;
>> he makes my feet like the feet of a deer,
>> and makes me tread upon the heights.

The poet fully acknowledges the threat to all creation caused by violence (v. 17) but then utters a profound "yet" of faith (v. 18), the faith formerly bespoken in 2:4. Thus the prophetic voice fully acknowledges the vexations of lived experience, but places in the very midst of them a confident affirmation that Yahweh can work through and beyond all such troubles to well-being.

These verses provide us the basic outline of faith that governs the more influential literatures of both Jeremiah and Ezekiel. While the historical specificities of Habakkuk are obscure, we cannot fail to notice the play upon themes that become characteristic of Judah's faith in its precariousness:

—There is a full and candid acknowledgment of disruption and the terrible consequences it produces.

—There is a confident affirmation that Yahweh is now and

will be in the end fully competent to govern in the midst of the disruption.

—The way of holding together the deep disruption and the deeper affirmation is in a "two-stage" notion of governance: (a) Babylon is Yahweh's instrument and (b) Babylon is Yahweh's enemy who will be destroyed. Babylon as instrument of Yahweh constitutes Judah's punishment. Babylon as destroyed enemy of Yahweh constitutes grounds for Judah's hope and deliverance. Thus Babylon, the penultimate reference here, is a cipher for speech about Yahweh's sovereign judgment and coming sovereign rescue.

Given the drama of judgment and rescue that can be neither evaded nor hurried, the faithful *wait*, honestly and confidently, while Yahweh's rule is enacted, in and through geopolitics. Habakkuk urges the faithful to wait, because in the long run, Yahweh will prevail and the arrogance of the empire will fail (2:3).

In this little corpus of Habakkuk, congruent with Jeremiah and Ezekiel, we have a succinct, albeit elusive, articulation of a theology of exile and hope. Everything for Judah depends upon the earth keeping awed silence before the Holy One.

Alongside the book of Jeremiah, *the book of Ezekiel* is the second great document of "the collapse" in the face of Yahweh's judgment effected through the invasive power of Babylon. The book of Ezekiel, unlike the book of Jeremiah, is carefully and symmetrically edited. As the book of Jeremiah concerns the twin themes of "pluck up and tear down, plant and build," so the book of Ezekiel has the comparable themes of "scatter and gather" (Ezek 11:17; cf. Jer 10). That is, both Jeremiah and Ezekiel articulate a "two-stage" notion of Judah's history in the sixth century: first, collapse into exile; and second, restoration into the land after exile. The book of Ezekiel speaks of "the scattering" into exile in chapters 1–24 (which we will deal with in the present section) and, in chapters 25–48, of the restoration. In taking up the first phase of this "two-stage" thesis, it is important not to permit the theme of restoration to seep into our consideration of the "scattering" in order to soften its impact, because the text itself allows for no such softening of the historical cost nor the theological gravity of the collapse. That is, in the voicing of the scattering, the text proceeds as though this is the end of the matter, that exile is the endpoint of Judah's life with Yahweh in the world. Thus,

> Now the end is upon you,
>> I will let loose my anger upon you;
> I will judge you according to your ways,
>> I will punish you for all your abominations.
> My eye will not spare you, I will have no pity.
>> I will punish you for your ways,
>> while your abominations are among you. (7:3-4)

The person Ezekiel is commonly thought to have lived and worked in Babylon among the exiles from 593 until 571, that is, like Jeremiah, both before and after the debacle of 587. The person of Ezekiel is pedigreed among the priests of Jerusalem, and there is no doubt that the book of Ezekiel reflects priestly concerns and perceptions and has an intimate connection with the Priestly tradition of the Pentateuch, which is commonly dated to this same period. This priestly mode of perception and articulation is particularly interesting to us, because it is very different from the tradition of Jeremiah, which is driven by Mosaic memories mediated through the Deuteronomists. Both Jeremiah and Ezekiel were priests, but they are informed by very different theological memories and perspectives. Thus together, the traditions of Jeremiah and Ezekiel are twin efforts to imagine the deep crisis of Judah through very different lenses, one through a Mosaic-covenantal accent upon obedience and covenantal sanctions, the other through a priestly-sacerdotal accent upon holiness and purity. The comparison and contrast of the two traditions makes evident the richness of Judah's resources in tradition. It makes equally clear that the "limit" experience of collapse and exile required exceedingly venturesome interpretation and commentary in order to make Yahwistic sense out of the events around the destruction of Jerusalem.

The "scattering" of Judah—the judgment against Jerusalem that culminates in deportation of more Jews to Babylon and the destruction of Jerusalem—occupies Ezek 1–24. In these chapters, with enormous variety and venturesomeness, this unwavering account of devastating judgment from Yahweh is pursued relentlessly. In reading this material one may pay attention to the rich variety that serves to voice this single, unqualified verdict that Judah—along with Yahweh—must vacate beloved Jerusalem.

1. The problem in Jerusalem, as Ezekiel voiced it in chapters 8–11, is that the temple, which is wholly and singularly devoted to Yahweh, has been hopelessly compromised by the worship of "vile abominations," "creeping things and loathsome animals," and finally even Tammuz, an alien goddess (8:7-15). Whether this is in fact a description of what happened in the temple or heated hyperbole in order to make a point, Jerusalem and its temple have so violated the holiness of Yahweh that Yahweh can no longer remain in residence. Two responses are made to the obscene defilement of the temple. First, a death sentence is asserted upon all those who have participated in the affront to Yahweh (9:5-10). Second, Yahweh cannot tolerate the affront and will bodily, physically fly away into exile (10:18-22). The vision of "wheels" in chapter 1 attests to Yahweh's mobility. This remarkable theological innovation breaks with any notion of Yahweh's permanence in the Jerusalem temple. The extreme case of exile is that even Yahweh is now exiled, far away from the temple, subject to the conditions and circumstances of deportation. In this remarkable imagery, Ezekiel has articulated the characteristic prophetic accents of judgment and sentence, but has done so with poignant reference to the temple, to Yahweh's uncompromising holiness and Yahweh's inestimable glory. The outcome is that Jerusalem now faces the abrupt absence of Yahweh, and when Yahweh is absent from Jerusalem, it is clear that the city and its people have no hope and no future.

2. In a second, very different set of texts (chaps. 4–6), the prophet tries to express in compelling imagery the coming, inescapable exile of Jerusalem, a city under judgment. These narrative accounts suggest that for the prophet, the fate of the city is a foregone conclusion, so offensive to Yahweh was its conduct. The city and its opinion makers, however, refused to see the threat. As a result, the prophet must resort to extreme measures in order to make that ominous, unexpected future clear.

The prophet does not rely merely upon speech but makes the point of impending exile and deportation by dramatic actions. His attention-getting actions include the construction of a small model of Jerusalem, shown to be under siege (4:1-3), his own lying down for a stated period in public, bound, in order to make clear the length of deportation and the hopelessness of the exiles (4:4-8), the preparation of food in an "unclean" way to anticipate the "unclean," defiled life of Israel in exile (4:9-15), and the use of hair from his head, blown in the wind to bespeak the scattering of Judah (5:1-4). In 12:1-16, the prophet stands by his baggage to signify that he himself is prepared for the exile that is sure to come soon.

These several enactments intend to assault the imagination of his contemporaries (and subsequent readers) with the hard reality of Yahweh's uncompromising holiness. Ezekiel, like Jeremiah, faced a Jerusalem ideology that assumed Yahweh was irrevocably committed to Judah, Jerusalem, its temple, and its king. In violent and daring ways, Ezekiel makes clear that all to which Yahweh has been committed is revocable and is now being revoked. It is not possible for Judah or its religious establishment to hold Yahweh in thrall to its own interests. Yahweh in freedom is now to act against Judah with profound severity.

3. In chapter 13, in a critique not unlike that of Jer 23, the prophet attacks his contemporary prophets who out of their imagination invent reassuring falsehoods in the name of Yahweh. The prophets themselves "whitewash" reality, making social reality look better than it is, by saying "peace" when there is no peace (v. 10; cf. Jer 6:14; 8:11). Such prophets, however, only give voice to the endless self-deception of the community, which imagines that somehow Yahweh's holiness and glory can be kept integrally connected to Israel's well-being. Such self-deception has placed Judah in an illusionary world, where it has no accurate sense of itself, and cannot see that Yahweh will terminate such a recalcitrant people.

4. The rhetoric of Ezekiel is noticeably stylized. Nowhere is this more evident than in the recital of classic curses against Yahweh's enemies—sword, famine, and pestilence (6:11-12; 14:12-20; cf. Jer 15:2; 24:10). In this triad of curses, the prophet may indeed be recalling an older curse recital. Or the triad may reflect realism about military invasion, for in the wake of a devastating army (here Babylon), the "sword" brings regularly in its wake famine, as food supplies are either confiscated or destroyed, the infrastructure of society breaks down, and disease breaks out. Thus the curses suggest a termination of Judah that is violent and wrought by human

agency. In the end, Judah will be helpless and exposed—all at the hand of Yahweh, who dispatches the human agents to effect Judah's end.

5. In chapter 18, the prophet speaks a familiar invitation to "turn and live." This teaching may be a wistful hope that Judah can, before it is too late, change its life enough to stave off the destruction. (Or it may be that this appeal is addressed later to those already in exile.) In either case, the urging of this chapter reflects the uncompromising conviction of this tradition that survival for Judah in the future depends upon responsible action in worship, economics, and sexual matters (Ezek 18:5-9). The prerequisite to "life" is to "turn." The offer and ominous invitation of this chapter strike one as provisional. While Yahweh has "no pleasure in the death of anyone" (v. 32), life is not freely given. Life is secured only by living in ways congruent with demanding Yahweh. Thus the offer of life, in the context of the book of Ezekiel, only points up the destiny sure to come from Judah's way of living, namely, death. Judah missed every chance for "turning," and so it forfeited every chance for life and for a future with Yahweh.

6. It is evident from the temple vision of 8–11, the enacted assertion of 4–6, the critique of deceiving prophets in 13, the recital of curses in 6 and 14, and the last chance to turn in 18, that this literature is unmitigated in its conviction that the end of Jerusalem, the end of Yahweh's presence in Jerusalem, and the end of Yahweh's commitment to Judah are now very near.

As though to relate this single conviction, rooted in Yahweh's holiness, in a most comprehensive way, the prophet offers three extended prose accounts of the entire history of Israel (chaps. 16, 20, 23). It had been standard practice in Israel, perhaps since early times, to retell its past as recital of Yahweh's acts of graciousness to Israel (as in Deut 6:10-14; 26:5-9; Josh 24:2-13; Ps 105). That graciousness is still acknowledged in Ezekiel (16:1-14; 20:6, 10-12). But now the main force of the retelling of "life together" is not an account of Yahweh's enduring graciousness.

Now the emphasis is upon Israel's lack of gratitude and responsiveness that issues in self-indulgent autonomy and a consequently profound affront against Yahweh. Thus in 16:15-34; 20:8, 13, 16, 21; and from the very outset in 23:3-49, the tables are turned. Attention is diverted from Yahweh's good initiatives to Israel's unseemly responses. While there are a variety of offenses that are identified, it is remarkable that the dominant images of affront are for sexual infidelities of a most "kinky" kind. This imagery is often noted to suggest that the prophet has unhealthy views of sexuality and of women and that his words reflect an uncritical patriarchal view of relational reality. While that seems to be beyond dispute, it is also likely that this imagery is utilized in order to express the most gross, obscene, unthinkable betrayal of Yahweh. That is, the poet here is required to use affrontive imagery because the point to be made is itself deeply affrontive. Thus we are able to see, yet again, the use of sexual imagery with incommensurate gender relationships utilized by the prophet. Again, we may note that the imagery is one that powerfully discloses, but also carries with it potentially destructive modeling of power relations. Any lesser imagery would have failed to match the point to be made.

It does not surprise us, given what we now know about Ezekiel's rhetoric, that Yahweh's heavy-handed response to the sexual affront of Judah is not simply punishment but the wild, irrational reaction of a wounded, shamed, humiliated lover who in rage will destroy the fickle partner on whom everything has been staked:

> So I will satisfy my fury on you, and my jealousy shall turn away from you; I will be calm, and will be angry no longer. (16:42, cf. vv. 35-43)

> Moreover I swore to them in the wilderness that I would scatter them among the nations and disperse them through the countries. . . . Moreover I gave them statutes that were not good and ordinances by which they could not live. I defiled them through their very gifts, in their offering up all their firstborn, in order that I might horrify them, so that they might know that I am the LORD. (20:23, 25-26; cf. 23:22-45)

The extremity of the rhetoric may indeed reflect a personal inclination of the prophet, as commentators suggest. The intent of the rhetoric, however, is to present to Israel an awesome God who will respond with devastation to an unspeakable, unbearable affront. This is not simply the breaking of a command or a rule but a profound emotional assault upon the very self of Yahweh. In Ezekiel's telling of the matter, Yahweh is right to be angry and affronted. The force of punishment, however, is driven by a deep and irrational fury, before which Judah is utterly hopeless. The punishment will come "from the north" (23:24), that is, from Babylon. Thus in the end, even this statement of intimate, personal outrage returns to the realities of geopolitics. Geopolitics, however, are only belatedly a tool for a relationship gone completely sour.

These poetic prophets—Habakkuk, but especially Jeremiah and Ezekiel—in a variety of themes and images, provide theological grounding for the harsh events wrought by Babylon. The experience of Judah, on the ground, did indeed match up with the rhetorical daring of these poets. Nebuchadnezzar and his armies did come. They came in 598 and took away 3,023 Judeans; in 587 they took away 832 Judeans; and in 581, subsequently, as a mop-up action, they took away another 745 persons. All told, they took away 4,600 persons, a harsh act of imperial policy (Jer 52:28-30).

That number, in itself, does not seem like very many. But of course to focus upon the number and the dates is to miss the point of these poets. An "outsider," one not committed to Yahwistic readings of events, could consider this crisis simply as an imperial act of misfortune. But "insiders" to the prophetic rhetoric of Israel know more and know better. They know that what seems like an imperial act is in truth an act of Yahweh. What seemed like a limited, disciplined deportation is in truth the displacement of all of Israel. What seemed like a "reason of state" is in truth an act of divine passion—rage, shame, hurt, indignation, righteousness. In that act, moreover, everything that seemed certain in Judah is terminated. The end was not of Nebuchadnezzar. It was of Yahweh.

And so ends Yahweh's scandalous experiment in history. Jeremiah voices the ending with pathos over the pitiful deported boy-king whose status signifies the failure of the experiment that is Israel:

> O land, land, land,
>   hear the word of the LORD! . . .
> Record this man as childless,
>   a man who shall not succeed in his days;
> for none of his offspring shall succeed
>   in sitting on the throne of David,
>   and ruling again in Judah. (Jer 22:29-30)

Ezekiel hears the news from a messenger:

> The city has fallen. (Ezek 33:21)

The tradition of Jeremiah had anticipated just this outcome:

> Thus says the LORD of hosts: So will I break this people and this city, as one breaks a potter's vessel, so that it can never be mended.
>
> (Jer 19:11)

Ezekiel had known well ahead of time (7:3-4). What had been uttered in this daring rhetoric is now enacted. It is finished!

Exile

The extremist rhetoric of the traditions of Jeremiah and Ezekiel is enough to make one conclude that Israel, as Yahweh's people in the world, was to be terminated and nullified. And no doubt that is what these traditions intended to communicate. No doubt, moreover, that is what was experienced by those who were seriously committed to covenant life (as in the circles of Jeremiah and the Deuteronomists) and to temple life (as in the circles of Ezekiel and the Priestly traditions), for both covenant and temple have been radically jeopardized in the lived experience of Judah and in the poignant rhetoric of the prophets.

But life goes on. In the years of devastation after 587, we have the odd situation of a rhetoric of nullification and a lived reality of continued existence as an ongoing community of faith with the marks of sociopolitical identity. To say that life goes on is to recognize that life, for the displaced community of Jews, went on in many places under many circumstances. There was, it is clear, a continuing community of Jews in the environs of Jerusalem, for the deportation by the Babylonians did not empty the land of those who understood themselves to be the people of Yahweh. There were, it is equally evident, scattered communities of displaced persons in various parts of that ancient world. The most prominent of these was Babylon, where Ezekiel was; but there was also an exilic community in Egypt, where Jeremiah was taken. The

Bible, however, gives only incidental attention to these several communities, which must have continued their worshiping and their hoping along with their suffering.

The Bible devotes almost all of its energies to the community of Jews deported to Babylon. This community, a subset of the larger community of Jews now living in many places, was likely an assembly of the most skilled, competent, and imaginative Jews, and it is these who became the central carriers and proponents of the traditions that were shaped into emerging Judaism. Indeed, such a focus in the textual traditions that became the Old Testament is not a disinterested enterprise, for we may believe that the texts were generated and preserved by the community of Babylonian Jews themselves, as a means of claiming for themselves the authority to be the normative interpreters and definers of Jewish faith, and therefore the central figures in the sociopolitical life of restored Judaism.

It is clear that for all of their rhetoric of nullification, the traditions of both Jeremiah and Ezekiel give attention to the plight and needs of the deported communities and seek to give resources to them for theological, that is, self-conscious, intentional survival. Thus in Jer 29:1-9, the prophet is said to write a letter to the exiles, urging them to accept exile in Babylon as the place where they must live their faith and develop sustainable modes of communal existence apart from Jerusalem. In a very different mode, moreover, Ezekiel offers his remarkable vision of a mobile God (Ezek 1:1-21), a God not rooted in Jerusalem, but quite capable of ranging the earth, with even a chance to be in exile and therefore present to the exiles. In both of these great prophetic works, provision is made that life in faith can be continued apart from the old institutional, now lost supports, though of course in quite altered forms.

The most remarkable theological aspect of the exile is that the profound losses of 587 did not lead to despair and a loss of faith. Rather, the exile became a remarkable moment in the life of the Jewish community for inventive and generative faith, which experimented with new articulations of that faith and which produced much of the more eloquent and more determined literature of the Old Testament.

The experience of loss and displacement evoked in exilic Israel profound questions of faith:

—Is Yahweh not powerful?

—Is Yahweh not faithful?

—How do we hope in exile?

—How do we move beyond exile?

—Is there life after exile?

These questions required clear and imaginative thinking. The process of rethinking and reformulating faith, however, was not simply an intellectual enterprise. The needs of faith were deep, immediate, and elemental, so that daring rhetorical and inventive theological formulations were responses to the most fundamental emotional sense of displacement, both as persons and as community, a sense of failure and disorder that impinged decisively upon every aspect of life. In speaking of a later Jewish crisis (the Holocaust), Alan Mintz speaks of the power of catastrophe

> to shatter the existing paradigms of meaning, especially as regards the bonds between God and the people of Israel. Crucial to creative survival was the reconstruction of these paradigms through interpretation, and in this enterprise the literary imagination was paramount.[1]

In the reconstruction of paradigms for faith through literary imagination, the first work for the deportees was to express the rage, sadness, grief, and deep sense of loss that permeated life. They had lost everything they valued and everything that gave life coherence. That is, the first ingredient in survival is an act of candor about the reality of the new situation. In voicing the truth of their lives, the community of exiles appealed to the old liturgic practice of lamentation, whereby all that is amiss in life is voiced out loud, directly to God. The voicing is, on the one hand, an indispensable catharsis. But on the other hand, it is a prayer addressed to Yahweh, drawing God into the trouble, protesting against God's neglect or ineffectiveness, and appealing to God for help. We should not, however, reduce the protest to excessively cognitive theology, because the protests are too raw and elemental to be flattened in a cerebral way. Here Israel tells its miserable truth, with artistry, but without emotional or theological restraint.

The most important such articulation is in the *book of Lamentations,* composed in response to the destruction and disruption of the temple in Jerusalem. This collection of poems consists of five poems, four of which are acrostic; that is, each line begins with a subsequent letter of the Hebrew alphabet. The purpose seems to express all of Israel's grief, from A to Z. The poetry is a sophisticated balance of acknowledgment of guilt and articulation of sadness that lives close to despair. In 3:21-33, there is a brief expression of hope and confidence in Yahweh, indicating that such hope is still available to and operative among exiles. But that voicing of hope is uncharacteristic of this poetry. Much more recurrent is the deep sense of loss and a lack of recourse. The final poem ends with a vigorous doxological affirmation (5:19) and an expectant petition (5:21). These positive statements, however, are in the midst of bewilderment and uncertainty (5:20, 22). Israel knows how to hope. But it will not keep silent about its present reality, unmitigated by positive theological conviction.

In addition to the book of Lamentations, we may mention several psalms that are congruent with the larger liturgical pattern of protest and complaint but that reflect the particular crisis of the exile. Best known of these is Ps 137, explicitly located in the exile, "by the rivers of Babylon" (v. 1). This psalm characterizes, perhaps in great hyperbole, the intolerable situation of the exiles (vv. 1-3). It voices the deep and nonnegotiable focus of exile on Jerusalem, in memory and in yearning (vv. 4-6), and it articulates, with merciless passion, resentment against Babylonian overlords (vv. 7-9). These last verses are often taken to be ignoble and unworthy of this community of faith. We may value them, however, both for the candor of this desperate community and for its readiness to submit its candor to the rule of Yahweh. That is, these resentful exiles do not propose, themselves, to "kill Babylonian babies." They only submit to Yahweh their depth of hostility, which is then left in Yahweh's capable hands. Such poetry evidences the way in which the biblical tradition lives in a world of violence. One can conclude that such violence in Israel is rhetorical rather than materially enacted, but the tone of violence is nonetheless prominent and powerful.

The same note of deep resentment and loss is evident in Pss 74 and 79. In both of these psalms we note recurring themes. The exiles dwell at length and in detail upon the affront of the destruction of the temple, thus voicing loss (74:4-8; 79:1-4). While the psalms focus upon the temple, they are prayers addressed to Yahweh. The involvement of Yahweh in the destruction of the temple is variously assessed. Sometimes Yahweh has indeed been the one who punished Judah by destruction (74:1; 79:5). At other times, however, the destruction seems to have happened by Yahweh's inattentiveness and by default (74:9-11). In either case, the very God who is credited with the destruction is the God to whom Israel must turn for hope. Thus in 74:2, 18, 22, Yahweh is urged to "remember," for if Yahweh pays attention, Yahweh will surely act to right the unbearable situation. This hope in Yahweh issues in a lyrical doxology directed toward Yahweh (vv. 12-17), counting on Yahweh's power to correct every dysfunction. Psalm 79, in like fashion, culminates with a series of petitions, for Israel in exile does not doubt that Yahweh is powerful enough to restore and return (79:9-13).

The most extraordinary of these is Ps 44.[2] This psalm reviews the past, when Yahweh performed deeds of rescue, victory, and transformation (vv. 1-8). After such an affirmation, however, in verse 9 the psalm abruptly changes tone. Now Yahweh is roundly accused and charged with damage to Israel (vv. 9-16). Moreover,

> All this has come upon us,
>> yet we have not forgotten you,
>> or been false to your covenant.
> Our heart has not turned back,
>> nor have our steps departed from your way,
> yet you have broken us in the haunt of jackals,
>> and covered us with deep darkness. (vv. 17-19)

In this assertion, Israel is innocent and does not deserve the brutality of the exile. In many places, exile is understood as Yahweh's just punishment of Israel. This is surely the case in the traditions of Jeremiah and Ezekiel. But not here. Here the exile is Yahweh's failure. And therefore, Israel issues to Yahweh a series of imperatives, urging that Yahweh has been neglectful, and must now act responsibly, as in the past of verses 1-8:

> Rouse yourself! Why do you sleep, O Lord?
>> Awake, do not cast us off forever! . . .
> Rise up, come to our help.
>> Redeem us for the sake of your steadfast love. (vv. 23, 26)

These verses evidence both the desperate need of Israel and its daring faith. Israel has found voice in exile and will, with great courage, expect and insist that Yahweh now act in a way appropriate to the needs of Israel.

What strikes one about these psalms is the fact that the prophetic assertion of nullification and termination has been completely overcome. Resignation has given way to insistence. Confession has yielded to expectation. Indeed, this is likely the characteristic route of Israel's faith, brilliantly enacted in exile. With its powerful tradition of protest and complaint, Israel is able to move toward a new hope. Long ago, in its liturgical activity, Israel practiced what psychotherapy has rediscovered in scientific formulation, that there is an inescapable requirement of *candor* that makes serious *hope* possible. These psalms are evidence that Israel moved through the entire sequence from accepted termination to anticipated restoration. It did so, moreover, fully aware that in each of its postures of defeat and expectation, it addressed Yahweh, who finally held the future of Israel in God's own hand. This is not to deny that in Israel's awareness the exile was punishment. But for the most part, Israel would not leave it at that. There arose in exilic Israel a buoyant insistence that is derived from and referred back to Yahweh. Yahweh is the one who caused exile; and yet it is clear that the exile has proximate causes that arise in the concrete realities of geopolitical interaction. In important ways, Nebuchadnezzar and the Babylonians are crucial in evoking exile. In the end, in any case, it is Yahweh who can and will end exile and permit homecoming to the land and full restoration. (As we shall see, as exile has a proximate human agent in Nebuchadnezzar, so homecoming has a proximate human agent in Cyrus the Persian.)

The Arena of Hope

One of the most remarkable features of the faith of the Old Testament is that the exile, the experience of historical disruption, displacement, and failure, produced not despair, but hope. That is, the texts generated in the exile (which became part of the Old Testament) are characteristically assertions of new historical possibility that are rooted in Yahweh's own good intention. These texts take the reality of exile, its defeat and dislocation, with great seriousness. They do not, however, accept that reality as the final outcome of Israel's historical destiny.

In the case of the two prophets to whom we have given primary attention, Jeremiah and Ezekiel, we may identify rhetorical moves that both embrace the exile as a serious theological datum about Yahweh and Israel and then promptly move beyond exile to make a very different affirmation about Yahweh and consequently about Israel. Thus Jeremiah understands exile as Yahweh's resolve to "pluck up and tear down," which happened in the exile. But these verbs are immediately followed up and overcome by two verbs of restoration and rehabilitation:

> See, today I appoint you over nations and over kingdoms,
>   to pluck up and to pull down,
>   to destroy and to overthrow,
>   to build and to plant. (Jer 1:10)

> And just as I have watched over them to pluck up and break down, to overthrow, destroy, and bring evil, so I will watch over them to build and to plant, says the LORD. (Jer 31:28)

Ezekiel, moreover, uses great energy to explicate the scattering of the exile, but then he promptly reverses the scattering with the verb *gather,* indicating homecoming:

> I will gather you from the peoples, and assemble you out of the countries where you have been scattered, and I will give you the land of Israel. (Ezek 11:17)

Thus our theme is the powerful and resilient assertion in Israel's faith that the terrible rupture in Israel's life caused by Yahweh is to be overcome by a new gift of well-being, also rooted in the resolve of Yahweh.

The ground for this determined conviction beyond exile is, to be sure, proximately located in the fall of the empire of Babylon. As noted above, the terrible power of Babylon withered away soon after the death of Nebuchadnezzar in 562. The residue of power in the empire lasted another two decades beyond the great king. By 540, however, Cyrus the Persian, the rising power to the east of Babylon, was able to enter the city of Babylon and incorporate the resources and territory of Babylon in his new and growing empire without meeting any resistance at all.

Surely the Jewish deportees could observe this profound change in geopolitics. They must have understood well that a prerequisite for return to their beloved homeland was the nullification of the power and policy of deportation practiced by Babylon. Thus the new possibility for restored Judaism in the region around Jerusalem is a function and outcome of geopolitical development. Persian policy toward subjected colonies was to permit local leadership great latitude and initiative, though of course in broad conformity with imperial needs and policy. That is, the Persians did not intend to do the Jewish deportees any special favor. The Persians did, however, make the strategic guess that recognized local leadership would better serve the empire than did the repression undertaken by Babylon. The effect of such policy was enormously positive for the Israelites, with the first returnees in 537, with the vigorous rebuilding of the Jerusalem temple in 520–516, and with the subsequent restoration of Ezra and Nehemiah. The later part of the Old Testament regards Persian policy as generally benign and generous, made more so by the inevitable contrast with its exploitative antecedent of Babylonian policy.

The theological interpreters of Israel's history in this period, however, did not find it adequate to offer geopolitical explanations for this remarkably positive turn in Israel's life. Thus it was no more adequate to speak of hope in terms of new Persian imperial policy than it had been to explain the fall of Jerusalem in terms of Babylonian expansionism. Israel insisted upon understanding its life and history in theological categories, in terms of Yahweh's intention and resolve enacted within the historical process. Thus Nebuchadnezzar (negatively) and Cyrus (positively) may be accepted as proximate agents of what happened to Israel. They may be regarded only as unwitting agents of Yahweh; and yet they are decisive agents, for Israel knows that what Yahweh does occurs in the nexus of human processes. Thus in his destructiveness, Nebuchadnezzar can be termed by Yahweh "my servant" (Jer 25:9; 27:6), and Cyrus can be termed by Yahweh "my messiah" (Isa 45:1).

In this regard, we may refer to two sets of texts that pertain, respectively, to the failure of Babylon and to the success of Persia, both understood Yahwistically. It is characteristic of the prophetic literature to include bodies of texts that are "Oracles Against the Nations." In these texts (cf. Amos 1–2; Isa 13–23; Jer 46–51; and Ezek 25–32), various states are dealt with by name and characteristically condemned for having acted in arrogance, for having practiced brutality, or for having defied Yahweh. In every case, the poetic oracle is an assertion that such resistance or opposition to Yahweh cannot stand, and so the named state will surely be severely punished or even nullified. These oracles are a daring, sweeping act of theological rhetoric, whereby it is asserted that Yahweh governs the nations.

Specifically, Jer 50–51 offers an extended, relentless condemnation of Babylon, much hated and regarded now as an enemy of Yahweh. (The tone here is not unlike the view of Assyria in the poem of Nahum.) It is important to remember that Babylon, that is, Nebuchadnezzar, was earlier regarded in the Jeremiah tradition as an agent and servant of Yahweh. Now, however, the erstwhile instrument of Yahweh has overstepped his mandate, and must be punished, that is, terminated, as Babylon was in 540. Notice that the Yahwistic assertion and the geopolitical experience converge. In a parallel poem from perhaps the same period, Isa 13:1–14:23 exults in the Yahwistic destruction of Babylon:

> I will punish the world for its evil,
>   and the wicked for their iniquity;
> I will put an end to the pride of the arrogant,
>   and lay low the insolence of tyrants. . . .
> And Babylon, the glory of kingdoms,
>   the splendor and pride of the Chaldeans,
> will be like Sodom and Gomorrah
>   when God overthrew them. . . .
> Its time is close at hand,
>   and its days will not be prolonged. (Isa 13:11, 19, 22*b*)

The poetry is an act of daring imagination that does not trade in historical, political, or military explanation but invites recipients of the poetry to notice that there is a purpose in the historical process to which even Babylon must yield.

It is of course a difficult question whether the anticipated destruction of Babylon is "after the fact"—simply reflective of what was observed "on the ground"—or if it is genuine anticipation. Since we cannot know the precise dating of this material, we cannot be sure. However, if we are to think theologically about this material, then it is completely credible to imagine that those in Israel who pondered Yahweh and Yahweh's intolerance of exploitative arrogance would conclude that such an empire cannot long stand in the face of Yahweh's governance. It is, however, the convergence of theological claim and lived reality that is celebrated in the Bible.

The disappearance of Babylon from history and the end of its threatening power, understood Yahwistically, is matched by a remarkable Yahwistic affirmation of Cyrus and the Persians. In the larger developed tradition of the book of Isaiah (to which we will come shortly), in a passage no doubt linked to the poem we have cited in chapters 13–14, Cyrus is named as the chosen agent of Yahweh:

> Thus says the LORD, your Redeemer, . . .
> who says of Cyrus, "He is my shepherd,
>   and he shall carry out all my purpose";
> and who says of Jerusalem, "It shall be rebuilt,"
>   and of the temple, "Your foundation shall be laid."
> Thus says the LORD to his anointed, to Cyrus,
>   whose right hand I have grasped
> to subdue nations before him
>   and strip kings of their robes,
> to open doors before him—
>   and the gates shall not be closed. . . .
> For the sake of my servant Jacob,
>   and Israel my chosen,
> I call you by name,
>   I surname you, though you do not know me.
> (Isa 44:24, 28; 45:1, 4)

Cyrus is designated to do Yahweh's will (which is the rescue of Israel), even though "You do not know me." That is, it is not required that Cyrus the Persian should know or acknowledge Yahweh, the God of Israel. Indeed, Cyrus surely did not know of such a God. But it does not matter for these hope-driven Jews. Yahweh uses agents without their intentional cooperation. Moreover, Cyrus is designated "his anointed," his "messiah," the one entrusted with royal power. This extraordinary identification of Cyrus is a model way in which historical reality and theological affirmation are held to converge.

Full appreciation of the biblical text requires that the two be held together, as two aspects of a single phenomenon, namely, the reality of Yahweh-governed public history. History does not happen without Yahweh. But Israel and Yahweh do not live in a theological cocoon, they live in the real world. Thus everything depends upon this convergence. As a consequence, the "collapse of Jerusalem" is effected, according to this faith, by the Yahweh-willed policies that converge with Nebuchadnezzar's Babylonian "reasons of state." Conversely, the hope of exiles is effected, according to this faith, by the Yahweh-initiated role of Cyrus and the Persians, who will accept the homecoming of deported Jews as an aspect of imperial policy. The judgment of Israel wrought by Yahweh in indignation and the future of Israel wrought by Yahweh in determined fidelity are accomplished in the public processes of history, so that judgment and hope become organizing themes for the way in which public history works. Both judgment and hope are fully credited to Yahweh. And yet in each case, Israel knows very well about decisive human agency, first Nebuchadnezzar and then Cyrus.

The texts themselves do not linger long over the geopolitical features of this new possibility for Jews in exile. Rather the texts, from the remembered utterances of these great prophets—poets who were deeply immersed in the reality of exile—offer exultant, daring, hyperbolic imagination of the newness Yahweh is about to work as the world is reordered into a "new world order" sanctioned by Yahweh. We may consider in turn the three major textual traditions in this matter.

Voices of Hope

First, the hope for Israel in and beyond exile is articulated in *the Jeremiah tradition,* especially in chapters 29–33. (These chapters constitute the specifically Israelite possibility that matches the negative dismissal of Babylon and the other nations in chaps. 46–51.) It appears that the materials in 29–33 have been edited, so as to group statements of hope together.

We have already seen that Jeremiah (and the derivative tradition) were deeply rooted in the memory of Moses. Consequently, Judah was seen to be under threat from the God of the covenant, who would punish blatant violations of the Sinai covenant. There can be little doubt that as the prophet uttered those threats, an end was announced. The tradition of Jeremiah, however, was alive and kept developing in the exile from the words of the prophet, no doubt after the prophet himself had died. As a result, it could be asserted that the God who had first loved Israel (cf. Deut 7:6-11) continued to love Israel in and through and beyond exile. Thus this tradition, which moves determinedly from "pluck up and tear down" to "plant and build," does so because it is able to discern that at the bottom of Yahweh's inclination for Israel is a reservoir of deep love that compels Yahweh to pathos, pity, concern, and finally to new action on behalf of Judah:

> The people who survived the sword
> found grace in the wilderness;
> when Israel sought for rest,
> the LORD appeared to him from far away.
> I have loved you with an everlasting love;
> therefore I have continued my faithfulness to you. (Jer 31:2-3)

The betrayed lover continues to love. The one who had anguished over Israel's terminal illness now decides to heal. In daring imagery, Yahweh has become the husband, father, doctor, lover, the one whose life is so committed to Israel that Yahweh will give this exile-deserving community a new life. Here and elsewhere in the rhetoric of hope, gender imagery is used in constructive and generative ways, without the dimension of violence noted in earlier usage:

> Is Ephraim my dear son?
> Is he the child I delight in?
> As often as I speak against him,
> I still remember him.
> Therefore I am deeply moved for him;
> I will surely have mercy on him,
>   says the LORD. (31:20)

In chapters 30–33, in a rich variety of images, the tradition of Jeremiah portrays Yahweh as resolved to give Judah a viable life beyond exile. And because this tradition is rooted in the memory of Moses, the hoped-for future is especially imagined to be a new covenant not unlike the covenant of Sinai, and a new land of well-being like the land of Joshua.

1. The best-known promise for the future in the book of Jeremiah is the anticipation of a new covenant rooted in forgiveness (31:31-34). The new covenant, which will be a practice of willing, glad obedience, is in that regard quite unlike the old covenant. The well-known phrase "write it on their hearts" (v. 33) likely refers to a new disposition of Israel whereby Yahweh's Torah requirements will no longer be imposed and extrinsic, evoking resistance, but now willingly embraced and enacted as Israel's own true character and disposition. It is important to note that already in Deut 30:14, Torah is made a matter of the heart. The covenant can be lived. It is, however, in continuity with the old covenant in that it focuses upon obedience to Torah. This anticipation is known and celebrated by Christians because the phrase "new covenant" has been taken to refer to God's new gift in Jesus Christ (Heb 8:8-12; 10:16-17). Such an interpretation of the text, however, is a quite secondary matter. What is in fact promised is a renewed relation of fidelity between Yahweh and Yahweh's people Israel, a relation now in good faith and trusting obedience.

2. That relationship, however, is not thinly "spiritual," as it could never be in Israel. And therefore, along with the new covenant, there is an assurance that the "landless," that is, the exiles, now would resettle securely in the land of promise. The narrative presentation of 32:1-15, concerning the securing of a regularized title to a specific piece of patrimonial land, is emblematic of the material promise made to the exiles. The concluding statement of verse 15 (cf. vv. 42-44) makes unmistakably clear that the specific piece of land in the story is a sign and token of the land of promise now secured for the exiles.

Along with the land—or, perhaps better, at the center of the land—it is anticipated that the devastated city of Jerusalem, the one left in shambles by Nebuchadnezzar and mourned in the book of Lamentations, will be restored to new splendor. This hope is articulated both with geographical precision (31:38-40) and with lyrical extravagance (30:18-22).

3. The restored covenant and the rehabilitated land signify the renewal of viable community life, expressed in a variety of images and formulations. Thus it is promised that there will be a full resumption of covenantal intimacy:

You shall be my people,
  and I will be your God.
  (30:22; cf. Jer 11:4; 24:7; 31:33; 32:38;
  Ezek 11:20; 14:11; 36:28; 37:23, 27)

It is asserted that "the fortunes will be restored," signifying all the blessings of a safe, prosperous, productive material existence as a result of a healthy relationship with Yahweh the Creator and blesser (30:18; 31:23; 33:11, 26). There will be a restoration of joy, as it is expressed in weddings, a measure of the confidence and buoyancy of the new community (33:10-11).

The culminating effect of this lyrical anticipation is to assert that all of life shall be restored to complete shalom:

There is hope for your future,
  says the LORD;
  your children shall come back to their own country. (31:17)

A hearer of these glorious texts can wonder if this is the same speaker—and the same God and the same people—who spoke so savagely of "plucking up and tearing down." The answer given in the text as we have it is that "yes, this is the same cast of characters." What has emerged now is the depth of love and the powerful resolve in Yahweh's life, as given us by the prophetic tradition, that creates new life for this bereft people. The tradition of Jeremiah understands both the deeply affronted love of Yahweh and the deeply resolved love of Yahweh, which in turn produce exile and then homecoming. While affronted, Yahweh enacts the ancient system of covenantal curses and sanctions that produce exile. Then, newly resolved, Yahweh moves powerfully beyond such a system of threat to a new possibility of life.

Second, in a parallel way, *the tradition of Ezekiel* moves through the exile from "scatter" to "gather," yet another vision of homecoming and restoration. The terms of articulation of Israel's new possibility, however, are very different in Ezekiel. As we have seen, Ezekiel's tradition is grounded in priestly holiness, and so the great threat is the absence of God brought about by the scandalizing of God's holiness. In priestly categories, the absence of God means that God's power for life is withdrawn, so that life becomes impossible. And therefore, if there is to be restoration, there will need first of all to be a restoration of Yahweh's presence to the city of Jerusalem, and so to the life of Judah. Yahweh, however, has been so deeply affronted that we may indeed wonder what would make restored presence possible.

Not for Ezekiel is there an appeal to the love of Yahweh for Israel, as in Jeremiah. Indeed, Ezekiel has nothing to say about Yahweh's love for Israel or even about Yahweh's relationship to Israel. Particular attention, however, should be given to chapter 18. In this chapter, the prophet provides that the new generation can "turn and live" and is not fated by the past. The chapter has a remarkably pastoral tone: "I have no pleasure in the death of anyone" (v. 32). But the new possibilities for Israel beyond exile are grounded in Yahweh's self-regard, that is, Yahweh's concern for Yahweh's own name, or reputation. Thus in Ezek 36:23, Yahweh is resolved to "sanctify my great name," that is, to restore it to its full holiness. In Ezek 39:25, Yahweh is "jealous for my holy name." In both texts, newness comes for Israel only as Yahweh acts for the enhancement of Yahweh's reputation. The "catch" for Yahweh, however, is that Yahweh can only exhibit holiness to the nations by doing something decisively positive for Israel that will impress the watching nations and the watching gods. Thus rehabilitation for Israel is a vehicle for the establishment of Yahweh's incomparable holiness in the eyes of the world. Yahweh will act for Yahweh's own sake, but to the great benefit of Israel.

Yahweh exhibits Yahweh's tremendous authority, sovereignty, and power by acting decisively against the other nations who have been arrogant, mocking, and autonomous (Ezek 25–32). These Oracles Against the Nations are not unlike the ones we have seen in Jer 46–51. Yet it strikes one that in this exilic document, there is not an oracle against Babylon. Perhaps it was too dangerous to utter. Or perhaps the community of Ezekiel knew itself privileged by the Babylonians. We notice, however, that Egypt receives special and extended attention in 29–32. We may wonder, because Ezekiel is in many ways odd and surrealistic, whether Egypt here is to be "decoded" as Babylon or if Egypt might be a cipher for all of the offending nations, including Babylon. In any case, these Oracles make clear the powerful intention of Yahweh to restore a fully Yahweh-oriented world.

It is on the basis of the resolve of Yahweh's holiness that there are articulated in 34–37, 38–39, and 40–48 rich anticipations of newness that Yahweh guarantees to Judah.

1. Among the most lovely of these is the promise of Yahweh to act as "the good shepherd" toward the lost, the strayed, the injured, and the weak (34:11-16). This vision of Yahweh's resolve to act in the place of failed kings is an anticipation of Yahweh's genuine pastoral concern for the exiles. This articulation is apparently taken up in the New Testament notion of "The Good Shepherd" (John 10:11-18), and is likely reflected in the ethical articulation of Matt 25:31-46. Restored Israel is now on a new basis with Yahweh, who is completely attentive at the point of Israel's need.

2. The familiar vision of "the valley of the dry bones" anticipates the restoration of Israel, who has been lost, dead, hopeless, and without possibility (37:1-14). While the text may be taken up in Christian tradition with reference to resurrection, it is most important to recognize that resurrection here bespeaks return of Judah from exile to the land:

> "Thus says the Lord GOD: I am going to open your graves, and bring you up from your graves, O my people; and I will bring you back to the land of Israel. And you shall know that I am the LORD, when I open your graves, and bring you up from your graves, O my people. I will put my spirit within you, and you shall live, and I will place you on your own soil; then you shall know that I, the LORD, have spoken and will act," says the LORD. (37:12-14)

The return from exile to full life in the land is indeed a resurrection to new life from the death and hopelessness of displacement. (It is this image that belatedly has caused some Jews to regard the recent founding of the state of Israel as a salvific act.)

3. In the same chapter (37), the vision of the "dry bones" (vv. 1-14) is followed by two other remarkable articulations about the future of Judah. In verses 15-23, we are offered a vision of the restoration into

"one people" of the tribes of Judah and Israel, divided since the death of Solomon. While the earlier specific political realities are not here important to us, the vision is crucial because it proposes the full restoration of the full, one people Israel. And in verses 24-28, the themes of hope are richly gathered together so that the future is fully Davidic, with Yahweh fully in the sanctuary of Jerusalem, with an assurance of a "covenant of peace" that will endure to all generations. This assurance, moreover, is supported by the reiteration of the covenant formula "I will be their God, and they shall be my people" (vv. 23, 27). This collage of promises anticipates a coming time when all of life will be securely established in the best, most life-giving categories that Israel has known in all its past.

4. The book of Ezekiel concludes with a quite extended provision for a full restoration of Israel in the land from which it had been deported. In general this is a priestly vision of the future in which the center of restoration is the fully rebuilt, reconstituted temple of Jerusalem, which will be an adequate place for the presence of Yahweh. That is, the substance of this elaborate and detailed vision is that it is now possible for Yahweh to be fully present, once again, in Jerusalem after an absence required by Israel's moral and cultic failure.

The Priestly tradition reflected in Ezekiel has a quite concrete notion of Yahweh's presence. As Yahweh's "glory" flew away to exile in chapters 8–11, so here the glory "flies" back into the temple, making a "sound . . . like the sound of mighty waters" (43:2). The coming community of Jerusalem now is assured, in this rendering, of the full powerful, attentive, life-giving presence of Yahweh. This tradition goes to some length to assign all of the accountability of the cult to the several priestly orders, which will make the new temple adequate and conducive for Yahweh. For when Yahweh again takes up residence, then all of God's power for life is available to Israel. This anticipatory statement is that Yahweh will again dwell in the temple and will not ever again leave this people:

> This gate shall remain shut; it shall not be opened, and no one shall enter by it; for the LORD, the God of Israel, has entered by it; therefore it shall remain shut. (44:2)

In addition to securing the proper priesthood that can implement the presence of Yahweh in the temple, we may identify three other features of this temple vision that pertain to the restoration of exiled Judah:

—There will be a prince *(nasî')* who will govern in Jerusalem, a regent for Yahweh the King (44:3; cf. 34:23-24). Thus some form of the restored Davidic monarchy is promised.

—As anticipated by the Ezekiel tradition, the envisioned future includes a renewal of all of creation. The prophetic tradition here has close parallels to the vision of creation in Gen 2:10-14, as it speaks of a stream of living water that flows out from below the threshold of the temple (47:1) to give living water to all the earth (47:7-12).

—The Ezekiel tradition gives major expression to the redistribution of the whole land, thus appealing to the Joshua account of the allotment of the land of promise (Josh 13–19). In the Ezekiel utilization of this tradition, land is allotted for the temple (45:1-5) for the city (45:6), and for the prince (45:7-8). More extensively, the land is to be reassigned to the several tribes within the borders of "Greater Israel" (47:13–48:29). It is commonly thought that this picture of the land is a highly schematic, artificial presentation, all of which is pointed to the final statement of 48:30-35, namely, the enhancement of the city of Jerusalem, which is Yahweh's true home. This remarkable declaration of new possibility culminates with a new name for Jerusalem, "The LORD is There" (48:35). This sure promise of presence is offered as a sharp alternative to the palpable experience of absence. Thus the fissure of the exile, during which time Yahweh abandoned both city and people, is completely overcome. It is remarkable that while the traditions of Jeremiah and Ezekiel have in common their conviction about the wondrous homecoming of the exiles that Yahweh now intends, they do so in very different imagery and on very different grounds. Between them the covenantal traditions of Deuteronomy and the sacerdotal traditions of the priests provide a rich variety of images, all of which are required in order to express the buoyant faith of Israel that emerged and found bold expression while still in exile.

The third major tradition of prophetic exilic hope is in Isa 40–55, a development of the Isaiah tradition that is rooted in the Jerusalem themes of king and temple, much older than the traditions of Jeremiah or Ezekiel. It is the common view of scholars that Isa 40–55 constitutes a major literary and theological effort that is informed and propelled by the earlier portions of the book of Isaiah but is situated in 540 near the end of the exile, when the force of Babylonian authority was ended and the coming of the Persians was well visible upon the horizon. As we have seen, at the center of this eloquent poetry is reference to Cyrus the Persian (Isa 44:28; 45:1), so that this poetry is located just at the moment when Persian power, with its more hospitable colonial policy, displaces Babylon as the superpower with which to reckon. In this poetry the advent of the Persians is regarded as the vehicle of the rescue of the exilic Jews by Yahweh.

With chapter 39 of the present form of the book of Isaiah, commonly taken to be the end of "First Isaiah," we arrive at an anticipation of the Babylonian exile (39:5-7). This chapter only looks over into the exile, which will come long after King Hezekiah. According to scholarly opinion, there is a long hiatus in the book of Isaiah between chapter 39 and chapter 40, corresponding to the long hiatus between the time of Isaiah and Hezekiah in the eighth century and the exile of the sixth century. The book of Isaiah is arranged so that there is, speaking dramatically, a long, somber waiting on exile after chapter 39.

And then, abruptly, the tradition of Isaiah begins again in 40:1. It begins with a staggeringly new assertion, said to originate in the government of God, whence come the sovereign decrees that are to be implemented in the history of the world. The decree that governs the poetry of Second Isaiah and is to govern the life of Judah at the end of the exile is that Jerusalem is to be comforted (40:1-2). The long night of anguish is near an end. The basis for this "gospel tiding" of good news to Judah in exile is that Yahweh, the God of Israel, is about to come in new power and new resolve, to rescue needy Israel in exile (40:9-11). The magnificent articulation of poetry in Isa 40–55 is dominated by the claim that Yahweh is at the threshold of a new, decisive intervention in the life of the world. Yahweh will do "a new thing" in the world on behalf of Jerusalem (43:19). It becomes clear that the radically new thing is not completely discontinuous from Israel's old faith memories, for the old and the new are delicately and dialectically related. That intervention will effect the nullification of Babylonian power and, consequently, the liberation of Israel from exile. There will be permitted a joyous, exuberant, exultant homecoming of Jews to Jerusalem. As one reads this assertion, one must see it intimately linked to the geopolitical reality of the end of Babylonian power and the rise of Persian hegemony.

In this rich and elegant poetic articulation, there is a variety of images and themes that merit close attention. We will focus only upon four of them.

1. Yahweh now is to govern as the powerful sovereign of all creation, who in great power will bring all recalcitrant forces to conformity to Yahweh's own will. The poetry of Second Isaiah utilizes sweeping doxological articulations in order to assert this sovereignty. Thus the celebration of the power of the Creator evokes the wondrous assertion of Yahweh, before whom all other powers, all other gods, all political powers, are "like a drop from a bucket" (Isa 40:15). The articulation of Yahweh as the dominant world power has two particular faces in this poetry. On the one hand, it is claimed that Yahweh is stronger than all other gods. Thus in 41:21-29, the other gods are invited to a contest of strength and authority. But of course they are mute and ineffective, because they are in fact no gods and can do nothing to counter the resolve of Yahweh. Indeed the poet delights to mock and dismiss other gods who are in truth powerless, phony pretenders (44:9-20). The mocking dismissal of other gods is marvelously asserted in 46:1-7, where the other gods are human products, not generative powers, and therefore they are burdens that must be carried around (46:1). They are utterly unlike Yahweh, who is a lively, active agent who will carry and does not need to be carried (46:3-4).

But note well, while this is a generic attack on other gods, in 46:1 the gods ridiculed are named. They are Babylonian gods—Bel and Nebo. That is, they are the ostensive legitimators of Babylonian imperial power. Thus we are able to see that this dispute with other gods is not an intellectual parlor game for theologians, but has as its purpose the criticism of phony pretenders to world power. The practical aim of criticism of the gods is the criticism of political power that these gods are said to legitimate.

373

For that reason it does not surprise us that in 47:1, on the other hand, the poetry turns from criticism of the gods to a criticism of earthly power, specifically a criticism of the "virgin daughter Babylon." The claims of Babylon to legitimacy are now nullified. Moreover, Babylon is indicted for practicing arrogant autonomy that culminated in brutality, in their showing "no mercy" (47:6). Babylon is a world power that did not conduct its power according to Yahweh's criterion of mercy in public affairs. And so its power is voided. There is in this poetry a poignant philosophy of history that asserts that legitimate public power does not arise through economic or military might, but through the practice of mercy. The doxological assertion of Yahweh's authority and sovereign power serves the purpose of nullifying Babylonian power, which to the exiles must have appeared to be absolute.

2. This nullification of Babylonian power is in the service of good news to the Jewish exiles. While Yahweh's sovereign power is voiced in large, boisterous, defiant doxology, the poetry utilizes a very different tone in addressing the exiles, a tone of pastoral attentiveness and gentleness that is a perfect counterpoint to the loud doxology.

Alongside self-asserting doxology, Israel in exile is given attentive assurance. For example, in 41:8-13 Israel in exile is addressed by the lord of the exile. The address of verses 8-9 includes a collage of treasuring names for Israel, looking back all the way to Jacob and Abraham, reminding the exiles that they are the chosen and beloved of Yahweh. The actual message to this cherished creature and subject of Yahweh is succinct: "Do not fear, for I am with you" (v. 10).

The utterance of Yahweh intends to counter and defeat all the negativities of exile—the fear, danger, loss of memory and rootage, and sense of hopelessness. Now it is asserted, in the face of the long-term circumstance of abandonment, that the Jews are not abandoned by Yahweh. They are in fact the very center of God's concern and activity. Indeed, Israel in exile has been like a wife long abandoned and shamed by a husband who forsook her (54:4-8). It is not denied that husband-Yahweh has abandoned Israel to exile—but only "for a brief moment" (v. 7), only in a moment of wrath (v. 8). Now the reassuring news is that into that very exile of abandonment, Yahweh comes to forlorn Israel with "great compassion" (v. 7), with "everlasting love" (v. 8).

The outcome of this new attentiveness on the part of Yahweh is that Israel is now wrested from the power of Babylon and is free to go home. The ground for the emancipation is that Yahweh's "plan" is not like the despairing plan of Judah nor like the abusive plan of Babylon (55:8-9). For Yahweh, it is all homecoming. The exiles are now authorized to be on their way rejoicing, going out in joy, being led back in *shalom* (55:12-13), as their life begins again.

It is important to recognize that this poetry is not presented as a commentary on world events. It is, rather, the sovereign utterance of Yahweh, who is not a prisoner of circumstance. Judaism, which made this poetry into canonical scripture, took this poetry as the true and decisive utterance of Yahweh, whose purposes guided the outcome of human history. On its own, the contest between pitiful Judah and mighty Babylon was no contest. Babylon would of course dominate. And then, in this poetry, Yahweh the heavyweight enters the contest on the side of Judah, and history takes a most unexpected turn. This poetry insists that public history is not reduced to economic, political, and military power. In the end, there is another purpose, rooted in God's fidelity and holiness, that turns history in inscrutable ways.

3. It is important to notice the remarkable convergence of theological claim and geopolitical reality. What Yahweh says here is what happens. The contact point between theological claim and geopolitical specificity here is said to be Cyrus the Persian. This new world power was of course engaged in raw imperial aggression. Cyrus certainly had never heard of Yahweh nor thought at all about the Jews. And yet, according to Israel's best poetry Cyrus works out the intention of Yahweh:

> Who has roused a victor from the east,
>   summoned him to his service?
> He delivers up nations to him,
>   and tramples kings under foot;
> he makes them like dust with his sword,
>   like driven stubble with his bow.
> He pursues them and passes on safely,
>   scarcely touching the path with his feet.
> Who has performed and done this,
>   calling the generations from the beginning?
> I, the LORD, am first,
>   and will be with the last. (Isa 41:2-4)

That is, Yahweh's work is in the world. Israel's faith is not a spiritual wish-world. Yahweh's resolve is seen to be effective in the real world of public affairs, so that the word of Yahweh "becomes flesh," that is, God's purpose takes public, historical form.

By identifying Cyrus as the convergence point of theological claim and geopolitical specificity, the odd coherence of faith and life that is characteristic of Israelite faith becomes evident. It is this coherence that produced the categories out of which Christians could later make the venturesome claim that God's purposes came to be "embodied" in Jesus of Nazareth. That "embodiment" may be taken by Christians to be more intense in Jesus, but it is not the first such "embodiment," of which Cyrus is such a prize example.

4. Finally we may notice one enigmatic element in this poetry that warrants our attention. Scholars have long noticed that in several of the poems of Second Isaiah, there is reference to "Yahweh's servant," who becomes a decisive agent in Yahweh's work (42:1-4; 49:1-6; 50:4-9; 52:13–53:12). This peculiar human figure is taken to be an agent whereby Yahweh's large purposes for history take effect. It is by no means clear who this "servant" is. A long-standing conviction of Jewish interpreters sees the community of Israel as the servant, which does Yahweh's purpose in the world. We pay attention to the question because, in the history of Christian interpretation the servant, especially in the familiar poetry of 52:13–53:12, is commonly taken as an allusion to and anticipation of Jesus. There is no clear way to identify the servant. Clearly it must be recognized that the poetry and the text per se do not have Jesus in purview, so that such Christian reading is surely a belated extrapolation.

More important is the awareness, shared by Jews and Christians, that this much discussed chapter probes a fresh and radical way whereby healing, perhaps healing among exiles, may be accomplished. It is asserted that in the historical process:

> Surely he has borne our infirmities
> > and carried our diseases;
> yet we accounted him stricken,
> > struck down by God, and afflicted.
> But he was wounded for our transgressions,
> > crushed for our iniquities;
> upon him was the punishment that made us whole,
> > and by his bruises we are healed. (53:4-5)

As David Clines has observed, none of the pronouns in this poem have clear antecedents. What is clear is that the way to newness in the historical process is through suffering taken on by some for others, whether the Jewish community or Jesus. This poet has seen that such embraced suffering does indeed break the vicious cycles of alienation and permits well-being. In the end, what counts here is not the identification of the servant, but the affirmation that the vicious cycles of displacement can be broken and healing made possible—but not without cost.

The poetry of Second Isaiah takes exilic Israel, in its liturgy and in its imagination, to the threshold of homecoming. It is anticipated that returning exiles shall soon be under way in joy, en route to Jerusalem:

> Break forth together into singing,
>   you ruins of Jerusalem;
> for the LORD has comforted his people,
>   he has redeemed Jerusalem. . . .
> Depart, depart, go out from there!
>   Touch no unclean thing;
> go out from the midst of it, purify yourselves,
>   you who carry the vessels of the LORD.
> For you shall not go out in haste,
>   and you shall not go in flight;
> for the LORD will go before you,
>   and the God of Israel will be your rear guard. (52:9, 11-12)

The poet goes no further. Beyond the lyric the expectant Jews now await the sober Haggai and Zechariah to rebuild, the insistent Malachi to correct, and the quarrelsome Nehemiah and Ezra to reform. These more visible actions will count enormously in emerging Judaism. They are all made possible, however, by these poetic figures who in their imaginative faith and eloquent tongues liberate Judaism from a closed world of defeat in order to permit the new world of Yahweh's gift.

The Continuing Testimony of Suffering and Hope

It is a very long sweep from the hate of Nahum through the hurt of Jeremiah to the hope of Second Isaiah. All of these traditions, plus many others, are drawn into and shaped by the matrix of exile and homecoming. That is because the exile is the overwhelming experience of Old Testament Israel and the defining reference point for ongoing Jewish imagination. In these texts, we are not dealing with literary reflections upon a historical moment that is over and past. The crisis of the exile has remained powerfully contemporary in the life of faith, and therefore continued grappling with this theological literature is urgent.

Israel discerned in this crisis and through this literature the truth that Israel shares life with a God who could not be presumed upon, but who in freedom would abandon those who presumed too much. This disclosure of God came to Israel through a profound moment of loss. Further, Israel discerned in this crisis that it is precisely in loss where this God may be astonishingly generative of new historical possibility, a willingness of God to create "a way out of no way." This disclosure of God came to Israel through a buoyant possibility of homecoming. The truth of abandonment by God and generative possibility from God emerge as the defining characteristics of a Jewish spirituality of candor in suffering and buoyancy of hope. Here we may suggest that this thematization evokes at least four lines for continued reflection.

1. The exilic themes of loss and possibility reference Jewish piety and spirituality as expressed in the book of Psalms. The Psalter is dominated by songs of lamentation and complaint and hymns of praise and thanks. Lament and praise are the most characteristic modes of transaction with this God, and they voice the extremities of faith and of life. Lament brings to speech the sense of loss that is focused in exile. Praise makes utterance available about the possibilities that are formed in homecoming.

2. The themes of loss and possibility are key reference points for Christian faith, which focuses upon the Friday death of Jesus and the Sunday of Jesus' new life. It seems plausible that the Friday-Sunday matrix of Christian faith is possible because in those deep days, Christian faith reiterates, albeit with its own intensity, the most profound loss imaginable and the most wondrous possibility that is thinkable. Indeed the Friday-Sunday paradigm is a Christian way of reengaging this demanding Jewish narrative.[3]

3. The thematics of loss and possibility provide perhaps the most helpful categories for thinking theologically about the Jewish Holocaust. To be sure, that scandalous happening finally defies all

explanatory categories, as Richard Rubenstein has said so well. Nonetheless, faithful people must think as they can in their traditions. It is this tradition of exile and homecoming that affirms that at the depth of the most ignoble loss, the Holy One of Israel may generate new life in the world. One must not trivialize the density, complexity, or quality of evil in the Holocaust. It is possible, nonetheless, to see in the Holocaust a recurrence of the God-crisis Israel has known for so long.

4. The modern world, with its technological commitment to consumer-militarism, is a mode of life that systemically produces exiles. In our time we witness the production of an endless parade of displaced persons—unwelcome immigrants, fugitives, refugees, and a permanent underclass. These social rejects are not the accidents of a commodity-driven society but an inevitable outcome. This "modern" account of reality concerns a conviction that there are no deep, God-caused losses that cannot be avoided. The parallel conviction is that there are no new possibilities beyond human, technical competence. That is, this is a tale of reality that has no place for suffering or for hope, both of which are programmatically excluded from the horizon of the modern world. And where suffering and hope are denied, exiles abound.

Contemporary readers of the Bible, at the edge of failed modernity, may notice that this biblical account of suffering and hope, which happens in concrete history but which pivots around a holy God, is an alternative to the suffering-denying, hope-excluding tale of modernity. Situated as we are, between these two compelling, irreconcilable accounts of reality, we may notice that given lived reality, Israel's account can make a claim as being "a more excellent way." Notice in the tension between these two accounts what a different social reality is possible in the biblical account, a different social reality that accepts at its center the God

who comes with might,
who gathers the lambs in his bosom.
   (Isa 40:10-11, author's paraphrase)

Notes

1. A. Mintz, *Hurban: Responses to Catastrophe in Hebrew Literature* (Columbia University Press, 1984), x.

2. On this psalm, see D. Blumenthal, *Facing the Abusing God: A Theology of Protest* (Louisville: Westminster John Knox, 1993), 85-110.

3. See G. Steiner, *Real Presences* (Chicago: University of Chicago Press, 1989), 231-32; and N. T. Wright, *The New Testament and the People of God* (Minneapolis: Fortress, 1992), 396-403.

Bibliography

Ackroyd, Peter R. *Exile and Restoration: A Study of Hebrew Thought of the Sixth Century B.C.* OTL. Philadelphia: Westminster, 1968.

Brueggemann, Walter. *A Commentary on Jeremiah: Exile and Homecoming.* Grand Rapids: Eerdmans, 1998.

―――. "Always in the Shadow of the Empire." In *The Church as Counterculture,* edited by Michal L. Budde and Robert W. Brimlow. Albany: State University of New York Press, 2000.

Klein, Ralph W. *Ezekiel: The Prophet and His Message.* Columbia: University of South Carolina Press, 1988.

―――. *Israel in Exile: A Theological Interpretation.* OBT 6. Philadelphia: Fortress, 1979.

Raitt, Thomas M. *A Theology of Exile: Judgment/Deliverance in Jeremiah and Ezekiel.* Philadelphia: Fortress, 1977.

Rubenstein, Richard. *After Auschwitz: Theology and Contemporary Judaism.* Second edition. Baltimore: Johns Hopkins University Press, 1992.

―――. "Job and Auschwitz." *Union Seminary Quarterly Review* 25. New York: Union Theological Seminary. Summer 1970 (pp. 421–37).

Smith, Daniel L. *The Religion of the Landless: The Social Context of the Babylonian Exile.* Bloomington, Ind.: Meyer-Stone, 1989.

Smith-Christopher, Daniel. *A Biblical Theology of Exile.* OBT. Minneapolis: Fortress, 2002.

Stevenson, Kalinda Rose. *The Vision of Transformation: The Territorial Rhetoric of Ezekiel 40–48.* SBLDS 154. Atlanta: Scholars Press, 1996.

Weems, Renita J. *Battered Love: Marriage, Sex, and Violence in the Hebrew Prophets.* Minneapolis: Fortress, 1995.

Westermann, Claus. *Lamentations: Issues and Interpretation.* Minneapolis: Fortress, 1994.

CHAPTER ELEVEN

WISDOM, ORDER, PROTEST

Proverbs, Job, Ecclesiastes, Selected Psalms

A careful reader of this book thus far will have noticed that our discussion has been roughly organized in a chronological way. That is, we have moved from the earliest memories of ancient Israel through the course of its history with all of its vagaries and crises. Indeed, chronology is one of the easiest, most accessible ways to acquire an overview of the Old Testament, even if that chronology is loaded with uncertainties.

Israel's self-understanding as a people engaged in the historical process operates on two very large assumptions. First, it is assumed that what happens socially, politically, economically, and militarily is the real stuff of life and the real agenda of faith. Israel knows that it lives in the real world. A student of the Old Testament, for that reason, must know about these worldly matters in some detail. This includes the course of Israel's own history as it is traced and interpreted in Israel's "historical books." It also includes knowledge about and reference to the larger history of the Fertile Crescent, with special attention to a series of formidable imperial superpowers.

Second, it is assumed in Israel that Yahweh, the God of Israel, is decisively at work in the historical processes of the world. God is deeply involved in the "rise and fall" of great powers. By its use of prophetic oracle and doxological celebration, Israel held together the *realities of public life and public power* and *the reality of God in its midst.* Israel refused to understand its political, historical existence *apart from God* and it refused, with equal passion, to imagine God *apart from the experience of its own public existence.*

The Horizon of Wisdom Teaching

In this chapter, however, our purpose is to consider literature in the Old Testament that is not a part of the nexus of "history and God." It now seems clear that along with faith as a "story line," there is another mode of faith in ancient Israel that operated in quite different interpretive categories and that proceeded with its own modes of discourse and reflection. This alternative mode of faith and discourse is referred to by the large, inexact term *wisdom* and eventuated in three "wisdom books" in the Old Testament: Proverbs, Job, and Ecclesiastes. (In the larger Greek canon, also included as wisdom books are Ecclesiasticus and Wisdom of Solomon.) The work of this chapter is to consider how this *alternative form of faith* operates and to recognize that its presence in the literature of the Bible attests to the theological pluralism of the Bible.

The category of *wisdom* is broad and imprecise, and in general refers in Old Testament studies to that literature that stands outside the primary flow of both historical narrative and law. We may identify five facets of this literature that are recurring and characteristic.

1. Wisdom literature is a reflection upon *lived experience* of quite mundane kinds. Whereas "historical faith" tended to focus on great public crises and transformations (like the Exodus, the entry into the land, and the exile), wisdom focuses on the daily routines of human interaction, and asks about the meaning and social significance of such matters as speech, money, friendship, work, sexuality, and land. It takes such matters with great seriousness and recognizes that the right use and enjoyment of these daily realities is the real stuff of human life.

2. Wisdom literature insists that each of these mundane matters is shot through with *ethical significance and ethical outcomes,* so that wise living consists in respecting the "givens" of daily life in making responsible choices about daily existence and in anticipating the consequences of those choices. The wisdom teachers recognize that life is a delicately balanced network of givens, choices, and consequences and that one cannot outflank or escape the requirements, disciplines, and demands of that dailiness of life. This simple calculus is succinctly expressed, "What you sow, you shall surely reap" (cf. Gal 6:7). One cannot move outside these systemic moral categories.

Nobody is exempt from lived reality, and so the wisdom teachers think long about being "wicked or righteous," being "wise or foolish."

3. Wisdom activity is the activity of *speech*. The wisdom books of the Old Testament are not simply inventories of experience but are *reflections and interpretations* of experience that are crafted in artistic speech that intends to be compelling and persuasive. That is, the wisdom teachers want to communicate to the young—those still to be inducted into the lore of the community—its distinctive sense of how life is to be lived well. In the interest of such persuasive communication, this artistic, carefully crafted speech engages in many rhetorical strategies that negotiate what is hidden and what is voiced. It is a way of speech that teases and invites playfulness, that utilizes images, metaphors, and figures of speech to suggest the large significance of daily options. This artistic speech seeks to communicate about experience what is not flatly and obviously available but is given only to the discerning who are patient enough to reflect, to notice recurring patterns, to pay attention to odd exceptions. Speech serves to discern lived experience shrewdly, knowingly, responsibly, faithfully.

4. Wisdom reflection is indeed *an intellectual enterprise*. Those who undertake it have a deep, trusting curiosity about how things work and a patience to observe that matches their curiosity. While their methods and modes of knowing do not correspond to modern science, it is fair to say that the wisdom teachers approximate a scientific understanding of reality. That is, they observe the orderly patterns of reality on the assumption of the constancy and reliability of reality. On the basis of their observations over time, they are able to make predictions about social integration. Thus, for example, people who act foolishly will lose their money. People who forgive make friends, but those who hold grudges do not. The teachers have seen the patterns over a long period of observation.

The intellectual activity of wisdom consists in a venturesome capacity to hold together observed experience, acknowledged ethical claims, and persuasive, winsome speech. It is no wonder that some scholars believe that the wisdom teachers were a recognizable social force marked by some qualities of elitism. Wisdom teaching is not simply common sense but is *studied reflective judgment about reality* that provides reliable lore transmitted to the next generation about how to live well, safely, responsibly, and happily. It has been suggested that in our time, folk like Ann Landers and Dr. Laura provide something like wisdom instruction, a reliable body of counsel to guide and assist present decision-making.

5. Wisdom teaching is *theological literature,* that is, it witnesses to Yahweh and Yahweh's large purposes for the world. It has been suggested that "early wisdom" in Israel was "secular," that is, not linked to God. In that ancient world, however, such "secular" thinking was surely not possible. What the wisdom teachers observe and reflect upon is a world order that is willed, governed, and sustained by Yahweh.

More specifically, it is widely recognized that wisdom theology is a "theology of creation," that is, a reflection of faith upon the world intended by the Creator. It is clear that the Creator God intends that the world should be whole, safe, prosperous, peaceable, just, fruitful, and productive, that is, that the world should be marked in every part by *shalom.* To that end, the Creator has given rich gifts of well-being. In the same way, the Creator God has set limits and built into creation rewards and punishments that are evoked and set in motion by wise or foolish actions. But these limits are not self-evident. They must be discerned over a long period of time by the study of many "cases," in order to notice what actions produce well-being and what actions produce trouble. The premise of all such observations and generalizations is that the large matrix of life and well-being is the creation of God. The Creator God has willed that all parts of creation are delicately related to one another, and therefore every decision, every act matters to the shape and well-being of the whole.

It is for that reason that Prov 1:7 may be taken as a motto for wisdom instruction:

> The fear of the LORD is the beginning of knowledge;
>   fools despise wisdom and instruction.

Serious recognition of Yahweh the Creator is the focal point for all true understanding of reality. Disregard of the will and purpose of the Creator will surely invite foolish behavior that contains within itself the seeds of destructiveness given as consequence.

As the student works through this chapter, we hope he or she will be dazzled and astonished at the intellectual-moral-rhetorical-theological achievement of wisdom. Note well that this theological perspective contains almost none of the "code words" commonly associated with biblical faith—nothing here of covenant or commandment, of cult or history, of miracle or exile, and certainly nothing that conventional, clichéd Christianity regards as biblical. We are here at a form of faith that is open to the world, that eschews authoritarianism, that has no interest in guilt, but that believes life in God's world is a way of faith to be celebrated. It is not surprising that for some who have been wounded by conventional forms of authoritarian faith, the teaching of wisdom is found to be an adequate alternative way to responsible life and joyous communion with God.

Common Sense Permeated by God's Holy Will

The book of Proverbs is the quintessential wisdom teaching in the Old Testament. The book of Proverbs, in its final form, is a rich, complex collection of wisdom sayings that range from very practical commonsense advice to lyrical, speculative, doxological assertions about mystery at the core of life. Obviously, *commonsense advice* and *celebration of mystery* are at a considerable distance from each other. It seems clear, nonetheless, that the entire spectrum of wisdom teaching in the book of Proverbs has a shared agenda, namely, to think, speak, and live in the world according to the given, demanding mystery of God the Creator.

The core unit of the book of Proverbs is the proverbial saying that is characteristically one or two lines long. Such proverbial sayings, when we are overly familiar with them, seem rather flat and obvious. Upon reflection, however, we will notice that the proverbial sayings often contain a shrewd presentation of something poignant but hidden that is true across many different experiences.

It is most likely that the proverbial sayings arise in the context of a family, clan, or tribe in which older members are constantly occupied with socializing the young into a set of assumptions, attitudes, and behaviors to assert, "This is how it is; this is how we do it." It is conventional in scholarship to say that proverbs, at the most elemental level, are expressed in two forms. One form is the more didactic mode of instruction, usually negative, that says to the young, "Thou shalt not." Every family or primary community has a consensus about attitudes and behaviors that are prohibited to all members and certainly to the young. Characteristically the prohibition in wisdom modes is simply asserted. No reason is given and no explicit punishment is stated for cases of violation, because the tone entertains no possibility of violation. The prohibition is a trusted truth of the community. It is widely accepted as necessary to the safety and well-being of the community, and the young are expected to comply. We may consider only one example. In Prov 22:28, it is asserted:

> Do not remove the ancient landmark
> that your ancestors set up.

That is all. No explanation, no sanction, no threat for violation. Presumably the community had learned (the hard way?) that moving land boundaries, either by stealth or by force or by shrewd legal, cunning maneuver, is destructive to the community. For that reason, the young are taught early to respect property arrangements. In 23:10-11, the same concern is presented more elaborately with a distinct emphasis:

> Do not remove an ancient landmark
> or encroach on the fields of orphans,
> for their redeemer is strong;
> he will plead their cause against you.

In this version of the instruction, the basic prohibition in the first line is made specific in the second line. Now it is clear that it is the property of the socially vulnerable orphan that is protected. The last two lines, moreover, suggest a sanction. "Their redeemer" likely does not refer to God but to a powerful kinsman who will go to court on behalf of the orphan. That is, there are heavy social risks to upsetting property arrangements. And the young are taught early not to do it. Notice that the "do not" is spoken with considerable authority, but that authority is not identified. The actual speaker may be a respected elder in the community. In substance, however, it is *the community* that speaks, enforcing its socioethical norm upon the listener in order to maintain equilibrium in the community.

The second form of proverb, called by scholars simply a *saying* or a *sentence*, is much more artistically voiced. And there are many more of them in the book of Proverbs that seem to arise from folk art. These are apparently the trusted, time-tested aphorisms of a community, designed to shape and govern social transactions. We ourselves are familiar with such sayings artistically wrought:

A bird in the hand is worth two in the bush.
Don't look a gift horse in the mouth.
Still water runs deep.
A stitch in time saves nine.
A penny saved is a penny earned.

In these utterances the community provides for the (young) listener an entire social code for acceptable attitude and behavior. Any reader of this book can multiply such sayings out of his or her own experience in a family community. We may identify several rhetorical strategies in the book of Proverbs for such sayings. One such accustomed pattern of speech is "better sayings," in which the teacher asserts that one option is "better" than another:

Better is a dinner of vegetables where love is
    than a fatted ox and hatred with it. (15:17)

Better is a dry morsel with quiet
    than a house full of feasting with strife. (17:1)

Better the poor walking in integrity
    than one perverse of speech who is a fool. (19:1)

Do not put yourself forward in the king's presence
    or stand in the place of the great;
for it is better to be told, "Come up here,"
    than to be put lower in the presence of a noble. (25:6-7)

Notice that the sayings do not tell *why* something is better than something else, or in what way better. But one can notice, with some reflection, that in a group of such sayings a certain code of behavior and a certain theory of social relationships are fostered that are on the side of modesty, tranquillity, and conformity. In sum, it is *better* not to rock the boat or call excessive attention to oneself.

A second rhetorical strategy is to make comparisons, so that "this" is like "that":

387

A word fitly spoken
   is like apples of gold in a setting of silver.
Like a gold ring or an ornament of gold
   is a wise rebuke to a listening ear.
Like the cold of snow in the time of harvest
   are faithful messengers to those who send them;
   they refresh the spirit of their masters.
Like clouds and wind without rain
   is one who boasts of a gift never given. . . .
Like a war club, a sword, or a sharp arrow
   is one who bears false witness against a neighbor.
Like a bad tooth or a lame foot
   is trust in a faithless person in time of trouble.
Like vinegar on a wound
   is one who sings songs to a heavy heart. (25:11-14, 18-20)

The teaching does not tell in what way "this" is like "that," but invites the hearer to complete the connection. Notice the pedagogic awareness that it is preferable to let the hearer reason out something that is implied. That is, these sentences are offered without any heavy, authoritarian insistence. It is as though the proverbs are invitations to reflection, in which the listener is expected to make connections toward which only hints are supplied. The strategy of comparison is subsequently employed by Jesus in his "kingdom" teachings, wherein "The kingdom of heaven is like . . ." (see, e.g., Matt 13:24, 31, 33, 44, 45, 47). One notices in these "like statements" the close attention to detail. These teachers clearly believed that the delicacy of creation brought the Creator's large vision to bear upon the most intimate dailiness of life.

A third pedagogic strategy consists in making lists and numbering them. This apparently is what happens in such texts as 30:15*b*-16, 18-19, 21-23:

Three things are never satisfied;
   four never say, "Enough":
Sheol, the barren womb,
   the earth ever thirsty for water,
   and the fire that never says, "Enough." . . .
Three things are too wonderful for me;
   four I do not understand:

the way of an eagle in the sky,
   the way of a snake on a rock,
the way of a ship on the high seas,
   and the way of a man with a girl. . . .
Under three things the earth trembles;
   under four it cannot bear up:
a slave when he becomes king,
   and a fool when glutted with food;
an unloved woman when she gets a husband,
   and a maid when she succeeds her mistress.

In each of these sequences, the teacher names four things that are quite unlike, except in the one aspect noticed. Thus in verses 15b-16, the thing never satisfied is fire. In verses 18-19, the thing most puzzling is how a man (in love) acts with a girl, more puzzling indeed than how an eagle flies or a snake moves. These rather remarkable inventories serve the purpose of inviting wonder about experience right at hand, of turning familiar experience by setting it in a new context and thereby causing it to be seen afresh in ways never seen before. The wisdom teachers are clearly alive to reality immediately available, insisting that even the ordinary needs to be pondered, because when noticed afresh it is indeed quite extraordinary.

In the fully developed wisdom discourse, perhaps the latest and the most self-conscious, there are also longer speeches or discourses that sustain a theme well beyond the simple true love proverb. These longer poems permit a more fully developed theological exposition that characteristically links Israel's faith to its lived experience.

The artistry of such articulation carries with it an authority all its own. It is evident that wisdom teachers never say, like prophets, "Thus saith the LORD." The sentences, moreover, do not even carry the tone of authority evident in the didactic prohibitions. The authority of these sayings is of another sort. To be sure, it is the gravitas of the community speaking that could not be taken lightly in a traditional society. But beyond that, the authority of the sayings depends upon the utterance ringing true to the experience of the listener. The authority of such wisdom teaching relies upon the authority of the utterance, an authority finally measured by the hearer.

This is not to suggest, however, that the wisdom teacher is democratic or intends the saying to be voted upon. It is an agency of socialization that asserts, before the listener is old enough or nervy enough to question, "This is how things work. This is how we do things. This is how things are." This process of socialization has been well described by Peter Berger and Thomas Luckmann.[1] They nicely characterize the process by which the "social world" of a community is externalized in teaching and then internalized by the young as a given that is to be appropriated and assumed and never questioned. The wisdom teachers, appropriately, "construct reality" not in large doses but one item at a time.

The accumulation of such interpretations of experience over time adds up to a reliable context for understanding and situating one's life. The "world" given in these teachings is a safe, settled world, perhaps agrarian, except that there is, in some sayings, the horizon of "the king" (Prov 16:10, 12-15; 20:2; 25:2). The world thus constructed and uttered is one of social equilibrium into which the young are expected to fit. The offer of such stability, moreover, spills over into social control, requiring that the young share this world if they are to share in its benefits.

While we can identify efforts at social equilibrium and social control, however, we remain mindful that creation theology is operative in these teachings, so that at its best, the world thus advocated is the world willed and intended by Yahweh. At times, there can hardly be any doubt that *the world willed by Yahweh* is equated with *the world in which we have advantage,* so that creation theology is confiscated and reshaped as self-serving ideology. No doubt this is a temptation for every socializing community. At the same time, however, we notice that *creation theology* acts as a check upon *ideological advantage.* Thus for example:

> It is better to be of a lowly spirit among the poor
> than to divide the spoil with the proud. (16:19)

> One who is slow to anger is better than the mighty,
> and one whose temper is controlled than one
> who captures a city. (16:32)

> Better is a dry morsel with quiet
> than a house full of feasting with strife. (17:1)

The "better" in each of these cases is consummately countercultural, suggesting that there are enduring human values, guaranteed by the Creator, that need to be valued more than self-advancement and quick personal advantage.

The collage of many proverbs in the book of Proverbs produces a *theodicy* for the community. The term *theodicy* refers to the insistence that God is just and good even when there are suffering and injustice in the world. The community in these sayings reaches a consensus about the distribution of pain and pleasure, need and comfort. That is, the book of Proverbs slowly sorts out who is entitled to what. The wise and the righteous are entitled to security and happiness; the wicked and the foolish are entitled to poverty and misery. The community works as long as this calculus of what each may expect and each must bear is generally accepted by all.

It is the socializing work of Proverbs to promote, sustain, and ensure such a general consensus and to ensure that the young of the community subscribe to this theodicy in positive ways. Something like this same theodicy is voiced in our own time by upwardly mobile middle-class people who tell our children, "Study hard so you get into a good college. Study hard in college so you can get a good job. Work hard at your good job to get a better job, to ensure a good retirement with a good health plan." Such instruction is a theodicy that assures that it is just and right and good (= willed by the Creator) that social goods rightly are merited and justified by the hardworking, deserving middle class. Such a theodicy is not far removed from the social perspective of Proverbs, though there the matter is stated more artistically and with more theological intentionality. The proverbs are not entertainment, even if cleverly put, nor are they idle, incidental chatter. They are serious, sustained advocacy, rooted in faith but with a pragmatic eye on the concrete future.

The Royal, Scribal Function

It is likely that many proverbs of the sort we have cited originated in familial communities. Scholars regard this point of origin as a "folk" setting, that is, relatively unreflective people commenting in discerning ways about the patterns of conduct and life that they are able to observe. It is likely that such sayings originated ad hoc and that they circulated in communities on a free-floating basis.

What we have in the book of Proverbs, however, is not a set of free-floating, ad hoc sayings. It is clear that these proverbs, from whatever sources, have now been collected and grouped into stable, intentional collections in order to create a durable body of interpretation and reflection. It is clear, moreover, that the process of collecting and editing is not the work of "relatively unreflective folk," but more likely is the achievement of a quite intentional intellectual community. Thus the initial utterance of proverbs and the collection of proverbs into intentional bodies of material are likely quite separate projects, undertaken by distinct groups of people in different contexts for different purposes.

It is conventional to identify in the book of Proverbs collections introduced and formed as distinct entities, as outlined in the following list. The student may want to notice especially the introductory formula for each collection:

—Proverbs 1–9, commonly thought to be the most sophisticated theological material in the book, perhaps closely connected to Egyptian modes of instruction and perhaps the latest among the collections;

—Proverbs 10:1–22:16, a collection of proverbial sayings ascribed to Solomon (see also 1:1 for a Solomonic assignation);

—Proverbs 22:17–24:22, ascribed only to "the wise," but with exceedingly close parallels to an earlier Egyptian collection, evidencing that Israelite wisdom teaching was situated in an international enterprise of such instruction and that this text may have been appropriated wholesale from Egyptian antecedents;

—Proverbs 25–29, a collection ascribed to Solomon but copied by officials of the regime of King Hezekiah;

—Proverbs 30:1-9, a collection credited to Agur;

—Proverbs 30:10-33, a collection without ascription;

—Proverbs 31:1-9, a collection ascribed to Lemuel;

—Proverbs 31:10-31, a collection without ascription, devoted to a model woman.

What becomes clear in such a review is that Proverbs is a collection of collections, not at all one piece, but instead made up of quite distinct elements. Several observations arise from this review. First, wisdom in the biblical book of Proverbs is part of an international project. The links to Egypt are transparent. We know both that Egypt had a considerable wisdom enterprise and that Egypt was heavily influential in royal Judah. Specifically it is often noted that Prov 22:17–24:22 is intimately linked to and likely derived from the Egyptian Instruction of Amenemope. The names of Agur and Lemuel clearly allude to non-Israelites in a larger wisdom tradition. This internationalism and its evident appeal to creation theology show a way of biblical faith that is removed from conventional Israelite categories. This material thus stands at a distance from the redemption-election traditions featured, for example, in the book of Deuteronomy. But for all of that, it is no less biblical.

Second, the process of collection is apparently under royal patronage. Both 10:1 and 25:1 make connections to Solomon, who is the quintessential wise person in the Old Testament. (Thus we are told of Solomon's patronage of wisdom learning in 1 Kgs 4:29-34.) The books of Ecclesiastes and Song of Solomon, moreover, are canonically credited to him. On the whole, critical scholars do not take the Solomonic connection to wisdom with historical serious-ness but do regard Solomon as an important interpretive cipher used to situate this material in royal, internationalist, accommoda-tionist Israel. By contrast, the connection of wisdom to Hezekiah in the eighth century in 25:1 is taken by scholars to be more reliable historically. Hezekiah's reign at the end of the eighth century was remarkably generative in the reform and revival of the Judean state. Thus it is not implausible that a codification of wisdom instruction took place under Hezekiah as a means of recovering what was allegedly remembered as the splendor of Solomon. In appealing to Hezekiah, we are of course a long remove from "folk art" and now deal with the work of paid, professional intellectuals.

Third, it is clear that Hezekiah and other kings like him—includ-ing Solomon if that connection is historical—were essentially patrons of the wisdom enterprise and not themselves practitioners. That is, the wisdom teaching attached to royalty was something like a professional responsibility that required learning and leisure, not likely the forte of kings. Thus we may propose that the collection of wisdom teaching was done by functionaries of the king whom we may describe as *scribes,* though other scholars sometimes use the word *sage.* The scribes are learned men (likely all men) who specialized in writing—a rare talent in ancient times—who gathered and consolidated the learning and the lore of the realm.

If we ask about the motivation and interest of such scribal activity, we may perhaps suggest three possible motivations that resulted in the collections. First, if we assume that these scribes had in their number genuine intellectuals driven by a profound curiosity about the world, we may imagine that there was an intrinsic interest in such collections, much as scholars in the contemporary world carry on research for the sake of research, for the love of learning, and the joy of amassing fresh data. Second and more obviously, we may imagine such scribes to be on the payroll in order to enhance the king and to add to the prestige of the regime. In the eighteenth and nineteenth centuries the several universities in Germany were sponsored by princes who delighted in their prestigious scholars and who took great pride in new learning. Given the international scope of such wisdom activity, it is entirely plausible that Israelite kings, when their energies were not drained off in war, put energy and resources into the wisdom enterprise as a way of self-aggrandizement.

Third, it is likely that such collection, consolidation, and organization also had practical functions. It was necessary for the royal enterprise to inculcate its own members into a manner and style befitting high office. For that reason, the scribes may have been managers of the socialization process whereby persons are nurtured in the arts of governance, in the management of resources, in the honoring of protocols that maintain privilege, in all those social arts appropriate to class. It is not at all clear that there were schools sponsored by the throne. If there were, the purpose of such schools would be socialization into the virtues of power and the scribes would be the teachers. If there were not such formal arrangements as schools, it is reasonable to assume such nurture and socialization on an informal basis. In any case, we may anticipate that the scribes, as the learned attendants of the king, exercised great influence.

That influence was further enhanced by the destruction of public institutions in Jerusalem in 587. When the king was deposed, the leadership gap required others to act in the place of the king. Among those who did so were scribes. Indeed, it may be suggested that by the fifth century, Judean society had become largely a scribal society. In parallel fashion, with the destruction of the temple, it appears that some liturgic functions were transformed into instructional functions, so that the scribes specialized in Torah instruction.

This scribal development in the public life of Judah placed a great value on scribal activity and upon the wisdom materials in which they specialized. For that reason, it is plausible to conclude, as much scholarship has done, that the actual work of the collection and the development of collections of proverbs into the book of Proverbs is a late, post-exilic achievement, perhaps as late as the fourth century. Such a dating, however, reflects only the culmination of a long process. It is likely that wisdom material, as a mode of interpretation and as a practice of theology, reaches back into family lore but culminates in the completed canonical book. Over all that time, Israel participated in the international interpretive act of wisdom, without appealing to Israel's distinctive theological categories. In Israel as in other wisdom communities, life in Yahweh's world is due cause for celebration. But such celebration is marked by attentiveness of a quite pragmatic kind, paying attention to the requirements of wisdom and the witness of "wise behavior."

Wisdom reflection, an alternative mode of theology in the Old Testament, tends to develop in two distinct directions that we will term *pragmatic* and *doxological*, both of which issue in proposals for theodicy.

The *pragmatic* development of wisdom reflection is to offer a model of ethical behavior that produces good for the community (and for the individual as a member of the community) because conduct resonates with the givens, gifts, and limits set by the Creator. Characteristically, Israel's wisdom is practical and not theoretical. We may cite two psalms (which could as easily be chapters in the book of Proverbs) that are clearly wisdom models. Both psalms, as it happens, are acrostic. That is, the first line begins with A (*'aleph*), the second with B (*beth*), and so on, suggesting symmetry, coherence, and completeness.

In Ps 37, the speaker "wanders through the alphabet" to teach behavior that will produce well-being, tranquillity, and prosperity. The listener is enjoined to eschew worry and envy (v. 1), anger (v. 8), violence and exploitation of the poor (v. 14), debt (v. 21), and oppression (v. 35). Positively the listener is urged to trust and delight in Yahweh (vv. 3-4), meekness (v. 11), blamelessness (v. 18), generosity (vv. 21, 26), justice (v. 28), righteousness (vv. 28-29), and just speech (v. 30). The consequence of a just, wise, righteous life is prosperity in the land (vv. 9, 11, 22, 29, 34), that is, a stable, prosperous, comfortable life in a settled community of well-being. The psalm witnesses both to the prudential concern of wisdom, that is, how to succeed, and to a deep sense of the ethical requirements of community that must be taken seriously because they are rooted in the purposes of Yahweh. What emerges is the model of a contributing member of the community who cares about the neighborhood in generous, active, intentional ways. It is *the enhancement of the neighborhood* that is the substance of righteousness and wisdom, which bring stability and prosperity. Conversely it is selfish, unthinking exploitation, and enhancement of self that constitute foolishness and wickedness, which bring misery and disorder to one and all.

The same model of *contributing humanness* is urged in the wisdom teaching of Ps 112. The responsible member of the community, the one sketched out here, is one who fears Yahweh (see Prov 1:7) and obeys the commandments (v. 1), who acts in ways gracious, merciful, and righteous (v. 4), practices generosity and justice (v. 5), and cares actively about the poor (v. 9). Such persons are richly blessed. They become influential, wealthy landowners (vv. 2-3), live in confidence and well-being without fear or anxiety (vv. 6-8), and are honored in the community (v. 9). As in Ps 37, so here also they invest generously and intentionally in the community; their effort produces a community of ordered existence from which they benefit greatly. The work of wisdom is to discern the kinds of action that will produce positive consequences of well-being. In a quite practical way, this tradition has concluded that *contributing neighborliness,* willed by the Creator, produces societal well-being. Conversely, the wicked neglect the community and therefore inevitably produce a conflictual society in which none are safe or finally prosperous.

The wisdom teachers do indeed engage in practical ethics. That is the primary work of the book of Proverbs. And they believe that one needs no "special revelation" or disclosure from Mt. Sinai to have adequate guidance. One can see what needs to be seen in the ongoing life of the community if one is attentive and discerning. But because the wisdom tradition is not merely pragmatic but wants to discern to the bottom of reality, the reflections of the tradition are not only practical but also seek to probe into the inscrutability of God's creation. We have termed this intellectual activity *doxological*, because the further this "science" of reality ventures, the more it ends in awe, wonder, and praise of the Creator.

In this regard Prov 8:22-31 may be taken to be the most awesome and venturesome theological articulation in the wisdom teaching. These verses are commonly regarded as a peculiarly important theological assertion, and special attention must be paid to them. In these verses it is clear that wisdom is not simply pragmatic discernment, but wisdom is a principle, a force, and an agent in the operation of creation. Here "wisdom" speaks as a dramatic voice, most probably a feminine voice.

The feminine figure of Wisdom is important in the book of Proverbs itself, and exceedingly important in contemporary interpretation. Because Wisdom as a feminine figure is said to be most intimately allied with God the Creator, the image has provided grounds for a feminist hermeneutic concerning a feminist dimension of God.

In a more critical vein, two important interpretations have been made of "the wise woman" and the counterpoint of "the woman of folly." Claudia Camp has explored the way in which the woman of folly —the strange woman—is perceived as a threat in Israel and so is condemned and excluded. The woman of foolishness becomes a metaphor for Israelite life that departs from the good order of the normative community of Torah. Conversely, the wise woman becomes a cipher for the maintenance of what is normative, a notion that is both theological and pragmatic. Thus the two women function as signals for social power and the management of social interpretation.

Christine Yoder alternatively has focused on the prudent woman in Prov 31:10-31 and has shown that the matter of concern for this woman is an economic one. The wise woman is one who manages public affairs well and so assures that her male partner can be comfortably sustained in a good economic situation. Yoder moves from 31:10-31 to the "wise woman" in Prov 1–9 to show how this concern for a good life makes a connection between wisdom and economics (Prov 4:7-9; 5:1-14; 7:10-27; 9:13-18).

It is evident in both Camp and Yoder that the image of the wise woman is enmeshed in issues of social power and does not yield an innocent feminist possibility for interpretation.

In Prov 8:22-31, wisdom asserts that creation is not raw power or the work of a rugged sovereign God, for along with power, there is sense, coherence, order, and beauty to God's creation. The claim of this "voice of wisdom" is that wisdom—sensible, life-producing coherence—is intrinsic to reality. Thus "before the beginning of the earth" (v. 23), before creation, wisdom was allied with the power of God. Wisdom was there before the depths, before the mountains, before the hills, before the earth and the fields, before the heavens, before the skies, before the sea (vv. 23-29). Wisdom is God's first ally, first assistant, first friend, and accomplice in the grand work of creation.

This lyrical statement, which must be left as lyric and not "decoded" into practical explanation, makes an important assertion about God; God is aesthetically sensitive and intends creation to be a place of lovely order. It also makes an important statement about the world, that the world is intrinsically, in its deepest fabric, designed and ordered to produce life. If one has life in created reality, one cannot escape or move outside this defining character that is both aesthetic and ethical.

This lyrical statement, in the end, turns to ethical import (vv. 32-36). One is happy, prosperous, and safe if attuned to the wisdom structures of creation, that is, attuned to the fabric of creation (vv. 34-35). To live life against the fabric of creation is to injure self and bring death (v. 36). Thus the choice of righteous/wicked, wise/foolish, life/death, is not an imposition of demanding duties. It is a given in the very functioning of reality. And even if one does not like the insistence of wisdom teachers, one must pay attention because the requirements are elemental and inescapable. One cannot by wealth, power, or knowledge outflank the requirements that are built in from day one. This is a lesson powerful people in the ancient world characteristically learned the hard way; and in our own technically advanced world, it is endlessly seductive to imagine one can move outside these old-fashioned requirements. This text is a quintessential reminder to the contrary. Public ethics is not a cranky human proposal. It is an insistence ordained from the outset. It will not yield to or be overcome by any human inventiveness. This is an ancient insistence, as ancient as creation itself, always again to be learned. Creation is ordered in uncompromising ways. To imagine that it is play-dough to be shaped as one wishes is a most destructive foolishness.

The wisdom teachers believe that (a) experience teaches us about reality, (b) reality is ethically ordered, and (c) ethical order is rooted in the purposes of God. The sum of this teaching is the articulation of a *theodicy*, whereby the rewards and punishments of reality are seen as appropriate and uncompromising consequences of actions taken and choices made. That is, the world has a good order guaranteed by God, and that order of responsible conduct must be taken seriously. In the end, the wisdom teachers reject moral relativism, even as they recognize that the precise discernment of that good order is an elusive and ongoing task. In the end, they teach that the world is a given—given by God the Creator—with which we must come to terms.

Theodicy as justification of a social system is a tricky matter, because the proponents of theodicy are never neutral, disinterested voices, but are characteristically those who have a decided view of the matter based on vested interest. Thus theodicy always runs the risk of becoming ideology, that is, of stating interest as objective reality. Thus the theodicy of the wisdom teachers tends to be partisan advocacy. The teachers of wisdom are perhaps established elders in the familial community who want to maintain equilibrium and privilege. Or in the royal environment they are privileged intelligentsia who value a social system that maintains and justifies their privilege. Thus theodicy tends to be a form of social control, urging the young to act in certain ways that sustain the advantages of the status quo, both for the teacher and for those whom they instruct. Proverbs is characteristically on the side of the status quo and tends to suggest that the present arrangement of social power and social privilege coheres with the will of the Creator. Any "boat-rocking" attitude or action that subverts power arrangements is not only unwelcome but is readily seen as a threat to creation.

Perhaps the most obvious statement of ideology in the guise of innocence is in Ps 37:25-28:

> I have been young, and now am old,
> yet I have not seen the righteous forsaken
> or their children begging bread.

They are ever giving liberally and lending,
   and their children become a blessing.
Depart from evil, and do good;
   so you shall abide forever.
For the LORD loves justice;
   he will not forsake his faithful ones.

It is asserted that the righteous are liberal and generous and are for that reason given prosperity. Moreover, those who live this way do good and promote justice and are never left begging. Conversely, those who do not live righteously will surely be reduced to poverty. Of course there is truth in this claim; but the statement comes very close to self-congratulation: live like us and become privileged like us. The statement sounds like a celebration of "our way" in the world, and a defense of "our system." Notice how ethics is intimately connected to economic advantage.

But of course the wisdom teachers are better than that, and in the end are capable of self-critical awareness. They know, in their best moments, that theodicy refers to God and is not to be reduced to any system of consequences. Gerhard von Rad has identified six proverbs in the book of Proverbs that deabsolutize the system of deeds-consequences that appears in much of Proverbs (16:2, 9; 19:21; 21:2; 20:24; 21:30-31). We may consider as representative only one of these sayings:

The human mind plans the way,
   but the LORD directs the steps. (Prov 16:9)

This proverb, like the other five mentioned, asserts that while human persons may intentionally and judiciously choose their futures by their "way," in the end there is something inscrutable about the future that is not automatically produced by our actions but belongs to the elusive ways of God. Thus it happens, as they know, that one may be a disciplined nonsmoker and get lung cancer; one may be a caring, responsible, wise parent and have a child who turns out "rotten." The ethical system advocated here explains a great deal. But not everything. And therefore at its best, the wisdom tradition is an awed, attentive reflection on God's governance, but it is not in the end an explanation. Explanation for much can be given, and it is the work of wisdom; but beyond explanation that is valued lies mystery that is to be treasured. Thus theodicy, like every explanatory theory, tends to be a mixture of practical observation, vested interest, and inscrutability. The prescriptive teaching of wisdom is on most days adequate and must be honored. In special times, however, pragmatics must yield to awe and finally to the relinquishment of control. The makers of Proverbs knew both the value of pragmatics and its limits, even if they sometimes failed to remember the second point.

Protest Against Conventional Settlements

We have spent so much time on the book of Proverbs because the theodic settlement voiced in Proverbs constitutes a baseline for all that we shall say about other Wisdom literature. That is, the other wisdom books we consider are either trying to come to terms with the theodicy of Proverbs or are seeking to get free of it.

The *theodic settlement* of Proverbs had insisted, in an endless recital of close, didactic observations, that the world works so that deeds have consequences guaranteed by the Creator in the very fabric of creation. Sowing leads to reaping. Righteousness and wisdom lead to life; wickedness and foolishness lead to death. And we, say the wisdom teachers, are living examples that it does work. "We" (either as established elders in the familial community or as privileged intelligentsia in the royal entourage) have done wisely and righteously and have been privileged. It works. And it will work for you. Every community, including the community of Yahweh, advocates a theodic settlement to order the daily affairs of society. The settlement works, moreover, as long as there is a general consensus affirming that a life of virtue is a recipe for prosperity and acknowledging guilt and failure in receiving negative consequences. Such a settlement makes communal life viable and relatively free of conflict.

The only problem is that the rawness and raggedness of lived experience do not uniformly adhere to theodic explanations. There is something slippery and unprogrammed about lived reality. It happens, more than rarely, that irresponsible people turn out happy and wealthy, and "good people" end up in suffering and misery. For a time such incongruities can be justified. But eventually, here and there, people notice. They challenge the theodic settlement that in any case is in part an ideology aimed at social control. They may become shrill in their protest and rejection, insisting that the social system of rewards and punishments is unfair and unacceptable. The social system, it may be loudly insisted, is not a gift from God but only a human contrivance to protect advantage. When this shrill awareness is voiced, there arises a *theodic crisis* that questions the distribution of social power and social goods.

The book of Proverbs is the elaboration of Israel's principle of *theodic settlement.* The book of Job may be regarded as the principal *theodic protest* in the Old Testament that challenges the serene justifications of social reality given in the book of Proverbs. And therefore one must be clear about the book of Proverbs in order to understand the book of Job as a dramatic and intense challenge to that explanatory literature. "Job" enters into dispute toward God, toward his "friends," and toward the entire theodic system that had become conventional.

The book of Job is dramatic fiction. That is, it does not purport to be history; it is theater designed to voice an alternative reality and to invite listening Israel to reimagine its explanation of reality, which had mostly gone uncriticized. Like all good theater, it is aimed at self-awareness that invites us to see our lives afresh from a new and different perspective. As dramatic fiction, the playwright takes two framing liberties. First, the drama is set in "the land of Uz" (1:1). The phrase may refer to a place in Arabia. What counts for us, however, is the fact that it is "not here," not Israelite. Uz is "no place," that is, out beyond the known world of Israel. The strategy is to create an alternative scenario of reality that has no point of contact with the familiar world of Israel. Further, the argument and formulation of the book of Job have nothing in common with Israel's characteristic expressions of faith. In this drama, it is intended that Israel should be transported out beyond itself and every common assumption. It is the work of such drama to hold us for a time suspended from the familiar, perhaps to be changed by the assault of fresh perception.

Second, the playwright takes the liberty of introducing the odd character "satan" in chapters 1–2 as a mysterious way to frame the ensuing crisis of Job. The figure of satan is scarcely known elsewhere in the Old Testament (only in 1 Chr 21:1 and Zech 3:1-2), and is not to be taken here with anything more than dramatic force. That is, the character satan is a dramatic device to pose in a most poignant tone the way in which lived experience disputes against settled religious conviction. It is enough to recognize that God or gods have a life of their own, hidden from human awareness and access, that need not conform to the restrictive theodicy of the book of Proverbs.

Thus the drama of the book of Job is a vigorous, artistic invitation in Israel to rethink in radical ways the theodic explanations that over time were undoubtedly reduced to moralistic clichés. Over time Israel had become too familiar with God, too much able to predict and control, so that ethics was programmed into a series of prepackaged consequences. The massive artistic, intellectual effect of Job is to undermine such certitudes and to reopen life with God to slippage and wonder and risk. In the end the truth of God is amazingly large, mysterious, stubborn, and elusive and cannot be reduced to a safe set of moralisms that are calculating and controlling. The student thus is invited to reflect upon *theodic settlements in Proverbs* and *theodic crisis in Job* as a format from which to consider the moral certitudes (religious and secular) in our own time and place, and the ways in which lived reality continually erodes the authority of such absolutisms.

The mounting of the dramatic crisis of Job takes place in chapters 1–2. Job is the key character. He is said to be "blameless and upright" (1:1, 8; 2:3). He is, as a dramatic figure, a pure product of the ethical program of the book of Proverbs. Thus compare:

> Do not be wise in your own eyes;
>   fear the LORD, and turn away from evil. (Prov 3:7)

> That man was blameless and upright, one who feared God and turned away from evil. (Job 1:1)

Indeed, the same terms, *blameless* and *upright,* are used in Ps 37:37 to summarize wisdom ethics:

> Mark the blameless, and behold the upright,
>   for there is posterity for the peaceable.
>   (See Ps 25:21 for the same terms.)

The "blameless and upright" are scheduled for "peace and prosperity." That is how it works. "Job" is the quintessential candidate for peace and prosperity. And indeed his tale begins so (Job 1:2-5). The drama begins with a reiteration of conventional theodicy. Job is a living example that it works.

That living example, however, is about to be disrupted. There is another drama under way in heaven, to which Job has no access (1:6-12; 2:1-7). The dramatic function of this counternarrative is to assert that there is something "on the loose" in reality about which Job knows nothing, but which is to undo Job's deserved "peace and prosperity."

Thus the issue of the book of Job is joined: a "happy" life, properly lived, and then an inexplicable assault on that happy, well-deserved life that is about to discredit all conventional ethical explanations. Job's wife is a dramatic voice who spots first the failure of the old explanatory system (2:9). Job, however, is firm in his moral position that is not only flawless but marked by a tenacious trust in God (1:21; 2:10). He is not only an *ethically* good man; he is also a *theologically* serious man. His confidence is not only in his own virtue (as popularly recognized) but in the reliability of God.

So the drama is set. The supporting cast consists of satan, an agent who will question conventional morality; Job's wife, who rejects the old scheme; and, belatedly, Job's friends, who defend the old system (2:11-13). In truth, however, the drama is a dispute between Job's *old ethical commitments* and *Job's present lived experience,* which simply does not conform to those old commitments. Wisdom teaching in general is the process of negotiating between old certitudes and present realities. This book, then, is a quintessential wisdom tract that takes the listener deep inside the tension that belongs, inescapably, to serious moral reflection. Wisdom teachers are endlessly preoccupied with making ethical sense out of a lived world that is endlessly underestimated and recalcitrant.

The long middle body of the drama of Job consists in a dispute between Job and his three friends that takes the form of three rounds of speeches in which Job and the three friends defend the old theodicy of Proverbs and critique it (3–27). The three friends, Eliphaz, Bildad, and Zophar, are agreed in the moral calculus that the righteous prosper and the wicked suffer. Some interpreters believe it is possible to distinguish between the arguments and positions of the three friends; some believe, moreover, that it is possible to trace a substantive development in the argument they make through the three cycles of exchange. These distinctions may perhaps be possible. But for our introductory purposes, such close differentiations are not necessary or important. What is more to be noticed is that the three friends adamantly hold to the thesis voiced by wisdom:

> For whoever finds me finds life
> and obtains favor from the LORD;
> but those who miss me injure themselves;
> all who hate me love death. (Prov 8:35-36)

That is, those who live a "wise life" obtain favor (peace and prosperity), and those who "miss and hate" a "wise life" will suffer. This is the established premise of conventional wisdom by the time of Job. This is the orthodoxy of the moral, privileged establishment. And who can say it is not true, because the world is indeed ethically reliable.

But the friends go one step further. They invert the calculus of:

righteousness $\Rightarrow$ prosperity,

wickedness $\Rightarrow$ misery.

Now, with reference to Job, it is:

misery $\Rightarrow$ wickedness.

Job suffers, so he must have sinned. And because he has sinned, he must repent.

The friends are convinced enough about this theodic equation that they become rather hard-nosed about it with Job:

> **Eliphaz:** Think now, who that was innocent ever perished?
> Or where were the upright cut off?
> As I have seen, those who plow iniquity
> and sow trouble reap the same. (4:7-8)

Bildad: Does God pervert justice?
    Or does the Almighty pervert the right?
  If your children sinned against him,
    he delivered them into the power of their transgression.
  If you will seek God
    and make supplication to the Almighty,
  if you are pure and upright,
    surely then he will rouse himself for you
    and restore to you your rightful place. (8:3-6)

Zophar: If you direct your heart rightly,
    you will stretch out your hands toward him.
  If iniquity is in your hand, put it far away,
    and do not let wickedness reside in your tents.
  Surely then you will lift up your face without blemish;
    you will be secure, and will not fear. (11:13-15)

The friends assume "the system." Consequently they assume Job's guilt. They must assume Job's guilt in order to sustain the system and in order to affirm that God is indeed a fair, reliable arbiter. Their "pastoral care" insists on the truth of the book of Proverbs.

It is important to recognize that Job does not reject the system of Proverbs any more than do his friends. He only wants the evidence against him. The argument is cast as a trial. He wants evidence. He wants to know what charges there are. He is prepared to submit, but he will not blindly submit. His defiance of the friends is a yearning to be answered with moral seriousness:

Teach me, and I will be silent;
  make me understand how I have gone wrong. (6:24)

The artist plumbs the depths of emotional exhaustion. The moral question is about to drive Job crazy. He does not ever ask for vindication. He asks only for evidence. He is exhausted by relentless moral assault that seems to lead nowhere:

I loathe my life; I would not live forever.
  Let me alone, for my days are a breath.
What are human beings, that you make so much of them,
  that you set your mind on them,
visit them every morning,
  test them every moment?

Will you not look away from me for a while,
   let me alone until I swallow my spittle? . . .
Why do you not pardon my transgression
   and take away my iniquity?
For now I shall lie in the earth;
   you will seek me, but I shall not be. (7:16-21)

As the argument progresses, Job gains courage. He realizes that in the end his argument is not with his friends, who are very little help or very little trouble. It is God whom he must meet, who is his real adversary. God is absent and silent, so that Job is left without an adversary with whom he can engage in disputation.

While the friends continue their defense of God, Job's own argument grows more intense and extreme. We may cite two remarkable utterances of Job.

First, in 9:1-24, Job launches yet another attack upon God, who in absence and silence is said to be grossly unfair. Job begins with a great doxology celebrating God's massive power (vv. 2-10). Nobody questions God's power. God is the strongest: "If it is a contest of strength, he is the strong one!" (9:19*a*). But the issue for Job is not power; it is justice. And on justice, the key subject of the wisdom tradition, God is not so hot. Indeed, Job dares to utter, in some of the most remarkable material in the Bible, that God is unjust:

If it is a matter of justice, who can summon him?
Though I am innocent, my own mouth would condemn me;
   though I am blameless, he would prove me perverse.
I am blameless; I do not know myself;
   I loathe my life.
It is all one; therefore I say,
   he destroys both the blameless and the wicked. (9:19*b*-22)

Job goes so far as to say that God is a perverter of justice, a dishonest judge who condemns the blameless. Or God is an indifferent judge who destroys indiscriminately. And if God is dishonest or indifferent, then the entire moral fabric of Proverbs is undermined. The way is left open to insist that if God is unjust and indifferent, then human persons are condemned to a moral anarchy in which there is no court of appeal.

The verdict of Job, however, is provisional. Job is too much schooled in conventional theology to leave it at that. So he must

407

continue to insist upon judicial engagement with God. Job wishes for a mediator between the two of them:

> There is no umpire between us,
>   who might lay his hand on us both. (9:33)

And eventually, Job insists on a direct confrontation in court:

> Oh, that I had one to hear me!
>   (Here is my signature! let the Almighty answer me!)
>   Oh, that I had the indictment written by my adversary!
> Surely I would carry it on my shoulder;
>   I would bind it on me like a crown;
> I would give him an account of all my steps;
>   like a prince I would approach him. (31:35-37)

Most astonishingly, in 19:25-26 Job issues a defiant warning to God:

> For I know that my Redeemer lives,
>   and that at the last he will stand upon the earth;
> and after my skin has been thus destroyed,
>   then in my flesh I shall see God.

In verses 23-24, Job wants his words permanently recorded as a testimony and challenge against God, so that later on it will be remembered that it was Job who did not flinch but told the truth. And now in verse 25, Job pushes the challenge to yet one more extremity. Conventional reading of this verse, reinforced by Handel's familiar expression in *Messiah,* takes Job's words to be a final reliance upon God. An alternative reading (here favored) is that "the redeemer" is not God but an advocate Job imagines who will take up his cause in court against God. The notion of *redeemer* used here is not of a "theological" word. Rather it refers to a member of one's family who will act vigorously to defend the honor of a kinsperson. Thus Job imagines someone who is connected to him who will act on his behalf toward God. On this reading, the statement about the redeemer is not an act of trust in God but a warning that Job will be back with a powerful ally who will more vigorously struggle against God and so vindicate Job.

This long series of exchanges comes to no settlement. The final word of the friends dismisses Job's claim and asserts that he is hopeless, his case without merit:

If even the moon is not bright
    and the stars are not pure in his sight,
how much less a mortal, who is a maggot,
    and a human being, who is a worm! (25:5-6)

Job's final address to his friends, in turn, is equally uncompromising:

Far be it from me to say that you are right;
    until I die I will not put away my integrity from me.
I hold fast my righteousness, and will not let it go;
    my heart does not reproach me for any of my days. (27:5-6)

In his sense of his own self, Job will accept no easy compromise and no conventional cover over his own innocence and his acute suffering. Job and his friends have laid out the issues but are incapable of adjudicating the issues between "orthodoxy" and the truth Job knows in his own bones.

The argument is escalated beyond the friends with a transitional chapter, 28. The chapter stands by itself and is a rumination upon the inscrutability of wisdom. It asks rhetorically, "Where shall wisdom be found?" (vv. 12, 20). The chapter ponders the amazing technical capacity of humankind to probe the earth, but concludes that all human investigations are bound to fail. The reason for human failure is that wisdom is not accessible to human discovery. Because

God understands the way to it,
    and he knows its place. (v. 23)

Only God. This is a staggering assertion among those who seek to voice wisdom, a quick way to undermine the confidence of Job's friends and the proverbial tradition to which they appeal. The friends think they know more than they know, because they trust the simple moral judgments of Proverbs. This poem is a large dismissal of human certitude. Except that in verse 28, after the exploration of all creation, we are brought back to the simplicity of Proverbs, for this verse seems to echo Prov 3:7:

Truly, the fear of the Lord, that is wisdom;
    and to depart from evil is understanding. (Job 28:28)

409

Wisdom consists in a life aimed toward Yahweh and responsibly lived.

But this is the very life Job has lived. And for that reason, the dispute is resumed after the interlude of chapter 28. Only now, it is different. Job no longer addresses his friends, who are not up to the argument. The dispute has moved beyond their clichéd responses. Now perhaps Job addresses God. Or perhaps he addresses no one in particular. Perhaps Job now speaks only because he must speak. His enigmatic suffering coupled with his undiminished faith refuses silence. Job, as a character in the drama, seems to know that it is precisely utterance that keeps him from being swallowed up by explanations too shallow.

Chapters 29–31 constitute the moral and rhetorical center of the drama of Job. Chapter 29 portrays "the good old days" when reality worked according to conventional explanations. Job was moral and honored. Chapter 30 characterizes the "bad present days." Now Job, still innocent according to his best understanding, is discredited and disregarded, humiliated and dismissed. He is a living embodiment of the failure of the system of Proverbs. His circumstance has changed massively. It should not change, because Job himself has been constant. He is the same wise/righteous, blameless, upright man he always was.

Chapters 29–30, however, are only prelude to chapter 31, the magnificent recital in which Job states his innocence, an innocence that is proactive for his community, an innocence not anywhere in the drama exposed as a hoax. So far as we know, he is indeed innocent. Here he makes his case in detail. The chapter is an important one, because it is the fullest, clearest articulation of ethics in the entire Old Testament. In this inventory, Job touches every phase of life and asserts his well-lived life. He has been responsible about sexuality (vv. 1, 9), in his treatment of his workers (vv. 13-14), in his concern for the poor, widows, and orphans (vv. 16-21), and in economic transactions (vv. 24-25); magnanimous toward his enemies (vv. 29-31); and generous toward strangers (v. 32)—and even in his care for the land (vv. 38-40). He has been not only pious but concerned for his community, taking care to contribute to the neighborhood. He is indeed a practitioner of the model of Ps 112.

His own assertion of innocence, however, is not enough. Because his life is focused in "fear of the Lord," he must be vindicated by the Lord who has smitten him. But he cannot be vindicated unless he knows the charges in order to refute them. And so he cries out for information about his case:

> Oh, that I had one to hear me!
>   (Here is my signature! let the Almighty answer me!)
>   Oh, that I had the indictment written by my adversary! (31:35)

Job is not humble or deferential. He refuses to crawl or to beg. He wants a hearing, because if he is heard, he will receive the vindication to which he is entitled by the tradition of Proverbs. Clearly the argument has moved beyond his friends.

Job is never indicted in the entire drama, never convicted, never shown to be guilty. Indeed, he is never seriously answered. He could dispute with specific charges. But now he is in an empty courtroom. God lives in a silent sky. Job's moral claims are not refuted but only disregarded. In this offering of theater, Israel is imagined outside the safe morality of Proverbs. This is indeed adult theater. Adults of serious faith are not readily answered. So much of life is moral silence, absence of explanation, only problematic cases out of which no sense can be made. Notice how inadequate Proverbs is to a morally serious person and how inadequate the God of Proverbs is to the moral insistence of Job.

So Job waits. He waits through the bombastic refutation of a fourth friend, Elihu (chaps. 32–37). And then he waits some more. Israel is accustomed to waiting for an answer from God, for God cannot be rushed or produced on demand. He waits because he is the lesser party in the exchange for which he hopes, an exchange that will happen only when God chooses.

And then, finally, God answers (38:1). It is an utterance of awesome power intertwined in the forceful destructiveness of the whirlwind. But it is an answer. Yahweh characteristically answers the needy petitions of Israel. And now Yahweh answers the passionate plea of Job. But what an answer (38:1–41:34)! Job has asserted his own innocence in chapter 31. Yahweh does not dispute the point. By disregard of the question, the innocence of Job is conceded. But the assertion of Yahweh is that questions of guilt or innocence are not

411

the defining questions of creation. Thus granted innocence, Job must still come to terms with God's greatness, which transcends the small moral categories of Proverbs.

This is the Creator who speaks. It is the Creator who in sovereign power created the earth (38:4-7), contained the sea (vv. 8-11), governed the light (vv. 12-15) and the deep places of darkness (vv. 25-30), the stars and the clouds (vv. 31-38).

It is the Creator who has wrought the animals—mountain goats, deer, wild asses, wild oxen, ostriches, horses, hawks (39:1-30). But all of these claims are preliminary. The self-celebration of Yahweh finally comes down to Behemoth (40:15-24) and Leviathan (41:1-34), creatures awesome in strength and splendor, so awesome that Yahweh must allow time to admire and dazzle and boast. The catalog is enough to cause the hearer to break out in praise: How great thou art!

But there has never been a debate about Yahweh's greatness, splendor, or sovereign power in the drama. Eliphaz has voiced that power in doxology (5:9-16), and Job had conceded as much in 9:4-12. The crisis is not about God's power. It is about God's justice. What strikes one about God's massive response to Job is not what is said but what is left unsaid. The most remarkable factor in the drama of Job is the *complete mismatch* between Job's demand and Yahweh's response. It is as though God has had no interest in Job—no interest in justice, no interest in the orthodoxy of Proverbs, no interest in theodicy. Astonishing: *God is not interested in the primal human question that drives the wisdom tradition, that haunts the human heart, and that has preoccupied Job.* All such moral calculations are here treated as irrelevant and uninteresting. Attention is given only to God's sovereign power, before which Job is reduced to silence. The question that so engaged Job and his friends has evaporated.

Thus God in the whirlwind does not seem to respond to Job at all; and yet it is a response. The answer is incommensurate to Job's protest. But perhaps it is precisely that incommensurability that is decisive for this theological statement.

Job yields to Yahweh (42:1-6). Job withdraws his argument. But what a yielding and what a withdrawal! Scholars take 42:6 to be the pivotal point of the entire drama. This final utterance of Job, however, is deeply enigmatic. It may be a yielding to power without conceding the point of justice. Or it may be an ironic statement, wherein God misses the irony that the listener is intended to perceive. Most likely it is a submission of Job as a man of faith to the reality of God, because he now is able to look beyond his own moral credentials to the words of God. Thus Job does not concede his claim of innocence, but he retracts his abrasive challenge to God. One cogent translation of the lines is that of Habel:

> Therefore I retract
> and repent of dust and ashes.

The theodic crisis receives no clear or satisfactory resolve, but questions of justice and injustice are overcome in a vision of the grandeur of God. Some scholars believe, moreover, that the lack of a good, clear settlement is intentional on the part of the dramatist—because the issue of justice cannot be settled, and Israel is the people that must live without any settlement. But without a settlement of the question of justice, Israel is left with a clear vision of the governance of God that is sure and reliable, a sure context in which such issues of justice can be lived with. The restlessness of Job is not resolved. But it is contained in an affirmation of massive faith in God.

Now it is time to leave the theater. The book of Job ends in something like a debriefing (42:7-17). Job is celebrated for speaking "what is right," as though the drama hints that Job's protest is not only correct, but welcomed by God, who appreciates a serious partner (42:7-8). In the end, God "restored the fortunes" of Job (42:10). Job receives back and dies "old and full of days" (42:17). We have come full circle. Job continues to be, as he has been all the way through, "blameless and upright." The drama seems to end by a return to the book of Proverbs and to the conventional conviction that good people get "twice as much" as before. It is as though the theodic crisis of Job is finally enveloped by the ancient theodic settlement of Proverbs. That may be enough, because on most days Israel lives conventionally in the world of Proverbs.

Except for two things. First, Israel has now been to the theater. Israel thought, as it entered the theater, that it would witness a neat, satisfying morality play in which both blameless Job and faithful Yahweh would be vindicated. But this theater is one of surprise if not of absurdity. The play does not quite work. There is a stupefying *mismatch* between Job's question and Yahweh's response. It is the mismatch that keeps thinking, caring people finally in crisis, because the world, even God's world, is not easily reduced to morality. This theater experience has caused Israel (and us) to look beyond conventionality into the abyss of life beyond explanatory morality. In the abyss there is the mismatch. There is Leviathan, monster of chaos, in whom Yahweh takes inordinate pride. And there is the unsettled "satan," who discomforts Yahweh and doubts Job's faith. In this hour of drama, Israel has lost its theological innocence. It has thought unthinkable thoughts. It may return to Proverbs, but it will not return innocently. It will return "for the sake of the children," to keep up appearances, and to get through the day. But from now on, it will always know that the question of justice has been asked and has been left unanswered. Perhaps not unanswerable, but as of yet unanswered. Departure from the theater is in a new sobriety. Israel can never again pretend, can never again imagine the world through unbothered proverbs.

There is a second "except." Emil Fackenheim[2] observes that while Job receives back from the Lord the same number of children—seven sons and three daughters—they are new children. They are not the same children. He has lost his children and they are not given back:

> This fact haunts, or ought to haunt, the religious consciousness of Jews and Christians alike. To Job sons and daughters are restored; but they are not the same sons and daughters. Children of Rachel have returned from exile; but they are not the same children.[3]

Israel leaves the theater, having watched and listened while the lost children of the divine enigma remain lost—forever. The playwright does not lie or deceive. Losses in the theater are real losses. One cannot undo what happens there. Israel cannot undo the loss, surely not by repeating proverbs of assurance.

The Enduring Question of Theodicy

An interlude:

The student may pause here after sitting through Job and after the undoing of all conventional moral and theological certitudes.

Job requires receptive pondering. This is not simply great literature by biblical standards. This is great literature by any standards. Here we are in the presence of greatness, an inexhaustible classic that holds together daring art and unthinkable human hurt.

Ponder especially that this is not only ancient literature dealing with ancient problems evoked by ancient conviction. The critical issue of *theodic settlement* and *theodic crisis* is as urgent today as the first utterance of Job. Serious biblical faith requires an engagement with the mismatch of God-Job and a continuing haunting by the issue. It will be important to think through how the question of theodicy is immediate for us. Consider three lines of reflection:

—The question of theodicy is *a daily struggle* for many people who live responsible lives and are surprised by grief and loss—cancer, unemployment, death, betrayal, violence—and the question of satan comes back: Is faith "for nothing" or is it prudential?

—The question of theodicy now haunts the West. The theodic settlement we have accepted for a long time is that *the imperial West* is "entitled" to the benefits of colonialism, colonialism now sustained by the economic structures and systems that "manage the debt" against "the underdeveloped." Or more closely that same justified privilege has guaranteed a theodicy of white advantage and male privilege, and now the shrill Joban voice of those long shut out of the Proverbs theodicy tends to undo all the privilege on which many have counted for so long.

—The question of theodicy haunts us with *the barbarism of the twentieth century,* with the regimes of Stalin and Hitler, the devastations of Hiroshima and Vietnam in which U.S. folk are implicated, the dramatic suffering of Biafra and Burundi, and finally—for theological thought, finally—*the Jewish Holocaust* in Germany. There is more undeserved suffering in the world than faith can contain. Job models the requirement that the suffering must be voiced boldly, even if the response of God is only a feeble, reneging mismatch.

Wisdom theology is not "theology lite." It puts us before questions that more conventional theologies of the establishment—ecclesial and secular—do not address. And once put there, we may never fully depart. It is the question that keeps us human. It is the God-uttered answer that gives us both the adequacy and inadequacy of our usual faith.

Hiddenness at the Brink of Futility

The third book commonly placed with Proverbs and Job as sapiential is Ecclesiastes. After the intense theological crisis of Job, the book of Ecclesiastes strikes a mood of resigned ease, in the awareness that the acute questions of Job are beyond resolution. One may as well return to a more conventional, less ambitious way of living. The book claims as its author "The son of David" (1:1), that is, Solomon, but that citation seems only to appeal to the tradition of Solomon as a wise man. It is not easy to date the book, though it is most plausibly to be located in the Persian period, when Israel faced a deep challenge to its old assumptions of power and meaning. It perhaps reflects a social situation when the economy had collapsed and all seemed lost to an erstwhile prosperous speaker. And if that socioeconomic judgment is too speculative, it seems clear that the book reflects a context wherein Hellenistic thought is available, and the speaker no longer expects a direct intervention of God, the expectation so characteristic of more robust Israelite faith. There is rather a mood of resignation that may reflect the malaise of a Jewish community in a Hellenistic environment that entertained no thought of possible new work by God.

The form of the book of Ecclesiastes is not unlike that of Proverbs, that is, a collection of wisdom sayings that comment on life, but with no obvious form or structure. While the form of the book is not unlike that of Proverbs, the mood and theological horizon are quite contrasted. Whereas Proverbs affirmed that human choice and human conduct would decisively influence one's own future and the future of the community, the voice of Ecclesiastes asserts that human conduct is meaningless and is a matter of indifference in relation to the future, which is blindly governed. Whereas Proverbs affirmed that God benignly ordered and guaranteed a viable life-world structured as a reliable sequence of deeds and consequences, Ecclesiastes can just barely affirm the reality of God. Indeed, the God who governs is remote, hidden, indifferent, and unmoved by human conduct. That is, the world is governed in inscrutable ways to which human reason has no access.

While the book has no obvious structure or order, we may suggest a series of teachings that evidence the general perspective of this literature.

1. God's governance is hidden, and there are no differentiations according to human conduct:

> Yet I perceived that the same fate befalls all of them. Then I said to myself, "What happens to the fool will happen to me also; why then have I been so very wise?" (2:14b-15)

> In my vain life I have seen everything; there are righteous people who perish in their righteousness, and there are wicked people who prolong their life in their evil-doing. (7:15; see also 3:14-15, 19-21; 7:16-18; 8:12-13)

God's decree about the world is all settled, even though we have no access to it. There is no interaction, no engagement, no impingement upon the divine will. The rhetoric is not unlike Job 9:22, cited above:

> It is all one; therefore I say,
>   he destroys both the blameless and the wicked.

The difference is that Job is in dispute, makes the statement in anger, and is prepared to reprimand God for the truth of the matter. By contrast, there is no fight left in Ecclesiastes. Everything is beyond reach though, to be sure, 8:12-13 seems a grudging acknowledgment that he may have overstated things. God has become profoundly remote and for all practical purposes irrelevant.

2. The inescapable consequence of this conclusion about God is a congruent conclusion about human possibility. Human possibility is an illusion:

> Vanity of vanities! All is vanity. (1:2)

These most famous lines of the book of Ecclesiastes are explicated in what follows: Everything is vanity, vapor, nothingness. Indeed, the speaker reviews the probes and efforts already undertaken, each ending in disillusionment. He has found in turn that: (a) wisdom (even wisdom!) is vanity, "a chasing after wind" (1:12-18); (b) pleasure

417

is a vanity—he pursued the desires of the heart and found no happiness (2:1-11); (c) labor is vanity (2:18-23); (d) self-indulgence is no better (2:24-26); and (e) money is a like emptiness (4:4-8; 5:10). The list is representative and intends to refer to every human possibility. Everything human persons can do is futile. None of these have ultimate significance. None of them are ultimately satisfying.

This conclusion, a remarkable one in Judaism, which characteristically believes that human life is invested with ultimate significance, is taken seriously even by God. Such world-weariness as given here may reflect either a specific context of disappointment or a general cultural malaise or both. In any case, Israel in these utterances has arrived completely emptied of passion.

The note of futility about human prospects is reflected in Ps 49, commonly taken to be a wisdom psalm. The psalm is a reflection upon the futility of wealth, asserting that in the end "you can't take it with you":

> Hear this, all you peoples;
>> give ear, all inhabitants of the world,
> both low and high,
>> rich and poor together. . . .
> Do not be afraid when some become rich,
>> when the wealth of their houses increases.
> For when they die they will carry nothing away;
>> their wealth will not go down after them. . . .
> Mortals cannot abide in their pomp;
>> they are like the animals that perish. (Ps 49:1-2, 16-17, 20)

The tone and the argument are not unlike Eccl 3:18-20.

3. Inside the context of resignation, however, the speaker does not decide upon suicide, which would seem to be the inescapable conclusion of such wholesale resignation. Rather the speaker urges making the best of it by investing life with modest joys and penultimate significance. We may identity three aspects of this penultimate embrace of life. First, in what is perhaps the best-known utterance of this material, the text offers a reflection upon time and the sense of appropriateness (3:1-8). The speaker does not, with the psalmist (Ps 31:15), assert that "my times are in your hand." Indeed there is no reference to God in this reflection, only a sense that different occa-

sions require and permit different sensibilities. If this saying is in the context of resignation, then it is clear that this is not an undifferentiated disavowal of life. Some things are more appropriate than others, though we are not here told why.

Second, the teacher offers a good bit of incidental practical advice, indicating that even in the context of blind fate, some things matter more than others. Thus he comments upon listening in preference to speaking (5:1-2), and on the keeping of vows (5:4-6). And as suggested above, 8:12-13 seems to signal a proximate valuing of one life over another.

Third, and most important, given the blindness of fate, one must still "seize the day" for the sake of well-being and enjoyment:

> Go, eat your bread with enjoyment, and drink your wine with a merry heart; for God has long ago approved what you do. Let your garments always be white; do not let oil be lacking on your head. Enjoy life with the wife whom you love, all the days of your vain life that are given you under the sun, because that is your portion in life and in your toil at which you toil under the sun. Whatever your hand finds to do, do with your might; for there is no work or thought or knowledge or wisdom in Sheol, to which you are going. (9:7-10)

Some parts of the text of Ecclesiastes sound like deep depression. But not here. For a time, the speaker is able to bracket out what is hidden and problematic and unresponsive, and proceed to live life in terms of what is given. In its own way, this also is creation theology, for there is the affirmation and reception of the abundant life given by the Creator. (See also 12:1 with reference to life with the Creator.)

4. It is commonly noticed that the final ending of the book, likely an editorial addition, is in contrast to much of the book, nearer to the main accents of Israelite faith:

> The end of the matter; all has been heard. Fear God, and keep his commandments; for that is the whole duty of everyone. For God will bring every deed into judgment, including every secret thing, whether good or evil. (12:13-14)

Indeed, the addition may be intended to correct a book that is for the most part "outside the pale." These final verses sound more like an echo of Proverbs and say nothing about blind fate or resignation or vanity. In the end, Israel is here admonished, even in its belated material, to keep to the course of what it knows best. Early on, wisdom had asserted that "the fear of the LORD is the beginning of knowledge" (Prov 1:7), and now, at the end of the canonical process, the same admonition is reiterated. For all its heaviness about God as it developed in Job and Ecclesiastes, in the end the wisdom tradition resists autonomy and insists upon referring life finally to God.

The book of Ecclesiastes is not a primary resource for Old Testament faith. Indeed it may reflect a time when the remoteness of God from lived reality placed in doubt the large claims made by conventional faith. The most that is claimed here is modest indeed, primarily a resolve to keep on living and to take life as best one can, a day at a time. In some situations, however, to *keep on keeping on* is no small resolve and may be reckoned, in its modest way, as an act of faithful resistance to a faith-denying culture.

We may make three observations about the crucial role of the book of Ecclesiastes for biblical faith.

First, that the book is in the Bible is an important testimony to the *candor* of Israel's faith. Because of loud and strident believers who prefer to cite only carefully selected references, one might conclude that biblical faith is always militant, upbeat, successful, and triumphant. That of course is not so. Here is a modesty of faith that lives close to depression. It is a measure of the honesty of the Bible that it does not cover over, deny, or exclude such a reality from the horizon of faith. There are many seasons in the life of faith, including downtime when God is remote and life is lacking in the characteristic passions of faith.

Second, Ecclesiastes is perhaps a *document of the absurd,* suitable for times of absurdity. Indeed technological modernity, if one notices, can almost eliminate the cadences of faith. In our current cultural setting we are witnessing much loud, bold, strident faith. But surely part of that boldness is an appeal against the cold emptiness that is so close at hand in our time. And while we may imagine a recovery of serious public faith, we are not so immune as not to notice that cold technology, in the name of scientific progress, may produce a silent world without communication, a lonely world without community, and an empty world without communion. Those who live in such a silent, lonely, emptied world may recall with wistfulness a former buoyancy rooted in faith. For many people there is now only a residue of that erstwhile faith. And when there seems no more access to what is ultimate, one may have determined recourse to what is penultimate. That is not much. But it is something, the very something given here in this text.

Third, it is important to recognize that Ecclesiastes, for all of its negativity, is engaged in the characteristic sapiential process of negotiating between *settled truth* and *new experience*. Roland Murphy[4] views the quarrel Ecclesiastes has with older proverbial wisdom as a "Yes, but" approach. That is, Ecclesiastes knows the old teachings well, but then counters them on the basis of current experience. The old claims are here much contradicted. But that is the way of wisdom theology. Ecclesiastes, like Job, will refuse to lie for the sake of old truth, will resist denying current experience in the protection of old conviction. And in any case, even with its minimalist approach, Ecclesiastes lives with the horizon of God.

This text is at the very margin of the Old Testament. At the margin, however, it performs an important theological function. It continually reminds established tradition that everything must be rethought and reformulated. One may not, in rethinking, end in resignation. But one is also not likely to end in a naïve buoyancy. Either way, it seems clear that what Ecclesiastes would most value is not a conclusion in resignation or buoyancy but the very process of rethinking. Faith of the kind the wisdom teachers practice is never settled but is endlessly rethought, because lived experience finally is the grist of faith.

Lived Experience as the Data of Faith

The valuing of experience as the material out of which faith is formed is a pervasive insistence of the wisdom teachers. The experience to be valued is *human experience* that causes the wisdom teachers to operate on a large human horizon of international reflection, with very little privilege given to Israelite tradition. It is likely that the Bible characteristically gives privilege to its own core of traditions. And that is necessary to the maintenance of a community that must be able to teach its young its precise memory.

At the same time, however, the Bible at its best knows that it must guard against producing an insular community that imagines it has a monopoly on God. One of the most important contributions of wisdom theology is to keep reminding the "internal traditions" that the world God governs is *out there* (among the peoples) as well as *in here* (with the Israelites). After all, the lived experience of Israel is not so peculiar. Like everyone else, Israel births, lives, and dies. Like everyone else, Israel worries about food, pays taxes, fights wars, and makes love. Like everyone else, Israel justifies its own existence and fends off threatening alternatives. The wisdom traditions are a reminder that Israel's lived experience is like the lived experience of its neighbors. And as the God of Israel judges and saves, so that same God, beyond Israel, gives life and presides over death.

There is in the ancient world a tension between faith turned inward and faith turned outward. And the tension must be preserved. So in our time, there is a deep urging to turn the faith of the church in, in order to exclude, even as there is a comparable exclusionary habit in our nationalism and in the history of the West. Such exceptionalism is understandable, but it is also continually undermined by an awareness that what we prize as peculiar is universally, humanly peculiar. And the wisdom teachers know that.

At the outset we opined that there was no such thing in the ancient world as "secular wisdom." In that ancient world, life begins in faith, even if the faith is inchoate and ill articulated. All across the spectrum of Proverbs, Job, and Ecclesiastes, these teachers began with a God premise. Wisdom theology is indeed "faith seeking understanding," trying to determine what it is about God's power and purpose that limits and permits, that authorizes and engages human meaningfulness in day-to-day interactions. The wisdom teachers want to make this guarantee of meaningfulness available. But they have a deep respect for what is and will remain hidden (as in Job 28).

It is possible that the same large enterprise of "faith seeking understanding" is what keeps this literature current. If searching questions are asked that are serious, they are rooted in something like faith, though I would not insist on "faith" being very precise. Such serious questions are minimally committed to the significance of lived experience, and the term *significance* pushes toward the realm of faith. In the context of wisdom teachers, this deep pulsing of significance seeks always to be understood, to see how it is, to discern interactions, interactions that will produce well-being or end in death.

It is not possible to make the wisdom teachers too "churchy," for they are not. But it is important to recognize that what they did, without any inclination to sectarianism, is still being carried on as a human enterprise in the modern, secular world. We want to know in order to trust; but we are able to know precisely because we trust. These ancient teachers knew that, and it did not lead them to easy confidences. But it did lead them to uncompromising honesty, a truth that is a form of faith. They resisted easy rejections in the form of self-indulgence. They also resisted easy acceptances in the form of certitudes. They refused to settle, because they knew that after the lived experience of today, there would be tomorrow with its own insistent questions and its undertow of affirmation. They stayed ready.

Notes

1. P. L. Berger and T. Luckmann, *The Social Construction of Reality: A Treatise in the Sociology of Knowledge* (Garden City, N.Y.: Doubleday, 1967).
2. E. Fackenheim, "New Hearts and the Old Covenant: On Some Possibilities of a Fraternal Jewish-Christian Reading of the Jewish Bible Today," in *The Divine Helmsman: Studies on God's Control of Human Events,* ed. J. L. Crenshaw (New York: KTAV, 1980), 191-204.
3. Ibid., 202.
4. R. Murphy, "Qohelet's 'Quarrel' with the Fathers," in *From Faith to Faith: Essays in Honor of Donald G. Miller,* ed. by Dikran Y. Hadidian (Pittsburgh: Pickwick, 1979), 235-45.

Bibliography

Camp, Claudia V. *Wise, Strange, and Holy: The Strange Woman and the Making of the Bible.* JSOTSup 320. Sheffield: Sheffield Academic Press, 2000.
Crenshaw, James L. *Old Testament Wisdom: An Introduction.* Atlanta: John Knox, 1981.
———, ed. *Studies in Ancient Israelite Wisdom.* New York: KTAV, 1976.
———. *Urgent Advice and Probing Questions: Collected Writings on Old Testament Wisdom.* Macon, Ga.: Mercer University Press, 1995.
Gammie, John G., and Leo G. Perdue, eds. *The Sage in Israel and the Ancient Near East.* Winona Lake, Ind.: Eisenbrauns, 1990.
Habel, Norman C. *The Book of Job: A Commentary.* OTL. Philadelphia: Westminster, 1985.

Murphy, Roland E. *The Tree of Life: An Exploration of Biblical Wisdom Literature.* ABRL. New York: Doubleday, 1990.

Newsom, Carol A. "The Book of Job: Introduction, Commentary, and Reflections." *NIB,* vol. 4. Nashville: Abingdon, 1996.

———. *The Book of Job: A Contest of Moral Imaginations.* Oxford: Oxford University Press, 2003.

Polanyi, Michael. *Personal Knowledge: Towards a Post-Critical Philosophy.* Chicago: University of Chicago Press, 1974.

———. *The Tacit Dimension.* Garden City, N.Y.: Doubleday, 1967.

Rad, Gerhard von. *Wisdom in Israel.* Nashville: Abingdon, 1972.

Seow, C. L. *Ecclesiastes: A New Translation with Introduction and Commentary.* The Anchor Bible. New York: Doubleday, 1997.

Yoder, Christine Roy. *Wisdom as a Woman of Substance: A Socioeconomic Reading of Proverbs 1–9 and 31:10-31.* Berlin: Walter de Gruyter, 2001.

CHAPTER TWELVE

NEW LIFE,
RENEWED COMMUNITY,
NEW CRISES

1–2 Chronicles, Ezra, Nehemiah, Remaining Minor
Prophets, Isa 56–66, Song of Songs, Daniel,
Ruth, Esther, Selected Psalms

Introduction

In this final chapter, we return to the history of those who worship Yahweh. The era about which we will comment is often called the post-exilic period, a phrase that is both useful and problematic. The phrase is useful because it points to a time in the mid-sixth century when some Yahwists were able to return from those places to which they had been forcibly removed earlier in the century. However, the phrase is problematic because the "post-exilic period" has no end. From the time of the Babylonian exile, there were Jewish communities outside the land. One could say that the post-exilic period continues down to our own time. Hence, some scholars have found it preferable to speak about "the Persian period," which commences with the imperium forged by Cyrus and concludes with the next empire to include Syria-Palestine, that created by Alexander the Great. (That next era may be called the Greco-Roman period.)

In this chapter, we will, as well, address the ways in which that history affected religious and theological developments in the literature of those people. We left our review of that history with mention of Deutero-Isaiah's view of Cyrus of Babylon. This king signaled a radical change in the ancient Near East. Hitherto, Semitic cultures (Assyria and Babylonia), had ruled Mesopotamia and exercised imperial influence on Syria-Palestine. Now Persia, a nation to the east of Mesopotamia, took that imperial mantle. (The contemporary nation of Iran includes much of the ancient heart of the Persian homeland.) Those Israelites in exile, as symbolized by Deutero-Isaiah, apparently believed that Cyrus would usher in a new age, enabling them to return to their homeland—a major group had returned by 520 BCE—and inaugurating a time of peace. In some measure, they were correct. This "Messiah" (Isa 45:1) is remembered by Israel as having promulgated an edict, authorizing the rebuilding of the temple in Jerusalem:

> A record. In the first year of his reign, King Cyrus issued a decree: Concerning the house of God at Jerusalem, let the house be rebuilt. (Ezra 6:2-3)

Thereafter, one faltering, unsuccessful attempt was made to rebuild the temple (Ezra 1:5–2:70). Then, under the leadership of Zerubbabel, the temple was finally rebuilt—supported by funds supplied from the regional Persian treasury. The dedication occurred in 515 BCE, the date that inaugurates what many call the second temple period.

To understand the second temple and its significance, one must refer to the first temple. That structure, conceived by David and built by Solomon, was an imperial expression of the united monarchy and, subsequently, the nation of Judah. It was physically joined to the royal residence and could be understood as a royal chapel with the king as the high priest. The first temple testified architecturally that God was present in Israel's midst.

With the destruction of that temple and with the theological work of Ezekiel on behalf of a people who worshiped Yahweh in Babylon, it would have been impossible to think about the second temple in the same way as had been the case with the first temple. To be sure, the second temple period saw the renaissance of sacrificial worship in Jerusalem. To that extent one could talk about a restoration. However, the old political order of monarchy had expired. There was to be no restoration of kingship (hints like Hag 2:20-23 to the contrary). So, the temple no longer symbolized a nation-state or the Davidic dynasty as it had in the past. As a result, it is no accident that new ways of talking about the temple, as a house of prayer (Isa 56:7), begin to emerge.

Those Yahwists who lived in Judah (also called Yehud during this period) experienced a political existence in which they had provincial status in the Persian Empire. There were governors, such as Nehemiah, but they hardly bore the glory of the former Davidic kings. As a result, the promise of a king to sit on the throne forever (e.g., Ps 72) is cast into the future. What should be happening in the present works itself out in a time when a messiah ("anointed one") will appear as a part of a truly glorious manifestation of a new Jerusalem (Dan 9:25).

Messiah is, of course, a powerful and complex term. It refers, literally, to someone who has been anointed with oil. We know that kings in Israel were anointed, as were priests. We have already noted that a Persian king, Cyrus, was viewed as God's anointed (Isa 45:1). Texts from the Greco-Roman period attest diverse Jewish expectations for a messiah. Some literature (Psalms of Solomon) talks about one messiah whereas the texts from ancient Qumran attest an expectation of two messiahs, one royal and another priestly. Such ambiguity about a messiah is consistent with the various models for political organization that we will note later in this chapter. The reader of this volume will recognize that ambiguity about messianic claims continues. Christians confess that Jesus was and is the Messiah, whereas Jews continue to expect the appearance of the messiah.

During the Persian period, the promises associated with David were understood in different ways. One tantalizing text suggests that the lyric prophet of the exile thought all Israel would stand as the beneficiary of God's promise:

> I will make with you [plural] an everlasting covenant,
>   my steadfast, sure love for David. (Isa 55:3)

Though we are not clear about what that transfer of the promise from David to the people might mean, the people as such become a prominent theological issue—and problem, particularly regarding the issue of who constitutes that group.

During the monarchic period, God's people were assumed to be those who lived within the territory of Israel, or more specifically Israel and Judah. And before the inception of monarchy, the people were understood to be those with whom God had covenanted—at Sinai and then with their descendants. Who composes God's people when Yahwists live in diverse settings creates a problem. The Old Testament literature indicates that those living early in the second

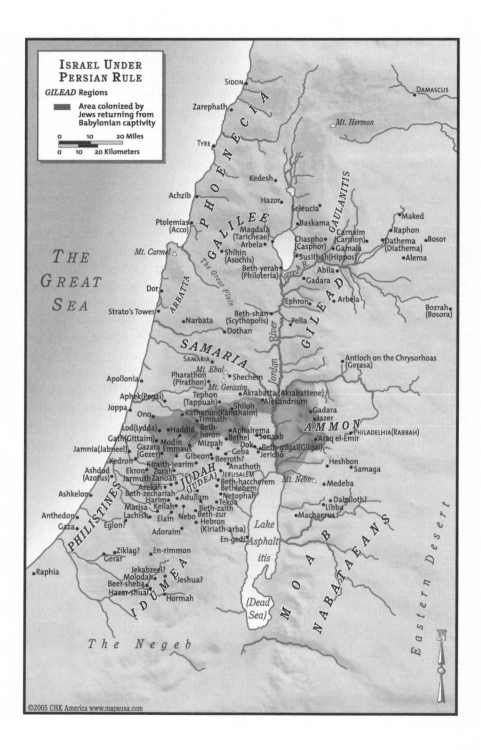

ISRAEL UNDER
PERSIAN RULE

GILEAD Regions

Area colonized by
Jews returning from
Babylonian captivity

0   10   20 Miles

0   10   20 Kilometers

THE
GREAT
SEA

THE GREAT SEA

PHOENECIA

GALILEE

GAULANITIS

GILEAD

SAMARIA

ARBATTA

JUDAH
(JUDEA)

PHILISTINES

IDUMEA

AMMON

MOAB

NABATAEANS

Eastern Desert

The Negeb

SIDON

DAMASCUS

Zarephath

Mt. Hermon

TYRE

Kedesh

Achzib

Hazor

Seleucia

Maked

Ptolemias
(Acco)

Magdala
(Taricheae)

Baskama

Raphon

Chaspho
(Casphor)

Carnaim
(Carnion)

Dathema
(Diathema)

Bosor

Arbela

Gamala

Mt. Carmel

Shihin
(Asochis)

Susitbah(Hippos)

Alema

Beth-yerah
(Philoteria)

Abila

Dor

Gadara

ARBATTA

The Great Plain

Ephron

Arbela

Strato's Tower

Narbata

Pella

Bozrah
(Bosora)

Beth-shan
(Scythopolis)

Dothan

SAMARIA

Mt. Ebal

Antioch on the Chrysorhoas
(Gerasa)

Apollonia

Pharathon
(Pirathon)

Shechem

Mt. Gerazim

Aphek(Pegai)

Tephon
(Tappuah)

Akrabatta (Akrabattene)

Joppa

Alexandrium

Ono

Rathamin(Ramthain)

Shiloh

Gadara

Lod(Lydda)

Timnath

Jazer

Haddid

Beth-
horon

Aphairema

Senaab

PHILADELHIA(RABBAH)

Gath(Gittaim)

Modin

Bethel

Dok

Araq el-Emir

Jamnia(Jabneel)

Gazara
(Gezer)

Emmaus

Mizpah

Beth-gilgal(Gilgal)

Kedron

Gibeon

Geba

Jericho

Heshbon

Beeroth?

Ashdod
(Azotus)

Ekron

Kiraith-jearim

Anathoth

Samaga

Jarmuth

Zanoah

JERUSALEM

Azekah

Beth-haccherem

Mt. Nebo

Medeba

Ashkelon

Beth-zechariah

Bethlehem

Harim

Adullam

Netophah

Marisa

Keilah

Tekoa

Dabaloth?

Lachish

Elam

Beth-zaith

Libba

Anthedon

Nebo

Beth-zur

Machaerus

Gaza

Eglon?

Hebron
(Kiriath-arba)

Adoraim

En-gedi

Lake
Asphalt-
itis

Ziklag?

En-rimmon

Gerar

Jekabzeel?

Raphia

Molodah

Jeshua?

Beer-sheba

Hazar-shual

Hormah

(Dead
Sea)

N

©2005 CHK America www.mapsusa.com

temple period were acutely aware of this issue. Moreover, this literature includes more than one answer to the question "Who are the
true Israelites?" The issue really involves a question of historical
experience. Some Israelites had been taken into exile, others had
remained in the land. Which of these experiences was to be normative?

We should note that such questions and their multiple answers
reflect the vigor of Judaism as it emerged in the Persian period. Jews
lived in diverse areas, including Egypt, Syria-Palestine, and
Mesopotamia. They preserved the testimonies of their forebears and
yet confronted conditions different from those described in that literature. As a result, it would be fundamentally inappropriate to
think about Judaism as some sort of monolithic entity. There were
multiple voices.

One should probably speak of a majority and a minority opinion,
thereby suggesting that the theological issue of religious identity was
at one and the same time a political one. The majority opinion is
represented in the books of Ezra, Haggai, and Zechariah. These
books attest to the prominent role played by those who returned
from exile. The reconstruction of the temple is attributed primarily
to the work of two political leaders, Sheshbazzar and Zerubbabel,
both of whom came back to Judah from Babylon. Zechariah makes
clear that major fund-raising efforts targeted donors either in
Babylon or who had just returned (Zech 6:9-15).

However, the key phrase is "the congregation of the exiles" (e.g.,
Ezra 10:8). The books of Ezra and Nehemiah make clear that the
leadership of the community in Yehud was undertaken by those who
had returned from Babylon. Only those who could trace their
genealogy to that experience were understood to be part of "the
congregation of the exiles." Only those who had endured removal
from the land could be enfranchised within the "ancestral houses"
(Neh 7:70). In sum, the true Israel, from this perspective, was the
group that lived in Mesopotamian exile. Ezekiel, who participated in
that exile, rather than Jeremiah, who was forcibly taken to Egypt, or
any of those who remained in the land (it is difficult to name any of
that group) symbolize the origins of "the congregation of the
exiles." The experience of the Babylonian exile became theologically and politically normative. According to this perspective, to be

part of God's people involved having lived through the exilic experience. Such was the majority report.

We have only hints from others. There are no texts that give explicit voice to those who remained in the land. That should not surprise us because it was the politically powerful and religiously influential people who went to Babylon. Those who remained—possibly known as "the people of the land" (e.g., Hag 2:4)—were not part of that elite. The book of Lamentations does seem to reflect the plight of the destroyed Zion. Zion, which is another name for Jerusalem, is personified in this poetry and even speaks:

> Is it nothing to you, all you who pass by?
>   Look and see
> if there is any sorrow like my sorrow,
>   which was brought upon me,
> which the LORD inflicted
>   on the day of his fierce anger. (Lam 1:12)

Moreover, this book also describes the fate of those who were left alive after the temple had been destroyed.

> The elders of daughter Zion
>   sit on the ground in silence;
> they have thrown dust on their heads
>   and put on sackcloth;
> the young girls of Jerusalem
>   have bowed their heads to the ground. (Lam 2:10)

Even more marginal than those who remained in the land were those who had not been part of the Yahwistic community at all—foreigners. At certain times in Israelite life, there had been positive concern for the so-called resident alien, as seen in Lev 19:34; Deut 10:18. Such concern was less pronounced in the exilic and post-exilic periods. Hence, Isa 56 presents what is truly a remarkable alternative answer to the question of who belongs to God's people. The author, who probably lived soon after the temple was rebuilt, addressed explicitly the situation of "foreigners" and "eunuchs," two classes of people who had not been permitted a full role in Israelite worship:

And the foreigners who join themselves to the LORD,
   to minister to him, to love the name of the LORD,
   and to be his servants,
all who keep the sabbath, and do not profane it,
   and hold fast my covenant—
these I will bring to my holy mountain,
   and make them joyful in my house of prayer;
their burnt offerings and their sacrifices
   will be accepted on my altar;
for my house shall be called a house of prayer
   for all peoples. (Isa 56:6-7)

Obviously, the doors to the temple are open wider here than they were according to Ezra and Nehemiah. Similar sentiments surface in Zech 14:16. What we see working itself out here is one way of understanding the promise to Abraham according to Gen 12:3: "In you all the families of the earth shall be blessed."

Visions of the Future

Israelites differed among themselves about what kind of community they should rebuild in the land. The Hebrew Bible presents evidence of diverse ways in which Yahwists envisioned their future. Haggai, Ezek 40–48, and Zech 1–8 present the most concrete options. But they were not the first to anticipate a future beyond destruction. Jeremiah's language about a new covenant (Jer 31:31), Ezekiel's anticipation of a new heart and spirit (Ezek 36:26), and Deutero-Isaiah's poetry about new things (Isa 43:18-19) demonstrate that Israelites were contemplating the future soon after the demise of Judah as a nation. However, the hard thinking about what it would mean for the people of Yahweh to live in radically changed circumstances came later.

The theological issue was nothing more or less than how Israel must organize itself, particularly in political and religious terms, in order to be Israel. The issue was particularly complicated since Israel had understood the previous polity—monarchy—as given by God. Must Israel remain a political entity, if only a subprovince of the Persian Empire? Must the civil authority be a Yahwist? What role should priests have in a new polity? What import did the promises

431

for an everlasting covenant with David as king offer in such circumstances? What was the relationship of those Yahwists living outside the land to those who resided in or around Jerusalem? All these questions were at one and the same time political and religious, since in earlier moments answers to such questions were offered with theological authority.

We will look briefly at the "theoretical" answers before turning our attention to what actually transpired. The restoration vision of Ezekiel offers the first alternative. Ezekiel 40–48 presents a dense but provocative description of life after the temple has been rebuilt. The vision is dated to 573 BCE. In it the prophet envisions a rebuilt temple as well as God's return to it. The vision also offers a description of the land and of priestly responsibilities and prerogatives. There is no place for a king, only for a prince or leader. As a result, this vision puts pride of place on the temple and its personnel. Ezekiel's restoration vision represents a judgment that Israel should be a hierocracy, a nation ruled by priests.

The other two concrete proposals are linked with the rebuilding of the temple; but they are more than a vision of its reconstruction. In fact, Haggai is as much a political strategist as he is an advocate for the rebuilding of the temple. For Haggai, the reconstruction of the temple is integral to life in the land. But Haggai also seems to believe in the importance of the restoration of the Davidic monarchy (Hag 2:20-23). He speaks to Zerubbabel, a member of the Davidic house, with language redolent of royal prerogative, for example, making Zerubbabel like a signet ring that David would wear (Hag 2:23). Haggai seems to think that for Israel to be Israel, they must have not only a temple but also a king of the Davidic line.

Zechariah's visions offer a third option, somewhere between the hierocracy of Ezekiel and the restored monarchy of Haggai. In an admittedly complex combination of vision and oracle (Zech 4), the prophet sees a golden lampstand with an olive tree on each side. Verse 14 identifies these two trees as "the two anointed ones," whom most commentators identify with Zerubbabel, the governor, and Joshua, the high priest. Zechariah apparently is advocating a dyarchic model of leadership in which responsibilities are shared by a political and a religious leader.

All three of these models—a temple community with a prince (Ezek 40–48), a reborn monarchy (Haggai), and a dyarchy of high priest and king (Zechariah)—are presented with the authority of a prophet. This theologically authorized diversity is indicative of the conflicted situation that Yahwists in the land were confronting near the end of the sixth century BCE. Ensuing decades saw none of these options develop in pure form. The challenging conditions of life as a subprovince of the Persian Empire required accommodation. In addition, the power exerted by one element of Israel—those who had returned from exile—influenced significantly all subsequent political developments.

Realities of the Present

Near the end of the sixth century BCE, there was a small community of Yahwists in Jerusalem. That community and its descendants were responsible for a consequential portion of the OT, including Chronicles, Ezra, Nehemiah, Jonah, Isa 56–66, Joel, Zech 9–14, and Malachi at a minimum.

Israel, or Yehud, was now a subprovince of the Persian Empire. But it was not the only place that Yahwists lived. Heretofore, those who worshiped Yahweh had lived in the land of Israel. Yahwism had been a state religion, with the king as its high priest. With the defeat of Judah in the early part of the sixth century, Yahwism was transformed due to the various places in which Yahwists lived—Mesopotamia, Egypt, Israel, even Crete. Aramaic documents dating to this era attest the existence of a community of Jewish mercenaries living at Elephantine, on the upper Nile. They worshiped not only Yahweh, but also Anath, a female consort. Moreover, the Septuagint, the Greek translation of the Hebrew Bible produced in Alexandria ca. 300 BCE, reflects a different ordering of the biblical books as well as different forms of several biblical books, most prominently Jeremiah. So, this dispersal of Yahwists allowed for the development of various forms of their religion.

In the midst of such pluralism there was, however, a countervailing force, one generated by concern for the core identity of Yahwism, which is related directly to the question we have just addressed: Who belongs to the people of God? Must they live in the land of Judah? Must they worship only Yahweh alone? Must they be born into that religion or could they convert to it? Were alternate religious calendars permissible? These and other questions were of such moment that, as they were addressed and answers were formulated, a new form of Yahwism emerged that allowed for worship in diverse geographical and social settings but insisted on a worship of Yahweh alone. Such a development is symbolized by the term *Judaism*.

Ezra and Nehemiah

The books of Ezra and Nehemiah offer a jumble of narratives and genealogies that depict the history of Yahwists, now called Jews (e.g. Neh 1:2), living in Judah in the sixth and fifth centuries. The early chapters of Ezra recount the rebuilding of the temple as a response to the edicts of Cyrus and Darius, a series of events we have already discussed. Ezra 7 offers a parallel event, another royal decree, this time from the Persian emperor Artaxerxes. This document authorizes Ezra to travel to Jerusalem and to institute a religious and a civil order based on "the [torah] of the God of heaven" (7:21). Later, Artaxerxes also permits Nehemiah to go to Jerusalem (though no decree is cited) in order to address security issues in Jerusalem (Neh 2).

There are severe historical problems related to the precise times that Ezra and Nehemiah were active. The date for Nehemiah's activity (Neh 2:1) is fairly certain: the twentieth year of Artaxerxes I is 445 BCE. The date when Ezra's work commenced is less clear. Ezra 7:7 refers to that date as the seventh year of king Artaxerxes. If the king was Artaxerxes I, the year was 458 BCE; if it was Artaxerxes II, the year was 398 BCE. The former date would place Ezra before Nehemiah; the latter date would place him after Nehemiah.

Even without resolving these chronological issues, it is possible to focus on central features of their activities, and in so doing to achieve clarity about critical issues facing Jews during the late sixth and fifth centuries. Preeminent was the matter of religious identity. If Yahwists no longer identified themselves by dint of national affiliation to the monarchic territorial state of Israel, Ezra personified a claim that to be a Jew involved adherence to Torah, which was present in the Pentateuch (so Neh 8:1). (The Pentateuch itself later came to be known as the Torah.) The norms and stipulations contained therein would, if lived out, create a religious community unlike any other. Of particular importance during this period, Torah-based living could occur anywhere (though to be sure temple ritual could be practiced only in Jerusalem). So, consistent with sentiments already appearing in Ezekiel, veneration of Yahweh was possible beyond the borders of the promised land. In fact, the very end of the Pentateuchal Torah describes an Israel outside the land, strongly suggesting that this "law" provided for religious activity anywhere Yahwists happened to live.

The literature associated with Ezra depicts him as highlighting one issue as of singular importance for a communal life based on Torah:

> The people of Israel, the priests, and the Levites have not separated themselves from the peoples of the lands. . . . They have taken some of their daughters as wives for themselves and for their sons. (Ezra 9:1-2)

Intermarriage, that is, marrying beyond certain stipulated lineages, was deemed to be a violation of Torah in and of itself, since it would lead to the mixing of "the holy seed . . . with the peoples of the lands" (Ezra 9:2). One should compare Deut 7:3-4, which prohibits marrying the inhabitants of the land since it would lead to veneration of gods other than Yahweh. Ezra, however, is less concerned with idolatry than he is with identity.

Nehemiah came to Jerusalem because he had heard about the plight of the city—it was now a "shamed" (Neh 1:3) place, a city without honor. When he arrived, he determined that the walls and gates needed to be rebuilt, explicitly to deal with the "disgrace" (Neh 2:17) of Jerusalem's condition. The issue was not so much one of defense against potential enemies but involved the need to address the matter of honor for God and God's people, secured through these highly symbolic walls. Once rebuilt, the walls resulted in shame for Israel's neighbors: "So the wall was finished. . . . And when all our enemies heard of it, all the nations around us were afraid and fell greatly in their own esteem" (Neh 6:15-16). When God's people rebuilt the walls, they created honor for the city and for themselves. Moreover, when the walls and gates were rebuilt, the city could be sealed off. Nehemiah 13 presents a picture in which foreigners were expelled from Jerusalem prior to the beginning of the sabbath and were kept outside until the sabbath ended (vv. 19-22). In so doing, Nehemiah created a way in which the sabbath could be kept as holy, since violations of the sabbath were associated with those who did not belong to the Jewish lineage.

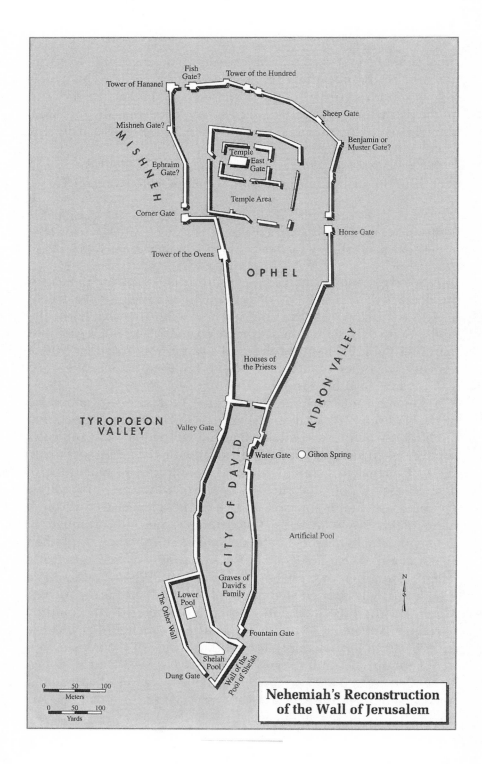

Fish
Gate?

Tower of the Hundred

Tower of Hananel

Sheep Gate

Mishneh Gate?

Benjamin or
Muster Gate?

MISHNEH

Ephraim
Gate?

Temple
East
Gate

Temple Area

Corner Gate

Horse Gate

Tower of the Ovens

OPHEL

KIDRON VALLEY

Houses of
the Priests

TYROPOEON
VALLEY

Valley Gate

Water Gate ○ Gihon Spring

Artificial Pool

CITY OF DAVID

Graves of
David's
Family

The Other Wall

Lower
Pool

Fountain Gate

Shelah
Pool

Dung Gate

Wall of the
Pool of Shelah

N

0   50   100
Meters

0   50   100
Yards

Nehemiah's Reconstruction
of the Wall of Jerusalem

Ezra, with his focus on intermarriage, and Nehemiah, with his concern for the rebuilding of walls, are both concerned with boundaries, ways in which the identity of Jews could be maintained. Crucial issues of identity (ethnicity) and status (honor and shame) were being addressed in these areas—family, community, and city structure. Such concern for establishing boundaries, putting in limits, may sound strange to modern ears, which are accustomed to hearing about the virtues of openness and inclusivity. And yet, with the earlier territorial boundaries gone, those Yahwists living in Yehud and elsewhere in the Persian Empire needed some identifiable way to stand in the great religious traditions of their forebears and to avoid religious and cultural assimilation.

The activities of Ezra and Nehemiah, along with what Ezra–Nehemiah tells us about the internal organization of the Jewish community, reflect a polity that might be described as a theocracy, a rule by God through the Deity's priests, but one that included a "populist" component. Decisions about key issues, such as intermarriage, are made or endorsed by an assembly. And there were various types of assemblies. On occasion, we are told about an assembly in which the entire community gathered (Neh 8:1). On other occasions, we are told about representative assemblies (Ezra 10:14), even with reports about votes on particular issues (10:15). Such behavior offers a quite different model for political activity than we have seen elsewhere in the OT. The people of Yahweh found it necessary to adopt various forms of political organization (chiefdom, monarchy, theocracy) at different points in their lives.

We should point to two other dynamics evident in the books of Ezra and Nehemiah. The first involves the prominence of community as such.[1] To be sure there are two leaders, Ezra and Nehemiah, but they are far less heroic than earlier judges and monarchs. Instead, they develop ways to help the Jews help themselves. Nehemiah does not build the walls, the people do. Ezra does not execute orders about foreign marriages, the people do. Second, the piety of prayer is prominent in the books. Ezra 7 and Nehemiah 1 and 9 offer examples of petitions to the God of heaven. These prose prayers stand outside the poetic petitionary discourse of the Psalms. The vocabulary often seems to derive from the Pentateuch, and the form is much less crisp than that of many psalms. One senses that new worship contexts, perhaps the household or an early form of the synagogue—in exile or in the land—were producing a new form of prayer, with its roots in the canonical Torah.

In sum, the books of Ezra and Nehemiah provide powerful testimony to the reconfiguration of religious traditions taking place in the early Persian period. The theological task was nothing less than whether Yahwism as a religion would survive the demise of the Yahwistic nation-state. The work of Ezra and Nehemiah attests to the means by which the move from Yahwism to Judaism occurred, with the pivotal pieces involving Torah piety and a closed lineage.

Chronicles

The literature leading up to Ezra and Nehemiah, Chronicles, is often viewed as a poor second to the books of Samuel and Kings. Spicy stories, such as the one involving David and Bathsheba, are present in Samuel but not in Chronicles. Such omissions in Chronicles might be viewed as pietistic censorship. However, we do well to remember that Chronicles was a history designed to meet the needs and concerns of the time in which it was written, which is true of virtually all good history writing. The Deuteronomistic History was composed, soon after 587 BCE, in considerable measure to explain how it was that the people to whom God had granted a promised land could be defeated and removed from that land. In contrast, the Chronicler's history focuses on the authorization of the temple. In this history, both David and Solomon are depicted as responsible for the planning of the temple and its maintenance. And the status of the temple was a key issue in the Chronicler's time. Monarchy was a thing of the past when Chronicles was composed, but the temple, especially for those in the land, was the focal point for religious and communal life. Hence, the Chronicler organizes his history around the importance of the temple for Yahwistic life. On a fairly mundane level such a concern works itself out on behalf of the Levites, who have a much more prominent role in Chronicles than they do in Samuel and Kings. These priests had tasks that included overseeing admission to the temple and performing in the temple choir. The temple and its priests, not changes in dynasty or battle reports, are the bellwether for the Chronicler.

On an even larger plain, the Chronicler shares a theological conviction with Ezekiel. Both authors were concerned to help Israelites understand that each generation stood afresh before its God. There were new possibilities before them, even as they lived in exile or in a backwater of the Persian Empire. The Chronicler's theology focuses on the ways in which God acts with regard to individuals or an individual in one generation and less on the effects of sin over many generations. The Chronicler conveys this theological perspective through his rehearsal of Israelite history.

It is instructive to compare and contrast the portrayal of Manasseh's reign in Kings and Chronicles. According to 2 Kgs 21, Manasseh acted in so impious a manner that his behavior served as the reason for the destruction of Israel in 587, some fifty-five years after his death, which was not a violent one. The Chronicler (2 Chr 33) presents a much different picture. Although Manasseh "did what was evil in the sight of the LORD" (2 Chr 33:2), he later "entreated the favor of the LORD . . . the God of his ancestors" (33:12). In no way is the future destruction of Jerusalem imputed to him. For the Chronicler, the key moment in Manasseh's life is his repentance, of which there is no mention in Kings. And, for the Chronicler, the destruction of Jerusalem is attributed not to someone who lived long before that event but to the circumstances of that period. For Kings, Manasseh is a distant cause of exile; for Chronicles, Manasseh is an example of repentance.

So, not only were the realities of the Persian period markedly different from those of the exilic and monarchic eras, but Ezra–Nehemiah and Chronicles—the "source material" for this period—offer a different theological vantage point than does the Deuteronomistic History or much of pre-exilic prophetic literature. The motif of repentance—a turning away from evil and a turning to God—looms large in the second temple period.

Psalms

Although it is terribly difficult to date individual psalms, most probably derive from the period of the monarchy, as is suggested by all the references to the king. However, we know that some psalms were composed in exile, for instance, "By the rivers of Babylon—

there we sat down" (Ps 137). Moreover, some no doubt derive from the second temple period. For example, Pss 12, 37, and 49 appear to reflect specific concerns from the time of Nehemiah.[2] Moreover, Ps 151, so numbered in a Greek manuscript, reflects the tradition of psalmic composition as it continued into the Greco-Roman period. (Psalm 151 is printed in the Apocrypha section of many study Bibles. It is part of the canon of the Eastern Orthodox Church.)

The magisterial center of the Old Testament, the Psalter, also reached its final form in the second temple period. Although the principles that lie behind that process of formation are only partially understood, the very fact that it is now configured into five books (1–41; 42–72; 73–89; 90–106; 107–150) surely reflects an attempt to have it mirror the structure of the Torah, a literary entity composed of five books. This arrangement of psalms betrays an interest in having diverse sections of the canon speak with confirming voices, a Pentateuch of five parts that resonates with a Psalter of five parts.

Another element of the Psalter provides further evidence of canonical integration. The first two psalms function as a prologue to the Psalter. That they work as a pair is suggested by the "Happy are . . ." sentences that enclose them, 1:1 and 2:11. The absence of a superscription for the second psalm points in a similar direction. Psalm 1 paints two contrasting pictures—the ways of the wicked and the righteous. The righteous person is securely rooted in "the [torah] of the LORD" (Ps 1:2). Such persons "meditate" continually on God's Torah. Torah piety has here the flavor of Wisdom literature: the righteous person not only acts out Torah but studies it as well. And since the psalms are structured in five books like Torah, we have the sense that psalms, too, have become the object of devout reflection. Such a sense is corroborated by the end of the second psalm, with its admonition to foreign kings, "Be wise" (2:10). In sum, in the second temple period, the Psalter is becoming a manifold theological resource, not only for worship but also for theological study and reflection. During this period, these words spoken by humans become—almost in dialectical fashion—words addressed back to humans.

Still, the psalms probably bore primary theological importance as individual poems—whether by one worshiper or by the entire community. We offer the following perspectives about the ways in which

440

individual psalms provided a theological resource for Yahwistic communities. In offering this vantage point, we build on but move beyond standard form-critical analysis of psalms, which has identified psalm types such as the lament, thanksgiving, hymn, wisdom hymn, and psalm of trust.

The psalms, when used by individuals, reinforce each other and provide a context in which the individual can understand both the good and the difficult times of their lives. Let us postulate an individual who is suffering serious illness. That person could use the resources of individual laments to give voice to the crisis. In that lament, the person would employ powerful poetic imagery to describe her or his situation. Psalm 6:6-7 offers a typical example (cf. 22:12-18):

> I am weary with my moaning;
>> every night I flood my bed with tears;
>> I drench my couch with my weeping.
> My eyes waste away because of grief;
>> they grow weak because of all my foes.

After asking God for help, the person would routinely offer to pay a vow or sing God's praise when healing occurred (56:12; 7:17). Hence, the lament not only involved a cry for assistance but a promise to God.

The psalm of thanksgiving constituted the fulfillment of that statement of promise. In it, the individual looks back to the past crisis and gives thanks for being delivered from it:

> O LORD my God, I cried to you for help,
>> and you have healed me. (Ps 30:2)

Then the individual looks around and speaks to the community,

> Sing praises to the LORD, O you his faithful ones,
>> and give thanks to his holy name. (Ps 30:4)

What began as an expression of thanksgiving for help for a particular problem moves on to more general praise.

Such general praise is the hallmark of the hymn, which typically commences with the call for the community to sing God's praises.

441

Make a joyful noise to the LORD, all the earth.
Worship the LORD with gladness;
come into his presence with singing. (100:1-2)

The calls for such collective behavior in the hymn are not grounded in a specific event such as we have described in the thanksgiving. Rather they are based on the nature of God, who has acted in many ways and times.

For the LORD is good;
his steadfast love endures forever,
and his faithfulness to all generations. (100:5)

These hymns offer general language about the nature of God more often than does any other kind of literature in the Old Testament.

With the resource of many hymns, it is possible for the individual to engage not only in praise but also in reflection about life as seen through the lens of the faith reflected in those psalms. So-called wisdom psalms offer advice about how to live that sounds very much like that which we read in Proverbs:

The wicked borrow, and do not pay back,
but the righteous are generous and keep giving. (37:21)

Or,

Better is a little that the righteous person has
than the abundance of many wicked. (37:16)

Moreover, such wisdom psalms attest to God's intimate relationship with the righteous,

The eyes of the LORD are on the righteous,
and his ears are open to their cry. (34:15)

and more generally, as with hymns, speak about the nature of God:

The LORD exists forever;
your word is firmly fixed in heaven.
Your faithfulness endures to all generations;
you have established the earth, and it stands fast. (119:89-90)

Such reflection and experiences lead to the final type of psalm we will mention, the psalm of trust. Thanksgivings, hymns, and wisdom psalms, when sung and studied, move the individual to certain dispositions and attitudes, primary among them the notion that God can be trusted—that the Deity will be there to respond to the plight of the Israelite and his or her community.

In the LORD I take refuge. (11:1)

The LORD is my light and my salvation;
   whom shall I fear?
The LORD is the stronghold of my life;
   of whom shall I be afraid? (27:1)

It is just such attitudes of trust that provide the Israelite with the theological resources to deal with illness, personal attack, and the like. Put another way, the song of trust sets the stage for the psalm of lament, since it is fitting that the one who believes God will deliver him or her is the one who will ask God for such deliverance.

In sum, the Psalter functions in many ways as a theological resource for the individual and the community. The Psalter gives graphic evidence of its ability to provide a theological context for the full range of human experiences—sorrow to joy, joy to sorrow. Moreover, during the second temple period, that resource was integrated both with the Pentateuch, in its Torah-like five-book structure (and cf. 19:7-10), and with the Wisdom literature, when the Psalter is viewed as a resource for reflection and meditation (so especially Pss 1 and 119).

Second Temple Prophetic Literature

For many readers of the OT, prophetic literature is associated with the named prophets who lived during the tenth through sixth centuries, roughly the span represented by Nathan (2 Sam 12) to Ezekiel. Prophecy did seem to be uniquely relevant to Israel when it was a monarchic state. Nonetheless, things prophetic continued in the Persian period. As we have seen, Haggai and Zechariah not only were instrumental in the rebuilding of the temple but also offered programs for the restoration of Judah. Haggai and Zechariah were, however, among the last of the named prophets; the Hebrew word *Malachi* really means "my messenger." In this section devoted to prophetic literature from the second temple period, we wish to offer two perspectives on the theological interpretation of this material.

First, the prophetic literature deriving from earlier prophetic figures was being interpreted in a new context. Israel perceived those words to have significance for ensuing generations. The identification of such reinterpretations is often a matter of scholarly debate. Nonetheless, it seems clear that many of the prophetic books have been edited and updated. We will note this process at work in Hosea, Amos, and Isaiah.

The books of Hosea and Amos offer some fairly clear examples. One indication that a text dates to a later period is the presence of the phrase "on that day," a phrase that is often used to introduce later material into earlier prophetic literature. In Hos 2:21-23, it introduces a brief poem, which recalls the names of the children identified in Hos 1 ("Jezreel," "Lo-ruhamah," and "Lo-ammi"). These three names were originally understood to involve a message of judgment. However, at the end of Hos 2, the negative significance is revised, so that pity and a restored relationship between God and people can occur. It is most likely that this redeployment of the children's names transpired after the destruction foreseen by Hosea. However, the imagery originally provided by Hosea, as well as theological perspectives present in the book, enabled a later writer to "update" the book to accommodate a time after destruction.

A similar phenomenon appears in the book of Amos. Amos 9:11 begins with that same phrase, "on that day." In Amos 9:11-15, the tone of the book shifts decisively—from the visions and oracles of judgment to reflection about a time after punishment. This oracle presumes a defeated Jerusalem, an exiled population, and a defunct Davidic dynasty—all of which may be associated with the time after the defeat of Jerusalem in 587 BCE, almost two and a half centuries after Amos had been active in Israel. Some later writer, probably during the mid-sixth century BCE, thought it appropriate for the book of Amos to conclude with this move beyond judgment. Moreover, this section returns to a theme struck in the first two chapters of Amos, namely, the place of Israel and Judah within the context of other nations. So, too, the imagery of the theophany with which the book of Amos begins (Amos 1:2) is reversed. In that first chapter, we read about desiccation on Carmel; at the end of the book, the poetry speaks of fertility on the mountains, which will "drip sweet wine" (9:13). The literary and theological imagery of the originating prophet are taken seriously as the book is reconfigured for a new generation of readers. Both Hosea and Amos were perceived as addressing Israel with new voices when the time of judgment had passed.

The book of Isaiah provides the most famous example of the way in which a prophet's words can exercise generative power over the years. Instead of several verses having been added, as was the case with Amos and Hosea, massive amounts of poetry have been integrated with the earlier words of Isaiah ben Amoz, who was active in the late eighth century BCE. We have already (chap. 10) commented on Isa 40–55, so-called Second or Deutero-Isaiah, which is one example of such updating. However, the book of Isaiah includes another eleven chapters, Isa 56–66, which are regularly attributed to the period soon after the second temple was completed.

The words of Isaiah ben Amoz offered a vigorous critique of Judah for not trusting in the God who was worshiped in its capital. Isaiah anticipated a severe response from Yahweh. After the destruction of that capital, a prophet familiar with those earlier words formulated rhetoric of promise, encouraging those taken into exile to return home (Isa 40–55). However, after some Israelites returned and rebuilt the temple, a new epoch commenced. And the book of Isaiah, which now included chapters 40–55, was reinterpreted again. For example, Isa 57:14 clearly builds on Isa 40:3-4.

Isaiah 56–66 addresses various topics, including the question of who is to be part of the community, as we have seen earlier in this chapter. As one might expect, a key issue throughout Isa 1–55 receives attention again in these latter chapters: Zion. Zion will be restored and vindicated (Isa 60–62). In these chapters, the second-temple prophet carried on the Isaianic legacy regarding concern for Jerusalem. Elsewhere, there are new emphases, which either pick up elements relatively unimportant in Isa 1–39, such as theological reflection on the temple and worship (Isa 66:1-5), or develop motifs prominent only in Isa 40–55, such as idolatry (Isa 57).

In sum, during the second temple period, earlier prophetic literature was being recast by a number of anonymous scribes. For the most part, they used motifs and traditions present in the earlier literature to address circumstances in the Persian period. Such scribes apparently believed that the earlier oracles and visions provided theological resources to address generations later than their original audience. Those who discern words of Amos as relevant to social and economic issues today stand in a long tradition of those who heard prophetic words speak afresh to their own time. In that regard, it is interesting to discover Hosea, Amos, and the other "minor" prophets were remembered in the Greco-Roman period as offering words of hope, which are often found in additions to the prophet's original sayings:

> May the bones of the Twelve Prophets
>   send forth new life from where they lie,
> for they comforted the people of Jacob
>   and delivered them with confident hope. (Sir 49:10)

Second, the very notion of prophecy itself—even from a theological perspective—was undergoing a transformation during the second temple period. The fact that we no longer hear about named prophets in the Persian period is itself significant. One primary venue for their activity, affairs of state, had disappeared. Put quite simply, there was no longer a king to address. Though priests would continue during the Persian and Greco-Roman periods in ways not dissimilar from those of their monarchic forebears, prophets and prophecy would not continue to model the pre-exilic pattern.

As we have seen, much of the critical and identity-bearing behavior of Yahwists focused on the temple. And so various forms of things prophetic began to appear in that venue. This process was, in a way, a natural transition, since prophets regularly were embedded in or had access to centers of power. Moreover, a number of the earlier prophets had themselves been priests, most notably Jeremiah, Ezekiel, and Zechariah. Still, the second temple period saw even more of this junction between prophecy and the realm of ritual affairs. For example, a group of minor priests, the Levitical singers, are, according to the book of Chronicles, to be viewed as prophets (1 Chr 25:1; 2 Chr 20:13-17). Also, prophetic elements appear in some psalms, for instance, Ps 81. However, the book of Joel offers the most compelling evidence of this tendency. (Many scholars think the book of Joel was written during the Persian period.)

In the book of Joel, we learn about a crisis confronting Israel. It is either a locust plague described as a war or a war described as a locust plague. In either case, the land was being devastated. Joel admonishes those in authority—elders, priests—along with the general populace—farmers, vinedressers—to undertake a full range of lamentation:

> Sanctify a fast,
>   call a solemn assembly.
> Gather the elders
>   and all the inhabitants of the land
> to the house of the LORD your God,
>   and cry out to the LORD. (1:14)

This summons extends until 2:18, at which point we are told that

> the LORD became jealous for his land,
>   and had pity on his people.

One may infer that Joel, like Haggai and Zechariah in their advocacy for the reconstruction of the temple, was a successful prophet. His admonitions apparently paved the way for a successful plea to God so that the people and land could survive.

> You shall eat in plenty and be satisfied,
>   and praise the name of the LORD your God,
>   who has dealt wondrously with you. (2:26)

Joel was not the first prophet to admonish the people to engage in proper behavior regarding ritual and religious matters. That was heard from the eighth-century prophets as well. That such should be the entire focus of this book, however, constitutes a turning point in the history of prophecy. God's direct words to the people were now appearing primarily in the world of ritual affairs.

If Joel's words appear within the ritual world, the book of Malachi (literally, "my messenger") regularly focuses on that world. The priests suffer severe indictment for dishonoring Yahweh in manifold ways, for example, offering "polluted food" on the altar (1:7), robbing God (3:8). The very tone of the book is strident, with the author quoting opponents and then refuting them abruptly. The book does anticipate that some, "those who revered the LORD" (3:16), will survive the coming catastrophe (see Mal 3:1-5), though probably with the help of an Elijah figure (4:5). A prophet will be necessary to enable some Yahwists to survive "the great and terrible day of the LORD." This tradition about a prophet who will come appears prominently in both Jewish and Christian expectations related to the appearance of a Messiah (see, e.g., Mark 8:28; 9:12).

Finally, we confront the oddest of prophetic books, Jonah, which poses a challenge to other prophetic books even as it sits among them. We ask two primary questions: what kind of literature is this book, and what sort of character is this Jonah? One powerful answer to the former question is that Jonah should be understood as a narrative parable, a story that throws the reader's world into turmoil. This book, almost certainly written in the Persian period, challenged the ancient Yahwistic reader to contemplate the ways in which God might relate to non-Jews. The reader encounters a world in which Phoenician mariners sacrifice and make vows to Yahweh (1:16) and in which Ninevites put on sackcloth, fast, and "believe God" (3:5). Moreover, the reader encounters a prophet who, in spite of his terse oracle (3:4), was stunningly successful. The people of Nineveh repent. However, this prophet, despite his success, is angry enough to die because this God showed concern about Nineveh, concern that made Jonah's words appear false. Jonah is a person of great theological integrity and filled with righteous anger.

All these elements create an ironic version of a prophetic book. Jonah (the name means "dove") was really a hawk. And the book calls into question theological hawklike sentiments. Such sentiments had appeared in other prophetic books, like the oracles against the nations in the major prophets or the book of Nahum, which is "an oracle concerning Nineveh" (Nah 1:1). In so doing, the book of Jonah conveys the idea of a Deity who responds to the plight of non-Israelite and Israelite alike. Just as the Deity responded to the Phoenicians and Ninevites, God shows concern for a hesitant prophet by rescuing him from the seas and by providing him with shade. The book of Jonah appears to be a cautionary challenge to standard theological formulations (4:2). The book asks Israelites to reflect on God's concluding question:

> And should I not be concerned about Nineveh, that great city, in which there are more than a hundred and twenty thousand persons who do not know their right hand from their left, and also many animals? (Jonah 4:11)

In sum, the great authority of the prophetic voices was manifesting itself in various ways, even as it was under attack from Jonah. Older theological traditions were being updated by those who preserved the words and visions of the earlier prophets. Moreover, intermediaries active in the Persian period, few though they might be, were related in diverse ways to the world of worship.

The Scrolls (Megillot)

Just as there are five books of Torah and five books of the Psalter, so, too, there are five books known as the *megillot,* or scrolls. This is a heterogeneous collection, two members of which—Ecclesiastes and Lamentations—we have already discussed. The remaining three books are Song of Songs, Ruth, and Esther. The alert reader will immediately ask: What do these books have in common? Lamentations and Song of Songs are composed entirely in poetry. Most of Ecclesiastes is poetry. Both Esther and Ruth are short stories. The five books derive from vastly different historical contexts. And, as we shall see, their theological impulses are quite different. However, they share at least two features: relative brevity and an association with a specific Jewish festival.

Song of Songs—Passover
Ruth—Pentecost
Lamentations—the 9th of Ab (the date on which the temple was destroyed)
Ecclesiastes—Tabernacles/Sukkot
Esther—Purim

In some cases, the connections between text and festival are self-evident. Esther mentions Purim explicitly (Esth 9:26). However, Ecclesiastes' association with Tabernacles/Sukkot and Song of Songs' association with Passover is less clear. However, such linkages reflect an interest in integrating scripture with the religious behavior of the people. This interconnectedness attests that all life, as attested in these diverse texts, was to be included within the ritual practice and calendar of ancient Israel.

Song of Songs

The Song of Songs is even more historicized than its association with Passover suggests. The first verse reads, "The Song of Songs, which is Solomon's." However, linguistic and other evidence suggests that these poems were actually composed in the second temple period, though they are similar to love poetry attested in earlier ancient Near Eastern cultures.

At first reading, the Song appears overtly untheological. There is reference neither to God nor to the religious traditions of ancient Israel. However, the very presence of such love poetry within the canon brings this realm of human experience into dialogue with other texts dealing with critical issues in human life. The language of human love is not particularly prominent in the Old Testament (cf. Gen 29:18). So the Song plays a special role in giving voice to this universal element.

In fact, several voices appear in the Song. One of the challenges the book presents is determining who is speaking at any given moment (such multivocality is also at issue in Lamentations). The book presents three speakers: a man (4:1-7), a woman (2:8-17), and a chorus (6:1). The man and the woman express their love for each other in various ways. Their speeches often appear in dialogue, with one following up on the expression of another (e.g., 2:1-2). There is a strong sense of mutuality—either one can take the lead. Each describes the beauty of the other. The Song is a subtle and wonderful presentation of human love expressed in a multitude of images (e.g., geography, fauna, flora) and settings (e.g., garden, city, countryside).

Though it is dangerous to identify one primary theme in a poem, the notion expressed in Song 8:6*b*-7*a* does seem to have pride of place.

> For love is strong as death,
>   passion fierce as the grave.

Its flashes are flashes of fire,
  a raging flame.
Many waters cannot quench love,
  neither can floods drown it.

The Hebrew text that is translated here as "a raging flame" could be translated "the flame of Yahweh," which hints at the divine origins for this powerful impulse. In any case, the poet offers three images—grave, fire, and flood—with which to understand the power of human love.

The canonical context for the Song provides one way in which to understand the language of love in the OT. That language is used by other authors (e.g., Hos 2; 11:8-9) to describe Yahweh's affection for Israel. Though there are dangers in such discourse, Israel came to believe that this powerful way to describe a human relationship was also apt for describing the way in which God related to the people of Israel (cf. Isa 5:1-7; Hos 2). The rich vocabulary of love complemented the quite different imagery that the language of covenant/contract provided.

The Song operates at several levels: as human love poetry, but also as poetry that participates in the language of divine love, which was also present in the traditions of ancient Israel. For example, the book of Deuteronomy uses the vocabulary of love to describe God's covenantal relationship with Israel (Deut 6:5; 10:12-19). As a result, it should not surprise readers to learn that later interpreters understood the poetry in quite diverse ways. In Jewish traditions, the book was often viewed as poetry expressing God's relation to the Jewish community, whereas in Christian traditions, the book was thought to express Christ's love for the church. Nonetheless, in the first instance, the Song offers primary expressions of a loving human relationship, which can itself stand in dialogue with biblical stories and prescriptions concerning humans in loving relationships.

Ruth

The book of Ruth, too, is built out of the stuff of human love and affection, though with a different diction than that of the Song. The language of love that involves the erotic and desire are prominent in the Song (dod, 'ahabah). In contrast, another term, hesed, which can be translated as "love" but also as "loyalty" or "kindness," is more prominent in Ruth. The book makes clear that both God and humans can be agents of such love. Naomi asks that God act in such a fashion toward her daughters-in-law (1:8). Similarly, Boaz asks God to deal in love toward Naomi. However, humans can act that way as well, as Boaz makes clear when he responds to Ruth (3:10) and Ruth demonstrates in her loyalty to Naomi (1:16-17).

Multiple agendas—theological, social, and political—work themselves out in the narrative. The following implicit questions lie behind the surface of this remarkable short story: Can a non-Israelite become part of Yahweh's people? How do women survive in a patrilineal culture? What is the lineage of David?

The plot focuses on the plight of two women: Ruth and Naomi, both widows, one an Israelite and one a Moabite, mother-in-law and daughter-in-law. Near the outset of the book, Naomi makes a declaration about her deep feelings of affection for Ruth:

> Where you go, I will go;
> Where you lodge, I will lodge;
> your people shall be my people,
> and your God my God. (Ruth 1:16)

Here the language about God, unlike that in the Song, is overt. However, it is human action rather than divine intervention that results in well-being for both Ruth and Naomi. The narrator has carefully noted that all the primary actors take initiatives within the story. Ruth decides to go out to the field and glean. Naomi offers Ruth a plan by means of which to attract Boaz. And Boaz takes the initiative in dealing with a kinsman in order to set the stage for his marriage to Ruth. And yet, such actions are complemented by apparent chance—as marked, for instance, by the phrase "as it happened" (Ruth 2:3)—which could also be interpreted as God's providential provision of care for Ruth and Naomi. It is almost as if the deity is a fourth major character—along with Ruth, Naomi, and Boaz—whose unspecified actions help move the story along.

By the end of the story, the questions mentioned above receive their answers: a non-Israelite can become part of Israel through marriage; women can survive by taking initiative, working together, and utilizing those structures (minimal though they might be) that can provide them with advantage; and David derives from Moabite as well as Israelite blood. Furthermore, all three human characters have achieved considerable blessing: Naomi has "a son" (4:17), Ruth has a husband and a son, and Boaz has a wife and an heir.

Esther

If the book of Ruth addresses the fate of a foreigner in Israel, Esther addresses the fate of Israelites in a foreign land, a topic of concern that became increasingly prominent during the second temple period. Like the stories of Daniel and Joseph, the tale of Esther sets this concern at a foreign court. And, as in Ruth, women figure as prominent characters in this short story.

The theological dimensions of Esther are not explicit. Although the book serves as an authorizing story for the Jewish festival of Purim, there is no overt reference to the Jewish God in the story. Jews are threatened but are understood to have the responsibility for working out their fates. When Haman, a Persian courtier, manages to have a decree promulgated according to which "all Jews" will be destroyed, Mordecai contacts Esther, recently become queen, to ask her to intercede with King Ahasuerus. Esther initially responds that such intercession would endanger her life, whereupon Mordecai responds:

> If you keep silence at such a time as this, relief and deliverance will rise for the Jews from another quarter, but you and your father's family will perish. Who knows? Perhaps you have come to royal dignity for just such a time as this. (Esth 4:14)

Such a judgment resonates with the comments in Ruth, which point to God's providence. The author of Esther, in effect, puts it this way: "as it happened, Esther was queen of the Persians and the Medes." However, the book of Esther makes more even explicit than does the book of Ruth the importance of responding to the potentialities built into such providential positioning. Had Ruth not continued to glean in the fields, had Esther not interceded with Ahasuerus, the potential for blessing would have been lost.

These two short stories may be understood as comedies to the extent that, as narratives, they describe an initial situation, an ensuing problem, and its resolution. There are heroines and heroes who act to secure their destiny. And, in both cases, those "personal" destinies directly affect the fate of the people of Yahweh. Similarly, the Song offers a lyrical assessment of human love. Indeed, all three "books" stand in dialogue with the sober acrostic expression of grief in Lamentations and with the resigned reflections of Ecclesiastes. All five of the scrolls attest to the potentialities built into human existence, possibilities known to far more than just those in ancient Israel. If the Song attests the joys and complexities of human love, Lamentations the devastation of and yet power to address grief, and Ecclesiastes the wisdom of age, then Ruth and Esther offer stories in which Israelites and then Jews live, love, and grow wise, particularly within a setting of the extended family.

Judaism in the Greco-Roman Period

Issues of identity that had been of critical importance for Judaism during the Persian period were raised again as the cultural force of Hellenism impinged upon Jews, both in diaspora, particularly Alexandria, and in the homeland. The books of Maccabees, reflecting conditions of the second century BCE, overtly attest to the struggle between enforced Hellenization and Jews in the land. The book of Daniel also reflects this crisis. However, the historical references in Daniel are less overt, a feature that enables the book to address a broader range of issues.

Daniel is made up of two types of literature, short tales in chapters 1–6 and apocalyptic visions in chapters 7–12. Each form of literature offers a religious perspective on the crisis faced by those who are challenged to remain loyal to their faith. The short stories, which predate the visions, set a Jewish hero, Daniel, or other pious characters in situations of cultural conflict. These individuals are faced with stark choices. Will they adhere to Jewish practice or will they succumb to that which is foreign? On occasion, the choice is one of life or death. The general tone of the stories is optimistic. According to Dan 1, for example, adherence to Jewish dietary practice enables Daniel and his colleagues to flourish at the royal court. However, in another tale (Dan 3), the heroes realize that their decision not to worship a golden image could cost them their lives.

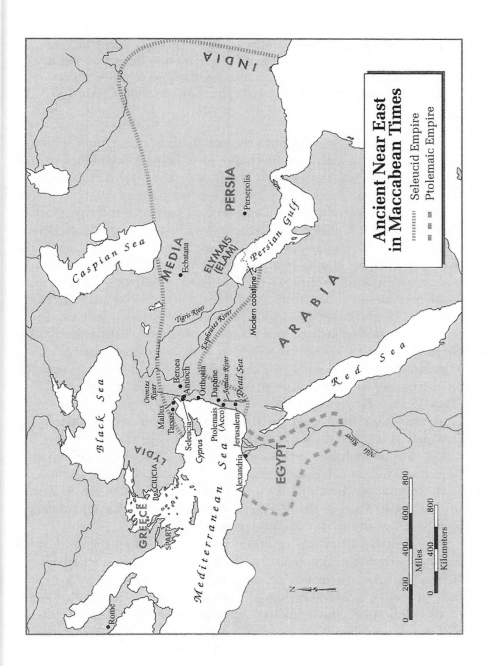

**Ancient Near East
in Maccabean Times**

Seleucid Empire

Ptolemaic Empire

> If our God whom we serve is able to deliver us from the furnace of blazing fire and out of your hand, O king, let him deliver us. But if not, be it known to you, O king, that we will not serve your gods and we will not worship the golden statue that you have set up. (Dan 3:17-18)

Such language clearly recognizes the possibility of martyrdom, which is quite another response to the challenge of being forced to worship other gods than was that offered by the Maccabees, who engaged in military activity in the first part of the second century BCE.

The visions, which make up the second part of the book, place these stories in a broader, even cosmic, perspective. Whereas the stories focus on human conflict, the visions, especially Dan 7, reveal that such conflict is part of larger historical processes (the several beasts represent different ancient Near Eastern empires). Moreover, conflict occurs in the heavens (vv. 21-25). Finally, however, justice is served through the actions of the heavenly court. Such concern for theodicy or divine justice on a cosmic scale fits well with the final chapter of Daniel, according to which after "a time of anguish. . . . Many of those who sleep in the dust of the earth shall awake, some to everlasting life, and some to shame and everlasting contempt" (Dan 12:1-2). Heavenly justice could have an impact upon humans, even after they have died. In this afterlife, some are accorded a favorable status based on past behavior, others are condemned.

Apocalyptic literature offers a new breadth of theological vision in Judaism. Whereas Job had been interested in theodicy, the ability to work out that problem in a future life was unavailable to the author of that book. Now, in the Greco-Roman period, life beyond death becomes part of the theological conversation.

The adjective *apocalyptic* can refer to both a specific type of literature and a theological perspective. First, an apocalypse is a narrative "describing the disclosure of otherwise inaccessible secrets to a human seer by a heavenly being."[3] According to a strict application of this definition, there are two apocalypses in the Bible, Daniel and Revelation. Fourth Ezra, which appears in the Apocrypha, and *1 Enoch* and *2 Baruch,* which are placed in the Pseudepigrapha, also exemplify apocalyptic literature.

Second, though apocalypses offer considerable diversity, they share some theological perspectives. They present a cosmic perspective on the entire world. God, though in control, often stands in conflict with destructive forces, whether human or divine. To this extent, one may speak of a kind of dualism that also manifests itself in the human realm, as with sons of light versus sons of darkness. Conflict of these various sorts will culminate in an eschatological cataclysm ("the end," Dan 12:1-4), after which a new age will dawn. Many apocalypses anticipate that this momentous end is imminent. The nature of this coming conflict and its outcome are revealed by a seer to righteous individuals. Such knowledge is, however, to remain guarded (Dan 12:9), available only to the elect. In the new age beyond death, those who have suffered will be rewarded, whereas those who have been oppressors will suffer.

This "apocalyptic imagination," to use a phrase coined by John Collins, has had a powerful influence up to our own time. It provides a template by means of which people in many periods can understand what is going on around them. It allows individuals, particularly if they are part of a group that suffers, or thinks they have been marginalized, to comprehend the source of their plight. Moreover, they understand that God is in control of their fates and that, ultimately, they will be victorious. The dualistic elements enable them to distinguish their own situation from that of others, whom they may perceive as their oppressors, creating an "us/them" mentality.

Important though this apocalyptic literature was, the Greco-Roman period saw the production of other kinds of Jewish literature. Although many study Bibles include the Apocrypha, which includes both nonapocalyptic and apocalyptic literature, this apocryphal literature is far less well known than are the books of the Old Testament as it exists in the canon of Judaism and Protestant Christianity. However, the Apocrypha remains a key resource for studying Judaism in the late second temple period, particularly the period after Hellenization swept over the eastern Mediterranean basin. Various traditions that invigorated the Hebrew Bible, for instance, the Wisdom literature, continued to generate literature in this new context. Several examples—Proverbs, Ecclesiastes, and Job—have already appeared in the Hebrew Bible. However, two other powerful examples of biblical Wisdom literature, Sirach and the Wisdom of Solomon, appear in the Apocrypha. Moreover, the short story, exemplified in the Bible by Ruth and Jonah, continues to appear in Tobit and Bel and the Dragon. These various forms of literature attest well to the theological diversity wrought out of the junction of Judaism emerging from the Persian period and the forces of Hellenism.

Conclusion

In this chapter, we have examined diverse literatures from the Persian and Greco-Roman periods. Diversity really is the hallmark of this era, since it was one in which the Old Testament was being created and used in varied settings. However, despite such tendencies, the theological beacon of Torah remained primary. Torah piety was necessary to accommodate the needs of Jews living both in and outside the land. Yet, the very notion of Torah was a flexible one, since it involved far more than the Pentateuch.

Notes

1. T. Eskenazi, *In an Age of Prose: A Literary Approach to Ezra–Nehemiah* (SBLMS 36; Atlanta: Scholars Press, 1988).

2. E. Gerstenberger, *Psalms: Part 1 with an Introduction to Cultic Poetry* (FOTL 14; Grand Rapids: Eerdmans, 1988), 31.

3. F. Murphy, "Introduction to Apocalyptic Literature," *NIB*, vol. 7 (Nashville: Abingdon, 1996), 2.

Bibliography

Albertz, Rainer. *Israel in Exile: The History and Literature of the Sixth Century* BCE. Atlanta: SBL, 2003.

Allen, Leslie C. "Chronicles: Introduction, Commentary, and Reflections." In *NIB*, vol. 3. Nashville: Abingdon, 1999.

Berquist, Jon. *Judaism in Persia's Shadow: A Social and Historical Approach.* Minneapolis: Fortress, 1995.

Blenkinsopp, Joseph. *Ezra–Nehemiah: A Commentary.* OTL. Philadelphia: Westminster, 1988.

Collins, John J. *Daniel: A Commentary on the Book of Daniel.* Hermeneia. Minneapolis: Fortress, 1993.

De Jonge, Marinus. "Messiah." *ABD*, vol 4. New York: Doubleday, 1992 (pp. 777-88).

Keel, Othmar. *Song of Songs*. Minneapolis: Fortress, 1994.

Klein, Ralph. *Israel in Exile: A Theological Interpretation*. OBT 6. Philadelphia: Fortress, 1979.

Levenson, Jon D. *Esther: A Commentary*. OTL. Louisville: Westminster John Knox, 1997.

McCann, J. Clinton, Jr. *A Theological Introduction to the Book of Psalms: The Psalms as Torah*. Nashville: Abingdon, 1993.

Mays, James L. *Psalms*. IBC. Westminster John Knox, 1994.

Nielsen, Kirsten. *Ruth: A Commentary*. OTL. Louisville: Westminster John Knox, 1997.

Trible, Phyllis. "Jonah: Introduction, Commentary, and Reflections." In *NIB*, vol. 7. Nashville: Abingdon, 1996.

SCRIPTURE INDEX

Old Testament

463

Apocrypha

TOPICAL INDEX

Aaron, 111, 117, 120-22, 123, 133, 138, 140, 221
Abel, 30, 51-52, 78
Abiathar, 225, 248, 252
Abimelech, 72, 73, 217
Abner, 237, 238
Abraham, 10, 35, 39, 56-58, 61-91, 96, 100, 105, 107, 129, 176, 185, 189, 374, 431. *See also* Covenant, between God and Abraham
Absalom, 245
Achan, 198
Adam and Eve, 30, 34, 45-46, 51, 168-69. *See also* fall, the
Adonibezek, 206
Adonijah, 248
Agur, 292-93
Ahab, 258, 268, 272-73, 279-80, 283
Ahasuerus, 453
Ahaz, 292, 320-21
Ahaziah, 272, 282
Ahijah, 261-62, 271, 284
Alexander the Great, 332, 425
Amalekites, 101, 123, 234
Amaziah, 265, 290
Ammonites, 71, 81, 83, 232, 243
Amnon, 245
Amorites, 73, 174-75, 188
Amos, 289, 299, 302-3, 312, 314, 319, 323
Amos, book of, 265, 304, 305, 307-11, 322
  edited and revised, 324n2, 442-46
Amun-Re, 47
Anat, 258
Anath, 433
Anathoth, 252
anger, 51, 119, 344, 417

divine, 102, 124, 130, 159
animals
  in the ark, 30, 53
  creation of, 39, 42, 45, 412
  in garden of Eden, 48
  killing of, 56
  laws regarding, 144, 159
  purity issues concerning, 133
  sin's effects on, 38
Apocrypha, 13, 25, 28, 255, 440, 456-57
apostasy, 102, 128, 130, 133, 136, 138, 149, 150, 167, 230, 250, 258-59, 267, 274, 279, 283, 285-86. *See also* idolatry
Aramaeans, 243, 273, 293, 308
archaeology, 179
ark of the covenant, 216, 218, 227, 239, 261
Artaxerxes, 434
Asa, 269
Asenath, 88
Ashdod, 273, 308
Asherah, 258
Ashkelon, 217
Assyria
  destruction of, 158, 160, 259, 283, 330-36
  empire of, 269, 289-324, 329
  as God's instrument, 280, 345
Astarte, 258
Athaliah, 269
Azariah, 27-28, 265, 268-69, 290

Baal, 258-59
  in confrontation with Yahweh, 277-78, 313-14
  and destruction of Samaria, 292
  signs of, 280
  in stories of Elijah and Elisha, 272-82

TOPICAL INDEX

TOPICAL INDEX

criticism, 4-7
  form, 33-35, 64-66
  historical, 4-7, 13
  literary, 68-69
  redaction, 66-67
  source, 31-33, 63-64, 97
crucifixion, 120
Crusades, 192
curses, 145, 153, 160, 298, 305, 367
Cyrus, 332, 359-61, 363, 372, 375-76, 425-27, 434
  as agent of Yahweh, 363, 375-76, 427

Dagon, 227-28
Dan, 211, 217, 261, 295
Daniel, 86, 454, 456
Darius, 434
darkness, 41, 113, 310, 412, 457
David, 235-48
Day of Atonement, 131, 135, 156
Deborah, 10, 208-9, 270
debt, 158, 276
Decalogue, 128, 141, 143-44, 162
Deuteronomy, 134, 141-47, 151-64
  as ending of Pentateuch, 164-70
  and reforms of Hezekiah and Josiah, 297-99
  wilderness traditions of, 122-24
Diasporanovelle, 86
Dinah, 79-80
disease. *See* illness
divorce, 313
Douglas, Mary, 134
doxology, 303, 308, 381
  in Genesis, 37
  in Job, 407, 412
  in Proverbs, 385
  in Psalms, 99, 224
  in response to exile, 357, 358, 374
  in response to the Exodus, 101, 115-16, 118
  in wisdom theology, 395, 397
  See also praise

earthquake, 280
Easter, 94
Eastern Orthodox Church, 440
Ecclesiastes, 255, 382, 416-21, 449-50
Ecclesiasticus, 482
ecology, 53, 131, 159-60, 314, 322
Eden, 44
Edom, 81, 83
Egypt, 111-12, 150
  exilic communities of, 354
  proverbial links to, 392-93
  See also Exodus, the; Pharaoh

Ehud, 208
Ekron, 217
Elephantine, 433
Eli, 216, 218, 223, 225, 226
Eliezer, 73
Elihu, 411
Elijah, 258, 272-74
  encounter with God, 279-81
  struggle with prophets of Baal, 258, 272-74, 277-79, 283-84
  symbolism and, 281-82
Eliphaz, 404-5, 412
Elisha, 272-74
  symbolism and, 281-82
Elkanah, 223
El names, 68, 107, 258
Elohim, 67, 77
Elohist (E) source
  in Exodus, 97
  in Genesis, 31, 63
  and Joseph story, 85
Enoch, 52
1 Enoch, 456
Ephraim, 261, 296-97
Epic of Atrahasis, 32
Esau, 78-84, 87
Esther, 10, 18, 86, 449, 453-54
ethics
  in daily life, 382-83
  and economic advantage, 399
  sexual, 129
  social, 395-97
Ethiopia, 57
ethnic cleansing, 145, 191
Eucharist, 94, 157
evil,
  historical, 110
  in Holocaust, 378-79
  tree of knowledge of good and, 45
evolution, 42
Exodus, book of
  composite character of, 97-98
  context of in canon, 94, 96-97
  historical context of, 98-99
  narrative flow of, 99-102
Exodus, the, 93-94
  dating of, 97
  and faith identity, 115-120
  geographic setting of, 95
Ezekiel, 254, 300-3, 336-37, 347-54
  tradition of, 367-69
  vision of future, 431, 432
Ezra, 81, 361, 377, 434-38
4 Ezra, 456

Fackenheim, Emil, 414

TOPICAL INDEX

TOPICAL INDEX

Ten Commandments, 128, 297, 314. *See also* Decalogue
Terah, 33, 62, 69, 70-78
testimony, 2-4, 8, 15-21, 377-79
Tetrateuch, 142
theodicy, 77, 391, 395, 399-401, 414-16, 456. *See also* Job
theology
  creation, 102, 390, 393, 419
  dogmatic, 13
  of grace, 345
  liberation, 94, 114
  royal, 238, 241, 242, 252
  of sin, 48
  systematic, 13
  wisdom, 384, 415-16, 421-22
Tiglath-Pileser III, 290, 321, 329
Tirzah, 261
Tobit, 458
Torah
  Deuteronomic, 186
  Mosaic, 96, 145, 178
  obedience to, 204, 207
  and piety, 438
  See also Pentateuch
tree of the knowledge of good and evil, 45
trust, 48-49, 122, 124, 243, 345
truth, 7, 183, 343

Uriah, 157, 244-45, 271
Uzziah, 265, 268, 269, 290

vegetation, 36, 42, 54, 159
violence
  in family of David, 245
  in Jacob-Esau story, 83
  in Jacob-Laban story, 83
  learned through suffering, 207
  legitimation of, 192-94, 213
  against noncombatants in war, 308
  against Pharaoh, 113-14
  of Pharaoh, 112
  in prophets, 322, 345, 365
  psalm about, 357, 395
  sin and, 51-52, 56
  toward women, 79
  and work of God, 113-14, 185, 192-94, 213, 273-74, 277, 314-15
vows, 140, 245, 419, 448

war, 196-97
  demonization of enemy in, 191-92
  religious rhetoric of, 192-93
waters
  of baptism, 93, 120
  of chaos, 219, 220

creation of, 41, 42, 371
  of flood, 54
  in lament psalms, 54
  provision of,
  walls of, 113
wealth
  defense of, 216
  futility of, 418
  and sacrifice and offerings, 156, 163
  in Solomon's reign, 250-51
weapons, 217-18, 227
Wellhausen, Julius, 31
Westermann, Claus, 76
widows, 145, 157, 274-75, 300, 309, 410, 453
wilderness
  stories of, 99, 119, 121, 137
  struggles in, 101-2, 122-24, 138
wind, 41-42, 103, 113, 280
wisdom
  as alternative form of faith, 382
  concerns of in Joseph story, 86
  ethics of, 403
  fear of the Lord as, 49, 77, 384, 411, 420
  intellectual activity of, 383-84, 397
  literature, 19, 86, 382, 401, 440
  proverbial, 255, 421
  of Solomon, 250, 254-55
  as vanity, 417
  voice of, 398
Wisdom of Solomon, book of, 255, 382, 457
wives, 10, 81, 210, 250
Wolff, Hans Walter, 63-64
women
  creation of, 38
  in Esther, 453-54
  Ezekiel's view of, 352
  perspective of, 10
  proverbs about, 397
  in Ruth, 452-53
  See also widows; wives
word of God, 32, 45, 129, 143, 168, 265, 282-84
work, 42, 51, 158-59, 382
world
  age of, 30, 31
  as creation, 37-38, 173-74
  God's relationship with, 35, 37, 54
  post-flood, 55-57
  of today, 16
worship
  calendars of, 129
  centralization of, 142, 144
  Israel's move from slavery to, 130
  and justice, 264
  and offerings and sacrifices, 131-32, 156-57
  responsible action in, 351

TOPICAL INDEX

statutes of, 131-36

Yahweh
in confrontation with Baal, 277-78, 313-14
graciousness of, 352
holiness of, 367-68
as king, 185, 219, 230
and land, 173, 184-89
loyalty to, 11, 129-30, 186-87
mobility of, 349, 355-56
name of, 108, 116, 303
opponents of, 188, 191, 210
presence of, 370-71
violence in name of, 192-94, 213
See also God
Yahwism, 91, 196, 258, 268, 281, 282, 341, 433-34, 438

Yahwist (J) source
and creation story, 32
in Exodus, 97, 109
and flood story, 52
in Genesis, 31-32, 46, 63-64
and Joseph story, 86
in Numbers, 137

Zadok, 225, 252
Zarephath, 274
Zechariah, 301, 377, 429, 432-33, 443, 446, 447
Zedekiah, 336
Zephaniah, 299, 322-23
Zerubbabel, 426, 429, 432
Zilpah, 82, 88
Zion, Mount, 241, 252, 316, 323
Zophar, 404

we are
enstoried against chaos